90 -0 885

The Common Good
and U.S. Capitalism

Oliver F. Williams
and John W. Houck
Editors

MURDOCK LEARNING RESOURCE CTR
GEORGE FOX COLLEGE
NEWBERG, OREGON 97132

UNIVERSITY
PRESS OF
AMERICA

LANHAM • NEW YORK • LONDON

Copyright © 1987 by

University Press of America,® Inc.

4720 Boston Way
Lanham, MD 20706

3 Henrietta Street
London WC2E 8LU England

British Cataloging in Publication Information Available

Co-published by arrangement with the
Notre Dame Center for Ethics and
Religious Values in Business

Library of Congress Cataloging-in-Publication Data

The Common good and U.S. capitalism.

"Co-published by arrangement with the Notre Dame
Center for Ethics and Religious Values in Business"
CIP t.p. verso.
Bibliography: p.
Includes index.
1. Industry—Social aspects—United States.
2. Capitalism—United States—Moral and ethical
aspects. 3. Business ethics. 4. Common good.
I. Williams, Oliver F. II. Houck, John W.,
1951- . III. Title: Common good and United
States capitalism.
HD60.5.U5C665 1987 306'.36'0973 87-8334
ISBN 0-8191-6364-3 (alk. paper)
ISBN 0-8191-6365-1 (pbk. : alk. paper)

For Theodore M. Hesburgh, C.S.C.

An Untiring Servant of the Common Good

Contents

iii

Preface

IN THE CLOSING PAGES OF THE PROTESTANT ETHIC AND *the Spirit of Capitalism,* Max Weber expressed serious misgivings about the future of capitalism in the United States. He feared that as people abandoned the interplay between religious and business values, civilization would be on the decline. Committed to affirming and improving the role of business in society, the Center for Ethics and Religious Values in Business of the University of Notre Dame takes Weber's warning as a challenge for continued reflection and action. To focus attention on religious thinking and the business world, the Center sponsors a biennial symposium on some aspect of the theme.

The 1980 Symposium resulted in the book *The Judeo-Christian Vision and the Modern Corporation,* which includes such scholars as James Gustafson, John C. Bennett, Michael Novak, Kirk Hanson, Denis Goulet, Christopher Stone, James Schall, S.J., Edward Trubac, Burton Leiser, William Sexton, Kenneth Jameson, Charles Wilber, Catherine Cleary, and Elmer Johnson. Of the conference, *The New York Times* reported: ". . . there would be no facile resolution of the conflict between the values of a just society and the sharply opposing values of successful corporations."

The 1982 Symposium examined John Paul II's encyclical letter *Laborem Exercens.* The meeting brought together eighteen distinguished scholars and corporate and labor leaders. In a lively and fruitful three days, some 150 persons shared in the discussions, which *Newsweek* characterized as a "free marketplace of ideas" exploring a religious vision of business power. The 1982 conference resulted in the volume, *Co-Creation and Capitalism: John Paul II's Laborem Exercens,* which includes essays by Michael Novak, Stanley Hauerwas, David Hollenbach, S.J., Bernard Murchland, Joseph A. Pichler, J. Bryan Hehir, Denis Goulet, Ernest Bartell, C.S.C., Andrea Lee, IHM, Amata Miller, IHM, George C. Lodge, Mark J. Fitzgerald, C.S.C., and Elmer W. Johnson.

In December 1983, the Center assisted the U. S. Bishops'

Committee charged to write a pastoral letter on the economy by convening a three-day symposium, Catholic Social Teaching and the American Economy. More than 250 people attended that symposium, including the five bishops who were to draft the letter. *The Los Angeles Times* observed that "About one-third of the major speakers represented conservative viewpoints, the remainder voiced moderate-to-liberal positions." *The New York Times* reported that ". . .contentiousness is commonplace here at Notre Dame, the home field of the Gipper. And when dozens of business leaders, theologians and academics lined up against each other at the university this week, the debate over the economy was fought as hard as any gridiron encounter."

In April 1986, a conference was convened to explore whether the concept of the common good might be retrieved and become central in contemporary religious social thought. It is this conference which is the subject of the present volume.

The Center for Ethics and Religious Values in Business is under the co-directorship of Oliver Williams, C.S.C., and John Houck, both of the Department of Management, College of Business Administration. It evolved from the University of Notre Dame Joint Committee on Business, Theology and Philosophy founded in 1976.

The Center seeks to build bridges between business, business studies and the humanities. Its programs are designed to strengthen the Judeo-Christian ethical foundations in business and public policy decisions by fostering dialogue between academic and corporation leaders and by research and publications.

Publications developed by the Center include: *Full Value: Cases in Christian Business Ethics, A Matter of Dignity: Inquiries into the Humanization of Work, The Judeo-Christian Vision and the Modern Corporation, Co-Creation and Capitalism: John Paul II's Laborem Exercens,* and *Catholic Social Teaching and the U.S. Economy: Working Papers for a Bishops' Pastoral.* Articles have appeared in *California Management Review, Business Horizons, Theology Today, Harvard Business Review, Business and Society Review* and *The Journal of Business Ethics.*

We wish to thank Daniel B. Walton for his assistance in preparing this manuscript. Father Austin I. Collins, C.S.C., Department of Art, University of Notre Dame, deserves special recognition for his sculpture photographed on the cover.

For guidance and support we wish to recognize our president, Father Theodore M. Hesburgh, C.S.C.; our dean, Frank K. Reilly; our associate deans, Yusaku Furuhashi and Vincent Raymond; and our chairperson, Robert P. Vecchio.

For the conference, *Catholic Social Teaching and the Common Good*, and the publication of this volume, we are most grateful for the encouragement and financial support provided by the Olin Foundation, The Hershey Foods Company and the General Electric Foundation; and at the University of Notre Dame: the College of Business Administration and the Center for Continuing Education.

Finally, it is our pleasure to dedicate this volume to Father Theodore M. Hesburgh. This academic year marks his 35th and final year as president of the University of Notre Dame. His untiring generosity and service to the common good have served Notre Dame and indeed the far corners of the globe well.

Oliver F. Williams, C.S.C.
John W. Houck
Co-directors, Center for Ethics
  and Religious Values in Business
University of Notre Dame
Notre Dame, IN 46556
December 1986

One

To Enhance the Common Good: An Introduction

OLIVER F. WILLIAMS, C.S.C.

The term "common good" is seldom highlighted in academia these days; it has not had one entry in the *Catholic Periodical and Literature Index* in almost twenty years. Why would two supposedly competent scholars invite over a dozen of the premier academics in the United States to come to the University of Notre Dame for three days and reflect together on the notion of the common good and U.S. capitalism? I will let my colleague speak for himself in the introductions to the individual essays but, as for me, perhaps some brief remarks outlining my concerns will be helpful.

Recently a front-page *Wall Street Journal* article recounted the sad story of a *Journal* reporter who was fired and was being investigated by the Securities and Exchange Commission for leaking information to traders for profit. The managing editor was obviously upset by the breach of professional ethics and he in-

1

sisted that the *Journal* had done all that is humanly possible to encourage appropriate behavior.

> In the final analysis, no matter how strong the ethical codes we issue and how carefully we check a reporter's background before hiring him, the only thing that prevents occurrences like this is the character and sense of commitment of each of our people. Even in retrospect, it is difficult to imagine what we might have done to avert Mr. Winans's acts.[1]

Mr. Winans, 35 years old, had worked one year for the paper before getting the highly sensitive column, "Heard on the Street." It would appear that the *Journal* had no sense of how moral character is nurtured—the need for mentors and time in rank before "morally risky" assignments are given, the sense that character is cultivated in a community of shared ideals and expectations.

Alasdair MacIntyre, in *After Virtue*, suggests that we may be beyond this community of shared ideals.

> The Supreme Court in *Bakke*, as on occasion in other cases, played the role of a peacemaking or truce-keeping body by negotiating its way through an impasse of conflict, not by invoking our shared moral first principles. For our society as a whole has none.[2]

While my assessment is not as pessimistic as MacIntyre's, he does lay bare a fundamental challenge of our time. For example, most of the work done in business ethics today focuses on providing a systematic framework to analyze the moral obligations of business people and their institutions. While this dimension is surely essential, in my view, what needs to be highlighted is the fact that moral obligations are, at root, an attempt to preserve a way of life and that an important task of the ethicist today is to spell out this way of life. Any account of morality is incomplete without a vision of what constitutes a good life—of the kind of persons we want to be and the kind of communities we want to form. Theories of obligation need a context, a vision of what constitutes the good life, and that vision ought to be the guiding ideal for the community.[3]

While the managing editor of the *Journal* was understandably upset that the employee in question lacked the common loyalty essential for running any enterprise, his analysis of the problem betrays the characteristic blind spot of our age. Traits such as loyalty, honesty, compassion are only cultivated in a community that cherishes social virtues. We have heard so often in our time that the primary goal is the protection and enhancement of individual autonomy, that many are actually coming to believe this foolishness. To be sure, individual autonomy is not unimportant, but this notion only has meaning in the context of a community that puts limits on *my* personal projects for the sake of the common life. When a society forgets this, it is on the path to self-destruction. The marketplace becomes a jungle and the community disintegrates.

Catholic social teaching has used the term "common good" to point to the challenge of creating the good society. The term takes on a concreteness specific to a historical context, but always in this view freedom is never an end in itself but rather the means to achieve the good society. Freedom to do the good, not merely the absence of limitation, is the cornerstone of this position. It may be helpful to outline briefly this religious teaching.

Catholic Social Teaching

The tradition of the Roman Catholic Church is that while the gospel message offers a vision of the sort of person one ought to become and the sort of communities one ought to try to form, this biblical vision requires human reason and the social sciences to become concrete.[4] The structures and institutions and the policies that ought to guide them are a product of disciplined reflection in the light of the biblical vision. Thus, the church has a long tradition of social teaching stated in encyclicals (pastoral letters written by the pope as the chief shepherd of the church) and the writings of theologians.

Catholic social teaching begins with the conviction that human nature is flawed, following on its doctrine of original sin, but that human freedom responding to God's grace can overcome the selfishness that destroys community. People need others to grow and develop as persons and there is a natural, God-given tendency to come together in various groups—families, churches, unions, businesses, professional associations and so on. "Society" is simply the sum total of all the various groupings. The role of the state is to facilitate cooperation among the natural groupings of society.[5] Legislation is always enacted with an eye to the "common good," a term used frequently in Catholic social teaching to refer to the total environment—cultural, social religious, political, and economic—required for the living of a humane life.[6] Legislation evokes the cooperation dimension of the person, setting up an environment for the basic goodness of the person to flourish.[7]

While Catholic social teaching would never endorse any one particular country's economic arrangements, it has repeatedly stressed that the role of the state is to be *in service of* society. Thus, for example, in Pope John Paul II's 1981 encyclical, "On Human Work," there is a vigorous defense of the workers' right to form unions. The term "solidarity" is used to defend this right.[8] In socialist Poland the state is *identified with* society and hence the government controls all dimensions of life and leaves little space for freedoms taking for granted in most of the western world. This all-pervasive control is clearly not in accord with Catholic ideals.

The sort of society envisioned by Catholic social teaching is one where private property is respected. Following the medieval scholar, Thomas Aquinas, the church assumes that private property enables the human development intended by the Creator. Yet the teaching has always insisted that private property has a social dimension which requires that owners consider the common good in the use of property.[9] This vision of society assumes that some persons will have more material goods than others but that the affluent will provide for the less fortunate, either through the channels of public policy or other appropriate groups of society. The emphasis is always on respect for the human dignity of the poor, even in their unfortunate situation. The ideal is to structure society so that all those who are able might provide for themselves and their families by freely employing their talents.

While a good case can be made that the mixed economy of the United States approaches the ideal more closely than most other nations, the teaching on common good may be a timely reminder about the basis of our common life. The need to go back to our roots is brought to the fore by the plight of the *Journal* reporter, a plight all too common in our time. Capitalism without a context in a humane community would seem inevitably to shape people into greedy and insensitive human beings.

To understand how the notion of the common good might set a favorable context for capitalism, it is helpful to refer to the work of the first, and probably the most compelling, apologist for capitalism, Adam Smith. Smith's *The Wealth of Nations*, although published over 200 years ago (1776), is still considered to be the bible of capitalism. Smith assumed the truth of the Judeo-Christian vision of a land where all might enjoy the fruits of creation. Smith's insight was that only certain places were generating sufficient wealth so that all might enjoy the good things of creation. What characterizes these places was what we now call a market economy. When each person pursues his or her own self-interest the common good is enhanced. The baker bakes the very best bread he can and sells it so that he can use the proceeds of his sale to buy what he wants. Although motivated by self-interest, the net result is that the community has quality products at a reasonable cost.

What Smith did was to show how economic action based on self-interest could be beneficial for the community. This was indeed a remarkable turn of events, for economic self-interest was heretofore not thought to be respectable. Smith assumed that economic self-interest would be kept in check by the moral forces in the community. His argument for the morality of a market economy was utilitarian: The end (a community where all could obtain the fruits of creation) justified the means (economic action based on self-interest).

What seems to be happening to a growing number of our

most talented managers in the business world is that the means has become the end, that is, making a profit has become an end itself with no reference to the humane community that Smith envisioned as the net result. Instead of an acquisitive economy enabling a humane community, we see an acquisitive economy *overwhelming* the community and shaping it into an acquisitive society. Respect for human dignity and the social virtues so essential for community are neglected.

It is my contention that more explicit reflection on the notion of the common good will raise our awareness of the crucial role of virtue in the community. Business education needs to examine carefully the question of what actually motivates business managers; business can be a noble profession. It is commonplace to assume that there is an inherent antagonism between the intellectual class and the business world. Intellectuals celebrate the heroic, the saintly, the noble, and the virtuous. The great intellectuals of the world—Aristotle, Thomas Aquinas, and the fathers of the church, for example—had a certain disdain for commerce. Business was never considered to be a noble profession. Consider Aristotle's definition of "noble":

> . . .those actions are noble for which the reward is simply honor, or honor more than money. So are those in which a man aims at something desirable for someone else's sake; actions good absolutely, such as those a man does for his country without thinking of himself; actions good in their own nature; actions that are not good simply for the individual, since individual interests are selfish.[10]

Adam Smith in *The Wealth of Nations* supposedly captured the dominant motivation of business people. For Smith, business is motivated by economic self-interest, the acquisitive impulse, and hence it is not a virtuous or *noble* endeavor. It is, however, a *respectable* occupation, he argues, because the aggregate of "self-interests" results in great benefits for the whole society. If each person pursues his or her own self-interest, then the common good will be enhanced, according to Smith. He saw that the sum total of individual self-interests resulted in a market economy that allowed all to better their own condition. A market economy is moral because it raises the level of living for all—even though it is based on acquisitiveness. In Smith's words:

> In civilized society he stands at all times in need of the cooperation and assistance of great multitudes, while his whole life is scarce sufficient to gain the friendship of a few persons. Man has almost constant occasion for the help of his brethren, and it is vain for him to expect it from his benevolence only. He will be more likely to prevail if he can interest their self-love in his favour, and show them that it is for their own advantage to do for him what he requires of them. Whoever offers to another a bargain of any kind proposes to do this. It is not from the benevolence of the butcher, the brewer, or the baker, that we expect our dinner, but from their regard to their own interest.[11]

The thrust of my remarks, however, is to say that Christians can and do participate in the market (business world) without being solely motivated by economic self-interest. The profit motive, that is, economic action based on self-interest, is not their single-minded concern. I suggest that business is a noble occupation when it is consciously concerned to enhance the common good, and not simply to make money. One can live a Christian vocation in the world of commerce. Christians, as an imperative of their faith, must consciously and deliberately work for the common good. The poor, the developing nations, pollution control, and the quality of life all need conscious care. We must make God's work our own.[12]

The essays that follow are by distinguished scholars reflecting on one or another dimension of the common good. Some share the vision I have outlined above, others have some questions about it. All the authors, however, give us cause for serious reflection on this most important theme of the common good and capitalism. The book is divided into four parts. Part one examines the historical roots of the notion of the common good, the second section presents some of the controversy over the term in the ecclesial community and the third part offers some new inquiries about the concept. The final part examines the common good from the various perspectives of business, labor, government and the media.

Notes

1. "SEC Investigates Charges of Traders Profiting on Leaks by Journal Reporter," *Wall Street Journal*, March 29, 1984, p. 3.

2. Alasdair MacIntyre, *After Virtue* (Notre Dame, IN: University of Notre Dame Press, 1981), p. 236.

3. For further reflections on the role of vision in moral life, see my article, "Can Business Ethics Be Theological: What Athens Can Learn From Jerusalem," *Journal of Business Ethics* 5(6), 1986.

4. See O. Williams, C.S.C., "The Catholic Teaching," *The Judeo-Christian Vision and the Modern Corporation*, eds. Oliver F. Williams, C.S.C. and John W. Houck (Notre Dame, IN: University of Notre Dame Press, 1982), pp. 76-80.

5. The 1931 encyclical *Quadregesimo anno* uses the verbs "direct," "watch," "urge" and "restrain" when speaking of the role of the state (#80). *Mater et Magistra*, the social encyclical of Pope John XXIII, identifies the role of the state as to "encourage, stimulate, regulate, supplement and complement" (#53).

6. For example, in the second draft of *Catholic Social Teaching and the U.S. Economy*, the term common good is used 24 times.

7. The work of Thomas Aquinas is seminal for Catholic thought on the role of law. See *Summa Theologica*, I-II, 90, 4; and *Summa Theologica*, II-II, 120, 1-2. For a contemporary retrieval of the theme that justification of law is the common good, see Karl Rahner, S.J., "The Dignity and Freedom of Man," *Theological Investigations* II (Baltimore: Helicon Press, 1963), pp. 235-64.

8. The word "solidarity" is used ten times in *On Human Work*, nine in paragraph 8 and once in paragraph 20. For reflections on this encyclical, see John W. Houck and Oliver F. Williams, C.S.C., eds., *Co-Creation and Capitalism: John Paul II's Laborem Exercens* (Washington, D.C.: University Press of America, 1983).

9. For the view of Thomas Aquinas on private property, see *Summa Theologica*, II-II, 66, 2. For a summary of the tradition, see E. Duff, "Private Property," *New Catholic Encyclopedia*, 2:849-55.

10. Aristotle, *Rhetoric*, 1, chap. 9.

11. Adam Smith, *The Wealth of Nations*, ed. Edwin Cannan (Chicago, IL: University of Chicago Press, 1976), p. 18.

12. The discussion of Adam Smith appears in my earlier essay, "The Professional Disciplines: Business and Management," *Justice and Peace Education: Models for College and University Faculty*, ed. David M. Johnson (Maryknoll, NY: Orbis, 1986), pp. 141-156.

Part I

The Notion of the Common Good:
Its History and Evolution*

JOHN W. HOUCK

From whence the common good? Charles West can trace it back twenty-four centuries to Aristotle, who said "The Good has been rightly declared to be that at which all things aim." Over two millennia later in the 1980s, the U.S. Catholic bishops describe the common good, "the dignity of the human person, realized in community with others," as the yardstick against which all aspects of economic and social life must be measured. Further, the bishops argue extensively for a social order "that guarantees the minimum conditions of human dignity in the economic sphere for every person." Part One, with five writers operating from several different disciplines and sources, i.e., the-

*Special thanks are due to Oliver F. Williams, C.S.C., my colleague, and Daniel B. Walton, my graduate assistant, for their editorial assistance.

ological, philosophical, ancient and contemporary, will sketch out the development of the concept over the centuries.

Charles West sees the common good as an ancient notion, yet one that entails a vital and attractive vision for any society. He further sees it coming under attack from many, including contemporary proponents of liberation theology on the left, as well as radical capitalism on the right. He is optimistic, however, "that despite the evidence of the centuries against it, it does not die."

John Collins, in his essay on the biblical literature and the common good, places the common good at the heart of Christian social principles. He views the role of biblical literature as telling us about God and God's relationship with us and how we personally and socially should live with these concepts embodied in our lives. Collins confronts the challenge of individualism by advocating an enlightened self-interest in accord with the biblical tradition, "identifying the benefits which would accrue to society as a whole from the pursuit of the common good."

Ralph McInerny writes that God is ". . . the common good *par excellence*." God is to be loved as a "good infinitely shareable," and to do so otherwise would be a defective love. He pointedly observes that the common good has primacy over the individual goods of capitalism or the collective goods of socialism.

In the next essay, J. Philip Wogaman argues for a very active and "full-throated" Church to speak out on social and economic issues. Wogaman explains the Protestant history of the common good by quoting from the documents of three major Protestant conferences:

[I]n the name of the Gospel, that industry should not be based solely on the desire for individual profit, but that it should be conducted for the service of the community. (Stockholm Conference, 1925)

[I]ndividual property rights must never be maintained or exercised without regard to their social consequences or without regard to the contribution which the community makes in the production of all wealth. (Oxford Conference, 1937)

[W]e must vindicate the supremacy of persons over purely technical considerations by subordinating all economic processes and
cherished rights to the needs of the community as a whole. (Amsterdam, 1948)

Charles Curran points out that the common good is an evolving concept subject to changing conditions. He quotes from *The
New Catholic Encyclopedia*: "It is simply impossible to define
the common good in a final way irrespective of the changing social conditions," and also *The Pastoral Constitution on the
Church in the Modern World* which refers to "the dynamically
conceived common good." Curran believes that if we want to
use the concept of the common good we must shift our thinking from being static to that of greater flexibility in order to allow for new insights as technologies and circumstances change.

The Common Good and the Poor

For Charles West, the common good is our attractive vision.
However, like cats, the vision has had many lives, whether found
in the Greek city-state, the philosophy of the Roman empire,
medieval Thomistic political writings, or modern humanistic
thought and optimism. In biblical literature there is a similar re-
invigoration for the common good: it challenges and empowers
us to live lives of shared trust and dignity as we rebuild a divine-
human relationship based on God's love and trust. We are told in
Genesis that humankind was made in God's image and that we
are to be "fruitful and multiply, and fill the earth and subdue it;
and have dominion over the fish of the sea and over the birds of
the air and over every living thing that moves upon the earth."
This mandate of stewardship, in West's view, is clearly communal
and entails sharing, and certainly is compatible with the common good.

On the other hand, West traces the way a concept like the
common good can lose its vitality in political and social con-

cerns. First, he points to an aspect of religious thought which paints the power of evil, whether greed or violence, so monstrously that any optimism about our capacity to live constructively is pushed aside. As West observes, for the common good to be effective, there must be a belief in the fundamental capacity of humans to persevere in doing good: "Good is who God is and what God does through and with his creatures."

Second, the expansion of human knowledge and power growing out of technology and western capitalism has slowly evolved into a form of radical individualism. There is considerable irony in this, given the need for cooperation and joint effort necessitated by the division of labor. (We forget that Adam Smith attributed the spurt in material output in his *The Wealth of Nations* to a communitarian revolution: workers specializing in the various specific tasks needed to manufacture a product, like the making of pins.) The same can be said for the contemporary division of knowledge with its fragmentation of all knowledge into highly sophisticated parcels of research and information, the organizational basis for both the university and technological advancement in the Twentieth century.

There are several consequences of this new radical individualism for the concept of the common good; in its place there has evolved the "assertion of private power and productivity as the basic fact and value of life." This is in tension with our ability to think in a communitarian manner which is at the heart of the common good. Second, this individualism has resulted in "the expression of human goals in terms of higher standards of living, technological progress, and more intense exploitation of the earth's resources." And finally, individual choices are legitimated socially by their aggregation in the market system with the rationale of "giving the customers what they want."

In addition, Charles West explores another important dimension of the common good, the place of the poor. He talks about the poor as being the penniless, who are the economic poor; the poor as being the oppressed, who are the victims of exploitation and domination; the poor as being the disabled, who will always need the help of others; and the poor as the meek, who are the poor in spirit. He concludes that the poor are the test of the integrity of economic and political systems. The poor are "the ultimate neighbors, to be loved, to be heard, to be empowered to correct and limit us as we face our common judge and redeemer, while we work out together the forms of just and promising community which reflect the divine work in the world's economy."

The Biblical Vision and the Common Good

John J. Collins, as a biblical scholar, explores the social and political implications of Yahweh's concern for the people of Israel. The lessons that can be drawn from Scripture, Collins believes, have great relevance for our present social and economic issues. To Collins, it is through the spirit, undergirding specific biblical laws and practices, that we obtain a vision of how religious people can make a contribution to the political and social order. Collins is very careful to avoid a literal meaning or interpretation of the sources; what is operational for him is "what it means," not "what it meant." For instance, the provision "when a man sells his daughter as a slave" cannot be construed to condone slavery, but must be interpreted in regard to the cultural environment of the day. He also illustrates this by discussing the various laws, like those dealing with the observance of the sabbatical year:

> . . .the intention of the law was evidently to protect the land from exploitation. There is also the implication that the natural fruit of the land belongs to all the people, and so the poor could enjoy it at least every seventh year. . . biblical laws do not provide a viable method for solving these problems in the modern world, but they suggest an attitude which is a prerequisite of any solution.

Collins argues that at the heart of biblical laws are the public consequences of personal ambition and actions, including private greed. If one views his or her good as part of the common good, God will bless the project; however, if he or she doesn't have this view, one may reap short-term benefits, but eventually these will turn to a curse. This is not to say that there is no role for wealth and enlightened self-interest in the biblical ethic. Rather, wealth was regarded as a good, but the prophets were opposed to any developments which would further increase the disparity between rich and poor. The biblical ethic served as a challenge for people with power and wealth not "to grab at everything they could. The ideal was to have enough and to leave whatever was extra for others."

The Primacy of the Common Good

Ralph McInerny, the philosopher, illustrates the importance of the common good by the detailing of a 1940s controversy in philosophic circles. Jacques Maritain believed it was useful to contrast "individual" and "person," with individual relating to material goods and almost a mechanical sense of humankind, while person, a larger concept in Maritain's thinking, related to a heightened spiritual capacity. Because of Maritain's emphasis on person, some thought he was deemphasizing the concept of the common good and the role of society. The Richter scale of this controversy hit the level of verbal characterizations like "monstrosities" and "vicious stupidities." But McInerny sees growing out of this debate a deeper understanding of a social vision that avoids individualism and collectivism.

Moving beyond the controversy, he feels that the common good is the absolute essential of Catholic social and economic teaching and should help us judge the signs of our times and society. It can "draw attention to flaws in our economic thinking and policies as well as to make positive suggestions that will be manifestly in line with our own tradition."

In the section entitled The Person and the Common Good, McInerny asserts that the human is by nature a political animal. Moral autonomy, according to McInerny, is not achieved by weakening our ties with others, but by strengthening them. Using this proposition, McInerny shows why the Church and Thomistic tradition reject both *laissez-faire* capitalism and command socialism, both of which reflect a defective notion of humankind and therefore of society.

Present-day capitalism has evolved away from its early radical ideology, with its unfettered pursuit of profit and tolerance for human exploitation, to a system (and rationale) which welcomes the test of the common good: which economic system best insures the welfare of members of a society? McInerny introduces the caveat that the common good be explicitly in the minds of the entrepreneurial capitalists when they act. "Of course it will not do to say that there is some law according to which the greedy pursuit of personal wealth results in the best for most others." He warns that there cannot be any moral justification of the system if wealth distribution is "an unintended accidental consequence."

The Protestant Tradition

In his essay, Wogaman first elaborates upon the traditional commitment of both Catholics and Protestants to achieving the common good. Wogaman argues, however, that there have been ambiguities in Protestant traditions that have clouded the perception of the commitment of Protestantism to the common good. (Certainly the philosophical writings of Protestants like John Locke and Adam Smith have been used to explain and support radical capitalism and individualism.) However, upon closer examination, the so-called warrants of self-centered individualism attributed to Protestant tradition are really not indicative of the Protestant attitude toward the common good. As an example, Wogaman quotes Calvin:

> When the Scripture enjoins us to lay aside private regard to ourselves, it not only divests our minds of an excessive longing for wealth, or power, or human favor, but eradicates all ambition and thirst for worldly glory, and other more secret pests. He who

has learned to look to God in everything he does, is at the same
time diverted from all vain thoughts. This is that self-denial which
Christ so strongly enforces on his disciples from the very outset.

Wogaman discusses the meaning of the common good, inter-
twining Protestant and Catholic social thought. The common
good is equated with the responsible society "where freedom is
the freedom of men who acknowledge responsibility to justice
and public order, and where those who hold political authority
or economic power are responsible for its exercise to God and
the people whose welfare is affected by it." And to the question
who are the "people whose welfare is affected," Wogaman
points out that we must consider not only the poor internally
and globally but the future generations who are part of the
moral community. There must be a balance between generations.

In his discussion of the "option for the poor" he sees that this
can mean different things, with much depending upon our understanding of poverty. Poverty can be a relative lack of the material basis of life, like food, clothing and shelter. And it can
mean a lack of power to influence the economic and social conditions that affect one's life. Wogaman wants to emphasize that
we need to define poverty in both perspectives: social participation and influence as well as material conditions. The problem,
then, in implementing the common good is more than a question of economic output and distribution. It is, for Wogaman,
the larger question of political power-sharing, whether in the
factory or in the society, for "all would be able to participate in
the process of deciding what the common life is to be."

The Catholic Tradition

Charles Curran asserts that since the Second Vatican Council,
Catholic social teaching has not given a significant role to the
concept of the common good. Curran believes there are several
reasons which can explain this:

1) The common good and Thomistic natural law have had a long history of mutual support; however, the latter is no longer the primary basis of Catholic social teaching and ethics.
2) The teaching itself incorporates "divergent" elements, for example, the preferential option of the poor by emphasizing a part rather than the whole, or rights and freedoms which seem to be in opposition to the common good tradition.
3) Neither the recent documents themselves nor the commentaries give much weight to the common good.

Curran interprets these developments, not as the end for the common good, but as challenges to our thinking about power, interest groups, competition, innovation and change—all part of the context of contemporary understanding about the concept. In a more realistic, conflictual model of society, the traditional emphasis on "harmonious cooperation," while idealistic, is not relevant to today's social dynamics. "Power and conflict can never become ultimate realities, but they do have a greater role in terms of tactics and strategies than has been recognized in the older Catholic tradition."

In addition, Curran sees another development in Catholic social teaching; this concerns political life. Today's documents portray political society as meaning the person living in community with others, participating and enjoying dignity and freedom, whereas the previous understanding envisions a society structured from the top down. There has been a shift toward recognizing that the common good requires religious freedom and the separation of church and state. Finally, there has been a refinement in the understanding of the role of the state; the state is not the totality of society but rather is an entity whose function is to achieve the public order, which is justice and peace, in concert with other institutions.

Two

The Common Good and the Participation of the Poor

CHARLES C. WEST

"The Good," wrote Aristotle some twenty four centuries ago, "has rightly been declared to be that at which all things aim."[1] The definition is so simple, so embracing, so grounded in a metaphysic which resolves all conflict, that it seems to transcend the limits of Ancient Greece and speak to the yearning of every age.

Aristotle's world view was synthetic. There are many goods, he recognized, that are pursued by many activities: health by medicine, structures by building arts, wealth by economics, or victory by military strategy. There are levels of good in the disciplined life: pleasure, wealth, honor, friendship, and justice. None of these is denied its validity. None is placed in conflict with the others, but all are proportioned and directed by true happiness which is found in rational contemplation of the goodness of the whole. There is, he knew, a distinction between the individual and society. The whole of the *Nicomachean Ethics* is devoted to the former. But from the beginning, Aristotle defines human life as destined for fulfillment in the *polis* . There, all persons — citizen and stranger, husband and wife, parent and child, master and slave — have their places according to the quality of their humanity. Aristotle was familiar with personal vices which disrupt the harmony of the soul. He knew the power of money to destroy true economy by stimulating the search for unlimited wealth. He understood how the opposing evils of tyranny and revolution provoke each other in the body politic. But for him, all these distortions are unnatural. They arise from a misconception of true desire and from the failure of reason to direct all things to their proper ends. The good is an inclusive order. It does not stand over, as with Plato against material things and human passions, but works in and through them toward a final harmony perceived by the theoretical understanding of human reason.

It is an appealing vision, so appealing that despite the evidence of the centuries against it, it does not die. Deprived of its roots in the Greek city-state, it was reborn in Stoicism as the philosophy of an empire, and thence entered the legal tradition of the western world. Thomas Aquinas synthesized it with the Christian tradition, and as Christian Democracy built on neo-Thomist foundations it has exercised a powerful direct influence on twentieth century politics. Indirectly, in various humanist forms, it has undergirded the optimism and confidence of liberal society from the eighteenth century until now. In simplest terms, it is by faith that the good is expressed in the order of being itself, which embraces nature and humanity. All desires move toward it by natural law. It is perceived and guided toward fulfillment in the personal and the common life by human reason. This reason participates in the divine or cosmic rationality by which all things are structured and directed toward their goals. Human beings, then, will direct their own ideas of the good to the harmony of the common good as they are educated by reason and disciplined by rational authority—because it is their nature and destiny to do so.

It is an attractive vision, but in the late twentieth century it is under attack from all sides. "Human reason is political reason," writes the dean of liberation theologians, Gustavo Gutierrez.[2] What he means by this is a reason utterly different from Aristotle's: an historical reason, a constructive reason, expressing a consciousness determined by the collectivities in which people find themselves and in which they struggle for liberation. On this basis he condemns the rationality of Christian Democracy as an ideology of the *status quo* . The common good will be found not in the projection of a teleological order, but by participation in the struggle of the poor to become subjects of their own history, and in reflection on that struggle.

Gutierrez and liberation theology are only one example. In recent years a growing ecumenical consensus on the principles of social ethics in the World Council of Churches, expressed in the search for a "responsible society," has been blown apart by a similar controversy. Even modest attempts to formulate in dialogue certain guidelines for social justice in a mixed economy, and for Third World development, have been attacked by those for whom priority lies with action in the power struggle on behalf of the oppressed classes of peoples.[3] Black theology sends a similar message to even the most open of the white churches in America. Meanwhile feminist thought, both theological and social, raises a continuing question mark after every formulation of the common good which a male-dominated church attempts.

All this reflects, of course, the condition of the modern world. At certain times in the twentieth century — after each world war, for instance — we have seemed to grasp an idea of a common good that might embrace the world: the dream of the League of Nations, the hope for some of a socialist society, the hope for others of an expanding economy led by science and technology in a free world. For a while it seemed as if there might be a slow convergence of the two great ideological-economic systems of the earth, capitalism and communism, as the one moved toward a welfare state and the other toward a more open society. But today, despite the valiant efforts of a few church leaders, the American Catholic bishops among them, competing visions of a common good vie less and less for the allegiance of the human race. There are interests which try to project themselves as universal. A whole industry has recently arisen of research institutes that build social philosophy on the welfare and power of industrial or financial clients. There are advocacy groups, each appealing to fundamental rights which it is denied, and each pursuing its own agenda. There are nations seeking freedom from debt and exploitation, classes within nations seeking freedom from their exploiters, ethnic groups fighting the oppression of others and peoples in mortal combat with one another for the same living space. Some of these define their good as common and commend their cause to the conscience of humankind. Others do not bother. Still others resist and resent all efforts to justify or judge them by universal standards which they claim are merely devices to keep them subordinate.

How did we arrive at this state of affairs? Let me suggest two reasons and elaborate upon each. First, the Aristotelian vision of a rationally discerned good toward which all things aim, has from the beginning faced competition, negatively, from philosophies with a deeper sense of the power of evil in the cosmos, and positively, from the Hebrew-Christian understanding of the election, covenant, and mission of the people of God for the healing of nations. Second, modern science-based industrial capitalist society, having turned divine calling into natural rights, covenant into contract, and mission into free enterprise, has dissolved the common good into a myriad of individual goods in competition for the material and social benefits of an expanding technological economy. It is not surprising that in reaction to this development a collectivist humanism has arisen to pursue the same material and social goals, expressing in its revolutionary method a parody of the Biblical drama, and in its realm of dominance a new Aristotelianism.

The Bible and the Common Good

Let me begin with a biblical analysis different from, but I think not at odds with that provided by the bishops' letter on Catholic social teaching and the U.S. economy.[4]

"And God saw everything that he had made, and behold, it was very good" (Gen. 1:31). In the beginning, there was no problem of defining a common good, for good and reality were the same. At the center of this reality was the human being, male and female, given dominion over all life on earth and called to cultivate and bring forth its fruits. The good resided not in the order or process of things, but in the relationship between God, man and woman, and created nature in an open-ended interaction. Jesus' rebuke to the rich young man, "No one is good but God alone" (Mk. 10:18), expresses this relationship well. Good is who God is and what God does through and with his creatures.

Adam and Eve did not, at first, know good; they lived it. The idea of knowledge that goes beyond the creative obedience of relationship with God was suggested by the serpent. But our first ancestors in the biblical story pursued that knowledge. They tried to become "like God, knowing good and evil," or, as the modern slogan goes, "Subjects of their own history". The result has been a broken relation with God, with nature, and with one another. In this condition we try in many ways to define the common good, but each effort is at once a testimony to the reality which we have lost and an effort to justify ourselves over against that reality.

God's response to this brokenness is, in Old Testament terms, covenantal. This means that it is first revealed by a calling, a command and a promise from outside the people's own desires and sense of the good. Second, it is specific, the election of one people for this relationship as a witness to all peoples. Third, it is total, embracing the whole life of the people and engaging the whole faithfulness of God. A covenant in the milieu of ancient Israel presupposes enmity and strife; it establishes peace. It assumes fear and destruction and brings about a new community of trust and shared life. "The covenant is the creator of all rights and duties."[5] It is the specific context within which the relationship of God, humanity and nature is known as calling and promise.

Covenant is therefore not a vision of the common good, not an order we can contemplate. At its least it is the promise of God's faithfulness in the conflict of humanity with nature that "while the earth remains, seed time and harvest, cold and heat, summer and winter, day and night, shall not cease" (Gen. 8:22. Cf. Ch. 9:1-17). In its fullness, it is the election of one people to hear and embody the judgment and promise of God for all peoples (Ex. 19:5-6), a rebuilding of the divine-human relationship in the people of God in order that it may spread to the nations of the world (Is. 49:6).

All of this has a label in modern thought. It is called the scandal of particularity. As long as this scandal was limited to one small nation in a corner of the Middle East, this seemed not to matter. But with the incarnation of God in the Jew Jesus of Nazareth, it became an issue for all of history. The called and chosen people of God were now no longer only one nation among others, but a people in and over against every nation. Yet they were a people united not by the pursuit of interests, welfare or a perception of the good, but in response to a calling. They expressed in their community that relationship with the serving, suffering and reigning Christ which gathered them around the communion table and sent them into the world. Their response to the question of the common good was a missionary invitation to the people of the world to come to Christ, to join the community and find there the peace which the world cannot give.

The early Christians were modest in their expectations for the world. The apostle Paul could send a slave back to his master "no longer as a slave but more than a slave, as a beloved brother" (Phil. 16). But he did not thereby expect to overthrow the worldly system of slavery. The early Christian community "were together and had all things in common and they sold their possessions and goods and distributed to them all as they had need" (Acts 2:44-45). But no suggestion was made that these should be the working principles of the first century Roman economy. Paul could chide his converts for going to the law with their disputes (I Cor. 6), and at the same time call for subjection to the authority of legal government (Rom. 13:1-5). Yet none of this was dualism. Rather the quality of justice and peace which the church was called to cultivate and show forth set a new reality over against the various "goods" which the world serves, as a witness to God's judgment and promise for the world. In the words of Ephesians, it was "the plan of the mystery hidden for ages in God who created all things, that through the church manifold wisdom of God might be made known to the principalities and powers in the heavenly places" (Eph. 3:9-10).

The expansion of Christianity to become the dominant, almost exclusive, religion of Europe tended to obscure his mission. Augustine still expressed it in his distinction between the city of God and the city of this world nearly a century after Constantine. The distinction between church and state which was preserved through the whole middle ages bears witness to it. Luther, Calvin, and the other Reformers dramatized it once again. But medieval society was a complex network of law, custom, civil and ecclesiastical institutions which did not allow an easy distinction between the witnessing community and what the New Testament called "world". In such a society it could be believed that a rational agreement about the human good expressed in the natural law needed only to be completed, not judged, by the means of grace in the Christian community. It was, after all, assumed by all that in the witness of the church and its guidance of the common life of Christians, the whole of society is called to recognize the quality of human relations promised and given in Christ. Why could it not also be assumed that in Christendom this was not inconsistent with the rational self-interest and mutual accommodation of society's members? On this basis, late medieval theologians developed complex moral structures of just-price, just-wage, just-return for labor and just-profit on the exchange of goods, not to mention the regulation of officially prohibited usury to control the burgeoning commercial economy of the cities. It is only slightly more surprising that Calvin, and his followers, the Puritans of England and early Massachusetts, took over and refined much of this ethic even while pursuing and promoting commercial enterprise. Not until the 20th century did the conflict between the covenant peace of God and the rational peace of human desires pursuing their ends, which was so clear to Augustine, come again into focus.

Liberal Society: The Disappearance of the Common Good

Meanwhile, an explosion of human knowledge and power occurred which changed the whole context of the problem. A case can be made that Christian faith in various of its forms prepared the way for the methods of modern science;[6] that the Lutheran Reformation with its focus on the faith of the believer opened the way to later individualism;[7] that Latin Western Christianity as a whole stimulated technological invention as a proper way to glorify God;[8] or that "this worldly asceticism" of Reformed theology produced the discipline and the motivation for the burst of efficient productivity which produced the modern economic system.[9] However this may be, the church did not control this revolution either intellectually or socially. Instead, the common good, in fact all final causes, were swept aside in favor of the efficient cause of dynamic creative human work, and community of all kinds was subordinated to the rights and powers of the individual. Even Christianity, in some of its expressions, has been co-opted by this spirit into projecting individual experience and discipline as the total sphere of the Christian life.

This had, it seems to me, five consequences. The *first* is the assertion of private power and productivity as the basic fact and value of life. The individual is set free to realize whatever goal she chooses or desires provided only that the right of others to do the same be respected. An expanding universe with an expanding economy is assumed in which there is no determinate limit on personal ambition or the progress which can result from the interaction of individuals seeking their self-interest by working with one another.

Second, the standard of good for the individual emerges from the person him or herself. It was crudely described by Jeremy Bentham as the seeking of pleasure and the avoidance of pain, but there is a recognition in this formula that in an individualist society the goods sought tend toward the material rather than toward the interpersonal. The result is the expression of human goals in terms of higher standards of living, technological progress, and more intense exploitation of the earth's resources.

Third, such common good as can be found in this philosophy is the result of individual forces and choices backed by effective demand in an open market. Goodness, in short, is measured by the price which a product or a service commands.

Fourth, there is a hidden assumption in this faith, namely, that the process as a whole is benevolent. Human beings entering the market will seek exchange and mutual benefit, not domination and control. Competition will result in cooperation and the mutual adjustment of persons to one another. Self-interest, rationally understood and pursued, will, through free exchange, enhance the public welfare. For John Locke this was expressed in a law of nature which is reason and "teaches all mankind who will but consult it, that being all equal and independent, no one ought to harm another in his life, health, liberty, or possessions."[10] For Adam Smith, it was the moral sentiments in human nature which give us each a natural sympathy with the welfare of others. For Milton Friedman, it is the natural tendency of the marketplace to decentralize power and promote uncoerced cooperation.[11] The qualities of human relations which permeate the society from centuries of biblical teaching and church experience still operate to make the system work. However, they are attributed to the nature of individuals themselves.

Fifth, defenders of this individualism, are however, quite prepared to accept the brutal and inhuman consequences of the system if necessary to its preservation. Labor was not only the source of all value but also had its price, and that price was the bare subsistence of the laborer and his capacity to reproduce. This is the source of Thomas Malthus' law that wages must always fluctuate around subsistence, never going far above or far below. It was David Ricardo who first set forth the theory of class conflict between workers, capitalists and landlords, and the necessary exploitation of the worker to provide capital for economic development. All this was generalized in the late 19th century by the Social Darwinism of Herbert Spencer which interpreted the whole society as a scene of struggle among individuals in which the human species is improved by the fact that the fittest survive. In the words of one commentator, two conceptions of the nature of things were in conflict here: "On the one hand was the belief that a natural order is inherently simple, harmonious, and beneficent; on the other hand that it is devoid of ethical attributes and that its laws have no relation to justice, reason or human welfare."[12]

The contradiction has not disappeared in the 20th century. Stripped of all dissembling and tendentious appeals to freedom, the argument might be stated thus: there is a mechanism in the free market by which millions of individual choices in pursuit of profit, pleasure and power, even at the cost of their neighbors, are converted into the general progress and prosperity of the human race. Despite the amorality of the process and despite the many injustices it leaves in its trail, most attempts to achieve the same benefits by responsible human policy will lead to disaster. We must depend on the science of economics to show us the way toward a common good that will emerge and be defined in the process itself.

The Collectivist Reaction

It is not surprising that there should be in modern society a reaction against all of this, nor that this reaction should develop on the same foundations that liberal individualism had laid. The movement founded by Karl Marx is liberalism both refuted and intensified.

First, Marxism shares the liberal understanding of human nature, but without the aura of divine providence at work in the process and without the illusions of private religiosity which tempered the contradiction in the liberal creed. Humanity, in Marx's view, is a self-creator by its own productive labor without determinate limits on its capacities to remold nature in its own image. But it is species humanity which has this character, not a collection of competing individuals. This term needs explanation. Collectivist is my word for it, but it would not be Marx's own. The human being in Marx's understanding is universal. There is no ultimate distinction between public and private, collective and individual. Each person embodies a species and realizes its destiny through his or her own productive self-expression. This solidarity was the character of primitive Communism as it will be of the Communism to come. The vision which has its roots in John Locke and Adam Smith, and which still operates in the technological optimists of today, is here absolutized and removed from all limits, whether nature or God or the teleological order of all being.

Second, Marx grasped the dark side of the science of 19th century economics and made it a key to understanding the dynamics of modern society. Class conflict was Ricardo's idea. Marx made of it a total explanation of the process. *Capital* is a brilliant restatement of Ricardian economics in all its scientific rigor as leading not to prosperity but to catastrophe. Labor is indeed the source of all value, but the price of labor is no more than the physical existence and procreation of the laborer. The difference between the two is the expropriation of the laborer's humanity in the form of capital. In the nature of the case, the rate of exploitation must intensify and the misery of the evergrowing masses must increase. The free choice of the worker in the marketplace is ever more restricted. The private economic power of a few, which is the source of political and all other forms of power in the society, is ever more concentrated, until the inhumanity of the system becomes intolerable. The logic of liberal economics is carried to its conclusion.

Third, Marx developed the liberal understanding of human power into an instrument of revolutionary transformation. The key was precisely the humanity of this power. The proletariat, deprived of all the private property, therefore of all that would individualize each member and give him or her a stake in the dehumanizing struggle for personal gain and status, becomes the negative image of species humanity. In deprivation, the solidarity of a new public humanity is formed. Human nature becomes human again and, as such, the instrument of revolutionary change. In Locke's terms, a state of nature is again created, but in a context of species humanity which makes the social contract irrelevant.

Fourth, in a strange continuity with the liberal vision of a *laissez faire* society, the new humanity after the revolution will be, in Marx's vision, without coercion, without power, yet fully developed as a prosperous technological society in which each member will naturally find his or her own place in the process of production while remaining in his or herself a universal human being. One cannot help but be reminded of Aristotle at this point. The good will indeed be that toward which all things aim. There will be a reason which all share and develop according to their capacities. It will be a *polis* though without politics. And the whole will be directed toward the *telos* of human mastery over nature.

Until that time, in Marx's faith, the good cannot be known; only the science which analyzes the dynamics of alienation, and the strategy of revolution. Yet even in the communist society the good will still be the efficient and not the final cause. It will be the product of the labor of species humanity.

Persistence of the Common Ideal

There is clearly no agreement in modern society about the common good, or even whether such a thing can be defined at all without reflecting the interest of one group against another. Still the yearning for it remains. Most modern defenders of a free enterprise economy defend the system not only because it is the law of human society, but because it works to human benefit better than any form of socialism. The Roman Catholic lay letter, *Toward the Future,* defines a dual standard with a clear priority: "A market system is validated because it is the only system built on the liberty of its participants. That it also works better to promote invention and yield an incredible bounty is a secondary, although not an insignificant, advantage."[13] It is the subordinate criterion however which gets the most attention in the letter. It is clear that the authors regard this bounty as to be shared by all. "No economic system can pretend to do everything sufficiently for a good society. Many human requirements must be met outside and beyond it: the young, the elderly, the disabled, those visited by sudden misfortune and many others who are, permanently or for a long time, unable to work. In a good society, the moral system and the political system must come to the assistance of such persons in ways the economic system alone cannot."[14] Milton Friedman is less circumspect. He would abolish such protections for the disadvantaged as price support programs for agriculture, rent control, minimum wage laws, social security, low-cost housing programs, and even national parks, all in the name of individual liberty. Even he, however, proposes a negative income tax for the relief of poverty, and in extreme cases his kind of liberal, he says, "may approve state action toward ameliorating poverty as a more effective way in which the great bulk of the community can achieve a common objective. He will do so with regret, however, at having to substitute compulsory for voluntary action."[15]

Only Robert Benne is something of an exception. He develops his justification of a free enterprise system entirely on the basis of a concept of justice of which individual liberty, including equality of opportunity, is a fundamental component. In this, informed by Reinhold Niebuhr, he shares as a Christian the skepticism of liberals and Marxists about the self-interested character of rational statements of the common good that are not worked out by the give and take of the power struggle in the democratic system. He advocates capitalism as a means of domesticating this struggle.[16]

Similarly Marxists, despite their doctrines of class consciousness and revolutionary action, are constantly seeking to legitimize their power in socialist societies and the policies of their parties elsewhere by reference to universal moral terms such as peace, justice, and people's democracy. This is not entirely hypocrisy. There is a hidden moral agenda, a yearning for the social system that will be truly universal in its appeal and benefits, which continually motivates and drives even the most extreme Marxist-Leninist parties. The common good, they say with one voice, is an idealistic concept which justifies the powerful and enervates the poor and the oppressed by relativizing their self-confidence in the struggle. But with another voice, they claim that a society of free universal participation in the power and progress of species humanity is now emerging in the oppressed parties, led by Marxists who know the laws of history, and that all people can join in allegiance to this emerging common good.

It clearly is Marxism that presents the strongest challenge at this point. It seeks to convict us of hypocrisy in all our definitions of what the common good is, and of justifying or ignoring the oppression and alienation of those who are excluded by our understanding and our system. Liberals have a basis for rejecting this attack. The private individual is their focus and they do not claim to define common values beyond those that regulate and provide access to free competition. Christians, however, have fewer defenses. We cannot help but be reminded by the Marxist charge of the dynamics of a relationship which sends us, with the Lord of the Covenant, out of our various structures and communities to seek those who are excluded and alienated from the community of promise.

At the same time, Christians and Marxists confront each other most sharply on a deeper level than defining the common good. The issue at stake is the character of human sociality and of human hope as it is expressed by the place and destiny of the poor in our midst. It is Marxism which has combined both the liberal and the Aristotelian challenge to Christianity in a new form. The individual becomes a collective universal humanity imbued with all the technological optimism and power which the world provides, but without the judgment and grace of interpersonal relations as both limit and liberation. At the same time Marxism projects an ultimate good as completely dominated by the order of the *polis* as anything that Aristotle conceived. Human freedom is totally subject to the rationality of that system in the name of the essence of true humanity. There is no covenant there. All of this is done in the name of oppressed and alienated humanity — the poor in Christian lingo — who are excluded from a community of benefits sanctified by appeals to moral order and the consolations of religion, which their exploiters enjoy.

The Place of the Poor

Who, then, are the poor? What is their relation to any possible definition of the common good? For Aristotle they simply were not a category. Women, slaves, alien workers *(metics)*, all had their subordinate places in the proper political order but the concept of the excluded as a basis for moral judgment was absent. For liberal individualism the poor are the unsuccessful, the casualties of freedom, possibly the objects of charity, but not the subjects of special rights or claims. Dialogue about the poor and their relation to the welfare of the whole community, is therefore primarily between Christians and Marxists. It turns, I believe, around four descriptions of who the poor are and what poverty means. They interact and the types are not pure. However, they represent distinctive emphases too often overlooked.

The Penniless.

There are the economic poor. This is the simplest and most common use of the word. These are the people who find the means of material life in short supply. They struggle for daily existence in a society where others are well off.

In both testaments of the Bible, poverty in this sense is constantly present. It is accepted as a fact of life and at the same time as a call to responsible community within the people of God. In the earliest Hebrew law code, protection for the poor is already built in. The justice of their suit may never be perverted (Ex. 23:3,6). The sabbath year must make provision for them (Ex. 23:10) and their debts must be forgiven (Deut.15:1-3). At any time "if there is among you a poor man, one of your brethren in any of your towns within the land which the Lord your God gives you, you shall not harden your heart or shut your hand against your poor brother, but you shall open your hand to him and lend him sufficient for his need, whatever it may be" (Deut.15:7-8). This message is carried forward throughout Old Testament history and into New Testament times. To deliver the poor and give them justice is the mark of a righteous man (Job 29:12-16). To exploit them ranks with idolatry in the prophets' condemnation (Amos 2:6;5:11). The Lord hears the call of the poor and even "stands at the right hand of the needy to save him from those who condemn him to death" (109:31). The writer of Proverbs sums it up: "He who oppresses a poor man insults his maker but he who is kind to the needy honors him" (14:31).

All of this rests, however, on a premise which goes back to the calling of Abraham. Material well-being, even prosperity, is a blessing of God and a part of his covenant promise to his people. Furthermore, God in his faithfulness to the covenant renewed this promise repeatedly in the history of the Hebrew people. The wealth of the patriarchs from Abraham to Joseph was a sign of this. In the land flowing with milk and honey into which the tribes of the Exodus were led, it was promised that "there will be no poor among you for the Lord will bless you with the land which the Lord your God gives you for an inheritance to possess" (Deut. 15:4). The people of the exile centuries later were promised restoration of an even greater prosperity (Is. 55).

There is a paradox here. It is expressed in two verses of the same chapter of Deuteronomy: "There will be no poor among you" (v. 4) and "The poor will never cease out of the land; therefore I command you, you shall open wide your hand to your brother to the needy and to the poor in the land" (v. 11). Gerhard Von Rad suggests that the lawgiver setting the principle and the preacher concerned with compassionate human conduct were wrestling through this passage in the mind of the writer.[17] The result in any case was to qualify the concept of wealth and the concept of poverty in the life of the covenant people. Material prosperity in this context is a blessing, not a source or standard of the good. It is absolutely dependent on the primary relations of the covenant, on faithful obedience to divine calling, and on the realization of love and justice in the community. The peace of God may be found in the wilderness (Deut.8:2-6), or in exile (Jer. 29:1-7). Economic enterprise is blessed but the direction of it is toward embracing all in the life of the community. The test of this is relations with the poor. The issue was not economic equality or even a structure of rights but participation in the work of God's justice reaching out to include the marginal and the destitute and to vindicate them as participants in the calling and hope of the Hebrew people. Even so drastic a redistribution of wealth as the jubilee year (Lev. 25) was part of the dynamic of this promise. If the whole nation suffers calamity because the rich "sell the righteous for silver and the needy for a pair of shoes, trample the head of the poor into the dust of the earth and turn aside the way of the afflicted" (Amos 2:67), this too is part of the drama. At stake here is not a just or good social order in any sense that can be generally described, but the dynamics of the spirit of God at work among God's people. Rich and poor are brought into a relationship of judgment and grace in which judgment serves the promise that never ends.

The New Testament continues this relationship and radicalizes it. The blessing and promise for human prosperity continues. The steward (in Greek *oikonomos*) is its agent, a responsible official in charge of the affairs of the household, an estate, or even in one case (Rom. 16:23) a city. The apostle Paul extends this concept to the faithful management of the mysteries of God (I Cor. 4:1-2) and the message of the gospel (I Cor. 9:17). The Letter to the Ephesians is the peroration of this: "the stewardship of God's grace that was given to me for you — to preach to the nations the unsearchable riches of Christ, to make all men see what is the plan (*oikonomia*) of the mystery hidden for ages in God who created all things" (Eph. 3:2,9). The faithful management of all the gifts of God, both spiritual and material, was the calling of the Christian.

Stewards were expected to be productive. The parable of the talents, despite its misuse by preachers in our individualistic society, is in the gospels. The basic test of stewardship, however, was not productivity but faithfulness in human relations. "Who then is the faithful and wise steward whom his master will set over his household to give them their portion of food at the proper time? Blessed is the servant whom his master, when he comes, will find him so doing" (Luke 12:42-43). Jesus' own example in the gospel stories illustrates by outrageous exaggeration what this means. He was productive in turning water into wine for a marriage feast, or multiplying the fish catch of his disciples or the loaves and fishes for his hungry listeners. He was, at the same time, prodigal, both in example and advice, where human relations or the promise of the kingdom were involved. Two thousand pigs was a fair price for the sanity of one man (Mark

5:1-20). Zacchaeus' four-fold restitution was a sign of salvation (Luke 19:8-9). The kingdom of heaven is like a treasure in a field or a single pearl which in order to buy everything else is sold (Matt. 13:44-45). A rich young man, himself a potential steward were he not a wealth addict, is told to sell all that he has and give it to the poor and become a follower (Matt. 19:20-21). And the dishonest steward is praised for cutting the debts to his master in order to have friends when he lost his job. "I say to you, make friends for yourself by means of unrighteous mammon so that when it fails, they may receive you into the eternal habitations" (Luke 16:9).

All of this is no way to run an economic system. But it makes the basic point: in the community of promise and the coming kingdom, faith working through love is the saving reality. Material well-being and economic enterprise are blessed as they are used for this purpose. "Do not be anxious saying what shall we eat or what shall we drink or what shall we wear. For the Gentiles seek all these things and your heavenly Father knows that you need them all. But seek first his kingdom and his righteousness and all these things shall be yours as well" (Matt. 6:31-33). The poor are blessed because in their deprivation they can receive this message more easily. The rich find it extremely difficult. The intention of God for the community, as for ancient Israel, is that no one should be in need within it. But the give and take between rich and poor was a part of the realization of this goal. "Listen my beloved brethren, has not God chosen those who are poor in the world to be rich in faith and heirs of the kingdom which he has promised to those who love him?" (James 2:5). The elimination of poverty or the redistribution of wealth is not in the New Testament message an end in itself, but a function of reconciliation and shared hope.

It is time for the contrasting view. "The history of all hitherto existing society is the history of class struggle." So wrote Marx and Engels in *The Communist Manifesto* . "Free man and slave, patrician and plebian, lord and servant, guildmaster and journeyman, in a word, oppressor and oppressed, stood in constant opposition to one another, carried on an uninterrupted, now hidden now open fight, a fight that each time ended in either a revolutionary reconstitution of society at large or in the common ruin of the contending classes."

This view is not so different from liberal individualism as is sometimes thought. It describes the state of nature as Hobbes might have seen it a century after his time. It is the world of free competition as Malthus and Ricardo described it. It is not far different from the view of the Social Darwinist of Marx's day. The only differences lie in differing judgments on the origin and the social destiny of the same economically determined humanity. For Marx and Engels, the starting point of history was not the social contract which orders the free competition of individuals but the division of labor and therefore the domination of one class by another which broke up primitive communism in which all property was held in common and individuals were unknown.[18] Since then history has been driven by the exploitation of the laboring poor, by the class conflict and breakdown that results and by the establishment of new, more dynamic systems of exploitation in place of the old. This process has been clothed in ideologies that obscure reality by describing, as did Aristotle, the dominant position of some as part of the natural order and the subordination of others as giving them status in the system. Religion, for Marx, is the most dangerous and potent form of this ideology because it combines the very protest of the poor against their exploitation with the promise of eternal bliss which leads them to accept it.

All this however, says Marx and Engels, has been stripped away by modern capitalism. It is worth quoting *The Communist Manifesto* at this point. "The bourgeoisie, wherever it has got the upper hand, has put an end to all feudal, patriarchal, idyllic relations. It has pitilessly torn asunder the motley feudal ties that bound man to his 'natural superiors,' and has left remaining no other nexus between man and man than naked self-interest, than callous 'cash payment.' It has drowned the most heavenly ecstasies of religious fervor, of chivalrous enthusiasm, of philistine sentimentalism, in the icy water of egotistical calculation. It has resolved personal worth into exchange value, and in place of the numberless indefeasible chartered freedoms, has set up that single, unconscionable freedom — Free Trade. In one word, for ex-

ploitation, veiled by religious and political illusions, it has substituted naked, shameless, direct, brutal exploitation."

The whole of society is determined in consciousness and
action by this economic struggle. The poor are a class created by
the system. They negate it by their very deprivation. They are
the historical agents of its overthrow and of their own liberation.
When they, the vast mass of humankind, bring about the revolution, there will be no more poverty because all will share as producers and consumers in the commonwealth.

There has not been until very recent years a direct encounter
between this view of economic poverty and the biblical perspectives we have described. This has been in no small degree
the fault of the church. When the Christian community became
the society of Christendom, it was all too easy for the dynamic
of the covenant community to become a sanctified social structure. The poor were institutionalized into subordinate status.
The prophets of protest were too few and their message too
mixed with apocalyptic enthusiasm. After due credit is given to
the late medieval Catholic and early modern Calvinist moral theologians who tried to contain the avarice of the rising commercial economy and render it more just, there was still too little appreciation in the church of the dynamics of good and evil that
were at work in that economy. At length, the surrender of Christian ethics to individualism or to spiritual idealism was so great
that Marx's picture of the function of religion in 19th century
capitalism: "the general theory of this world — its enthusiasm,
its moral sanction, its solemn complement, its general basis of
consolation and justification," was a recognizable description.[19]
The few Christian socialists he met could be dismissed as irrelevant. The Christian economic ethic of the 20th century is post-
Marxist.

Nevertheless, the Marxist concept of economic determinism
extends a biblical insight into the contemporary world. The
drive for security and wealth does determine human actions and
the result is that poverty is a structural, not just a personal, problem. To bring the poor into full participation means curbing the
autonomy of economic power and creating a community of full

employment in the kind of work that makes a contribution to society.

This having been said, the question remains about the poor as a class, the agents of their own liberation, and the arbiters of the common good. To answer this we turn to a second understanding.

The Oppressed

The poor have been defined as those who are oppressed, who are the victims of the exploitation and domination of others, and who are alienated from the society in which they live. They are passively or actively in conflict with the powers and values that dominate that society, and this conflict defines their very being.

This is at heart a social rather than an economic definition. The basis of alienation may be class. It may also be race, culture, language, religion, or condition of servitude. It is also a definition that requires us to look into the particular circumstances in each society, because members of these categories may or may not be oppressed, alienated, rebellious and therefore poor by this understanding.

Nevertheless, this condition is as old as the story of human conquest and domination. The Hebrews were born as a people in the experience of it and in rebellion against it. Their entire history was dominated by the sense of being poor in this meaning of the word. They were surrounded and at times decimated by stronger enemies, exiled, restored and then conquered again first by the Seleucid and then by the Roman Empires. They were sustained in all this only by the power and loving kindness of God. It was a condition made ecumenical by Roman domination which was the socio-political context of Jesus' ministry and the mission of the early church. In one sense the whole Jewish nation was oppressed, waiting for the messiah's deliverance. The same could be said of other subject peoples to whom the gospel came. In another sense the common people were victimized by rulers who were tolerated and sometimes disciplined by Rome.

In a third sense the truly oppressed were the rebels, the Zealots, who fought in the hills and were hunted down by the authorities. Jesus' message had to be addressed to all these levels of indignation. His church in the early centuries had the same relation to the victims and the rebels throughout the empire, even while it shared their fate.

Nor has poverty as oppression and rebellion been missing from the history of Christendom. It was an element of many of the heresies of the middle ages and in their millennial hopes it challenged the reformation through its militant radical sects.[20] Out of this experience the Dutch fought a war to become Protestant and the Irish became passionately Roman Catholic. One could multiply examples.

The issue is furthermore still internal to the life of the church today. Missions spread throughout the world in the 19th century in a thoroughly ambivalent relation to European-American imperialism. They were at various times and in various ways bearers of the liberating message of a new humanity in Christ and symbols, even instruments, of a new domination. They planted the church, and then controlled it beyond their time. Third-World Christianity is still today trying to define its identity in relation to this heritage. It is joined in this by black churches in the United States and South Africa and by advocacy groups for the disadvantaged of all kinds.

To all of this ferment, both Christian and secular, Marxism has made one tremendous contribution. It has universalized the consciousness of oppression, providing the victims with tools of analysis and strategies in their struggle. It is a curious fact that the appeal of Marxism has had very little relation to the accuracy of its economics. It has succeeded in countries with weak capital development and few industrial workers but where the feeling of being victimized by the dominant system was most strong. Marxism communicates the hope and strategy of total revolutionary systemic power change, wherever this need is felt. No other faith or ideology in history has played this role.

There is also of course the great weakness, some would say the menace, of Marxism. It gives one systemic solution to the problem of human oppression. This solution is based on a collective vision of true humanity and on unlimited confidence in collective human struggle. The result is that neither the complexity of oppressive systems under which the poor suffer, nor the wonderful plurality of human goals which the poor seek, is rightly understood. The subtlety of human freedom is overridden in a massive assertion of human power.

What then can Christians say out of their faith concerning the victimized and rebellious? Let me offer three comments.

First, a sense of being victimized, of suffering unjustly and rising in protest against it, is common not only to the external condition of the Hebrew people of the Old Testament, but also to their internal life. Many of the Psalms seem to be written by such victims. "Why doest thou stand far off O Lord? Why dost thou hide thyself in times of trouble? In arrogance the wicked hotly pursue the poor. Let them be caught in the schemes which they have devised" (Ps. 10:1-2). "Because the poor are despoiled, because the needy groan, I will now arise, says the Lord. I will place him in the safety for which he longs" (Ps. 12:5). "Give the king thy justice O God — may he defend the cause of the poor of the people, give deliverance to the needy, and crush the oppressor" (Ps. 72:1, 4). Nor is the word "poor" in any of its Hebrew forms always used to describe the victims. For the prophet Micah it is simply the people who suffer at the hand of the wicked. "They covet fields and seize them and houses and take them away. They oppress the man in his house, a man and his inheritance — you rise against my people as an enemy. You strip the robe from the waist of those who pass by trustingly with no thought of war" (Mica: 2:2, 8). The awful fact was that for the people of ancient Israel the enemy was within and without. And it was the enemy within against which the Psalmist and prophets most often called down the judgment of the Lord.

This, however, also defined the nature of the protest. The Psalms were recited by all the people of the temple. Prophets spoke to those whom they condemned. The protestors were themselves subject to the judgment of the same God they called on to condemn the oppressors. They were bound in one community seeking the form of its obedience.

Second, in the story of the Exodus and the calling of Israel into nationhood, rebellion and covenant go together in a divine purpose. "If you will obey my voice and keep my covenant, you shall be my own possession among all peoples for all the earth is mine, and you shall be to me a kingdom of priests and a holy nation" (Ex. 19:5-6). The liberation is not an end in itself but the beginning of a responsibility which will include even the oppressing nations. Reminders of this calling are built into the Hebrew law. "You shall not wrong a stranger or oppress him for you were strangers in the land of Egypt" (Ex. 22:21). In freeing a slave, "you shall remember that you were a slave in the land of Egypt and the Lord your God redeemed you" (Deut. 15:15). But the real test of this calling comes after the destruction of Jerusalem. "Seek the welfare of the city where I have sent you into exile," writes Jeremiah to the Jews in Babylon, "and pray to the Lord on its behalf for in its welfare you will find your welfare" (Jer. 29:7). It was a foretaste of the vision of the suffering servant who bears the sins of many and makes intercession for the transgressors, and in this ministry becomes a light to the nations. The calling of God to the oppressed poor, if Israel is the model, it is not to liberation as such but to an obedience which in prosperity or suffering intercedes for the oppressor and reaches out to bring him into the covenant.

Third, the New Testament church was a church of the poor in large part. It too suffered at the hands of the powers of the day. Its witness was, however, remarkably free, as was the ministry of Jesus, from preoccupation with the conflict. In Christ's resurrection a new reality had dawned whose aim was the reconciliation of the world in him. Christians in this community were already free, although in the world they might be slaves, already called into life although in the world they might face suffering. This placed the struggle against oppression in perspective. The principalities and powers of the world must still be resisted (Eph. 6:12). But the resistance is a witness to the Lordship of Christ which shows them their proper function and place. Even submission (Rom. 13) and intercession (I Tim. 2:2) are in this sense forms of resistance. They are also forms of transformation which aim at a new, juster social peace.

Does this mean that the Church in New Testament times or

now is on the side of the oppressed? No if this means participation in their own revolution. Yes if it invites them to a resisting and transforming responsibility for the powers and the system of which they are victims.

The Disabled

There are two more forms of poverty which must be mentioned, although it is only the biblically informed tradition that gives them status. First, there are the poor who are so because they are disabled, the victims not first of oppression or lack of funds but of disease or of physical, mental or emotional handicap. These are the poor of every society regardless of its structure. They will always need the help of others to bring them into such participation in the community as they can sustain. These poor play at least as large a role in the biblical story as do the others. Hebrew has a special word, *dal,* to describe them. It can also be translated "weak." Everything the Old Testament says about God's concern for the economic poor applies to them with emphasis. They need help in their defenselessness: "How long will you judge unjustly and show partiality to the wicked? Give justice to the weak and the powerless, maintain the right of the afflicted and the destitute, rescue the weak and the needy from the hand of the wicked" (Ps. 82:2-4). Yet they like all others are called to full participation in the covenant community. They too are bearers of the calling of God.

In the New Testament, the picture of this group is stronger and more vivid. Indeed, one commentator suggests that it may be the dominant meaning of the Greek word *ptokos.*[21] In matthew 11:4-5, the poor are listed along with the blind and the lepers, the deaf and the dead. Luke 4:18 quoting Isaiah identifies the poor with the captives, the blind, and the bruised. Poor Lazarus was probably a leper (Luke 16:20). These with other texts suggest that a poor person in the New Testament sense was not a permanent social class but persons who were for various reasons, some physical and some mental, some circumstantial (e.g. widowhood Mark 12:42), cannot survive as independent participants in society. Jesus' healing ministry, but also his preaching ministry were directed at these with special consideration, as has been the ministry of the church ever since.

There is, however, a subtle danger in this ministry. It has taken advocacy groups in our own generation to remind us of this. It is the danger of moving only in one direction. Compassionate help may go out to the disabled. A context of care may be established. Indeed in communist as well as in capitalist countries, the church is often encouraged to establish this community of care because neither Marxism nor liberal individualism has a role for the permanently poor. But the covenant community does not move simply from our strength to their weakness. It involves their ministry to us as well. Poverty is indeed a scandal; one must work to eliminate it. Disease is to be healed and disabilities are to be overcome. But there are people who will not be made whole, and who in their weakness can communicate to us something of the patience and faithfulness of God. Without them, we are not made whole. "The poor you have always with you" is not only a call to duty; it is a promise.

The Meek

The last form of poverty to be mentioned is basically spiritual. It is rooted in the Hebrew word *anav* meaning humble or meek. The related word *ani* is used many times in the Old Testament for the poor and carries something of the same connotation. Gutierrez calls it spiritual childhood.[22] "For I will leave in the midst of you a people humble and lowly. They shall seek refuge in the name of the Lord, those who are left in Israel; they shall do no wrong and utter no lies nor shall there be found in their mouth a deceitful tongue" (Zephaniah 3:12-13). The meek may be economically poor or disabled, but their basic characteristic is a humbleness to God's leading and a renunciation of personal claim. They are the poor in spirit of the Beatitudes, participants in the servanthood of Christ. In this sense Christ himself was poor and his followers are "as poor yet making rich" (II Cor. 6:10).

This dimension epitomizes the paradox of the church's relation to poverty as a whole. Christians are stewards of the unsearchable riches of Christ for the world. This involves us in the struggle to minimize all poverty, especially when rooted in exploitation and injustice. Yet we know that our real goal is not this but the building of free communities of persons informed by the love of God through the witness of the church, in which the good can be continually rediscovered and defined in the mutual correction and service of the members, including the full participation of the poor. In this ministry, however, concern for our own economic and social rights may be a barrier. Before God, we are poor. This is not an option; it is a calling. Only so can we witness to God's covenant which embraces and gives hope to us all.

The Promise of Community

Is there then a common good? The answer must depend on the way in which it is sought. As a rational order common to all humanity it is clearly an illusion, however much we yearn for it. The vital forces of human ambitions, ideals, loyalties and creative projects have made it obsolete in a world of scientific-technological revolution. This much at least we must learn from the liberal transformation of human consciousness during the past three centuries. No longer can we impose on all society the goals and values, however reasonable or good, which for one group in society seem to define the meaning of the whole. Where religious authorities attempt to do so — one might mention the diverse cases of Iran and South Africa — the consequences are monstrous. Where romantic nationalists try it they stifle freedom in their own countries and heighten world tensions. The Leninist form of Marxism has been the most ambitious attempt in our time to recreate a good that would be common, by using and subverting the forces of an individualist competitive world, defining it as alienation, and building a single unified humanity on its ruins. The results, though they seduce many Christian idealists, have been disastrous. We must start with the liberal premise: the search for a common good must start with the particular goals and values which many different persons and groups pursue, and seek, in mutual respect, some accommodation.

For those who do not share the liberal optimism about human cooperative competition or the liberal indifference to the plight of the poor, this can sound like endless conflict and movement from one tenuous compromise to another—at the cost of justice. Christians, however, are graced with another perspective. God is good in an active sense, establishing his covenant with his people and through them with all people. Exploration of this relationship, and its implications for human relationships throughout the world, is the substance of the church's witness and mission. It is the hope for the realization of relative but dynamic forms of justice and good in the world. These cannot be known beforehand. They are discovered in the three-way dialogue between the God whom the biblical history reveals, the neighbor, and the self.

It is the poor who test the integrity of this process, in the various forms of their poverty. They are the ultimate neighbors, to be loved, to be heard, to be empowered to correct and limit us as we face our common judge and redeemer, while we work out together the forms of just and promising community which reflect the divine work in the world's economy.

Notes

1. *The Nicomachean Ethics* , Book I, paragraph 1.

2 Gustavo Gutierrez, *A Theology of Liberation* (Maryknoll, N.Y.: Orbis Books, 1973), p. 47.

3. The conflict had its roots in the World Conference on Church and Society, Geneva 1966. Cf. C. West, *The Power to be Human* (New York: Macmillan, 1971), Part One, Chapter 1. It has continued down to the present, reflected in contrasting emphases in reports from the World Conference on Faith, Science and the Future in Cambridge, Mass., 1979 (Cf. *Faith and Science in an Unjust World* , Vol. 2, *Reports and Recommendations,* Part One, Chs. II-VII vs. Ch. VIII, and Part Two, Chs. II-III, Geneva 1980), and in the VI Assembly of the World Council of Churches in Vancouver, 1983 (Cf. C. West. "Before and After Vancouver," *Theology Today,* Vol. XL, October 1983, pp. 336-346.)

4. See *Catholic Social Teaching and the U. S. Economy* , The Second Draft, as reproduced in *Origins* , Vol. 15: No. 17, October 10, 1985. For several commentaries see the volume, *Catholic Social Teaching and the U.S. Economy: Working Papers for a Bishops' Pastoral,* editors John W. Houck and Oliver F. Williams (Washington, D.C.: University Press of America, 1984).

5. Johannes Pedersen, *Israel: Its Life and Culture* (London: Oxford University Press, 1959), I-II, p. 309.

6. Michael Foster, "The Christian Doctrine of Creation and the Rise of Modern Natural Science," *Mind* , 1934, or more recently Mary B. Hesse, *Science and the Human Imagination* (New York: Philosophical Library, 1954) and Carl Friedrich von Weizsacher, *The Relevance of Science* (New York: Harper and Row, 1964).

7. Oddly, there is agreement here between some Roman Catholic writers, e.g., Jacques Maritain, *Three Reformers* (New York: Scribner, 1929) and Karl Marx, *Critique of Hegel's Philosophy of Right* (various editions available), see especially the Introduction.

8. Lynn White, Jr., *Machina Ex Deo* (Cambridge, Mass.: MIT Press, 1968).

9. Max Weber, *The Protestant Ethic and the Spirit of Capitalism* (London: Unwin Paperbacks, 1985).

10. John Locke, *Of Civil Government, Second Essay* (various editions available), Chapter II, No. 6.

11. Milton Friedman, *Capitalism and Freedom* (Chicago: University of Chicago Press, 1962), ch. I.

12. George H. Sabine, *A History of Political Theory* , 3rd. edition (New York: Holt, Rinehart and Winston, 1961), p. 688.

13. *Toward the Future: Catholic Social Thought on the U.S. Economy* . (Lay Commission on Catholic Social Teaching and the U.S. Economy, 1984), p. 26.

14. *Ibid.* , pp. 32-33.

15. Friedman, *Capitalism and Freedom* , p. 195.

16. Robert Benne, *The Ethic of Democratic Capitalism* (Philadelphia: Fortress Press, 1981).

17. Gerhard Von Rad, *Deuteronomy* (Philadelphia: Westminster Press, 1966), p. 106.

18. K. Marx and F. Engels, *The German Ideology* (various editions available), Part 1.

19. K. Marx, *Critique of Hegel's Philosophy of Right: Introduction.*

20. Marxist historians delight in tracing the revolt of the poor in Christendom through these figures and movements from the early

Gnostics through Joachim of Flora, the Cathari, the radical Hussites, and Thomas Muntzer. Cf. Ernst Bloch, *Man on His Own* (New York: Herder and Herder, 1970) and F. Engels, *The Peasant War in Germany* (various editions available).

21. Bruce J. Malina, *The New Testament World (Atlanta: John Knox Press*, 1981), p. 85.

22. Gutierrez, *A Theology of Liberation* , p. 296.

Three

The Biblical Vision of the Common Good

JOHN J. COLLINS,

The Relevance of Scripture to the modern debate

In their recent pronouncements on *The Challenge of Peace* and on the U.S. Economy, the Catholic bishops begin with reflections on the teaching of Scripture. Since the relevance of the biblical texts to contemporary problems is not always obvious, it is well to begin here with some reflections on the significance and force of this appeal to Scripture.

Scriptural citations are a conventional part of ecclesiastical rhetoric. Since Vatican II they have generally replaced the traditional appeals to natural law as the basic moral grounding for Catholic social teaching.[1] The citation of scripture is usually taken to imply a claim to transcendent authority, like the claim previously based on natural law. Indeed Catholic moral teaching often gives the impression of exploiting the claim to divine revelation, without then being bound by the content of that revelation. From the viewpoint of critical biblical scholarship, however, the Bible cannot support the claim to transcendent authority. The study of the Bible over the last two centuries has amply demonstrated that it is the record of an historic people, through the vicissitudes of its very particular history. The social message of the Bible, like everything else in it, is historically conditioned and relative. The Bible can no more provide us with objective, transcendent moral certainties than can natural law.

Nonetheless, the Bible is relevant to our present discussion for two reasons. The first is broadly humanistic. The Biblical ethic has had a profound and long-lasting influence on human civilization especially in the west. It deserves our consideration on its own merits, just as Plato's *Republic* or any other classic text from the past does.[2] The second is specific to the Catholic, or other Christian, community. Christianity is not a deposit of timeless truth but a religious tradition which derives its identity from continuity with the past. The Bible is the foundational document of that tradition and so occupies a fundamental place in the definition of Christian identity. This does not oblige us to accept everything in the Bible, but *de facto* if we were now to reject the Bible completely we would have cut ourselves off from the root of our tradition and it would be misleading to persist in calling ourselves Christian at all.

The Bible then is a controlling factor in deciding what constitutes Christian, or Catholic, social principles. Principles should not be called Christian unless they are in continuity with the Bible in some significant way.

To decide what is in continuity with the Bible, however, is neither simple nor straightforward. The Bible consists of historically specific texts which were composed to address the problems of the day in the ancient Near East. Nowhere is this more apparent than in the Pentateuchal laws on social and economic matters, where we encounter such provisions as "when a man sells his daughter as a slave . . ." (Exod 21:7). Any modern appropriation of the Bible must find a way to distinguish between "what it meant" and "what it means,"[3] between the specific ancient laws and the principles which can be adapted to new situations. The problem of historical distance can not be by-passed by mystifying appeals to the status of the canon or the role of the spirit.[4]

The Bible itself offers some clues as to how it may be adapted to new circumstances. It is not a unified composition but the collected documents of a tradition that spans more than a thousand years. Already in the laws of the Mosaic covenant we can distinguish between the apodictic laws of the Decalogue, which provide sweeping general principles ("thou shalt not kill," "thou shalt not steal") and the casuistic laws which tailor these principles to fit varying circumstances.[5] ("Whoever strikes a man so that he dies shall be put to death. But if he did not lie in wait for him . . . then I will appoint for you a place to which he may flee." Exod 21:12-13). We can also see how biblical laws evolved in the various Pentateuchal codes, and how the prophets interpreted traditional law in specific situations. There are, then, biblical warrants for seeking to distinguish between the historically specific biblical laws and their underlying principles. The bishops are well advised when they maintain that our attention should focus, not on the specifics of biblical law, but on "the Bible's deeper vision of God, of the purpose of creation, and of the dignity of human life in society."[6] Nonetheless it is only through the specific applications that we can properly grasp the underlying principles. The Bible is not a perfectionist document which is content with proposing moral ideals. It is rather the record of a tradition which constantly addressed specific problems and was concerned with practical results.[7] There is no foolproof method for correctly inferring the right application of biblical principles to new situations. Nonetheless the tradition demands that the attempt be made. The bishops are at least faithful to the biblical process in attempting to address concrete contemporary problems.

The Place of Social Ethics in the Bible

On questions of social and economic justice, it is primarily the Hebrew scriptures which demand our attention. The teaching of Jesus in the New Testament, is to be sure, greatly concerned with the problems of wealth and poverty, especially in the Gospel of Luke; as the bishops note. Yet Jesus was not a legislator, and his teachings bear mainly on the conduct of individuals. He presupposes a vision of the social order which he inherited from his Jewish tradition and which is today the common heritage of Jews and Christians.

There is no doubt that a vision of the social order is at the very heart of biblical faith. There is at present little consensus on the historical question of how Israel emerged as a distinct entity in Canaan.[8] There is widespread agreement, however, that earliest Israel was distinguished by its particular social order, most especially by the fact that for a time "there was no king in Israel." (Judg 19:25) The great law codes of the Pentateuch had their origin in this early period. They are not royal proclamations but tribal law. They certainly underwent development at later times but they remained independent of royal authority. The Hebrew Bible has often been characterized as "salvation history" or as "revelation in history." It might equally well be characterized as "revelation in law." One scholar, Norman Gottwald, has gone so far as to argue that Yahweh, God of Israel, should be understood primarily as a symbol for an egalitarian model of society.[9] Gottwald's formulation is extreme, but he is right that the worship of Yahweh was understood from the outset to imply a commitment to certain social values.

The Covenant

The laws of the Pentateuch are presented in the context of a covenant between the god Yahweh and the people Israel. Modern scholarship has shown that this covenant was conceived on the model of international treaties in the ancient Near East, specifically of vassal treaties whereby one people became subject to another.[10] These treaties followed a conventional format, three aspects of which concern us here:

First, there was an historical prologue which rehearsed the events that led up to the making of the treaty and clarified the reasons for it.

Second, there were stipulations—the specific behavior required by the treaty. The subject or vassal must pay tribute, support the overlord in time of war and not become the vassal of any other lord. In return the overlord promised to protect his subjects.

Third, the treaty was confirmed by curses and blessings, of which the gods were guarantors.

There was, then, a simple logic to the covenant form. The essence of the relationship was defined by the stipulations or requirements. The history, on the one hand, and the curses and blessings on the other, supplied a supporting framework which was conducive to the observance of the laws.

The covenant between Yahweh and Israel was focused on the right of the people of Israel to possess their land. The historical retrospective claimed that they had received the land as a gift from Yahweh. The greatest curse with which they were threatened was loss of the land. Their continued enjoyment of the land was contingent on their observance of the covenant laws.

Divine Ownership of the Land

The most fundamental principle of biblical ethics is the belief in the reality of a God who is lord of the covenant. Vassals in the ancient Near East pledged their loyalty exclusively to one overlord and even promised to "love" that lord in the practical sense of faithful allegiance. Israel, with equal exclusivity, pledged its loyalty to Yahweh. Deuteronomy is especially insistent on this point: "Hear, O Israel, Yahweh is our God, Yahweh alone, and you shall love Yahweh your God with all your heart, with all your soul and with all your might" (Deut 6:4). The land was a gift of God, not something Israel had earned, or to which it had an intrinsic right: "Beware lest you say in your heart, My power and the might of my hand have gotten me this wealth! You shall remember Yahweh your God for it is he who gives you power to get wealth . . ." (Deut 8:17-18). The land is ultimately the property of Yahweh. This point is expressed most directly in Leviticus 25:23: "The land shall not be sold in perpetuity for the land is mine; for you are strangers and sojourners with me." Consequently, there are constraints on the ways in which the human tenants may use the land.

The religious faith of ancient Israel is not widely shared in contemporary America. Few, even of those who profess to share it, conceive of divine ownership of the land with the realistic seriousness of Leviticus. The belief in divine ownership can no longer serve as a common basis for public dialogue. If we wish to relate this principle to contemporary issues, we must demythologize it, i.e. understand it in terms of its practical consequences for Israelite society. Most basically, the emphasis on the unity of God symbolized the unity of the people. The command to love God entailed a command to serve the common good, or in biblical idiom, to love one's neighbor as oneself. The affirmation that the land belonged to God meant that in principle it belonged to all, not only to all the people at any given time but also to all generations. The covenant was addressed to the entire people of Israel and the morality of individuals was viewed only in that context.

The Sabbatical Laws

The practical implications of divine sovereignty for social ethics were spelled out in the Pentateuchal law-codes. Perhaps the most striking stipulations are the so-called "sabbatical laws."[11] The idea of the sabbath rest is familiar from the Decalogue. It is attested by the prophet Amos in the eighth century (Amos 8:5) and so is verifiably ancient. It was not prescribed for the leisure of the wealthy. The commandments repeatedly insist that it also applies to "your manservant, or your maidservant or your cattle, or the sojourner who is within your gates." Exodus 20:11 gives a theological reason for the commandment: "for in six days the Lord made heaven and earth, the sea and all that is in them, and rested on the seventh day." Elsewhere however we find a more socially-oriented explanation: "Six days you shall do your work, but on the seventh day you shall rest; that your ox and your ass may have rest, and the son of your bondmaid and the alien may be refreshed." (Exod 23:12) Deuteronomy is more emphatic: "the seventh day is a sabbath to the Lord your God; in it you shall not do any work, you, or your son, or your daughter, or your manservant, or your maidservant, or your ox, or your ass, or any of your cattle, or the sojourner who is within your gates, that your manservant and your maidservant may rest as well as you. You shall remember that you were a servant in the land of Egypt . . ." (Deut 5: 13-14). In this latter case the rationale is evidently to prevent the exploitation of servants, or slaves.

In the Book of the Covenant (Exod 20:22-23:33), which is usually regarded as the oldest of the Pentateuchal codes,[12] the sabbath rest is extended to the land: "For six years you shall sow your land and gather in its yield; but the seventh year you shall let it rest and lie fallow, that the poor of your people may eat; and what they leave the wild beasts may eat. You shall likewise with your vineyard, and with your olive orchard" (Exod 23:10-11). It is not certain whether the whole land was originally supposed to observe the law simultaneously, or whether it could be staggered for individual fields.[13] Deuteronomy 15 clearly envisages a fixed sabbatical year for the remission of debt, but does not mention letting the land lie fallow. The practical difficulty of a fixed sabbatical year is obvious. It is acknowledged in Leviticus 25: "And if you say, 'what shall we eat in the seventh year if we may not sow or gather in our crop?' I will command my blessings upon you in the sixth year, so that it will bring forth fruit for three years." (Lev 25:20-21). This answer is idealistic rather than practical, and this is even more true of the Levitical legislation about the jubilee year in the same chapter.[14] We simply do not know how, or how far, the law was observed. After the exile Nehemiah tried to enforce observance of both the sabbath and the sabbatical year (Neh 10:31) but the only time we read of the actual observance of a sabbatical year is in the time of the Maccabees (1 Mac 6:49, 53).

Regardless of the actual observance, the intention of the law was evidently to protect the land from exploitation. There is also the implication that the natural fruit of the land belongs to all the people, and so the poor could enjoy it at least every seventh year. These intentions are reflected in several laws in Deuteronomy: the forgotten sheaf is to be left for the sojourner, the vineyard and olive trees should not be gleaned a second time (24:19-22), the ox that treads the grain should not be muzzled (15:4).

The practicality of the sabbatical laws, even for antiquity, is open to some question. The objectives, however, were important, and remain matters of concern for our own time: how do we preserve the land for future generations and how do we provide for the poor in society? The biblical laws do not provide a viable method for solving these problems in the modern world, but they suggest an attitude which is a prerequisite of any solution. The landowners of ancient Israel were forbidden to think primarily in terms of their individual profits but were directed to think instead of the common good. They were not to grasp at everything they could. The ideal was to have enough and to leave whatever was extra for others.

A second area where the distinctive methods of the Hebrew Bible can be seen concerns the treatment of slaves.[15] Leviticus 25:39-46 explicitly forbids Israelites to take their fellow Hebrews as slaves, for the obvious reason—"for they are my servants, whom I brought forth out of the land of Egypt" (25:42). Instead they should be treated as hired servants. Like many of the social laws of Leviticus, this one probably reflects a (fairly late) ideal, rather than actual practice. The older laws in the Covenant Code (Exod 21:2-6) and Deuteronomy (15:12-18) allow the possession of Hebrew slaves, but require that they be released in the seventh year.[16] This law provides a good illustration of the importance of historical context. The logical implication of the Exodus story, which was clearly perceived in Leviticus, was not drawn out in Exodus or Deuteronomy. It is difficult to be sure whether this was due to a lack of vision or was rather a compromise with the prevailing custom. Deuteronomy clearly provides for an element of compromise. At the outset of Deuteronomy 15 we read that "there will be no poor among you . . . if only you will obey the voice of the Lord." (15:4). Yet the next passage in 15:7 begins "If there is among you a poor man . . ." and follows with the realistic admission that "the poor will never cease out of the land" (15:11). The next passage (15:12) deals with the case where people are forced by poverty into slavery. The Deuteronomic writers did not expect, or even attempt, to eliminate poverty, but only to set limits to it and thereby to alleviate it.

A third law which may serve to illustrate biblical social ethics concerns lending practices.[17] All the Pentateuchal law codes prohibit taking interest from fellow Israelites (Exod 22:24; Lev 25:35-37; Deut 23:20), although it is permitted to take it from foreigners (Deut 27:21). It was permitted to take pledges, but again there were restrictions. For example, the creditor was forbidden to enter the debtor's home to seize the pledge, and garments taken in pledge should be returned before night-fall (Deut 24:10-13). We can infer from the prophets that this law was not always observed, but the intention is clear. Moreover, debts were supposed to be remitted in the seventh year. In all, biblical law was not conducive to a profitable banking industry. Here again, we must distinguish between the objective and the means used to attain it. It is evident from Deut 15:9 that the sabbatical release sometimes backfired, making it more difficult to obtain a loan at all.[18] The objective, however, was to do whatever would actually help to relieve the poverty of the debtors.

Some variation and development can be seen in the biblical laws, but the general principles are clear enough. On the one hand, they place restrictions on the aggrandisement of individuals and on the other they provide protection for the weaker members of the society.

There is evidently a strong egalitarian impulse in the Israelite tradition, based on the recollection that "we were slaves in the land of Egypt." Yet at no point do the laws envisage a complete elimination of wealth and poverty. It is assumed that there will always be rich and poor. The objective is rather to maintain equilibrium. Accordingly, every provision was made to keep the allotted lands within the family or tribe even if the individual owner had to part with them.[19] The laws were designed to prevent monopolies and situations which could force the poor into slavery.

The Rationale for Social Ethics

The preceding sample of biblical laws may suffice to show that a communitarian ethic was at the heart of the religion of Israel. The good of the individual is always viewed in the context of the community. The welfare of the community determines the welfare of the individual. We must now consider the kinds of rationale on which this ethic rests.

In the context of the Sinai covenant, three warrants are provided for obedience to the commandments:—divine command, appeal to history and appeal to consequences.

The appeal to divine command is perhaps the most obvious warrant for the covenantal laws. Fundamental though it was in antiquity, this appeal can bear no weight in a modern retrieval of biblical ethics. The point here is not only that people are now less likely to accept the force of such an appeal. More fundamentally, we now recognize that the claim to divine authority was conventional for lawgivers in the ancient Near East.[20] Such claims were a rhetorical device which could be used to legitimate any ideology. Within the Bible, divine authority sanctions the slaughter of the Canaanites as well as the release of slaves. This warrant offers no way of distinguishing which principles have enduring validity. It does not provide a constructive basis for a modern discussion.

The most serviceable warrant for ethical behavior in the Bible is the appeal to consequences. The "bottom line" of the covenant is that obedience is rewarded with a blessing; disobedience is punished with a curse. In this sense the covenant appeals to the enlightened self-interest of the community. We should emphasize that self-interest here is communal self-interest; there is no question of opposing the interest of the individual to that of the community in the biblical laws. We should also emphasize the importance of the adjective "enlightened." The covenant claimed to disclose a moral order in history which was not always evident in the short-term. Appreciation of the force of the covenant required the wisdom to take a long-term view. In this regard the Sinai covenant is fundamentally similar to the other great ethical tradition of ancient Israel, the wisdom literature, which, as is well-known, relied on a highly pragmatic theory of reward and punishment.[21]

The other warrant supplied by the covenant, the appeal to history, also includes an element of enlightened self-interest. The typical reminder that "you were slaves in the land of Egypt" implies the possibility that you might find yourselves in that situation again. Accordingly, as you would that men should do to you, so should you do. The recollection of Israel's particular history, then, serves as a reminder of human commonality. No one is exempt from the possibility of being a slave or an alien. There is also an appeal to the intuition of human sympathy here, but this in turn rests on the recognition that we are all vulnerable to the vicissitudes of life.

The various warrants of the Sinai covenant are complementary and not in tension. It is important to recognize that biblical law does not rest only on an apodictic appeal to divine authority. There is also an attempt to persuade, by recollection of the past and by positing a moral order in history, so as to argue that obedience to the divine commandments was, in fact, in the enlightened self-interest of the people.

Illustrations from the Prophets

The practical implications of the covenantal social ethic can be seen most clearly in the preaching of the eighth-century prophets. While it may be that the Pentateuchal laws reflect to some degree the practice of pre-monarchic Israel, it is quite clear that different social patterns prevailed in the monarchic period.[22]

The upper classes began to expand their holdings and force the smaller owners off the land. We get our first illustration of the problem in the story of Naboth's vineyard in 1 Kgs 21. The king of Samaria wanted the vineyard "for a vegetable garden, because it is near my house." However, Naboth was unwilling to sell or exchange his ancestral heritage. The queen, Jezebel, resolved the problem by having Naboth stoned and his land confiscated. Elijah the prophet pronounced a blistering curse on the king, but he was powerless to prevent the seizure of the land. This incident seems to be all too typical of the situation addressed by the eighth century prophets such as Isaiah and Amos.[23] "Woe to those who join house to house, who add field to field, until there is no more room and you are made to dwell alone in the midst of the land." (Isa 5:8). The expansion of the rich was only the converse of the oppression of the poor. Amos denounces those who "sell the righteous for silver, and the needy for a pair of shoes" and "trample the head of the poor into the dust of the earth." The people "lay themselves down beside every altar upon garments taken in pledge, and in the house of their god they drink the wine of those who have been fined." (Amos 2: 6-8). Small landowners were forced to sell themselves into slavery because of their debts. The expanding landowners were more interested in vineyards and wine than in producing the staples of life to feed the peasants.

The charge which Amos and Isaiah bring against the rich of their day is not only that they are doing wrong to the poor but that they are violating the common good. By the common good I mean that which is ultimately in the best interest of all the society, rich and poor. Specifically, they claimed that social injustice would cause the Assyrian invasions, which would lay waste both Israel and Judah, bring an end to the northern kingdom of Israel and send its ruling class into exile. Ironically, then, the rich in Israel were fashioning their own destruction by their behavior.

A Moral Order in History?

We touch here on another basic presupposition of the Israelite social ethic: the belief that there is a moral order in history. The Mosaic covenant was founded on the belief that the material welfare of the people is directly influenced by their moral behavior. This belief is pervasive in the account of the so-called Deuteronomic history from Judges to Kings, and also in the prophetic books. It gives the social ethic of the Bible a pragmatic, consequentialist orientation.

Here again the biblical presupposition is not widely held today, and indeed the moral order of history was perceived to be problematic as early as the Book of Job. The belief that history, even the history of the people of Israel, follows a convenantal pattern has been undermined by the apparent randomness of weal and woe through the centuries. We should not, however, go to the other extreme and posit utter randomness. Human actions do indeed influence the course of events, even if the correlation is not as simple as the covenant would seem to suggest.

When the prophet Isaiah said that Assyria was the rod of Yahweh's anger (Isa 10:5) to punish Israel and Judah, he was speaking in mythological idiom of divine intervention in history. Modern critical historiography requires that events be explained in terms of human causality, thus Isaiah's analysis must be de-mythologized. Since the prophet spoke of God acting through human agents (the Assyrians), this move does no real violence to the biblical text. Isaiah saw the root of Judah's problems in the pride of its rulers, who aspired to superhuman status by the pursuit of wealth and military power.[24] He denounced attempts to form international alliances, which served only to attract the punitive force of Assyria (Isa 31:1-3). In the prophetic view the rulers were led to oppose Assyria, and so court disaster, by their desire for power and status as an independent nation. The same ambition led to social exploitation within the society, so that wealth could be concentrated in the hand of the rulers. There was then an intrinsic connection between internal social abuses and the policies that led to confrontation with Assyria. This analysis of history was probably over-simplified, since it takes too little account of Assyrian greed and aggression, but it was not entirely mistaken. The social abuses in eighth century Israel and Judah were related to the political actions that led to national disaster.

The biblical view of a moral order in history cannot now be affirmed without qualification, but it should not be completely dismissed either. Precisely because we see the greater complexity of historical causality, we should recognize that economic policies are interwoven with other social and political issues and the social ethic we espouse may indeed have reverberations in other areas of society. The biblical view of history can at least serve as a reminder that social and economic problems can not be isolated form the political welfare of the society as a whole.

The Social Ideal

The prophetic critique of individualist profiteering in monarchic Israel shows that even in the ancient world there were competing visions of the national interest. In one view, the national interest entailed independence and respectability as a nation and the development of wealth and luxury for the upper classes. Amos sketches this ideal vividly, though only to denounce it, when he describes "those who are at ease in Zion and feel secure on the mountain of Samaria, the notable men of the first of the nations . . . those who lie upon beds of ivory, and stretch themselves upon their couches and eat lambs from the flock and calves from the midst of the stall; who sing idle songs to the sound of the harp, and like David invent for themselves instruments of music; who drink wine in bowls, and anoint themselves with the finest oils . . ." (Amos 6:1-6). These people could probably be described more sympathetically by someone less passionate than Amos. Their luxury was not intrinsically evil: it was simply their view of the good life. Equally those who "joined house to house and field to field" (Isa 5:8) and had "a thousand vines worth a thousand pieces of silver" (Isa 7:23) could be viewed as the progressive developers of their day. Their wealth presumably brought some employment, and some of it must have trickled down to their servants. They had succeeded in creating wealth which was unknown to pre-monarchic Israel. Yet the prophets were outraged by the inequity it involved.

Their outrage arose from a different set of values. The issue was not only whether the peasants of Israel were better housed and fed as slaves under the monarchy or as free land holders in the earlier period (although such considerations were important). There was also the question of human dignity, which was violated by slavery and even by the extreme contrast between rich and poor. The prophetic ideal was that each family live under its own vine and its own fig-tree. (Micah 4:4). Theirs was an ideal of material sufficiency, but not of luxury, and also of the dignity of independence.

Neither the prophets nor the legislators of the Bible condemn wealth as such, and all regard material prosperity as a good. There is no preferential option for poverty in the Hebrew Bible. Both the legislators and the prophets are opposed to developments which magnify the gap between rich and poor. In a society with limited resources, if some people have more, others must have less. Given the inherent selfishness of human nature, one cannot assume that the rich will take care of the poor. The biblical legislators realized the need to protect the rights of the poor by laws. The experience of the prophets shows that laws alone were not enough. When there is an extreme division of wealth and power, injustice is virtually inevitable. The prospect of a just society then depends not only on legislating rights for the poor, but on restraining the acquisitive instinct of the rich and promoting an ethic of moderation. This ethic is radicalized considerably in the New Testament Sermon on the Mount, where we are urged to consider the birds of the air and the lilies of the field. Jesus was not legislating for a society as Deuteronomy was, but his message about fundamental attitudes to material goods also goes to the root of the problem of social inequity.

The laws of the Pentateuch often provide protection for the weaker members of society—the widow, the orphan, the alien, etc. The major prophets too, regularly speak up for the rights of the poor. Accordingly the modern slogan, "a preferential option for the poor," has some biblical warrant—most evidently in the case of a prophet like Amos. The phrase is less appropriate for the Pentateuchal laws—Leviticus 19:15 admonishes; "you shall not be partial to the poor or defer to the great but in righteousness shall you judge your neighbor." The bishops adopt the slogan with a qualification that "option for the poor" . . . "is not an adversarial slogan which pits one class against another. Rather it states that the deprivation and powerlessness of the poor wounds the whole community."[25] In short, the "option for the poor" is a strategy for restoring the balance to the common good. It is, of course, the poor and vulnerable members of a society, "the widow, the orphan and the alien," who need special legislation and the voice of a prophet to protect them. The presupposition of biblical ethics, however, is that the treatment of these people will ultimately determine the welfare of the nation as a whole.

Conclusion

The laws of the Pentateuch and the preaching of the prophets were born out of the very practical attempts of the people of Israel to regulate their society. They constitute a religious vision, founded on a belief in divine sovereignty and divine ownership of the land. The religious vision, however, is not an apodictic demand for altruism, but claims to represent the best interest of the community and of the individuals in it. The special provision for the poor and the restraint and moderation in the pursuit of material goods are recommended because they ultimately enhance the peace and prosperity of all.

Modern attempts to retrieve this biblical vision encounter many obstacles. On the one hand, there is the innate propensity of human nature to short-sighted individualism—a tendency which was also present in ancient Israelite society, as we know from the prophets. On the other hand, the problem is aggravated in modern times by the decline of belief not only in a sovereign God but in any moral order in the universe or in history. Beginning with the New Testament, Christianity relied on belief in an apocalyptic judgment, beyond the bounds of history, to provide the ultimate sanctions or ethics.[26] Apocalyptic imagery remains an important resource for the Christian tradition,[27] but if we want our ethic to serve as the basis for public discussion of economic policy, we need to demonstrate its value for this world too.

While the biblical conceptions of a moral order must now be qualified and revised, the attempt to ground ethics in the ultimate self-interest of the community is of fundamental importance. Enlightened self-interest is undoubtedly the most widespread rationale for all kinds of policy in contemporary American society. It often results in policies that are shortsighted and individualistic, but the fact that self-interest is often misconstrued is not a reason why it should be abandoned as a rationale for ethics. Pragmatic appeals to self-interest are fully in accord with biblical principles. The claim of the biblical tradition, however, is that concern for the poor and restraint in using material goods are ultimately in the best interest of all sectors of the community. The challenge to both the contemporary ethicist and economist who want to maintain this biblical tradition is to validate this claim in contemporary terms, by identifying the benefits which would accrue to society as a whole from the pursuit of the common good.

Notes

1. See the reviews of Catholic social teaching by Frs. Bartell and Curran in this volume. I am especially indebted to my colleague, Professor Leslie Griffin, for orientation to the issues in contemporary moral theology.

2. Compare David Tracy's definition of a classic as "any text, event or person which unites particularity of origin and expression with a disclosure of meaning and truth available, in principle, to all human beings." ("Theological Classics in Contemporary Theology," *Theology Digest* 25 [1977] 349) and his discussion of the New Testament as a classic

in *The Analogical Imagination* (New York: Crossroad, 1981), pp. 248-304.

3. The phrase of Krister Stendahl, *Meanings. The Bible as Document and as Guide* (Philadelphia: Fortress, 1984), p. 14.

4. Against the "canonical approach" advocated by B. S. Childs in several books, most notably his *Introduction to the Old Testament as Scripture* (Philadelphia: Fortress, 1979).

5. The distinction was formulated by A. Alt. "The Origins of Israelite Law," in *Essays on Old Testament History and Religion* (Garden City: Doubleday, 1968), pp. 101-171. For recent surveys of biblical law see D. Patrick, *Old Testament Law* (Atlanta: Knox, 1985) and L. Epsztein, *La Justice Sociale dans le Proche-Orient Ancien et le Peuple de la Bible* (Paris: Cerf, 1983).

6. *Pastoral Letter on Catholic Social Teaching and the U.S. Economy* (Washington, D.C.: National Conference of Catholic Bishops, 1985), para. 35.

7. On the "traditio-historical" approach to the Bible, which views the biblical material as a tradition in process, see J. A. Sanders, "Adaptable for Life: The Nature and Function of Canon," in F. M. Cross *et al.* eds., *Magnalia Dei: The Mighty Acts of God* (Garden City: Doubleday, 1976), pp. 531-60; D. A. Knight, ed. *Tradition and Theology in the Old Testament* (Philadelphia: Fortress, 1977). Compare the "historical contextual" approach advocated by T. W. Ogletree, *The Use of the Bible in Christian Ethics* (Philadelphia: Fortress, 1983).

8. The main approaches are summarized by N. K. Gottwald, *The Hebrew Bible. A Socio-Literary Introduction* (Philadelphia: Fortress, 1985), pp. 261-276.

9. Gottwald, *The Tribes of Yahweh. A Sociology of Liberated Israel* 1250-1050 B.C.E. (Maryknoll: Orbis, 1979), pp. 700-709.

10. The initial demonstration was made by G. E. Mendenhall, *Law and Covenant in Israel and the Ancient Near East* (Pittsburgh: The Presbyterian Board of Colportage, 1955). For a recent discussion see J. D. Levenson, *Sinai and Zion. An Entry into the Jewish Bible* (Minneapolis: Winston/Seabury, 1984), pp. 15-86.

11. R. de Vaux, *Ancient Israel* , vol. 1. *Social Institutions.* (New York: McGraw Hill, 1961), pp. 173-177; R. Gnuse, "Jubilee Legislation in Leviticus: Israel's Vision of Social Reform," *Biblical Theology Bulletin* 15 (1985), pp. 43-48.

12. S. M. Paul, *Studies in the Book of the Covenant in the Light of Cuneiform and Biblical Law* (Leiden: Brill, 1970).

13. de Vaux, *Ancient Israel* , p. 173.

14. de Vaux, *Ancient Israel* , p. 175: "There is no evidence that the law was ever in fact applied."

15. de Vaux, *Ancient Israel* , pp. 80-90.

16. The sabbatical release did not apply to foreign slaves, but Deuteronomy defies ancient Near Eastern custom by forbidding the extradition of runaway slaves (Deut 23:16-17).

17. de Vaux, *Ancient Israel* , pp. 170-173.

18. In the Roman era Hillel allegedly had to devise a legal ruse to bypass the sabbatical law and make it possible for borrowers to obtain loans. He decreed that a loan would not be cancelled in the seventh year if it was secured by a *prosbul* which explicitly declared that it could be collected at any time. See R. A. Horsley and J. S. Hanson, *Bandits, Prophets and Messiahs. Popular Movements in the Time of Jesus* (Minneapolis: Winston/Seabury, 1985), pp. 59-60.

19. de Vaux, *Ancient Israel* , pp. 166-67. See Num 27: 9-11 for the law of succession. Daughters could inherit (Num 27:7-8) but had to marry within their tribe. See also Lev 25:25, which requires the next of kin to "redeem" property sold because of poverty, by buying it and keeping it within the tribe. See Jer 32: 6-9, where Jeremiah buys the field of his cousin and the Book of Ruth, where Boaz buys the land of Elimelek.

20. The major ancient near eastern law-codes can be found in J. B. Pritchard, *Ancient Near Eastern Texts* (Princeton: Princeton Univ., 1955), pp. 159-198.

21. See J. Blenkinsopp, *Wisdom and Law in the Old Testament* (Oxford: Oxford University, 1983).

22. An ideal of justice was of course maintained in the monarchic period. See K. W. Whitlam, *The Just King. Monarchical Judicial Authority in Ancient Israel* (Sheffield: JSOT, 1979), pp. 29-37.

23. See R. Coote, *Amos among the Prophets* (Philadelphia: Fortress, 1981), pp. 24-32; B. Lang, "The Social Organization of Peasant Poverty in Biblical Israel," in *Monotheism and the Prophetic Minority* (Sheffield: Almond, 1983), pp. 114-127.

24. J. J. Collins, *Isaiah* (Collegeville: Liturgical Press, 1986).

25. *Pastoral Letter* , para. 90.

26. So the famous passage "I was hungry and you gave me food . . ." is framed in an apocalyptic judgment scene in Matthew 25. See J. R. Donahue S.J., "The Parable of the Sheep and the Goats: A Challenge to Christian Ethics," *Theological Studies* 47 (1986), pp. 3-31.

27. On the relevance of apocalyptic imagery see J. J. Collins, *The Apocalyptic Imagination* (New York: Crossroad, 1984), pp. 214-15; A. Yarbro Collins, *Crisis and Catharsis: The Power of the Apocalypse* (Philadelphia: Westminster, 1984), pp. 165-75.

Four

The Primacy of the Common Good

RALPH McINERNY

As a mere philosopher, I cannot and will not be expected to contribute anything that would have immediate applicability to the concerns of the U.S. bishops' pastoral letter on economic matters. Nonetheless, because in such documents our spiritual leaders are engaged in a reading of the signs of the times in the light of faith and of the Catholic intellectual tradition, a study such as this, devoted to the common good and its implications for business and the economy, can accomodate a contribution like mine, which concentrates exclusively on the presupposed doctrine.

Professor Houck and Father Williams are to be congratulated for putting their finger on this absolutely essential note of Catholic political and economic teaching and to have drawn our attention to the uses of the notion of common good already present in drafts of the pastoral. I suspect they would like to see an even greater emphasis put on the notion of the common good, and I could not agree more that this is indeed essential to our tradition. Indeed, it is precisely the traditional understanding of the common good that will enable the bishops, as well as others, both to draw attention to flaws in our economic thinking and policies as well as to make positive suggestions that will be manifestly in line with our own tradition.

The title I have chosen for my essay recalls a famous controversy of some forty years ago that involved Jacques Maritain, Yves Simon, Father Eschmann and Charles DeKoninck. Three of these men were connected with this university. Jacques Maritain, as some of us remember, regularly lectured here and in 1957 he was present at the inauguration of our Jacques Maritain Center of which I have the honor of being director. Yves Simon was a professor in the philosophy department at Notre Dame before going to Chicago — though he never left South Bend — and Charles DeKoninck, in the late 50's and early 60's, divided his academic year between Notre Dame and Laval University in Quebec. By coming at the doctrine of common good by way of a review of some aspects of the controversy that involved these three, I hope to make my ideas somewhat less esoteric than they might otherwise be.

The men who were involved in the controversy over the common good were all Thomists. That is, having taken note of the Church's naming St. Thomas Aquinas as, in a special way, the guide and patron of Catholic intellectual life, they devoted themselves to a study of his work, not as historians, not as antiquarians, but as seekers after truths that travel, truths that while encountered in a medieval setting could, with appropriate linguistic and conceptual adjustments, be made to speak to modern man and his problems.

Maritain once wrote, *"Vae mihi si non thomistizavero"* [Woe is me were I to cease to be a Thomist] and DeKoninck wrote "I hope so to understand Saint Thomas as always to remain a disciple who trusts his master." Well, the French express themselves differently than you and I, and so do the Flemish. But let no one imagine that these statements express a policy of intellectual servitude or dogmatism. Neither man held any position *because* St. Thomas held it.

I mention this first of all to suggest the ambience within which the best Catholic intellectual work has been done. Within a tradition, certainly, but interpreting, expanding and developing that tradition. (T. S. Eliot's essay dealing with the way in which a major poet both belongs to and alters the poetry of his language is pertinent. "Tradition and the Individual Talent" is a theme which could have engaged Maritain, Simon and DeKoninck.) That a sympathetic reading of the same sources does not produce identical results is clear from the dispute that arose over Maritain's effort to develop a Catholic, even Thomistic, personalism.[1]

Individual and Person

Maritain's efforts to develop a personalism were intended to provide an alternative to what he did not shrink from calling the divinization of the individual in modern thought and practice which had led to a divinization of the state. In "La conquete de la liberte,"[2] Maritain wrote of the false political emancipation and a false conception of human rights which derive from the anthropocentrism of Rousseau and Kant based on the autonomy of the human person. One is free if he obeys only himself. Maritain cited three political and social consequences of this divinization of the individual: (1) a practical atheism in society, since God appears as a threat to the autonomy of the individual; (2) the theoretical and practical disappearance of the idea of the common good; (3) the theoretical and practical disappearance of the idea of authority. The notion of Mass Man and of a leader who is an inhuman monster follow. Bourgeois liberalism thus paves the way to revolutionary totalitarianism.

This is stern stuff. Maritain is asserting that the political horrors of this century are a consequence of a false understanding of person and society and that they can only be effectively combated with a true understanding. Let us have before us Maritain's summary statement of that true alternative.

"La vraie emancipation politique, au contraire, ou la vraie citè des droits humains, a pour principe une conception conforme à la nature des choses, et donc 'theòcentrique,' de l'autonomie de la personne: d'après cette conception l'obèissance, quand elle est consentie pour la justice, n'est pas opposèe à la libertè, elle est au contraire une voie normale pour y parvenir; et l'homme doit progressivement conquèrir une libertè qui dans l'ordre politique et sociale consiste avant tout pour lui a devenir, dans des conditions historique donnees, aussi independant que possible à l'ègard des contraintes de la nature materielle. En bref la personne humaine, pour autant qu'elle est faite pour Dieu et pour participer à des biens absolus, dèpasse la sociètè terrestre dont elle est membre, mais pour autant qu'elle tient de la sociètè ce qu'elle est, elle est *partie* de la sociètè comme d'un tout plus grand et meilleur."[3]

A theocentric view, one that sees man as part of society but also as ordered to absolute goods, provides both a sounder conception of man as citizen of the earthly and heavenly cities. The essay from which I have quoted was published in 1944, but the thoughts of the passage were by no means late entries in Maritain's writings. In *Scholasticism and Politics*, citing a distinction between *individuality* and *personality*, Maritain urges that "*humanism of the individual* and *democracy of the individual*, in which the twentieth century had placed its hopes, must be replaced today — if we want to save civilization — by *humanism of the person* and by *democracy of the person*."[4] The distinction between individual and person is already present in the essay on Luther in *Three Reformers* (1925) and *Du regime temporel et liberte* (1933) and *Humanisme integral* (1936) as well as *Les droits de l'homme et la loi naturelle* in 1942. Already a prominent element in his thought, it was to continue to play a significant role.

Any student of Jacques Maritain will know that conceptions

that appear early in his thought (and continue to be used throughout his long career) sometimes develop over the course of time, becoming clearer and more subtle. It is sometimes also the case, that in later writings Maritain will simply take over passages from earlier ones, thus expressing satisfaction with the previous effort. Sometimes, however, an idea will wax and wane as far as clarity goes, and then it seems to be a good principle of interpretation to let passages comment on one another without exclusive regard for their chronology. In the case of Maritain's contrast between individual and person, which has such a long career in his writings, I think we find an instance of the third case. It is not always the later expressions which are the clearest. There are some expressions of the contrast which invite criticism.

The contrast between individual and person is used for a variety of purposes, but an abiding note is that it enables us to avoid a anthropocentric humanism or personalism, one that is effectively atheist, and to embrace in its stead a theocentric humanism or personalism. The social and political consequence of the contrast is that man is a part of civil society when considered as an individual, but transcends it when he is seen as a person. Man relates to the common good of civil society as individual, but as person he transcends that common good.

Furthermore, man as individual relates to material goods, but as person he relates to spiritual goods. "It is this material pole, and the *individual* becoming the center of all things, that the words of Pascal aim at. And it is on the contrary with the spiritual pole, and with the *person*, source of freedom and of goodness, that the words of St. Thomas are concerned."[5] Pascal had said "the ego is hateful" whereas Thomas wrote the person is that which is noblest in the whole of nature. The individuality of things is rooted in matter; matter sets off thing from thing; it is an appetite for what benefits the individual as such. "In so far as we are individuals, each of us is a fragment of a species, a part of this universe, a single dot in the immense network of forces and influences, cosmic, ethnic, historic, whose laws we obey. We are subject to the determinism of the physical world. But each man is also a person and, in so far as he is a person, he is not subject to the stars and atoms; for he subsists entirely with the very subsistence of his spiritual soul, and the latter is in him a principle of creative unity, of independence and of freedom."[6]

Since Maritain works with the definition of person that had been bequeathed to the Scholastics by Boethius — a person is an individual substance of a rational nature; that is, a person is a kind of individual — the contrast he is drawing presents difficulties. It is not simply a matter of distinguishing those individuals who are persons from those who are not — men from monkeys, say, but two ways of looking at man.

The contrast is not meant to point to two distinct *things* — man as individual, man as person — so much as to draw a moral contrast. Man as individual is grasping, acquisitive, egocentric; man as person is open to the spiritual. Maritain quotes with approval this passage from Garrigou-Lagrange: "Man will be fully a person, a *per se subsistens* and a *per se operans*, only in so far as the life of reason and liberty dominates that of the senses and passions in him; otherwise he will remain like the animal, a simple *individual*, the slave of events and circumstances, always led by something else, incapable of guiding himself; he will be only a part, without being able to aspire to the whole."[7] To be an individual thus appears to be a morally defective state for which one is responsible and to be a person a morally praiseworthy condition.

It is this that renders other passages which make social and political applications hard to understand. "Thus the individual in each one of us, taken as an individual member of the city, exists for his city, and ought at need to sacrifice his life for it, as for instance in a just war. But taken as a person whose destiny is God, the city exists for him, to wit, for the advancement of the moral and spiritual life and the heaping up of divine goods."[8] Here what pertains to man as individual and what pertains to him as person seems fixed and more or less definitional.

But what is puzzling about Maritain's position is that he seems to hold that man is both subordinate to the common good and that he transcends it. We must have before us a somewhat extended statement, again from *Three Reformers*:

"On the contrary, according to the principles of St. Thomas, it is because he is first an individual of a species that man, having need of the help of his fellows to perfect his specific activity, is consequently an *individual* of the city, a member of society. And on this count he is subordinated to the good of his city as to the good of the whole, the common good which as such is more *divine* and therefore better deserving the love of each than his very own life. But if it is a question of the destiny which belongs to man as a *person*, the relation is inverse, and it is the human city which is subordinate to his destiny. If every human person is made directly, as to his first and proper good, for God, Who is his ultimate end, and 'the distinct common good' of the entire universe, he ought not therefore, on this count, in accordance with his law of charity, to prefer anything to himself save God. So much so that according as personality is realized in any being, to that extent does it become an independent whole and not a part (whatever be its ties on other grounds.)"⁹

A puzzling position. Human development seems portrayed as a matter of escaping the net of society and its demands and relating oneself to spiritual goods, preeminently to God, with the result that only God could be preferred to oneself.

The Controversy

The difficulties and complexities of Maritain's contrast of individual and person with its implications for the common good invited criticism. And, in 1943, that criticism came in the form of a small book, Charles DeKoninck's *La primaute du bien commun* published in Quebec.¹⁰ The nub of the book had already been presented to L'Academie Canadienne Saint-Thomas d'Aquin in October, 1942, but the issue of the proceedings in which it appeared was not published until 1945 under the title "La notion du bien commun".¹¹ The 1943 book contained this essay and another "The Principle of the New Order." The subtitle of DeKoninck's book was significant: Against the Personalists. Was it an attack on Maritain? Maritain is not mentioned either in the original presentation nor in the book. Nonetheless, two defenders of Maritain rose to the defense.

Yves Simon, writing in *The Review of Politics*,[12] had praise for DeKoninck's efforts, finding that "it constitutes a very sound foundation for any further development of the theory of the common good"[13] adding, "insofar as DeKoninck's essay vindicates the primacy of the common good and carries out the criticism of definite positions, it is entirely praiseworthy."[14] Simon characterizes the target of DeKonick's attacks as "vicious stupidities" and "monstrosities." We are not surprised, accordingly that Simon does not consider Maritain's views to fall within the target area. But Simon laments the fact that the book's subtitle "Against the Personalists" could invite the interpretation that Maritain *is* its target or one of its targets because Maritain has embraced a kind of personalism. The views attacked by DeKoninck are as odious to Maritain as to anyone else and it would be pure calumny to suggest otherwise.

Up to this point, we have a possible interpretation of DeKoninck's title that could have been cleared up in a quince. Alas, the Dominican I. Thomas Eschmann decided to enter the debate with "In Defense of Jacques Maritain."[15] Eschmann maintained that the position DeKoninck attacked was that of Maritain, indeed of St. Thomas and all the Fathers for two thousand years, and Eschmann proceeds to defend it.

Did DeKoninck intend to attack Jacques Maritain anonymously, as a personalist? Is the position he attacked accepted or rejected by Maritain? I really do not know the answer to the first question, but I am confident the answer is no. He meant to attack Personalism. Eschmann's attack could scarcely be ignored, since the criticism was that DeKoninck had misunderstood St. Thomas, fighting words to any Thomist, and he replied in a lengthy piece, "In Defense of Saint Thomas," whose tone, unfortunately, echoes that of Eschmann.[16] The reply is longer than the original book and is guided by Eschmann's charges. Maritain does not figure in this exposition. It is fair to say that Eschmann was demolished by DeKoninck. It is also clear that Maritain nowhere holds the positions Eschmann embraces, certainly not in the explicit way of the Dominican. When Maritain wrote *The*

Person and the Common Good in 1947,[17] the controversy prompted him to greater clarity on matters that had hitherto been somewhat ambiguous.

It is nonetheless puzzling that the only allusion to the controversy is oblique, in the form of a note of thanks to Eschmann in the course of which Maritain says the positions attacked were not his!

> "Je remercie l'auteur de ces lignes d'avoir pris ma defense dens un débat qui a été assez vif au Canada et aux Etats-Unis, et où il s'était curieusement trouvé qu'en critiquant des idées qui ne sont pas les miennes on avait cependant, même quand on prenait soin de ne pas prononcer mon nom, donné à penser que j'étais obliquement visé. Je voudrais espérer que le présent essai, tout on rectifiant certaines formules excessives dont moi-même je n'ai pas fait usage, mettra fin aux malentendus et aux confusions dus au vice originel d'une telle controverse."[18]

That is an extremely Delphic note. Maritain thanks Eschmann, who ascribed to Maritain the positions DeKoninck attacked, but which Maritain says he does not hold, and hopes in the present work to rectify some excessive formulae, which he himself never used (Eschmann had?) And, without mentioning DeKoninck, Maritain suggests that DeKoninck was attacking him, though DeKoninck did not name him. The temperature of this controversy was raised by Eschmann and prevented what might have been a fruitful exchange. Simon's review is straightforward and civil and one can imagine a quite different sequel if Eschmann had not muddied the waters.[19]

Person and Common Good

Beyond the fine points of difference of expression, this controversy conveys the centrality of the common good, the primacy of the common good. What these Thomists are as one in opposing is the liberated individual of modern thought, the

Kantian person who has become his own end, the autonomous individual presupposed by contract theory, the Marxist person for whom all claims other than private ones are alienations to be overcome — society and God limit me and must be overcome.

Such a view of the human person, of the individual of a rational nature, tends to look at societal relations, politics and political economy, as devices whereby the good of the individual as such can be most prudently achieved. The social contract is something I enter into for my own good, my own proper good. The notion of common good is thereby denatured, becoming at best a mere abstraction. By that I mean some such claim as this: it is common to individuals to look after Number One.

In our tradition, on the contrary, man is by nature a political animal. He is a part of a larger whole or he would not exist. Human persons do not fall out of the sky and then confront the possibility of entering into social contracts. They are born to mothers, nurtured at the breast, raised and educated by father and mother, brought from total dependency to the point where they can be responsible members of the social groups to which they cannot not belong. Moral autonomy, according to this view, is not a matter of progressively weakening our links to others, but of developing them in terms of what is truly perfective and fulfilling of the kind of entity a human person is.

Even this beginning of a sketch makes it clear why the Church is opposed both to *laissez-faire* capitalism and to socialism. Both are grounded on a defective notion of the person and therefore of society. An economic system that aimed at profit only and saw others merely as objects of exploitation on the way to amassing greater and greater wealth would put the private good of the pursuer of wealth not only above the private goods of all others but above the goods shared by many. But of course such a view would deny that there is a good perfective of members of society which is not the private good of any of them, such as peace and order. One who wants peace and order simply as means to self-aggrandizement does not want them as common goods.

Classical socialism sees persons as mere units, without history, without family, without any features independent of their being parts of the invented social whole. Any discrimination between persons on the basis of property or talent or gender becomes abhorrent. It is Mass Man who becomes the ideal — the featureless constituent of the social machine.

It will be rightly pointed out that present day capitalism has developed away from this condemned capitalism, and the same could be said for present day socialism. To suggest that whatever nowadays is called capitalism or socialism comes under 19th century condemnations would betray a singular lack of subtlety.

What the traditional doctrine of the common good requires is that our defense of the capitalist system include the recognition of the primacy of the common good. And indeed most defenses of entrepreneurial capitalism maintain that this system best insures the welfare of members of a society and that it is this that motivates the entrepreneurial capitalist. Of course it will not do to say that there is some law according to which the greedy pursuit of personal wealth results in the best for most others. If this were merely an unintended accidental consequence it could not be introduced as a moral justification.

What the traditional doctrine of the common good requires is that any defense of even a modified socialism include the primacy of the common good. Not the collective good, not the greatest good of the greatest number, not some abstract criterion of particular acts no one knows how to apply. The recent attacks on Consequentialism must be confronted by those who would defend even a modified socialism.

Our bishops are wise to see the defense of the family as their most fundamental task, since if we do not learn the primacy of the common good in the family it is doubtful that we will see it in the political and economic orders. The good of the family is my good, one I share with other members of the family, and it takes precedence over my merely private good. I must love this shared or common good precisely as shareable by many but if I make sacrifices for it is not because I put the private goods of others above my private good. Rather, I acknowledge the primacy of a good common to many and more important than the individual or collective private goods of the many.

It is because human persons are ordered to a variety of common goods that the assertion of the primacy of the common good can sometimes seem to imply unacceptable consequences. When Maritain wrote of man as a person transcending the common good of society, what he meant is not that in the crunch, *qua person*, my private good takes precedence over the common good. Rather his concern was with the common good that transcends the common good of the city, the supernatural end to which we are called. The human person is ordered to God as to his happiness, his ultimate end, his supreme good. But God is the common good *par excellence*. It is not the Catholic view that human persons relate to God one-to-one, so to speak, with God being *my* good in an exclusive sense. Indeed, to love God merely as *my* good would be a defective love, it would be to turn God into my private good, as if there were commensurability between my finite will and infinite goodness. The only appropriate way to love God is as a good infinitely sharable. The rule of charity makes this clear. I must love my neighbor as, like me, ordered to a common good.

Envoi

The conception of the human person as chiefly and primarily perfected by common goods because he is naturally, inevitably, a member of society, as opposed to the view of man as chiefly a monad whose good is a private one such as societal arrangements are for his private good and nonetheless always diminishing of it, has implications for political theory and for political economy. This doctrine functions as a guide or measure. It is not the case that one can simply deduce from such considerations the best political or economic arrangements. More likely than not, such principles can be embodied in a variety of arrangements whose desirability or preferability has to be decided on other grounds. But any economic or political system which collided with the primacy of the common good would be to that degree unacceptable from the point of view of traditional Catholic doctrine.

Notes

1. The most pertinent books of Maritain are *Three Reformers*, published in Paris in 1925, English translation, 1929; *Du régime temporel et la liberté*, Paris, 1933; *Humanisme integral*, Paris, 1936, 2nd ed. 1947; *Scholasticism and Politics*, New York, 1939, *La personne humaine et la société*, Paris, 1939; *Les droits de l'homme et la loi naturelle*, Paris, 1947; *La personne et le bien commun*, Paris, 1947.

2. *Principes d'une politique humaniste*, New York, 1944.

3. *Ibid.*, p. 30.

4. *Scholasticism and Politics*, p. 56.‘

5. *Ibid.*, p. 58.

6. *Ibid.*, p. 62.

7. *Three Reformers*, p. 24.

8. *Ibid.*, p. 22.

9. *Ibid.*

10. *De la primaute du bien commun*, Quebec, 1943.

11. Pp. 51-108.

12. *The Review of Politics*, Vol. VI, (Notre Dame, IN, 1944), pp. 530-533.

13. *Ibid.*, p. 531.

14. *Ibid.*, p. 533.

15. *The Modern Schoolman*, Vol. XXII, no. 4, (St. Louis, Mo., 1945), pp. 183-208.

16. *Laval theoloqique et philosophique*, Vol. 1, no. 2, (Quebec, 1945) pp. 3-103.

17. *La personne et le bien commun*, Paris, 1947.

18. *Ibid.*, p. 12, note.

19. Yves Simon, in a letter to Jacques Maritain written December 11, 1945 relates a conversation he had with Jacques de Monleon in Quebec the previous summer in which he summed up the doctrine of the common good in five propositions on which "il y avait accord parfait entre vous, moi, Dek et lui meme." The five points are: "1. Any good of a higher order is greater than any good of a lower order. 2. Within a given order, there is absolute primacy of the common good over any private good. 3. When a person is an absolute person (God) there is an absolute coincidence of common and personal good. 4. To the degree that a created person is a person there is a tendency toward a coincidence of personal good and common good. 5. There is no restriction on the primacy of the common good in its order; when this primacy

disappears (3 and 4), this is not because the primacy then belongs to a private good, but that the problem of primacy disappears." (my translation) Simon was convinced from first to last that there was this accord and that the suggestion there was not was libelous. There is little doubt of Simon's agreement with DeKoninck and that, here as elsewhere, Simon's expression of Maritain's position gives it a new clarity.

cial church documents including those of Pope John XXIII in the early 1960s insist on a greater role for the state than did the earlier documents. As mentioned before, these later documents still refer to the principle of subsidiarity, but this principal is now used to justify a greater role for the state than in the past. Pope John XXIII in *Mater et Magistra* still cautions against the danger of the state taking away the rightful role of individuals and voluntary associations. But he recognizes that public authorities are requested to intervene in a wide variety of economic affairs, and are called to a more extensive and organized way than heretofore to adapt institutions, tasks, means, and procedures to the common good (par. 54; O'Brien and Shannon, p. 63). These two emphases are not necessarily incompatible; however, there is need for the official teaching to recognize both of them and to show how they are compatible. The danger is that in talking about religious liberty, one will stress a lesser role of the state; whereas in talking about social and economic concerns one will speak about a greater role for the state.

Another important characteristic of the understanding of the content of the common good in more recent church documents concerns the world-wide nature of the problems facing humankind. In the beginning of *Populorum Progressio*, Pope Paul VI insists: "Today the principal fact we must recognize is that the social question has become worldwide" (par. 3; O'Brien and Shannon, p. 313). Subsequent church documents in their treatment of the contemporary issues well illustrate this fact. No question today can be discussed merely in terms of the problems affecting one country or one area of the world alone. The obligations of the first world vis-a-vis the Third World are very significant. In this context of the growing recognition of the solidarity of all human beings in the world there is much less emphasis on the common good within individual countries. The greater emphasis on ecological problems throughout the world also illustrates this same development. This very significant new emphasis will of necessity tend to see all problems in terms of the universal solidarity of all human beings in all parts of the globe rather than in light of the common good of a particular nation.

Five

The Common Good and Economic Life: A Protestant Perspective

J. PHILIP WOGAMAN

The commitment by Christians to a "common good" transcending purely individual interests enjoys deep support in both Catholic and Protestant traditions. Protestant Christians who share this commitment must, however, admit to certain ambiguities in their traditions that have clouded public consideration of the common good. It is well-known that some kind of relationship exists between Reformation moral theology and the emergence of modern capitalism, and it is well-known that modern capitalism has often eroded communitarian values in a sea of individual self-interest. Friedrich Engels interpreted Protestantism in part as an expression of bourgeois class interests in the epoch of capitalism.[1] Max Weber, while not attributing capitalism to Protestantism—as he is sometimes erroneously blamed for doing, did find a certain affinity between the Lutheran and (especially) Calvinist conceptions of vocation and the emerging new economic system.[2] As the theological restraints of Luther and Calvin progressively faded in the modern era, capitalism could "escape from the cage" of such restraints and purely secular versions of vocational freedom could find more individualistic assertion in unrestrained *laissez-faire*.[3]

Luther and Calvin had both emphasized the importance of service in the economic life of Christians. Even though their respective versions of the doctrine of vocation are quite different, both insisted that we are "called" in our economic existence to serve others. It is utterly impossible to find warrants in either Luther or Calvin for self-centered individualism in our economic life. A characteristic passage from Calvin's institutes makes the point:

> When the Scripture enjoins us to lay aside private regard to ourselves, it not only divests our minds of an excessive longing for wealth, or power, or human favor, but eradicates all ambition and thirst for worldly glory, and other more secret pests. He who has learn to look to God in everything he does, is at the same time diverted from all vain thoughts. This is that self-denial which Christ so strongly enforces on his disciples from the very outset. Self-denial has respect partly to men and partly (more especially) to God. For when Scripture enjoins us, in regard to our fellow men, to prefer them in honor to ourselves, and sincerely labor to promote their advantage he gives us commands which our mind is utterly incapable of obeying until its natural feelings are suppressed.[4]

While there may be a certain spiritual individualism embodied even in such a condemnation of economic selfishness, the Calvinist influence inspired the founding of holy commonwealths, such as the Commonwealth of Massachusetts, in which the common good was taken to be the common objective of all participants.

Later Protestant leaders, such as John Wesley, expressed this same abhorrence of personal selfishness; but by couching economic ethics in individualistic terms, a Wesley could open the door to a substitution of charity and private philanthropy for the deeper sense of common enterprise. (Wesley asked his early Methodist followers to gain all they could, in order to save all they could, in order to give all they could. Many Methodists, no doubt, were more successful in the first two of these than in the third!)[5] Still, it could be argued that even this was a subordination of private well-being to the economic needs of others. And the so-called "left-wing of the Reformation," the "diggers" and "levelers" and such groups, were quite intentionally communitarian in their conceptions of the common good.[6] It is a fair generalization that virtually no Protestant theologian prior to the 19th century can be cited in support of unrestrained economic individualism.

That may not be as true if we throw in Protestant philosophers, for two of the latter, in the 17th and 18th centuries, made enormous intellectual contributions to the emergence of *laissez-faire* capitalism. John Locke, with his conception of property as deriving from the essentially individual act of a person's withdrawing something from the state of nature through his/her own labor, did much to legitimize the notion of private property as an absolute derived from the natural moral order.[7] That notion continues to infuse the work of libertarians, such as Robert Nozick, who hold that it is theft for government to tax the property of those who have worked for what they have.[8] And it was a Protestant moral philosopher, Adam Smith, who developed the view that the public good is best served by individuals seeking their own self-interest, provided this is done in a capitalistic market system. In such a system, according to Smith, even one who is concerned with only self-interest "is led by an invisible hand to promote an end which was no part of his intention."[9] Smith follows this famous quotation with a remark contemptuously dismissing the idea that one could "trade for the public good." There is a sense, of course, in which Smith's view is formally governed by the objective of public good. It can be argued that the individualism of Smith reflects only his empirical finding that the public good, the "wealth of nations" from which all economic good is derived, is best served by individual self-interest in a free market system. Nevertheless, if we are indeed counseled to think only or primarily of our personal self-interest—trusting that somehow this will inure to the public good through the work of the "invisible hand," then we are at least let to sub-

ordinate the common good at the level of our conscious intention. We are free to be as self-seeking as we wish in the conviction or illusion that is also the essence of economic morality.
The 19th and 20th centuries have been the full-throated expression of this philosophy on the part of a few theologians and
many lay Christians.

Twentieth-century Protestant economic doctrine has largely
been a reaction against the individualism of *laissez-faire* capitalism, particularly if one consults the official statements of mainline Protestant denominations and ecumenical bodies. The Social Gospel Movement, spanning roughly the years between the
U.S. Civil War and World War I, was largely a Protestant response
to the economic distress suffered by many people in the wake of
the Industrial Revolution.[10] First led by a few venturesome souls
and isolated groups, the movement came to influence the denominations themselves early in the 20th century. For instance,
the Methodist Episcopal Church (one of the forerunners of the
present-day United Methodist Church) adopted a "Social Creed"
in 1908 which vigorously advocated a set of economic rights
for people who were especially vulnerable in the new industrial
system.[11] These included the "abolition of child labor," such
"regulation of the conditions of labor for women as shall safe-
guard the physical and moral health of the community," and
"the most equitable division of the products of industry that can
ultimately be devised." Apart from a vague call for "complete
justice for all men in all stations of life," this document could not
be said to articulate a conception of the common good. But
clearly it was a rejection of unrestrained individualism in economic life. The Social Creed was promptly adopted by the new
Federal Council of Churches, a forerunner of the present National Council of Churches, as an expression of ecumenical economic teaching.[12]

Following World War I, Protestant and Eastern Orthodox com-
munions joined in ecumenical expression of social witness, first
through the Life and Work Movement (essentially begun at the
Stockholm Conference on Life and Work, 1925, and continued
in the great Oxford Conference of 1937) and then through the

post-World War II development of the World Council of Churches. Particular economic teachings varied with the historical development of this ecumenical tradition. But a common theme throughout is the subordination of private interest to public good. Thus, for instance, the Stockholm Conference affirmed, "in the name of the Gospel," that "industry should not be based solely on the desire for individual profit, but that it should be conducted for the service of the community,"[13] And the Oxford Conference, while affirming the importance of private property, argued that "individual property rights must never be maintained or exercised without regard to their social consequences or without regard to the contribution which the community makes in the production of all wealth."[14] The First Assembly of the World Council of Churches (Amsterdam, 1948) insisted that "we must vindicate the supremacy of persons over purely technical considerations by subordinating all economic processes and cherished rights to the needs of the community as a whole."[15] The Oxford Conference and the Amsterdam and Evanston (1954) Assemblies of the World Council of Churches developed and refined a measured criticism of both cases insisting on the subordination of ideological commitments to deeper Christian values.[16] The Amsterdam and Evanston Assemblies also developed the normative idea of the "responsible society," a formula emphasizing the accountability of economic as well as political power "to God and the people whose welfare is affected by it."[17] This formulation was not understood as an alternative ideology but as a criterion of all systems and ideologies. Following the Fifth Assembly (Nairobi, 1975), the World Council of Churches developed a new normative conception, the "Just, Participatory, and Sustainable Society," with the noteworthy addition of concern for future generations.[18] In harmony with its predecessors, the Sixth Assembly (Vancouver, 1983) saw the unity of the church—a persistent ecumenical objective—as an instrument and sign of the unity of all humanity: "The Lord prays for the unity of his people as a sign by which the world may be brought to faith, renewal and unity."[19] This theological perception, that we all belong to one another as we belong to God, has profound implications for economic and political policy when taken seriously.

The informed critic can discern through the sixty-year history of statements by the Life and Work Movement and the World Council of Churches the imprint of many individual Christian thinkers. The earlier statements reflect considerable influence from American and European versions of the Social Gospel Movement. During the middle decades of this ecumenical history, creative theological minds of the stature of Karl Barth and Reinhold Niebuhr were notably influential. In more recent years, the liberation theologians have had substantial impact. It is not as easy to trace direct connections between the papal conciliar versions of the "common good" theme and the World Council's work, but plainly all have been addressing the same problems and all have, to a considerable extent, been fed by similar sources of theological insight. We will note some similarities and differences in these two broad streams below. But whatever the differences of source and development, it is noteworthy that one can gain very little support from either Roman Catholic or Protestant/Eastern Orthodox ecumenical statements for the proposition that the common good should be subordinated to individual good in economic and political life.

The *meaning* of common good, and how it is to be related to individual good, remains, however, to be considered. Ecumenical and Roman Catholic efforts offer us negative as well as positive insights in our quest to understand the meaning of common good. But both agree that the good of the wider community—indeed, of all humanity—is the inescapable implication of Christian faith and the unavoidable objective of Christian discipleship. There is room for much difference of opinion over questions of fact and strategy, as there are wide variations in the Christian interpretation of the meaning of common good; but there appears to be a real consensus among Roman Catholic, Protestant, and Eastern Orthodox Christians that the common good has an overriding claim upon the Christian conscience.

The Meaning of "Common Good"

We have already noted that common good at least means the

repudiation of any purely individualistic conception of economic life. In defining the common good more fully, however, much depends upon the normative sources upon which we depend. Leo XIII, whose encyclical *Rerum Novarum* is rightly credited with initiating and shaping subsequent Catholic social teaching, presents us with a doctrine of property which is largely derived from Lockean sources (in spite of Leo's repudiation of the excesses of individualism)[20] and with an emphasis upon family and social hierarchy which is largely derived from Thomistic versions of natural law.[21] In that version of social good, economic responsibility does not appear to go much farther than the obligation of employers to provide wages large enough to sustain the families of their employees[22] and for persons of means to be generous to the poor—but only with what is left over "when necessity has been supplied, and one's position fairly considered."[23]

The Stockholm Conference, while unaffected by traditional Catholic natural law conceptions, was clearly influenced by personalistic versions of natural law. That conference appealed to "the soul" as "the supreme value," and insisting on "the rights of the moral personality, since all mankind is enriched by the full unfolding of even a single soul."[24] The good society can here be understood as whatever is required to enable personality to blossom forth, to be all that it was created to be. That personalistic way of putting it can also be traced through subsequent ecumenical doctrine, at least through the period in which the idea of the "responsible society" was most influential. It can be argued that the "responsible society" formulation was, itself, greatly influenced by Lockean thought, more in terms of the latter's social contract than his view of the natural right of property. The responsible society, it will be remembered, is "one where freedom is the freedom of men who acknowledge responsibility to justice and public order, and where those who hold political authority or economic power are responsible for its exercise to God and the people whose welfare is affected by it."[25]

Translated into the "common good," this would appear to mean that the whole society benefits when persons are not treated only as means to the ends of others. Each of us should have some "say" in the determination of economic and political policies that will affect us. Otherwise, our personhood is violated fundamentally. As the Amsterdam Assembly went on to apply the concept of responsible society, it specified "that the people have freedom to control, to criticize and to change their governments, that power be made responsible by law and tradition, and be distributed as widely as possible through the whole community."[26]

Whether this moves beyond a contractarian view of mutual self-interest depends in part on how one interprets the "justice" component of the formulation. If it is seen in contractarian terms, it may still be rather individualistic. The more recent formulation of the meaning of justice by John Rawls illustrates what I mean by this. Rawls defines justice as the social arrangement that would be chosen by the least privileged members of society as being in their interest.[27] This could mean a society with great inequalities, but only if these inequalities are necessary to better the condition of the least favored. If, it is argued, absolute equality meant only absolute misery for every member of the community, it could be in the interest of poor people to tolerate a good deal of inequality if, at the same time, they could better themselves materially. But such a view of the common good does not treat the common good as a good in itself so much as a necessary means to the realization of the individual good of individual people.[28]

The individualism implicit in this notion of justice is even more marked in theories of justice that are more compensatory in character—with justice defined as a rendering to each of us exactly what we deserve in the way of rewards and punishments. Such a view of justice is not necessarily complacent in face of the inequalities and sufferings of the contemporary world, since it is difficult to defend either the riches of the wealthy or the sufferings of the poor solely in terms of their respective deserving. We surely ought not to "blame the poor" for their plight any more than we should congratulate the rich for their well-doing. Much depends upon inheritance and good or bad luck. So "justice" structured entirely along the lines of human deserving would require vast redistribution of wealth and income, with many of the poor becoming wealthy and many of the rich becoming poor.

In context and vague as they often are, most ecumenical appeals to justice appear to be more egalitarian—a call for more equal distribution of the world's goods, giving each person a fair or fairer share. The "Just" part of the World Council's more recent "Just, Participatory, and Sustainable" formula (JPSS) strikes as one as being egalitarian in this sense, as do the writings of the more recent Popes. It is a standard feature of such documents to contrast the prosperity of the rich countries with the distress of the Third World, while also noting the vast and indefensible gaps between rich and poor within countries. Some should live more simply that others may simply live. It is unfair for some to be so close to utter destitution while others live like kings.

The recent ecumenical call for a "sustainable" society suggests a dimension of common good that one does not find emphasized much in the papal tradition.[29] We are responsible, under God, for what we hand on to future generations. Justice for people now living is not enough; we must also be just in our relationship to those who will come after us. They, too, are to be referred to when we speak of the "common" good, for they, too, are a part of our moral community. Therefore, policies and practices which are not "sustainable" for the long future are to be questioned, even if they contribute to personal and social well-being in the present setting. This, too, can be expressed in rather individualistic terms. The concern can be limited to the future well-being of individuals as individuals, although the "participatory" element in the JPSS formula suggests a quality of communal life that transcends purely individualistic interest.

The social character of our life is doubtless implied in most of the declarations of Popes and church bodies over the past century. But can this be taken for granted? It is possible to define "justice" or "common good" in quite individualistic terms as what is good or just for individuals, as what moral claims individuals as individuals have upon one another based upon their essential humanity and their personal relationship to God.

But something very important may be missing when we limit our view of the common good in this way. The watershed question is whether our view of the common good moves beyond individual rights and well-being to a conception of our "being-in-community." Is there not a fundamental sense in which we belong to one another in our very being? Are we not, as Aristotle said, social by nature? Is not the idea of a purely individual persona an abstraction?

As we have said, Protestantism is partly to be blamed for the excesses of individualism in the Western thought of the past few centuries. At the same time, ecumenical formulations like the "Responsible Society" and the "Just, Participatory, and Sustainable Society" at least point toward the social dimension of human fulfillment, as do many of the papal teachings about common good. Several recent Protestant theologians emphasize the point; one thinks of Joseph Haroutunian, with his conception of "fellowman,"[30] Paul Lehmann, with his Koinonia Ethics,[31] and L. Harold Dewolf, with his emphasis upon love defined as koinonia.[32] The idea is developed in the Barthian stream and in the work of Emil Brunner, both of which emphasize the complementary character of human beings in community.[33] Such thinkers do not think of society simply as individuals serving one another or relating to one another out of self-interested motives. In a deeper sense, they think of our very being as social. To be fully human, in this sense, is to identify with others as "we" and not simply as "I and you" or even "I and thou." Individualism, in this perspective, represents the fragmentation of our being.

The first and second drafts of the American Catholic bishops' pastoral letter on "Catholic Teaching and the U.S. Economy" emphasizes the social dimension of life quite fruitfully, employing this as a criterion of poverty:

> . . . poverty is not merely the lack of adequate financial resources. It entails a more profound kind of deprivation, a denial of full participation in the economic, social and political life of society and an inability to influence decisions that affect one's life. It means being powerless in a way that assaults not only one's pocketbook but also one's fundamental human dignity.[34]

Poverty, thus, is not simply a *material* condition, it is a social, a relational condition as well. One can be well-off financially while remaining very poor relationally. In providing for the good life, one must attend to more than the questions of physical well-being. It is even possible to be poor in material terms while finding rich fulfillment in the life of community—although it must be remembered immediately that there are levels of material destitution so great as to overwhelm any possibility of social fulfillment.

A clear implication of such an understanding of poverty is the complementary notion that the relational impoverishment of some is the relational impoverishment of all. If poor people are deprived of the material conditions necessary to their finding relational fulfillment, this means that rich people are also deprived at exactly the same point but for exactly the opposite reason. Poverty can alienate us from those better off, but wealth can alienate us from the poor. Martin Luther King, Jr. understood this point and applied it to the problem of racism: "In the final analysis the white man cannot ignore the Negro's problem, because he is a part of the Negro and the Negro is a part of him. The Negro's agony diminishes the white man, and the Negro's salvation enlarges the white man."[35] Hegel had a grasp on this problem in his observation that slavery diminishes the slaveholder, possibly more even than the slave, because it robs him of the one thing the slaveholder needs to fulfill his humanity—namely, the acknowledgement or affirmation of his (the slaveholder's) humanity by the slave.[36] When we reduce the human dignity of another, through racism, or slavery, or poverty, we reduce our own humanity by the same token. We cannot treat another person as a thing without treating ourselves as a thing.

One of the problems with the way conceptions of the common good or of social justice are often framed is that they imply that there are and have been both "winners" and "losers" in the unjust state of society. But if we frame the question in this deeper way we can understand that there can be no "winners" as long as there are "losers." The common good, thus, means that the good of each is contained in the good of all.

Does this mean, then, that the more individualistic affirmations of private property (Leo XIII, Pius XI, etc.) or of freedom and self-determination (Amsterdam, Evanston, John Paul II, etc.) are to be excluded from the norm of the common good? By no means. If we are social by nature, so are we also personal and individual. The very idea of mutuality of life in society presupposes free centers of personal consciousness and activity who are capable of entering into interpersonal relationship. To rob people of their freedom is also to dehumanize them. Participation in society does not mean simply that one is a unit of the social whole; it means that we are enabled to participate as responsible beings. Social justice entails recognition of the social whole, but it also implies respect for the civil and material rights of individuals who are a part of that social whole. The 19th- and 20th-century debates between various forms of socialism or collectivism and the various forms of individualism are profoundly misplaced to the extent we are asked to surrender either the social or the individual aspects of our being. When either is lost, both are lost.[37]

The "Preferential Option for the Poor"

In this context, we must ask whether the "option for the poor," as articulated by Pope Paul VI[38] and the Bishops' Pastoral on the U.S. economy, is in tension with the idea of the common good. It can be asked whether the "option for the poor" has replaced concern for *all* of society. What about our option for the nonpoor? Did Christ die only for the poor? Are not the nonpoor also within the circle of God's boundless love, and therefore also possessed of a moral claim upon the ministries of the church?

To the extent that "option for the poor" continues to think of the poor as the only "losers" in economic life, these may be the right questions. For surely the gospel depicts all humanity as embraced by the love of God. We cannot even think of the poor as being more deserving morally. We cannot depict them as "better" people than their more prosperous sisters and brothers. Are there not innumerable instances of marginalized people gaining power and then oppressing others in their turn? Have there not been revolutions that, in their turn, "devoured their own"? Recent Popes have warned against the dangers of revolution at this point. One notes, in particular, Paul VI's warning that "revolutionary uprisings—except where there is manifest, long-standing tyranny which would do great damage to fundamental personal rights and dangerous harm to the common good of the country—engender new injustices, introduce new inequities and bring new disasters."³⁹ He is right to warn that "an even worse situation" can result. This does not mean that the poor do not have a moral claim upon us for change, even for radical change—as Paul makes clear. It does mean that we should be under no illusion that the poor are the only ones having a moral claim upon us and other Christians. All have a moral claim upon us; and since the claim has its roots in God's own unbounded love, we may say that all have an equal moral claim upon us. Preferential option for the poor cannot mean a judgment that poor people are morally preferable.

But the "option for the poor" can mean something very different. It can mean that dealing with the material distress and social oppression of the poor first is also the way to attend to the relational impoverishness of the more prosperous. It we are to think of society as a chain, the impoverished are its weakest links. If they are not attended to, the whole chain is, as such, at risk. Giving priority to the poor and their needs is, thus, the correct approach to dealing with the needs of the rich. Seen in this way, "option for the poor" is "option for all." But if we say "option for all" the tendency of many people is to interpret that as an affirmation of things as they are.

Thus, there is no necessary conflict between an affirmation of the common good and a preferential option for the poor since the latter is an inescapable condition of the former. A conflict between these two can only occur where the prosperous are taken to be the enemies of God, on the one hand, or where the plight of the poor is not understood to contain the plight of the nonpoor. If, along with the draft Bishops' Pastoral, one takes the capacity to participate in society seriously as criterion of the common good, then one can hardly be surprised to find the bishops lavishing so much attention on the twin, interrelated problems of poverty and unemployment. For these conditions represent the points at which people are not able to participate in the normal life of the community. These points are, therefore, the points where the common good has broken down.

At risk of belaboring the point, I wish to reemphasize just how important a watershed it is to define poverty in terms of social participation and not simply in material terms alone. The moral significance of economic life is not limited to the meeting of everybody's purely material needs for food, clothing, housing and health care—even though it would represent startling progress for us to do so. It is also the provision of those material conditions without which some people are practically excluded from the relational fabric of community, and along with them the rest as well.

The Economic Role of Government

It is a striking thing that when people become concerned about such fundamental problems as poverty and unemployment, they also often find themselves looking at the possibilities of government in a new way.

We should remind ourselves that this is not a necessary relationship. It is not necessarily inconsistent for one to be deeply concerned about poverty and unemployment and, at the same time, to feel that the best way to deal with such problems is through the workings of the unfettered free market mechanism and private philanthropy. Adam Smith plainly thought the competitive market would work best in securing the economic well-being of society. That mechanism alone, he held, matches the felt needs of people to their productive genius. Hence, by serving ourselves we also best serve others. Smith may have been the first theorist of the "trickle-down" effect, although he has had many followers who also believe that the free market is the best way to handle economic distress. Again, it is not necessarily inconsistent to hold that (a) the alleviation of poverty and unemployment are overriding moral objectives for persons of Christian conscience and (b) the best way of achieving the objectives is to free the market of constraints, including governmental constraints. Belief in the two propositions simultaneously is not necessarily to be in self-contradiction. There are, however, two problems.

First, at the cultural level something happens to people when they come to identify their personal material self-interest as a necessary condition of the common good. It is a very easy move from this complacent attitude to a thoroughly selfish one. Beginning with a kind of principled selfishness, in the Adam Smith sense, we drift toward a thoroughly unprincipled self-centeredness. Personal and cultural materialism become our idols. Even if one could be assured, empirically, that principled selfishness does best enhance the material well-being of all, this materialistic idolatry would remain a serious problem for Christians who believe, after all, that they cannot serve God and mammon.

Secondly, however, at the factual level it is more than disputable whether the unrestrained market really does produce the best results. No question, the industrial revolution in the era of capitalism has yielded vast material benefits. Never before in human history has there been so rapid and dynamic a development of material well-being as this era of two or three hundred years. Even Marx and Engels pay great tribute to capitalism in their Communist Manifesto! But these few centuries have also contributed vast waste and misery to large numbers of people. Karl Polanyi makes and illustrates the point that, from the very beginning of modern capitalism, society has had to intervene in the market mechanism to protect important social interests.[40] Among other interesting illustrations, he points out how British society found it necessary to adopt the ineffective, inefficient Speenhamland policies in order to slow the pace of people leaving agriculture and to protect the minimal economic well-being of those forced off the land who were yet unable to secure industrial employment. The experiment, a kind of guaranteed income scheme, was inefficient only in the purely economic sense. It probably did slow the pace of industrial development. But at the same time it preserved the fabric of British society at a time when anything less might have torn it apart.

Governmental interventions in U.S. economic life have often

similarly had less than beneficent effects on the developing gross national product while, at the same time, preserving people and society from catastrophe. The legislation of the Progressive Era to preserve product safety and insulate children from economic exploitation may have slowed the pace of industrial development, but who would argue that they were unnecessary in human terms? New Deal legislation, largely in response to the catastrophe of the Great Depression, was widely, and I think rightly, seen as necessary to protect people. Indeed, in this case it is arguable that absent the New Deal, the economic system itself might have collapsed.

It may be quite debatable at the present time whether the high rates of poverty and unemployment are attributable to the Reagan-era retrenchments of the role of government.[41] But those who believe the unrestrained market capable of dealing with poverty and unemployment without governmental interference have got to face the empirical problem that the social pathologies persist even in the face of a prolonged economic "recovery." If the dynamic market alone is to be trusted to abolish poverty and unemployment without serious intervention from government, it had better do so quickly!

The U.S. Catholic bishops garnered some criticism for urging a more positive attitude toward governmental economic interventions and planning in the first two drafts of their economic pastoral. The critics may have mistaken the bishops' intent. Certainly they were not arguing the case for governmental intervention as some kind of higher principle, nor had they taken leave of the principle of subsidiarity. But, true to that principle, they were pointing out that it is the moral obligation of the higher collectivity (such as government) to act when lower levels of institutional life are unable to deal with a compelling human problem.[42] Their response was to an empirical problem, not to a narrow ideology. My impression is that their critics were more prompted by ideological motives. For the critics, the free market principle seems to override other considerations, even in the face of hard, empirical evidence that the free market is not serving the needs of the poor and the unemployed. Those who agree with the bishops that the need of the poor and the unemployed to have the economic basis for full participation in the life of the community are invited to come up with some other way of achieving that objective. Perhaps government programs are not the best way. But those who are opposed to governmental programs to alleviate poverty and unemployment had best not offer only the abstract alternative of the free market principle, for that abstraction has not yet yielded the concrete result of a poverty-free, full-employment society at any time, anywhere on earth.

Of course, the advocates of pure *laissez-faire* (like the advocates of pure socialism) can always argue that we have never tried the real thing in its purity. Milton Friedman has argued that the persistence of the Great Depression was more due to wrong-headed governmental intervention than to the failures of the free market.[43] Since ideological visions can seldom be tried out in pure form in the real world, it is generally possible for the purist to say that it is our failure to live up to the vision that is at fault. It is barely conceivable (just barely) that government action did delay economic recovery in the 1930s, although it is clear that it was the truly massive governmental interventions occasioned by World War II that really brought the U.S. out of the depression. It is also conceivable that straighter doses of free enterprise will bring an end to unemployment and poverty today. Have not George Gilder and Charles Murray indicted governmental welfare programs as the real source of the persistence of poverty and the breakdown of family life in America?[44] But the continuing realities of poverty belie the hope that still further erosion of governmental programs will help.

I have quarreled with Gilder and Murray elsewhere in greater detail than space permits here.[45] But we must ask ourselves the general question whether we can or should allow the common good to come only as a by-product of our headlong quest for personal wealth. For one thing, the people who must bear the greatest risk that this will not, finally, work are the very ones who are must vulnerable. For the unemployed, the unemployment rate is not 7.3%; for them, it is 100%! The destitute may not be a majority of the population, but for them poverty is an all-consuming reality. All of us are diminished by the suffering of any, but the risks of failure in trusting *laissez-faire* are concentrated precisely at the points where people are marginalized from full participation in the life of the community: with the powerless and the poor.

We must also ask the general question whether society as a whole should not assume some responsibility for defining and implementing visions of the common good. To the extent we accept this responsibility we must acknowledge government as the primary institution giving force to the will of the people. The ecumenical documents and the teachings of the more recent popes reinforce the notion that government should be accountable to the people. This at least means that people should have some say in the economic and social policies that are bound to affect them. In a larger sense, this surely means that all of us should have some say in the overall shaping of society. We should all have a part to play in the shaping of history.

When we act privately, of course, we also participate in shaping history. But private decision-making, no matter how benevolent its motives, misses some of the reality of public policy debate and democratic decision. We cannot always have our own way, in this process, and no one should argue that democracy always produces good results. The majority is very often wrong. But the democratic process of shaping the life of the community gives each of us a voice and a vote. To be denied the institutions of democratic government themselves is to be denied that broadly based distribution of social power which ecumenical and recent papal teachings both affirm. When wrong, democratic decision-making can be reversed by sufficiently committed people. When absent, the institutions of democratic government can only be replaced by the largely irresponsible concentrations of private power.

I have not wished to affirm here that economic and social decisions should *only* be taken at the level of government. The principle of subsidiarity continues to embody much wisdom, and it is doubtful whether democracy itself would be possible without some mediating institutions[46] and a good deal of personal freedom. In the economic sphere, I would not go as far as a Milton Friedman in touting the benefits of private enterprise.

But within due limits the free market principle has made and can continue to make enormous contributions to economic well-being. The point is that it is a mistake to take it for granted that total reliance on the free market will enhance the common good. The definition of common good is the proper object of the ongoing debate of a free people, and the implementation of common good is no less important an object of that debate.

The Proposal of "Democratic Capitalism"

A number of writers in recent years have advanced the proposal of "Democratic Capitalism," partly as an alternative to democratic socialism and the existing authoritarian versions of capitalism and partly as a constructive idea for the further development of society. What is to be said for and against this proposal in light of a Christian understanding of the common good?

There is, first, a certain ambiguity in the phrase "Democratic Capitalism" that needs to be understood. Michael Novak's treatment of the theme illustrates my point. Arguing for a pluralistic vision of the social good, rather than a unitary one, Novak writes that there are three independent though interacting elements in the democratic capitalist social order: the economic, the political, and the moral-cultural. "Every other form of society the world has ever known," he writes, "imposes a collective sense of what is good and true. In all other systems, every decisive economic, political, and moral-cultural power is exercised by one set of authorities." "Democratic capitalism," he continues, "is unique among all forms of political economy by reason of its pluralism."[47] The question presented by the term "democratic capitalism" is just what is meant by the adjective "democratic." Is it that the economic institutions are run democratically? Novak plainly does not think it necessary for them to be democratic in themselves.[48] Is it simply because such a society is pluralistic, so that the government cannot run the moral-cultural or economic aspects of society? Is it because the political aspect is handled democratically? Is it because the democratically constituted government has formal control over the other two sectors, the economic and the moral-cultural?

A careful reading of the book does not entirely dissipate the ambiguity. At points, the pluralistic character of such a society is almost taken to constitute its being democratic, for such a society has respect for multiple centers of power and its people are free to pursue their lives without the interferences of a unitary state. At points it is the fact that government is chosen democratically, although Novak often treats government, with its "new class," as though it were an irresponsible institution. Is it that government, elected democratically, has formal control over the economic sphere? To some extent that is clearly Novak's argument. ("Like states, centers of economic power are tempted to abuse their power. That is precisely why the state retains ultimate legal and coercive power, and why the moral-cultural system is kept free of direct dependence either upon the state or upon the economic system."[49]) But the main thrust of his discussions of the relationships between government and the economic order strongly emphasizes the latter's independence of the former.

The root of the ambiguity of such a conception of "democratic capitalism" is, I believe, in its attempt to characterize the political, economic, and moral-cultural spheres as conceptual equals. There is a sense in which a democratic society must respect the conceptual equality of the political and what Novak calls the moral-cultural. For if the political can determine the moral-cultural, there is no ground of transcendence upon which the people can stand to exercise democratic control over the state. If the moral-cultural views and values we hold are subject to governmental determination, then there is no longer a basis for protection of the free expression of views, without which democracy itself is impossible. In this book and elsewhere Novak has attempted to assert similarly that without capitalism there can be no democracy. But that does not follow, at least as an *a priori* principle. I can see no *a priori* grounds for excluding the proposal of a democratic socialism—a socialist economy owned by and run by a democratically constituted government. Or, more to the actual point, there seems to be no reason *a priori* why some aspects of the economic order might not be directly accountable to government, so long as government in turn is accountable to the people. So the case for the independence of the economic sphere is not quite the same as the case for the independence of the political or moral-cultural spheres. Moreover, a proper road map of a pluralistic society would (disregarding questions of relative degrees of independence) also have to include a social sphere which is neither political, economic, nor moral-cultural in the sense in which Novak uses those terms. Depending on how one constructed the typology one might suggest still further spheres.

But laying Novak's version of "democratic capitalism" aside, is there a simpler, clearer way in which one might find this acceptable in light of the principle of "common good?"

I believe there is as long as one is willing to retain the formal superiority of the political to the economic intact. As long as we are willing to accept governmental regulation of economic life and a legitimate governmental role in the planning of production, the distribution of economic benefits, and the ownership of common facilities for the health, education, cultural enrichment, and recreation of the community, we may legitimately speak of a democratic capitalism. The distinguishing mark of such a capitalism, as over against *laissez-faire* or authoritarian versions of capitalism, is that it makes the capitalist economy directly accountable to the people through the democratic political process. This understanding of "democratic capitalism" coincides with many Western versions of "mixed economy," "welfare capitalism," or "social market capitalism" except in that it deliberately emphasizes the democratic accountability of government.

I have argued elsewhere that the case for such a capitalism in opposition to democratic socialism is not yet clear.[50] I am intrigued by the tentative approval Pope John Paul II has given to some forms of democratic socialism,[51] although he certainly has not advocated its adoption everywhere or even anywhere. Perhaps the best posture for the church is to retain an openness to much experimentation in this dynamic era of history, while insisting upon certain criteria to be used in judging all systems.

Among these criteria, the preservation of democratic political institutions must loom large, as must the adequacy of any system in making it possible for all members of the community to have a sufficient level of material well-being to enable them to participate meaningfully in the life of the community.

Priorities in Economic Life

I have also argued elsewhere, at greater length than this paper affords, for the importance of Christian participation in the setting of economic priorities.[52] Economic life affects all other aspects of existence powerfully. The advocates of *laissez-faire* capitalism urge us to trust the free market to establish the common good, trusting that the market mechanism will best translate the actual wishes of the people into economic reality. To some extent the market mechanism may indeed help establish the right priorities; but overall that will not do. People are too unequal in the power they bring to the market—their skills, their inherited wealth, their present income. If dollars are the votes of the marketplace, some clearly have far more votes than others. But all should be able to participate in the process of deciding what the common life is to be.

Momentous problems face us today: What is to be done, and done soon, to draw fellow citizens out of poverty and unemployment? What is to be done to overcome the enormous gulf between the relatively rich countries and the relatively poor ones? What is to be done to overcome the economic burdens imposed by an international arms race long spun out of control? What kind of infrastructure does society need for transportation and communication, and how are we to get it? How are we to deal with the educational needs of a profoundly demoralized generation of inner-city youth? What kind of health-care system should be developed to ensure adequate health care for our people without undermining other aspects of their economic life? How are we to preserve the future of unborn generations from the hazards of environmental pollution and the waste of limited resources? What population size is optimal for the sake of the common good?

Such questions are not easily and perhaps not permanently answered. But they help define the more detailed agenda which must be addressed by all who care deeply about the common good.

NOTES

1. Friedrich Engels, "On Historical Materialism," in Lewis S. Feuer, ed., Max & Engels *Basic Writings on Politics and Philosophy* (N.Y.: Doubleday Anchor, 1959), pp. 55-56.

2. Max Weber, *The Protestant Ethic and the Spirit of Capitalism*, Talcott Parsons, trans. (N.Y.: Charles Scribner's Sons, 1958 [1904-5]).

3. *Ibid.,* pp. 181-3.

4. John Calvin, *Institutes of the Christian Religion*, trans. Henry Beveridge, in Waldo Beach and H. Richard Niebuhr, eds., *Christian Ethics: Sources of the Living Tradition* (N.Y.: The Ronald Press Co., 1955), p. 284.

5. John Wesley, "The Use of Money," in Beach and Niebuhr, eds., *Christian Ethics*, pp. 572-577. Cf. Richard M. Cameron, *Methodism and Society in Christian Perspective* (N.Y. and Nashville: Abingdon Press, 1961), pp. 67-72.

6. Ernst Troeltsch, *The Social Teaching of the Christian Churches 11,* Olive Wyon trans. (N.Y.: The Macmillan Co., 1931), pp. 710-711.

7. John Locke, *An Essay Concerning the True Original, Extent and End of Civil Government* (1690), Chapter V.

8. Robert Nozick, *Anarchy, State and Utopia* (N.Y.: Basic Books, 1974), selections in Robert H. Hartman, Ed., *Poverty and Economic Justice: A Philosophical Approach* (N.Y.: Paulist Press, 1984), esp. p. 129.

9. Adam Smith, *An Inquiry into the Nature and Causes of the Wealth of Nations* (1776), Book V, Chap. II.

10. Cf. Charles Howard Hopkins, *The Rise of the Social Gospel in American Protestantism*, 1865-1915 (New Haven: Yale University Press, 1940).

11. Walter G. Muelder, *Methodism and Society in the Twentieth Century* (N.Y. and Nashville: 1961), pp. 48-49.

12. *Ibid.*

13. Nils Ehrenstrom, ed., *Ecumenical Documents on Church and Society (1925-1953)* (Geneva: World Council of Churches, 1954), p. 3.

14. *Ibid.*

15. World Council of Churches, *Man's Disorder and God's Design*, Vol. III on *The Church and the Disorder of Society* (N.Y.: Harper and Brothers, 1948), Report of Section III, p. 200.

16. Against Marxian communism, the Amsterdam Assembly lists "(1) the communist promise of what amounts to a complete redemption of man in history; (2) the belief that a particular class by virtue of its role as the bearer of a new order is free from the sins and ambiguities that Christians believe to be characteristic of all human existence; (3) the materialistic and deterministic teachings, however, they may be qualified, that are incompatible with belief in God and with the Christian view of man as a person, made in God's image and responsible to Him; (4) the ruthless methods of communists in dealing with their opponents; (5) the demand of the part on its members for an exclusive and unqualified loyalty which belongs only to God, and the coercive policies of communist dictatorship in controlling every aspect of life." *Ibid.*, p. 202. Against capitalism are listed as problems that "(I) capitalism tends to subordinate what should be the primary task of any economy—the meeting of human needs—to the economic advantages of those who have most power over its institutions. (2) It tends to produce serious inequalities. (3) It has developed a practical form of materialism in western nations in spite of their Christian background, for it has placed the greatest emphasis upon success in making money. (4) It has also kept the people of capitalist countries subject to a kind of fate which has taken the form of such social catastrophes as mass unemployment." *Ibid.*, pp. 202-203.

17. *Ibid.*, p. 200.

18. Leon Howell, *Acting in Faith: The World Council of Churches Since 1975* (Geneva: World Council of Churches, 1982) and David Gill, ed., *Gathered for Life: Official Report VI Assembly World Council of Churches* (Grand Rapids, Mich.: Eerdmans, 1983).

19. Gill, ed., *Gathered for Life*, p. 2

20. Leo XIII, *Rerum Novarum*, in *Seven Great Encyclicals* (Glen Rock, N.J.: Paulist Press, 1963 [1891]), paragraphs 7 and 8, pp. 4-5.

21. *Ibid.* Cf. paragraphs 9, 11, 16.

22. *Ibid.*, paragraphs 34-35, pp. 21-23. The attempts to define "just wages" is worthy of respect and, indeed, badly in need of refinement in the present situation. Leo's effort, commendable as it was, fell short

even for his own time because it did not relate the needs of the family to the demands or disciplines of the competitive market.

23. *Ibid.,* paragraph 19, p. 11.

24. Ehrenstrom, ed., *Ecumenical Documents,* p. 3

25. WCC, *The Church and the Disorder of Society,* p. 200.

26. *Ibid.,* p. 201.

27. John Rawls, *A Theory of Justice* (Cambridge: Harvard Univ. Press, 1971), pp. 14-15.

28. While I believe this to be the main tendency in Rawls' thought, later in the book he does acknowledge that "it is a feature of human sociability that we are by ourselves but parts of what we might be. . . . The collective activity of society, the many associations and the public life of the largest community that regulates them, sustains our efforts and elicits our contribution." *Ibid.,* p. 529.

29. See Gill, ed., *Gathered for Life* and *Faith and Science in an Unjust World: Report of the World Council of Churches' Conference on Faith, Science and the Future* (Philadelphia: Fortress Press, 1980). For a helpful discussion of the sustainability problem as a problem in Christian ethics see Robert L. Stivers, *The Sustainable Society: Ethics and Economic Growth* (Philadelphia: Westminster Press, 1976).

30. Joseph Haroutunian, *God with Us: A Theology of Transpersonal Life* (Philadelphia: Westminster Press, 1965).

31. Paul Lehmann, *Ethics in a Christian Context* (N.Y. and Evanston: Harper and Row, 1963), pp. 57 ff.

32. L. Harold DeWolf, *Responsible Freedom: Guidelines to Christian Action* (N.Y.: Harper and Row, 1971), pp. 102-110.

33. I am particularly impressed by the profundity of the analysis accompanying Barth's discussion of the doctrine of creation, in which he discusses the relationship between creation as the external basis of covenant and the covenant as internal meaning of creation. The covenant with God, which establishes the meaning of our humanity, also establishes our fellow humanity. See Karl Barth, *Church Dogmatics* III/1 (Edinburgh: T. & T. Clark, 1958.)

34. *Catholic Social Teaching and the U.S. Economy,* second draft. *Origins: National Catholic Documentary Service,* Vol. 15, No. 17 (October 10, 1985), at paragraph 186, p. 276.

35. Martin Luther King, Jr., *Where Do We Go from Here: Chaos or Community?* (Boston: Beacon Press, 1968 (1967)), p. 101. King also applied the point to economics: "In a real sense, all life is interrelated. The agony of the poor impoverishes the rich; the betterment of the poor enriches the rich." p. 181.

36. G. F. Hegel, *The Phenomenology of Mind*, trans. J. B. Baillie, 2nd rev. ed. (London: 1949), pp. 229-240. Cited by Andrew J. Reck, "The Metaphysics of Equality," in W. T. Blackstone, ed., *The Concept of Equality* (Minneapolis: Burgess Publishing Co., 1969), p. 138.

37. The individual/social polarity is one of several polarities I have discussed at greater length in *A Christian Method of Moral Judgment* (Philadelphia: Westminster Press, 1976). The mark of true polarities of this kind is that either side is the necessary precondition of its opposite.

38. Pope Paul VI, *Octagesimo Adveniens*, in Michael Walsh and Brian Davies, eds., *Proclaiming Justice and Peace: Documents from John XXIII—John Paul II* (Mystic, Conn.: Twenty-third Publications, 1984). "In teaching us charity," the Pope declares, "the gospel instructs us in the preferential respect due to the poor and the special situation they have in society . . . " Paragraph 23, p. 175.

39. Pope Paul VI, *Populorum Progressio*, in Walsh and Davies, *Proclaiming Justice*, at paragraph 31, p. 150.

40. Karl Polanyi, *The Great Transformation: The Political and Economic Origins of Our Time* (Boston: Beacon Press, 1957 [1949]), pp. 76-85.

41. At the present time the number of persons below the poverty line remains in excess of 33 million—a number substantially in excess of the 24 to 26 million of the period roughly from 1968 to 1978. Unemployment, fluctuating recently between 6.7% and 7.3% of the available work force (those actively seeking employment), and at this writing the figure is 7.3%. By comparison, unemployment during the 1960s was below 5%. It is noteworthy that the higher rates of poverty and unemployment at the present time are recorded in the third year of a highly touted economic recovery.

42. That principle has often been used only to protect lower-level institutions and private persons from encroachment by government and other large institutions. But subsidiarity has always included the possibility of intervention by the higher to protect the lower. Pope John XXIII invoked the principle in admittedly vague support of the development of international institutions to effect a better world order. See *Pacem in Terris*, paragraphs 131, 134, 135. The Bishops' Pastoral notes that "The market alone will not automatically produce full employment. Therefore, the government must act to ensure that this goal is achieved by coordinating general economic policies, by job-creation programs and by other appropriate policy measures." *Catholic Social Teaching and the U.S. Economy*, paragraph 153, p. 273.

43. Milton Friedman, in *Capitalism and Freedom* (Chicago: Univ. of Chicago Press, 1962) remarks that "the Great Depression in the United States, far from being a sign of the inherent instability of the private enterprise system, is a testament to how much harm can be done by mistakes on the part of a few men when they wield vast power over the monetary system of a country." p. 50.

44. See George Gilder, *Wealth and Poverty* (N.Y.: Basic Books, 1981) and Charles Murray, *Losing Ground: American Social Policy 1950-1980* (N.Y.: Basic Books, 1984). Gilder writes that in order to succeed, the poor need most of all the "spur of their poverty." p. 118.

45. See J. Philip Wogaman, *Economics and Ethics: A Christian Inquiry* (Philadelphia: Fortress Press, 1986), esp. Chapter 6.

46. See Michael Novak, *Democracy and Mediating Structures: A Theological Inquiry* (Washington, D.C.: American Enterprise Institute, 1980) for a diversity of views on the need for mediating institutions in a democratic society.

47. Michael Novak, *The Spirit of Democratic Capitalism* (N.Y.: Simon and Schuster, 1982), p. 49.

48. *Ibid.,* p. 175.

49. *Ibid.,* p. 91.

50. J. Philip Wogaman, *The Great Economic Debate* (Philadelphia: Eastminster Press, 1977), pp. 155-166.

51. Pope John Paul II, *Laborem Exercens*, in Walsh and Davies, eds., *Proclaiming Justice*, at paragraph 14.2, p. 293: "one cannot exclude the socialization, in suitable conditions, of certain means of production." John Paul goes on to warn that merely taking property out of private hands "is not enough to ensure their satisfactory socialization." Paragraph 14.5, p. 294.

52. J. Philip Wogaman, *Economics and Ethics*.

Six

The Common Good and Official Catholic Social Teaching

CHARLES E. CURRAN

Official Catholic social teaching in the modern era is usually understood as beginning with the social encyclicals of Pope Leo XIII at the end of the nineteenth century, especially the encyclical *Rerum Novarum* . Other benchmark documents which are usually included in this tradition are the following: Pope Pius XI's *Quadragesimo Anno* (1931); Pope John XXIII's *Mater et Magistra* (1961) and *Pacem in Terris* (1963); *The Pastoral Constitution on the Church in the Modern World* and *The Declaration on Religious Freedom* of the Second Vatican Council (1965); Pope Paul VI's *Populorum Progressio* (1967) and *Octogesima Adveniens* (1971); the Synod of Bishops' *Justitia in Mundo* (1971); and Pope John Paul II's *Laborem Exercens* (1981).[1]

There has been a selection process in determining what belongs to this body of official social teaching. Pope Leo XIII, for example, wrote many encyclicals on the social order, but today

111

most of his encyclicals on political ethics are generally ignored. Subsequent papal acceptance and reception by the universal church have had a great role to play in determining this unofficial canon of what constitutes modern Catholic social teaching.

Modern official Catholic social teaching began with Pope Leo XIII, who also presided over the renewal of Thomistic philosophy in Catholic schools and scholarship. Thomas Aquinas was made the patron of Catholic theology and philosophy which, according to the pope, were to be taught according to the method, the principles and the teaching of Thomas Aquinas. Thomistic theology was understood to be the perennial philosophy which undergirded Catholic theology and selfunderstanding.[2]

In this context Pope Leo XIII obviously based his social morality on Thomistic teachings and principles. A very central element in Thomistic political ethics is the concept of the common good, which deals with the fundamental question of the nature of political society and the relationship between the individual and society. The common good is the end or the purpose of society, but the common good ultimately redounds to the good of the individuals involved. In this Thomistic concept the human being is by nature social, and civil and political society are natural. The individual's quest for perfection as well as the weakness and incompleteness of the human being call upon the individual to live in society, including political society. Thus society and the state are based on human nature. The pre-Vatican II papal documents, as one might expect, do not go into the philosophical grounding of the common good in great depth, but the early encyclicals use this understanding of the individual and society to condemn the two positions of individualistic liberalism on the one hand and collectivism on the other. The communitarian and social nature of the individual serves as the basis for the principles and more specific applications made in the official Catholic social teaching. Thus, for example, the principle of subsidiarity sees the role of the state as a help (*subsidium*) to enable individuals and lesser groups in society to do and accomplish what they can do. The state should not take over what can be done on the level of the individual or of lesser groupings in society, but at times the state must intervene and act for the good of all concerned.

In explaining the official Catholic social teaching, commentators emphasized the Thomistic foundation of this teaching and developed the understanding of the common good, the role of the individual in society, and the fact that the state is a natural society based on human nature as social and not on sin and evil. The well known book of Calvez and Perrin originally published in French in 1959 illustrates the understanding of the Thomistic teaching on the individual, society, and the common good as the basis for official Catholic social teaching.[3] There would seem to be little or no argument against the position that official Catholic social teaching up to the time of the Second Vatican Council (1965) gave great importance to the concept of the common good and generally accepted the Thomistic foundations of this teaching.

The Common Good and Catholic Social Teaching

A case can be made for the position that since Vatican II official Catholic social teaching has not given that significant and important a role to the concept of the common good, especially as rooted in Thomistic thought. Four generic reasons connected with official Catholic social teachings since Vatican II can be proposed to support this thesis:

1) Thomistic natural law method no longer is the primary basis of Catholic social teaching and ethics;
2) The teaching itself incorporates elements that seem to be in opposition to the common good tradition;
3) The documents do not explicitly give that much attention to the common good;
4) Catholic social thought as developed by contemporary theologians seems to have neglected the concept of the common good.

First, the methodology of the official Catholic social teaching since the *Pastoral Constitution on the Church in the Modern World* of Vatican II has definitely changed from the natural law methodology employed in the earlier documents. There are two significant methodological developments that have taken place in the official Catholic social teaching since Vatican II. These two developments might be generally described as the theological and philosophical aspects of the methodology of social ethics.

The older documents were based almost totally on the natural law approach which prescinded from the supernatural, grace, faith, and the Gospel.[4] However, more recent documents appeal very often to the Gospel. Action on behalf of justice is seen to be a constitutive dimension of the preaching of the Gospel and the mission of the church for the redemption of humankind.[5] These documents very correctly recognize that faith and the Gospel, and not just reason and natural law, have something to say about political and economic realities. However, the Gospel must always be mediated in and through the human. This newer methodology does not see social and political ethics only in the light of human reason and natural law. This theological aspect of methodology can also be called the question of the sources of ethical wisdom and knowledge for the Christian.

A second methodological change concerns the philosophical understanding of human reason and human nature. It is impossible here to document all the changes which have occurred within official Catholic social teaching, but the two most significant developments are a greater emphasis on historical consciousness (as distinguished from classicism) and on personalism. Historical consciousness gives more importance to the individual, the contingent, the particular, the historical, and the changing, and is associated with a more inductive methodology. Since the *Pastoral Constitution on the Church in the Modern World* in 1965, these documents have given greater emphasis to the signs of the times and have developed a more inductive methodology. Thus, for example, *Octogesima Adveniens*, perhaps the most radical of the later documents in its methodology, recognizes—that in the midst of widely varying situations throughout the world—it is neither the ambition nor the mission of the Pope to put forth a solution which has universal validity. It is up to the local Christian communities in the light of the Gospel and the social teaching of the church to discern the options and the commitments that are called for in their situation (par. 4; O'Brien and Shannon, pp. 353-354). *Octogesima Adveniens* thus illustrates the influence of historical mindedness in contemporary official Catholic social teaching.

A second changed aspect of the philosophical understanding of the human being has been the greater emphasis on personalism and all that is connected with it, such as human rights. This personalism is present in all the recent documents and is the hallmark of Pope John Paul II's *Laborem Exercens* . It can be maintained that Pope John Paul II has tended to move away from the historical consciousness of Paul VI, but there is no doubt about his emphasis on personalism. Two important examples of this contemporary personalism developed in *Octogesima Adveniens* are the aspirations to equality and to participation (par. 22 ff; O'Brien and Shannon, pp. 364 ff.).

These two developments in the understanding of the human differ from the earlier approach based on the scholastic notion of natural law. Thus, the understanding of the human and human reality found in the recent documents differs somewhat from the older natural law approach. The theological and metaphysical bases for the common good approach are no longer the same as those proposed in earlier documents.

Second, the newer documents introduce elements and approaches that seem to replace or even go against the basic concept of the common good. The more recent documents emphasize equality, but the classical Catholic common good concept was fearful that equality could too readily be seen as an individualism which destroys the organic unity of society. The image or metaphor of the body with its many different parts was often used to describe the unity of the state with unequal functions and operations contributing to the good of the whole. The stress on such concepts as rights, freedom, and participation seems to be opposed to the classical Catholic notion of the common good. More recently the preferential option for the poor and solidarity with the poor have come to the fore. By emphasizing a part rather than the whole, these expressions seem to go against the very nature of the common good.

Third, an examination of the more recent documents reveals that the common good is not a central theme in many of these writings. There is no real development of the common good in John Paul II's *Laborem Exercens* or the Synodal document *Justice in the World*. However, *Octogesima Adveniens* devotes a short section to political society, and appeals to the common good as the basis for a condemnation of both individualism and collectivism (par. 23-25; O'Brien and Shannon, pp. 364-366). *The Pastoral Constitution on the Church in the Modern World* of Vatican II discusses political life in the fourth chapter of the second part and relies on the fundamental concept of the common good. In this connection it is important to remember that even the earlier documents in the body of official Catholic social teaching did not develop the concept of the common good in great philosophical depth or detail. Such an approach is really not that appropriate in documents destined for all and not just for academics and specialists. Certainly the common good is occasionally mentioned in these documents, but it does not seem to play a very central role in them.

Fourth, the commentaries on contemporary Catholic social teaching and Catholic philosophy in general no longer give great importance to the concept of the common good. A check of the *Catholic Periodical and Literature Index* is most revealing. There is no entry under "common good" from Volume 13 (1965-66) to the present. There are many entries under "common good" in Volume 12 (1963-64) and in the preceding volumes. This certainly indicates that Catholic scholars are not paying much attention to the notion of the common good. A comparison of commentaries on Catholic social teaching points in the same direction. As already pointed out, Calvez and Perrin, writing in 1959, included a long chapter on person in society with a section on the common good. Donal Dorr, in his recent *Option for the Poor: A Hundred Years of Vatican Social Teaching,* has no development of the concept of the common good, and the term does not even appear in the index.[6] Thus, the case can be made that recent official Catholic social teaching has moved away from the emphasis of the earlier social teaching on the common good and its importance for political and social teaching.

New Developments

The opening section of this paper developed the reasons for maintaining that recent official Catholic social teaching has downplayed the concept and role of the common good. This section will try to indicate that such a picture is not totally accurate. Yes, there are some discontinuities with the earlier teachings, but there is also continuity on the fundamental ideas involved in the traditional understanding of the common good. Second, some of the discontinuity with earlier Catholic social teaching can be explained by the recognition that the concrete content of the common good by its very nature is subject to change and development. Third, some developments which appear to go against the concept of the common good are not necessarily opposed to this notion. Each of these three parts will now be developed in greater detail.

First, official Catholic social teaching since Vatican Council II has continued to uphold the basic and essential aspects of the common good tradition. As mentioned above, the concept of the common good is highlighted when these documents discuss political life. This tradition is rooted in an anthropology that stresses the social nature of humankind, resulting in an approach to political society which tries to avoid both extremes of individualism and collectivism. There can be no doubt that this basic meaning continues to be at the heart of recent Catholic social teaching. This teaching serves as the basis for an attack on individualism, which does not recognize the social aspect of human beings. The drafters of the bishops' pastoral letter on the United States economy recognize that the major difference between Catholic social teaching and the American ethos is the latter's emphasis on individualism. There can be no doubt that the church has learned many things from the American experience, but it properly should point out the dangers of individualism in our society. At the same time recent Catholic teaching with its greater emphasis on personalism strongly opposes any collectivism which subordinates the person to the collectivity.

The more recent documents do not call the state a natural society, but they do insist that the state is basically something good and has a positive function. Here again is a conviction of Catholic social teaching which at times differs sharply from the approach that sees government as something evil and believes that the government which governs least is the best form of government. The state is not something negative which unduly restricts human freedom, but rather the state has the positive function of promoting justice and true freedom for all.

Contemporary Catholic social teaching continues to put into practice the principle of subsidiarity, which is intrinsically connected with the core of the common good tradition. This principle recognizes a rightful role for individual persons and for voluntary associations in society as well as for the state itself. This practical principle attempts to put flesh and blood on the basic approach which tries to avoid both individualism and collectivism. The state should do everything possible to support and help individuals and the smaller voluntary societies to do what they can. However, at times the state itself must intervene to accomplish what individuals and smaller groups cannot do.

Thus, in my judgment, there can be no doubt that recent official Catholic social teaching continues to maintain the basic core and central aspects of the common good tradition. In a sense this should not be surprising, for the Thomistic common good tradition never really saw itself as an absolute but as an understanding of the basic Biblical and Christian vision in the light of the circumstances of the time. This basic Biblical vision should always be controlling and guiding. Of course, it is possible to interpret the Biblical view in different ways, as is evident in the difference between the classical Lutheran and Roman Catholic approaches. However, the Catholic tradition has always interpreted the Biblical vision as stressing the communal and social dimension of human existence. Even in political society we are not just individuals, we are a people and a community. Robert

Bellah and the other co-authors of *Habits of the Heart* have recognized that the Biblical vision is communitarian and opposed to the individualism so often prevalent in contemporary American society.[7] With that same controlling Biblical vision, contemporary Catholic social teaching continues to emphasize the social and communitarian dimension of human existence in the political sphere.

Second, there can be no doubt that there have been some changes and developments in the understanding and content of the common good in the more recent official Catholic social teaching. The fact of such change and development, however, should not be surprising.

Even before Vatican II there were changes in the understanding of the common good, as found in official Catholic social teaching and in Catholic philosophy and theology. The best illustration of this development is the emphasis on personalism during the period of the 50s and 60s. In the 1940s an interesting debate occurred in Thomistic philosophy on this same issue. Jacques Maritain was stressing the personalistic aspect of Thomistic thought and showing how it was compatible with more contemporary emphasis on democratic forms of government.[8] However, some other Thomists objected; they argued that Maritain, by stressing personalism, was denying the primacy of the common good in Thomistic political ethics.[9] This discussion is mentioned here only to point out that there were changes and developments in the understanding of the elements of the common good even before Vatican II.

The emphasis on personalism also grew in the papal documents as the twentieth century progressed. Dignity, freedom, and even rights of the human person became more central realities in the papal understanding of the content of the common good. Nineteenth century Catholic social teaching strongly opposed the excesses of individualistic liberalism, but in the twentieth century a greater danger was now coming from the rise of totalitarianism. As a result, Catholic social teaching began to defend the dignity, freedom, and rights of the individual. Only in *Pacem in Terris* in 1963 does there appear the first fullblown treatment of human rights in the Catholic social tradition (par. 9-

37; O'Brien and Shannon, pp. 126-133). Vatican II sees this emphasis on human dignity and rights as part of the common good.

Even before Vatican II there was a recognition that the content of the common good is bound to change. The article on the common good in *The New Catholic Encyclopedia* was written before the documents of Vatican II were issued, but it concludes with the following recognition: "It is simply impossible to define the common good in a final way irrespective of the changing social conditions."[10] *The Pastoral Constitution on the Church in the Modern World* refers to "the dynamically conceived common good" (par. 74; O'Brien and Shannon, p. 254).

It is obvious that there has been a major shift in the understanding of political life in Catholic social teaching from the time of Pope Leo XIII in the nineteenth century to the present. An even greater change marks the difference between the understanding of Thomas Aquinas and that of contemporary Church documents. The earlier understanding saw society as structured from the top down while the contemporary documents see political society as centered on the human person living in community, with great emphasis on the dignity, freedom, and rights of the person. It is only natural that the concrete content of the common good will be different in these two diverse understandings of society. The next section will develop some of the more significant changes which have occurred in the contemporary official Catholic understanding of the common good.

One of the most significant developments in the Catholic tradition concerns the relationship between the temporal common good and the spiritual common good. This question was generally discussed under the rubric of the union or separation of church and state and the acceptance or denial of religious liberty. Only at Vatican II did Catholic teaching accept religious liberty. Many factors contributed to this change in Catholic social teaching, but a major aspect was the growing importance given to the freedom, rights, and dignity of the person. The state has no direct competency in matters of religion. The proponents of religious freedom at Vatican II in no way accepted the notion that the church and religion were private realities with no role in influencing human individual and social life. However, the new approach saw that the common good of human political society did not call for the union of church and state.[11] In subsequent years the debate has shifted from the relationship of church and state to the relationship of church and society, and how the church should address and be present to human existence in this world. But the Catholic Church today strongly recognizes that the temporal common good demands religious freedom and the so called separation of church and state.

Another significant development concerns the precise end of the state and its function. Here there have been two significant developments which have existed simultaneously within the recent teaching but have not been coordinated in that teaching itself. The first development arose in the context of the religious freedom debate, and concerns the distinction between the common good and public order. The state is only one part of the total civil society. Precisely because the contemporary Catholic understanding recognizes the freedom, dignity, and rights of individual persons and the role of lesser associations within society, the state can never be identified with the totality of society. The end of society is the common good, whereas the end of the state is much narrower — the public order. *The Declaration on Religious Freedom* accepts this distinction in light of its recognition of the lesser role of government in the life of society (par. 6, 7; O'Brien and Shannon, pp. 296, 297). There is a public role for religion in affecting human society, but this role lies beyond the legitimate reach of government, which by definition is limited. Public order in this understanding is an order of justice, of public morality, and of public peace. So that the role of the state is not unduly limited, I would add that the role of justice also includes social justice. Despite the insistence on public order as the end of the state in the document on religious liberty, this concept is not developed in any other official church document after 1965.

In the discussion on religious liberty there was an insistence on a more limited role for the state precisely because the aspect of religion and its effect on society lies beyond the competency of the power of the state. At the same time the more recent offi-

The emphasis on personalism has had a great impact on the concrete content and context of the common good. As already mentioned, Catholic social teaching only recently has developed the important concept of human rights. The first full blown treatment of human rights appeared in Pope John XXIII's encyclical *Pacem in Terris* in 1963 (par. 9-37; O'Brien and Shannon, pp. 126-133). There can be no doubt that this represents a significant change in Catholic self-understanding. The older tradition emphasized duties and not rights. Some see in this development the proof that contemporary Catholic social teaching is moving away from the common good traditions associated with Thomas Aquinas.[12] However, Vatican II sees this as a legitimate and necessary development of the concrete content of the common good in the light of changing circumstances.

There is no doubt that the Catholic tradition has learned much from the emphasis on human rights in the American ethos, but to its credit the recent Catholic teaching also explicitly criticizes the individualistic tone of the rights tradition as often found in the United States. An emphasis on rights and freedom easily results in a one-sided individualism. While trying to appreciate the importance of fundamental human rights, contemporary Catholic social teaching has also attempted to avoid the dangers of excessive individualism. *Pacem in Terris* recognizes the need for duties as well as rights. In addition, Pope John XXIII insists on the existence of economic rights as well as political and civil rights. Economic rights recognize the social and communitarian aspects of human existence. People have rights to basic food, clothing, and shelter; and society must protect and promote these rights.

The insistence on personalism has also stressed the primary importance of equality and participation. *Octogesima Adveniens* makes this point: "While scientific and technological progress continues to overturn man's [sic] surroundings, his patterns of knowledge, work, consumption and relationships, two aspirations persistently make themselves felt in these new contexts, and they grow stronger to the extent that he becomes better informed and better educated: the aspiration to equality and the aspiration to participation, two forms of man's dignity and freedom" (par. 22; O'Brien and Shannon, p. 364).

The recognition of the importance of equality raises some problems for the Catholic tradition. Traditionally, Catholic social teaching did not give much importance to equality. An emphasis on equality was looked upon as inimical to the organic nature of political society and community. Within society as an organism each one had a different task and function to fulfill. Society needed the different functions and roles of different people. Here again one finds a new emphasis in the more recent social teaching which, without some nuances, might go against a more traditional emphasis. A flat equalitarianism seems opposed to the communal and social nature of human existence which has been a hallmark of the Catholic and Thomistic traditions. *Octogesima Adveniens* recognizes the problem: "Without a renewed education and solidarity, an overemphasis on equality can give rise to an individualism in which each one claims one's own rights without wishing to be answerable for the common good" (par. 23; O'Brien and Shannon, p. 365). However, more work needs to be done to indicate how the acceptance of equality will not ultimately destroy the solidarity and communal nature of human social existence.

The emphasis on equality raises a somewhat related question concerning the relationship of recent Catholic social teaching to its Thomistic roots and origins. What is the understanding of justice operative in the recent documents? The traditional Thomistic understanding stressed distributive justice, according to which the burdens and goods of society should be properly divided. In distributing goods, human need constitutes a basic level or floor. All human beings have a right to the basic goods of this world which are necessary for a minimally decent level of human existence. Above and beyond this basic minimum level for all there can be differences and inequalities connected to other titles such as labor, creativity, scarcity, etc. The Thomistic tradition did not insist on an equalitarian justice demanding total equality for all.[13] The contemporary documents without a doubt give much more emphasis to equality and point out the glaring inequalities of our age. However, in my judgment the category of distributive justice, and not equalitarian justice, still remains at the heart of recent social teaching. Other commentators put more emphasis on equalitarian justice.[14] There is no doubt that recent documents rightly stress equality, but the emphasis is almost always nuanced in the official documents to speak about the dangers of excessive, inappropriate or glaring inequalities. As a result I think the concept of distributive justice still plays the central role. Without a doubt, distributive justice is the controlling concept in the recent draft of the bishops' pastoral letter on the United States economy.[15] The older concept of distributive justice, as well as the common good, still continue to be important concepts in recent Catholic social teaching even though there have been significant developments.

Another development in the understanding of the common good in practice concerns the growing recognition of a somewhat more conflictual model of society. The common good tradition sees all the members working together for the good of the whole, which ultimately redounds to the good of the individual. The emphasis in the past was often on harmonious cooperation. Now there is more emphasis on challenging the inequities among various parts of the world and within different sectors in the same national society. More recent church documents recognize a greater role for power and accept revolution as a last resort.[16] In my judgment a greater emphasis on human sinfulness as well as the realities of our modern world point to the recognition of more conflict in the political and social order than was recognized by the older Thomistic tradition. The recent documents rightly talk more about power and the need to overcome the powerlessness of so many people. I personally have made the point that contemporary Catholic social teaching should give even greater recognition to a more conflictual model of existing society and the need for a more theoretical development of the understanding and role of power. Power and conflict can never become ultimate realities, but they do have a greater role in terms of tactics and strategies than has been recognized in the older Catholic tradition.

Certainly there have been a number of important changes in the context and concrete content of the common good throughout the whole history of official Catholic social teaching. These developments have become even more prominent since 1961, but they in no way go against the basic thrust of the common good tradition.

The Preferential Option for the Poor

The next point concerns the discussion of those aspects in recent Catholic social teaching which might be opposed to the common good tradition. The emphasis on inequalities in the modern world has already been discussed. The development in recent social teaching which seems at first sight somewhat opposed to the common good tradition concerns the preferential option for the poor. Is such an option compatible with the common good tradition or does it so emphasize a part that the whole suffers? In general, I do not see the preferential option for the poor as opposed to the common good tradition. Such an approach recognizes a more conflictual model of society. The language of powerlessness also supports this emphasis, but it does not necessarily deny that political society is natural for human beings and all must work for the common good. Note the emphasis on the *preferential* option for the poor as distinguished from an exclusive option for the poor which would definitely deny the common good tradition. By preferring the poor one does not necessarily exclude all others in society.

The preferential option for the poor is putting into contemporary and even somewhat Biblical language a point which was enshrined in the older Thomistic tradition's notion of distributive justice. Distributive justice insisted on a basic minimum necessary for all human beings. This fundamental floor or basic level had priority over other considerations. Such an understanding is also totally compatible with the traditional insistence which has become even more prevalent in contemporary times that the goods of creation exist to serve the needs of all. Thus the preferential option for the poor is in continuity with many of the emphases that have been a part of the Thomistic and Catholic social teaching traditions.

The emphasis on the preferential option for the poor without simultaneously downplaying the common good is analogous to what Leo XIII in *Rerum Novarum* said about the plight of workers and the poor. "Whenever the general interest, or any particular class, suffers or is threatened with harm which can in no other way be met or prevented, the public authority must step in to deal with it." "The richer class has many ways of shielding themselves and stand less in need of help from the state; whereas the mass of the poor have no resources of their own to fall back upon, and must chiefly depend upon the assistance of the state" (par. 36, 37; Gilson, pp. 225-226). A preferential concern or option for those worse off in no way destroys the basic understanding of the common good.

Significant Questions to be Answered

The first section of this paper tried to make the case for saying that recent official Catholic social teaching has moved away from the concept of the common good. However, the second section has tried to prove that the basic realities of the common good tradition are still found in contemporary Catholic social teaching. The common good tradition itself recognized that the concrete content and context would change over time. An examination of the recent official teachings has tried to point out the more significant changes which have occurred, especially in more contemporary times. Nor can one maintain that the introduction of new emphases such as that of equality or the preferential option for the poor is opposed to the core of the common good tradition.

The primary purpose of this paper has been to analyze the understanding of the common good in the documents of official Catholic social teaching. This analysis, however, raises some significant questions for further study. To what extent should the contemporary documents make more explicit their dependence on basic notions of the Catholic tradition such as the common good? To what extent can the common good tradition exist without all of its Thomistic metaphysical grounding? There is no doubt that the draft of the pastoral letter on the United States economy definitely appeals to the common good and bases its teaching explicitly on this concept. There are also important questions that need to be studied as a result of the developments that have occurred in the understanding of the content and context of the common good. How precisely can the recognition that human beings are by nature social and civil society is basically good be reconciled with the growing emphasis on freedom, equality, and rights? How much of a role should be given to power and conflict as strategies and tactics without destroying the common fabric of society? How is distributive justice related to the contemporary emphasis on equality?

Notes

1. There are a number of unofficial collections containing many of these documents. See especially David J. O'Brien and Thomas A. Shannon, eds., *Renewing the Earth: Catholic documents on Peace, Justice, and Liberation* (Garden City, New York: Doubleday Image Books, 1977); David M. Byers, ed., *Justice in the Marketplace: Collected Statements of the Vatican and the United States Catholic Bishops on Economic Policy, 1981-1984* (Washington: United States Catholic Conference, 1985). Future references to official documents will be to O'Brien and Shannon wherever possible.

2. Leo XIII, *Aeterni Patris* , in Etienne Gilson, ed. *The Pope Speaks to the Modern World: The Social Teachings of Leo XIII* (Garden City, New York: Doubleday Image Books, 1954), pp. 29-54.

3. Jean-Yves Calvez and Jacques Perrin, *The Church and Social Justice: The Social Teachings of the Popes from Leo XIII to Pius XII* (Chicago: Henry Regnery, 1961), pp. 101-132.

4. Calvez and Perrin, pp. 36-53.

5. 1971 Synod of Bishops, *Justitia in Mundo* , in O'Brien and Shannon, p. 391.

6. Donal Dorr, *Option for the Poor: A Hundred Years of Vatican Social Teaching* (Maryknoll, New York: Orbis, 1983).

7. Robert N. Bellah *et al., Habits of the Heart: Individualism and*

Commitment in American Life (Berkeley: University of California Press, 1985).

8. Jacques Maritain, *The Person and the Common Good* (New York: Charles Scribner's Sons, 1947; paperback ed., Notre Dame, Indiana: University of Notre Dame Press, 1966).

9. Charles DeKoninck, *De La primaute du bien commun* (Quebec: Editions de l'Universite Laval et Montreal: Fides, 1943); Jules A. Baisnee, "Two Catholic Critiques of Personalism," *The Modern Schoolman* 22 (1944-45), 59-74; I. Th. Eschmann, "In Defense of Jacques Maritain," *The Modern Schoolman* 22 (1944-45), 183-208; Charles DeKoninck, "In Defense of St. Thomas: A Reply to Father Eschmann's Attack on the Primacy of the Common Good, *Laval theologique et philosophique* I, no. 2 (1945), 9-109; Yves R. Simon, "On the Common Good," *Review of Politics* 6 (1944), 530-533.

10. A. Nemetz, "Common Good," *New Catholic Encyclopedia* , 1967, IV, 15-19.

11. For a study of the debates at Vatican II see Richard J. Regan, *Conflict and Consensus: Religious Freedom and the Second Vatican Council* (New York: Macmillan, 1967).

12. Ernest L. Fortin, "The New Rights Theory and the Natural Law," *Review of Politics* 44 (1982) 590-612.

13. For a contemporary appreciation and application of the Thomistic tradition on justice, see Daniel C. Maguire, *A New American Justice: Ending the White Male Monopolies* (Garden City, New York: Doubleday, 1980). However there is a dispute among contemporary Catholic thinkers. Some with Maguire see three particular kinds of justice —individual, legal or social, and distributive. For the opinion that legal justice is a general virtue and not a particular kind of justice see Normand Joseph Paulhus, "The Theological and Political Ideals of the Fribourg Union," (Ph.D. Diss., Boston College-Andover-Newton Theological Seminary, 1983).

14. E.g., Drew Christiansen, "On Relative Equality: Catholic Equalitarianism after Vatican II," *Theological Studies* 45 (1984), 651-675.

15. *Pastoral Letter on Catholic Social Teaching and the U.S. Economy* , Second Draft (Washington: National Conference of Catholic Bishops, 1985), par. 6, p. 23.

16. Congregation for the Doctrine of the Faith, *Instruction on Christian Freedom and Liberation* (Vatican City: Vatican Polyglot Press, 1986), par. 78, p. 47.

Part II

The Role for the Church

JOHN W. HOUCK

The three essays in this part are written by authors well-versed in religious-social thought. Interestingly, they each tackle a different aspect of the immensely challenging issue of the relationship between the church and economic and social issues in society. How should the church speak to contemporary issues embedded in society? Should the church only raise questions or should it go on to advocating specific policy solutions? In the first essay, Richard John Neuhaus' concern is that the church might be understood as advocating particular social and political policies as *the* Christian solution to a problem. This approach would transform prudential judgments about strategies to achieve the common good into an Absolute Good; this would be "spiritually idolatrous and politically disastrous."

In the second essay by Dennis McCann, we are presented with a whole new view of the church's role, growing out of the democratic, pluralistic American experience. The church, ac-

131

cording to McCann, does not speak with its traditional authority, but rather as one interest group speaking to other interest groups; in this account, the church's persuasiveness stems from the strength of its arguments. "In a secular pluralistic society, in which by definition there is precious little consensus in matters of substance, the common good should be understood procedurally: it conveys the church's commitment to a genuinely public discourse seeking to define the good to be pursued in common."

In the final essay, the economist-ethicist Ernest Bartell, C.S.C., writes about the influence and resiliency that Catholic social teaching has exhibited. Starting with Leo XIII in 1891 and up to the present day with the U.S. Catholic bishops' Pastoral Letter on the U.S. Economy, Catholic social teaching has had significant influence in this country and around the world. However, he points out that there has been a discernable evolution in Catholic social teaching that "alters the relationship of social sciences to the social teaching of the church."

A Theology of Politics, Not Political Theology

In Neuhaus' essay, we are advised that the greatest danger facing the church today is the assimilation of the tenets of liberation theology, which holds that all theology must be political. And for Neuhaus the differences between a theology of politics and political theology is critical. The latter is heavily ideological and topical, drawing its agenda from social changes and struggles. Whereas a theology of politics "grants a large measure of integrity to politics itself; it speaks more of creation and preservation, of the public rules by which social life is to be ordered and which are accessible to all rational actors."

To illustrate his point, Neuhaus provides an extensive case study of a situation in Hitler's 1930s Germany. During that period, Emanuel Hirsch, a well-respected Protestant theologian, argued that the German Protestant church should throw its support behind the National Socialist Party (Hitler's movement) in order to achieve the goal of revitalizing the German state along religious lines. Hirsch stated his case: "There exists between German *Volkstum* and Christian belief absolutely no division or contradiction to make it difficult as a German to be a Christian, or as a Christian a German."

The challenge to Hirsch's view came from Paul Tillich, a friend and fellow theologian. Tillich argued that Hirsch failed to leave the Christian any space for a yes or no to the political program; and that any political movement is subject to the independent judgment of God's word. Tillich accused Hirsch of consecrating political events and movements instead of discriminating amongst them: "you have approximated the year 1933 so closely to the year 33, that it has gained for you the meaning of an event in the history of salvation." The essence of Richard John Neuhaus' perspective is that the church and its members keep their autonomy (space) to judge any proposal for the common good, and not to yield to a political movement the power to discern the good in the common good.

The Good to be Pursued in Common

In Chapter Eight, Dennis McCann, a theological ethicist at DePaul University and the author of *Christian Realism and Liberation Theology*, questions the proposition that there is a consensus in religious circles, especially Catholic, about the meaning of the common good. If, in fact, it was fairly clear in the writings of Leo XIII what was meant by the concept of the common good (1891), this clarity was short lived. Pius XI's encyclical letter *Quadragesimo Anno* (1931) destroyed those elements there that were in the consensus by his justly famous "principle of subsidiarity" which granted to intermediate groups freedom to pursue different, if not conflictual, goals. McCann writes:

> I will argue that the common good, as commonly understood, does not provide a very helpful perspective for challenging the American economy. The perspective is not very helpful because,

once its content is stretched far enough to establish continuity between its origins in a traditional, paternalistic view of society and the church's growing appreciation for the virtues of the modern, democratic state, it inevitably becomes so nebulous that nothing very well focused by way of a moral agenda can be inferred from it. And what sort of challenge to American capitalism could that possibly represent?

For Dennis McCann, the common good is no longer a substantive, objectively knowable, major premise which can give guidance and answers. The certainty has given way to a process, the elements of which are: First, within the spirit of the church, the members work out social-ethical propositions that are within their respective church traditions; "they are recognized as the fruit of a particular community's moral deliberations, now presented to society as a whole for public consideration." Second, the church lobbies with the larger society to explain and justify a specific set of social policies and rules. In our liberal, pluralistic, and democratic society, the role of the church, along with other groups, is to participate in a civil consensus through public dialogue. McCann uses phrases like "adult moral dialogue" and "the church's commitment to a genuinely public discourse" which convey for the reader the seriousness of the public conversation. The discernment of the common good is resolved through "public argument about conflicting interests and discordant moral agendas, some of which may eventually be recognized as generalizable and, hence, as essential to social justice."

This new state of affairs in which, to say the least, the process is as important as the dialogic conclusions, leaves McCann "cautiously optimistic" about the recent performance of the American Catholic Church. He cites the two recent pastoral letters, "The Challenge of Peace" and "Catholic Social Teaching and the U.S. Economy" as evidence of the institutionalization of the dialogic process. These pastorals encouraged inquiry and discussion both within the confines of the church and in the broader public debates. The bishops realized that the possibilities for a true consensus, both within the church and the larger public sphere, depended on a vigorous debate. The implication of this new process for American Catholic social thought has yet to be fully understood. McCann questions whether the church can be "authority-centered" in its own realm and "democratic" in the public weal. This raises for McCann the serious issue of dissent within the church.

How Do the Social Sciences Affect Religious-Social Thinking?

Father Bartell explores new answers to the challenges raised by the social sciences for religious-social thinking. He does this by tracing the history of one branch of religious-social thinking, the Catholic social teaching tradition which started in 1891 with Leo XIII's encyclical *Rerum Novarum*. Underlying what Leo XIII wrote was the assumption of a coherent body of natural law principles from which could be deduced a properly ordered society. The meaning of the common good could be discovered from these natural law principles and could be understood apart from any knowledge or information about the dynamics of social reality then prevalent in the society under consideration. The spirit of *Rerum Novarum* was followed in Pope Pius XI's *Quadragesimo anno*, 1931.

In 1963, even John XXIII maintained the usefulness of the natural law tradition in his *Pacem in Terris*. However, in *Pacem in Terris*, John XXIII acknowledged the wide diversity of economic institutions, policies and systems, which suggested a greater openness to a plurality of solutions to concrete problems. This should not be surprising when applying ethical principles to real situations and in analyzing the effects of economic activity on human well-being.

Two years after *Pacem in Terris* was issued, the Council (Vatican II) Fathers authored *Gaudium et Spes*. The Council document was notable for its reduced reliance upon natural law principles and more emphasis upon sacred scripture in grounding the social teaching of Church. Ascertaining the common good

now became less a matter of deduction from generalized principles and more a question of induction based on observations of
what is going on in society and included a sense of the trade-offs
entailed in a decision. To John XXIII, the common good is "the
sum of those conditions of social life which allow social groups
and their individual members relatively thorough and ready access to their own fulfillment."

In *Octogesima Adveniens* Paul VI acknowledged the growth
of the social sciences and their role in "subjecting to critical examination the hitherto accepted knowledge about man." However, Paul VI suggested the crucial need for the positive human
sciences to be open to principles and values outside their own
field; according to Paul, methodological requirements and ideological presuppositions "too often lead the human sciences to
isolate, in the various situations, certain aspects of man, and yet
to give these an explanation which claims to be complete or at
least an interpretation which is meant to be all-embracing from a
purely quantitative or phenomenological point of view."

Bartell believes that the recent Pastoral Letter of the U.S. Bishops on the economy, while grounded solidly in what has been
traditional Catholic social teaching, reflects in itself new characteristics and trends in Catholic social teaching. For one, there are
the practical policy recommendations the bishops have in the
document. Also, the bishops are quite open to a dialogue of religious-social thinking and the social sciences; for example, the
document repeatedly emphasizes the distribution of income,
wealth, and opportunity, and calls attention to the international
perspective on a number of complex issues. Bartell is pleased by
the willingness of the Church to use more effectively the social
sciences to affect religious-social thought. Nevertheless, the new
methodology presents a challenge to the Church as it tries to
link the new empirical ways with natural law and scripture.

Seven

No Space for Yes and No: The Obligations and Limits of Political Commitment

RICHARD JOHN NEUHAUS

A discussion of the common good does not get very far unless there is some shared idea of the good. It is almost a commonplace today to observe that our culture does not possess such a shared idea of the good. Without an idea of the good, the notion of the common good readily degenerates into being no more than an amalgam of the desires and interests of the commonality. The common good may end up meaning simply the accumulation of goods. When all is relative and all desires and interests are equal, the common good becomes a euphemism for a social stew of aspirations and discontents. The stew may be given the elevated name of democratic pluralism, but it is stew nonetheless.

The common good without reference to the good results in a

137

politics that assumes that man is the best thing in the world. Indeed, it assumes that man is the only thing in the world, or at least the only thing that matters. (If other things matter, they matter because man has determined they matter.) The corresponding consequence is that there is then no "ought" in politics. That is, there is no "ought" other than the "ought" that results from the interaction of human interests and desires. What will be will be, and what will be will be declared to be what should be. The "ought of results," however, is no "ought" at all, for it lacks the prescriptive force of the word "ought."

Without the prescriptive "ought," there is finally no politics at all. Not at least in Aristotle's sense, for he understood politics to be the project in which free and reasonable persons deliberate the question, How ought we to order our life together? Regardless of how they felt about Aristotle, most Christians over the centuries have agreed that there ought to be an "ought" in politics. Even New Testament Christianity, with its minimalist expectations of the state, assumed that political power should have something to do with the punishment of the wicked and the reward of the good (Romans 13). By the fourth century, Christians such as Eusebius of Caesarea would promote a much more intimate connection between politics and the good. And so it continued through Aquinas and Calvin, and through the Protestant social gospel movement in this country, with its celebration of the "holy trinity" of Progress, Democracy and America.

The good to which the "ought" is related in Christian thought is finally the Absolute Good who is God. That is, politics, along with everything else, ought to be in accord with the will of God. The ways in which the will of God is known is variously stated in the several traditions of Christian thought: in Jesus above all, in Scriptures, in divinely guided tradition, in natural law, in the orders of creation, in common grace, in general revelation, in human reason. Most Christians have conditioned their political expectations by an "eschatological proviso" which makes clear that everything will not be ordered according to the will of God short of the End Time. Humanity and all of creation are still yearning toward their intended form (Romans 8), which will not be revealed until the time when every knee shall bow and every tongue confess that Jesus Christ is Lord, to the glory of God the Father (Philippians 2).

On this nether side of the End Time, Christians have tried in different, and frequently contradictory, ways to relate the good and the common good. In what is called the "sectarian" option, Christians have seen a very close connection between the good and the common good, but the commonality in that case is limited to the "new humanity" of the community of faith, which is sharply marked off from "the world." Apart from the politics of its own community, the sectarian option is typically apolitical or antipolitical, and is therefore somewhat marginal to our present considerations.

The more classical traditions have employed concepts such as natural law in order to affirm a convergence or congruence between God's will as perceived by faith and as perceived by reason. In this sense the classic or catholic tradition is a more truly public tradition. Within the Church, humanity receives by grace a further measure of fulfillment, but it is emphasized that this humanity is the common humanity of all, believer and unbeliever alike. In other words, grace does not destroy but crowns nature. It is further emphasized that the one Lord is Lord over all, so there is a will of God both for the redeemed and the unredeemed. Within the catholic stream, Lutherans have spoken of the "two kingdoms," or, better stated, the "twofold rule of God." Calvinists in the Abraham Kuyper tradition speak of "spheres of sovereignty" by which the world is to be rightly ordered. And of course Roman Catholics speak of natural law. What all have in common is a theologically-based understanding of the good which gives substance to the "ought" of Aristotelian politics and makes it possible to speak of the common good.

What all have in common is a theology of politics. A theology of politics affirms the political enterprise itself and gives assurance that the "ought" that is pursued in that enterprise can be congruent with the will of God. A theology of politics means, in the present context, something different from a political theology. The term "political theology" has been variously employed. By political theology I mean theology that entails a political direction or course of action. A political theology is more closely tied to political ideology. A theology of politics grants a large measure of integrity to politics itself; it speaks more of creation and preservation, of the public rules by which social life is to be ordered and which are accessible to all rational actors. It is with this understanding of a theology of politics that Luther could say he would rather be ruled by a wise Turk than by a foolish Christian. A political theology is something else.

A political theology speaks more of "reading the signs of the times" (Matthew 16) than of obedience to abiding definitions of the good. Put differently, the good is not so much that which God has decreed as it is that which God is doing. History is the story of the "God who acts," to use the phrase from an older school of biblical theology, and it is the Christian's responsibility to get with God's action. Political theology readily becomes politicized theology and theologized politics. It is susceptible to confusing whatever is happening — or whatever we think is happening — with God's acting. Thus the World Council of Churches proclaimed the slogan, "The world sets the agenda for the Church." Such political theology frequently turns into the paths of enthusiasm and fanaticism.

All that said, however, political theology has been with us for centuries and is not likely to disappear before the Kingdom Come. And that for very good reasons. Whatever the specifics of its politics, political theology speaks of change in a world that manifestly needs changing. In addition, almost no Christian has such a static understanding of God's will for the world that he does not believe that God is still acting in history. Believing that, he seeks to discern and participate in God's acting. Even the most convinced proponents of natural law or of God's twofold rule have at times read the signs of the times and discerned God's judgment and leading in the events of history. Thus the common good is to be determined not only by eternal rules but also by the active ruling of the One who is the Absolute Good.

Today, as usual, there is heated controversy among Christians over political theologies in conflict. Almost nobody today advances the political theology of the earlier social gospel movement as represented by, for instance, Walter Rauschenbusch. The afterglow of that movement is still evident in the fussy benevo-

lence of old-line Protestantism, but seldom is substantive theological argument mustered in its defense. A more vibrant, if not
very persuasive, political theology is advanced by the religious
Right today. Here one encounters strong theological assertions
about God's law for the ordering of society and lively apocalyptic readings of how God is acting, as revealed by "Bible proph-
ecy," in the contingent events reported on the evening news.
There are also today cautious probings toward a political theology of democratic capitalism and of liberal democracy. But these
are likely to remain very cautious indeed, since those who are
sympathetic to the effort have been made suspicious of political
theology itself.

One reason for their suspicion is the influence of the most aggressive form of political theology today, namely, liberation theology. Of course there are different liberation theologies, as is
routinely and sometimes misleadingly noted. But there is an
identifiable, indeed self-identified, common project which
makes it possible to speak of liberation theology in the singular.
That project is led by, *inter alia*, Gustavo Gutierrez, Juan Luis
Segundo, Hugo Assmann, and Jose Miguez Bonino. It is to them
that we owe a great debt for forcing us to think again and more
clearly about the difference between a theology of politics and a
political theology, about the connections between the common
good and the Absolute Good.

Political Theology: A Case Study

As indicated earlier, the problem and promise of political theology are hardly new in Christian history. In this context it is instructive to consider the case of Emanuel Hirsch.[1] Hirsch is little
known today but at one time he was ranked as a giant of 20th-
century German theology, along with such as Barth, Bultmann,
Brunner and Tillich. He was, among other things, a preeminent
authority on Kierkegaard and sought with existential urgency to
discern and act upon the signs of his times. Born in 1888, Hirsch
was, as a student and young teacher, an intimate friend and intel-

lectual soul-mate of Paul Tillich. Both were the product of the best of 19th-century theological liberalism, and both rejected Karl Barth's stringent reaction to that heritage. They were not prepared to say with Barth that there is an "infinite qualitative distinction" between God and man, between God's ways and man's ways in history. Together they searched for the convergences between the Divine and the human, for the correlations, as it were, between theological theory and social praxis. Although their paths were to diverge dramatically in the 1930s, they were asking many of the same questions and coming to many of the same answers.

Hirsch, Tillich, and most of the leading intellectuals of the time shared a passionate contempt for liberal, bourgeois democracy. This was also the case, although it is often forgotten, with the theologians who produced the Barmen Declaration in 1934 and became the heroes of the Confessing Church under Hitler.[2] The Weimar Republic, they were all convinced, was a time of deepest crisis, what Tillich termed a "Kairos" of monumental historic importance. Tillich developed what was called a Kairos theology, and Hirsch shared fully his sense of almost apocalyptic urgency. To understand the turn that Hirsch took, one must know that he was a deeply committed Christian, a modern man devoted to reason and unwilling to jettison the fruits of science and intellectual inquiry. In addition, he was politically committed to "the people," the *Volk*, and sought Germany's liberation from what was viewed as the oppressive yoke imposed by the victorious powers after World War I. Hirsch saw reality from "the underside of history" and thus saw through the ways, or thought he saw through the ways, in which the vaunted "freedoms" of liberalism disguised and legitimated continuing exploitation.

Hirsch wanted a political ethic rooted in Christianity, although borrowing freely from other sources for purposes of analysis. Liberal democracy, he believed, was riddled with internal contradictions and, in its chaotic give and take, truth had been reduced to "a party matter." Hirsch wanted a potent truth, a revolutionary truth, that could cut through the debilitating relativities of liberalism. "What we are missing today," he wrote, "is contemplation of the ultimate bases of all our political as well as social historical judgments." A radical struggle was required to discover "guidelines for the life of the individual and the society as a whole." The people are hungry for a sense of purpose, a great cause. The sense of crisis is to be welcomed because "crises make us young," according to Hirsch. The revolution "would be a hard path" but at least it would be "a path which has a destination." The new order that Hirsch desired must agree with the Marxists in rejecting the "old Hegel" who elevated the state to the point where the free act is made impossible. At the same time, it must reject the loose and atomizing individualism of liberal democracy. The alternative is freedom that is in solidarity with the people and thus in the service of authentic community. The revolution must be led by a vanguard that constitutes itself as a "community of conscience" leading the entire society to become such a community of conscience.

In this struggle, violence could by no means be ruled out. Hirsch had little patience for pacifists and others who "sentimentally" distorted the liberating force of authentic Christianity. In any event, violence between oppressed and oppressor is inevitable. "War," he wrote, "is a tool of history" and history has its own laws. Against the socialism of the Left, Hirsch would choose the "socialism" in National Socialism. In this socialism the state would not disappear but would closely regulate the lives of all its citizens and provide for their needs. (In this respect, the state would do in principle what the state attempts to do in practice where Marxist socialism has come to power, always remembering that the party-state decides what people need.) The struggle must be advanced by people who believe that God is at work in it. Against Barth and his followers, Hirsch declared his refusal to view history "as a region abandoned by God."

Hirsch underscored faith and action in the concreteness of history. He was suspicious of liberal abstractions and for this reason opposed participation in the ecumenical movement of the time. Whatever the "subjective" good intentions of well-meaning Christians, the "objective" consequence was to distract energies from the struggle of the people. The time, he insisted, was not one for pious universalisms but for deepened commitment to the concrete cause. The conventional distinction between "the sacred" and "the secular" must be challenged. The Church is indeed holy, but it is not an ethereal and disembodied holiness; it is a holiness that intersects with the tasks of history. The Confessing Christians of Barmen were wrong to set their holiness against history. The *Deutsche Christen*, on the other hand, understood that it is precisely Christian faithfulness that requires taking sides. As for those who say that the Church should transcend partisanships, or offer some kind of "third way," or be a forum for the critical engagement of all proposed ways, this is not possible according to Hirsch. The withholding of commitment, he said, can only result in the continuation of what Kierkegaard dismissively called "the all-encompassing debate about everything."

Hirsch did not claim to know the future. His analytic tools included no "scientific laws of history" by which it was certain that the revolution would succeed in history. The future, he said, "lies in that which comes." He did not take lightly National Socialism's restrictions of freedom, but he dared to believe that "all tensions within our new restrictions upon freedom are tensions of an encounter with God." Hirsch asked, "Is it then true that such an encounter with God is the ultimate secret of the German turning point?" If the answer is Yes, then a price must be paid without liberal compunctions. Hirsch read the signs of the times and answered Yes. Moreover, those who refused to answer the question were in "objective" fact answering negatively. As Hirsch said again and again in his own way, not to decide is to decide; or, as a later generation would put it, if you aren't part of the solution you are part of the problem.

Unlike the Marxists, Hirsch had no dogmatic consolation that, developments notwithstanding, he had chosen the right side. "Only in the depths of belief in justification by faith was it possible to allow the ethical involvement of the Christian in the historical community. This is not built on the basis of a law, but out of merciful responsibility based on the general self-testimony and rule of God in nature and history." Political commitment, in this view, is to accept Luther's familiar (and usually misunder-

stood) invitation to "sin boldly." Although Hirsch urged the
Church to be partisan, he did not go so far as today's liberation-
ist proponents of "the partisan church." That is, the true Church
and the struggle were not coextensive in Hirsch's view, nor were
the grace and mercy of God to which the Church witnessed
equated with the doctrine of the struggle. The struggle remained
in all its parts always under judgment. It may be *an* encounter
with God in history but, according to Hirsch, there is no theological warrant for saying it is *the* encounter with God in history.

The critical thing, according to Hirsch, is that we make concrete choices in history. Barth, he said, thought the Church
could and should proclaim its message "as if nothing had happened." Hirsch rejected this as nonsense. "God does not speak
to my heart today as if nothing has happened...He carries the
danger that lies therein: He is the Lord and does not need to fear
for his truth." Nor, contra the Confessing Church that opposed
Hitler, need the Church fear the revolution's encroachment on
what had traditionally been Church responsibilities in areas such
as education, health care, and tending to the needs of orphans
and the mentally ill. None of these activities are integral to the
Church's essential mission, Hirsch argued, and were only necessary as band-aid ministries so long as the state was not living up
to its total responsibility for the society. The Church should not
complain, but should rather acclaim the revolution's assumption
of its proper responsibility in these areas. Indeed the entire posture and structure of the Church should be changed in order to
reflect "leadership as passionate will" in support of the revolution. "If that is not easily understood nor understood by all today, that is because it has not yet gone into everyone's blood that
National Socialism, based on the right of historical change, is becoming the self-evident and binding form of life for all Germans." Against the counterrevolutionary Confessing Church,
Hirsch tirelessly argued that the *Deutsche Christen* movement
was the true people's church of the historical moment. But even
then he could not bring himself to explicitly excommunicate
from "the true church" those who read the signs of the times
differently.

"There exists between German *Volkstum* and Christian belief absolutely no division or contradiction to make it difficult as a German to be a Christian, or as a Christian a German," Hirsch wrote. Those who claimed such a division or contradiction were in fact missing Christianity against the common good as represented by the people's movement and its Fuehrer. Hirsch well understood that his argument required a new theology to accommodate the new historical moment. This requires also a reformulation of the Church's self-understanding, it requires what Leonardo Boff would later call "ecclesiogenesis." "The fate of Christianity in Western civilization depends on this," Hirsch wrote: "that in Protestant Christianity the men do not die out who offer this crisis of reformulation as the path ordained by God to our veracity. In this crisis and with its means, they become bearers of a historical process which will build a new Christian concept of history consistent with the new circumstances and the new understanding." Despite his theoretical statements about the uncertainty of historical outcomes, Hirsch ended up giving a moral and theological *carte blanche* to the Nazi regime. He did not deny that the revolutionary leadership made "mistakes" nor that the leaders were themselves "imperfect," but to focus on these was to run the risk of being "paralyzed by uncertainty" and thus to miss the historical moment and its imperative which, it must be remembered, were also God's moment and God's imperative.

Paul Tillich's Response

Robert Ericksen, a student of the period, believes that between Tillich and Hirsch there was not all that much theological difference. He writes that "Tillich jumped left, believing he had interpreted God correctly, and Hirsch jumped right." Either jump, Ericksen suggests, was not theologically mandated but based upon a prudential judgment of historical contingencies. Of course "the judgment of history" has gone against Hirsch but, according to Ericksen, neither theology nor reason could at the time have settled the dispute between historical actors such as Hirsch and Tillich. Ericksen seems to suggest that they paid their theological money and made their political choice, and some won and some lost. Not surprisingly, Tillich himself had a somewhat different view of the matter.

Writing from Union Seminary, New York, Tillich addressed a long open letter to his friend and colleague.[3] It is dated October 1, 1934, and goes on for more than thirty published pages. The letter is at times hostile and at times cordial, reflecting the pain of having come to a parting of the ways with an intimate. Also, Tillich reveals both resentment and embarrassment. Resentment because he claims that Hirsch has stolen from his own "Kairos doctrine" without giving him credit, and embarrassment because he implicitly recognizes that his "Kairos doctrine" could be taken in the direction that Hirsch had taken it. Of course Tillich claims that Hirsch has distorted what he, Tillich, intended to say, and the letter is in large part an effort to clarify just what he had intended to say.

Tillich's basic argument is that Hirsch had collapsed theology into politics, giving an uncritical spiritual legitimation to his judgment of contingent events. "I can summarize my critique...in this sentence: *You have perverted the prophetic, eschatologically conceived Kairos doctrine into a sacerdotal-sacramental consecration of a current event.*" (The emphasis is his.) Hirsch had, according to Tillich, turned theology into ideology. Tillich quotes Hirsch's claim that true theology is possible "if it is altogether open from within to the great and the new, which has broken through with the National Socialist movement. Its world view should be the sustaining, naturally historical basis of life for the German man of evangelical faith." In making such claims, Tillich wrote, "you have approximated the year 1933 so closely to the year 33, that it has gained for you the meaning of an event in the history of salvation."

By refusing the Church its own space in which to say both No and Yes to historical developments, said Tillich, "You consecrate instead of disclosing." Indeed Christians must make historical judgments and take the resulting risks, but in doing so they must "acknowledge the relativizing of what is risked in all its consequences." Tillich accuses Hirsch of historical myopia, of apotheosizing a specific historical moment as *the* moment of definitive change, to the neglect of two thousand years of Christian history, to the neglect of the longer reaches of human experience, and, most particularly, to the neglect of *the* definitive revelation in the Christ event.

The question of ecclesiology is also critical to Tillich's argument. The role of "the blood-bond" in Nazi ideology denied to Jews who had become Christians full standing in Church and society. Tillich's point is that unity in Christ must transcend any other bond of race or nation or class. A partisan church that denies this transcendence is a repudiation of the Church. "Are you, precisely as a theologian, called to subordinate the sacramental consanguinity of Christianity, which is given with the Lord's Supper, to the natural historical consanguinity?" Tillich asks. In other words, does solidarity with "the people" take precedence over the solidarity established by God in Word and sacrament? In asking such questions, Tillich is pressing Hirsch to make explicit the radical ramifications of his position.

In his letter Tillich may also be regretting some of his own strident condemnations of liberal democracy, condemnations which had been a commonplace among intellectuals during the Weimar period. Tillich presses Hirsch on what follows "the destruction of democracy." It is fine to talk about a new order and a more just society but, by refusing to be specific and believable about the shape of that new order, such talk "drives you into a mysticism from which nothing concretely follows." Or, more likely, what follows is "despotism." It is not enough, writes Tillich, to issue "a declaration of hate...against everything democratic." Tillich even asks whether Hegel might not have been right after all when he posited "the Christian-Germanic notion of freedom in opposition to the Asian and pre-Christian principle of despotism." Even the so-called negative freedoms of bourgeois liberalism begin to take on great value when one contemplates the alternatives, Tillich suggests.

But the gravamen of Tillich's letter is not whether Hirsch is right or wrong in his political judgment, as such, but whether he understands what is at stake theologically and spiritually. When the idea of the good is subsumed in a partisan definition of the common good, there is no room for the spirit. In order for the spirit to assert itself, "it must have a space in which it can come to yea-saying through nay-saying." "The first step of spirit is to say no to what is immediately given. Does it not contradict the totalitarian ideas, as you portray it, to provide space for the development of an existential no? There have been states that have denied spirit this space and have destroyed spirit in itself. Has the seriousness of this question never disturbed you in your enthusiastic portrayal of the total state and in the demand of ruthless intervention, which is said to be better than persuasion?" In appealing to historical experience with totalitarianism, of course, Tillich did not have the advantage of knowing the Soviet Gulag or the despotisms of Cuba, Vietnam and Cambodia. And, of course, neither he nor Hirsch knew at the time what the Nazi regime would become. But Tillich did have a larger measure of prescience in understanding the historical consequences inherent in and invited by totalitarian principles.

The principle for Christians, Tillich argued, is that there is both a *reservatum* and an *obigatum*, a No and a Yes, in all political commitments. Hirsch, like contemporary totalitarians, was prepared to affirm a place for the *reservatum* in the privacy of the individual's personal relation to God. But he does not grant the right of such a *reservatum* to the Church and its "independent historical place." But in refusing that, says Tillich, Hirsch also cancels the personal *reservatum*, for "you make it impotent over against the *Weltanschauungen* or myths that sustain the totalitarian state." Tillich takes pains to absolve his own version of socialism from this totalitarian crime against the spirit: "Religious Socialism knew, when accepting the doctrine of the *reservatum religiosum*, that the religious can never be dissolved into the socialist, that the church is something quite apart from the *Kairos*, that is, from the promise and demand that Religious Socialism saw in the broadly visible irruption of the new social and spiritual arrangement of the society. You took over the *obligatum* but gave up the *reservatum* — the charge that is basically the theme of my whole letter."

At the end of his letter, Tillich says his hope is that "enthusiasts could be made into believing realists." As an example of enthusiasm, he cites Hirsch's words: "When we have the courage, on the basis of the faith that obeys this truth [of the Gospel], to enter into something human-historical with our yes, then the unfathomable sublimity of the truth accompanies us and, in its way, reigns in this human-historical thing." That claim, Tillich makes clear, is not simply an instance of enthusiasm but of idolatry.

Now many years ago, in *The Origins of Totalitarianism*, Hannah Arendt made the case for the similarities and frequent identities between National Socialism and Marxist-Leninism. Many intellectuals, including theologians, still resist that argument although it has been reinforced by scholarship and historical experience since Arendt. I believe that Karl Dietrich Bracher, for instance, is correct when he argues in *The Age of Ideologies*, that the significant line of division from the 19th century through to the present is between those who support and those who oppose the idea of liberal democracy.[4] But our more specific concern here is the theological contribution to maintaining the tension between the good and all definitions of the common good, between a theology of politics and a political theology. Essential to that contribution, I believe, is what Tillich describes as the tension, even dialectic, between *obligatum* and *reservatum*, always remembering that the *reservatum* is prior and more certain. In the absence of the *reservatum*, the *obligatum* becomes spiritually idolatrous and politically disastrous.

The Issue Today

As with Emanuel Hirsch and the *Deutschen Christen*, so with much liberation theology today, the *obligatum* has swallowed up the *reservatum*. As Hirsch believed that the truth "reigns in this human-historical thing," so Juan Luis Segundo declares that faith is "the spirit of *freedom for history, of taste for the future, of openness for the provisional and relative*," in short a "*freedom for ideologies*."[5] The critical distance from all ideologies which makes possible the prophetic witness of the Church is eliminated. As Dennis McCann puts it, "From Segundo's perspective, this religious reservation represents not an ultimate principle of criticism, but one more outmoded Christian ideology. Since it tends to 'throw a dash of cold water' on the political enthusiasm necessary for 'real-life revolution,' it in turn must be relativized...." Segundo rejects the traditional idea of the Kingdom of God as "something metahistorical and a disgusted turning away from real-life history."[6] Segundo favorably quotes James Cone: "There are no universal truths in the process of liberation; the only truth is liberation itself."[7] One might say it is an assertion worthy of Emanuel Hirsch, but Hirsch was a careful thinker and never went so far in eliminating the *reservatum*.

Christian realism, as represented by Reinhold Niebuhr, and liberation theology, as represented by Segundo, "dramatize the current impasse in practical theology," according to McCann. It is the same impasse reached by Tillich and Hirsch. To some political definitions of the common good Christians must say an unequivocal No. There can be little or no reservation, for example, in our condemnation of National Socialism or the regimes of today's Cambodia or Iran. Such regimes are evil in principle and practice, and we should not hesitate to say so. The tragic truth is that history has thrown up numerous distortions of the common good to which the Church can and must say No. Short of the Kingdom of God, however, there is no politically established definition of the common good — nor any candidate for such establishment — to which the Church can say an unequivocal Yes. In the exercise of the political *obligatum* Christians can and do take risks, but we have no right, indeed it is not too much to say that it is apostasy, to risk the surrender of the critical *reservatum*. Against all despots — whether or not they are totalitarian in principle — the first spiritual and political obligation of the Christian community is to struggle to maintain its space for saying Yes and No.

We have, I believe, not done justice to contemporary liberation theology until we recognize that it is indeed as radical as many of its theologians claim it is. A careful evaluation of arguments suggests that, compared with the claims of Segundo and others, Emanuel Hirsch was temperate in his endorsement of National Socialism. Tillich was right to criticize Hirsch for neglecting the *reservatum* implicit in the "eschatological proviso." Dominant forms of liberation theology do not neglect but explicitly deny both the proviso and the reservation. Indeed the "dialectic" employed in such liberation theology has already anticipated and annulled the criticism that Tillich tried to bring to bear in the case of Hirsch. It is a dialectic that, to use its own terms, has negated the negation. McCann is surely justified, I believe, in describing this as "the impasse" in contemporary theological thought about politics and ideology.

There are no doubt many reasons why theologians in this country have failed to address this impasse with greater lucidity and candor. One reason no doubt is understandable feelings of insecurity and guilt about our more favored placement in the global scheme of things, especially when it is alleged that our economic and political well-being is purchased at the price of the misery of most human beings on earth. Another reason is a laudable sympathy for the social and political crises experienced by the people for whom such liberation theologians claim to speak. Yet another and less edifying reason is that there is a certain condescension among us North Americans. It may be that we hesitate to criticize people whom we do not really view as peers in theological discourse. This is evident when we refuse to take them at their word, even though they insist again and again that they mean exactly what they are saying. Finally we fail to criticize because we are afraid. I suspect that more than a few of us are morally intimidated by their claim that, if we are not more or less uncritically on their side, we must be on the side of their oppressors, real or alleged.

In September of 1985 more than 150 professional and lay theologians in South Africa issued "The Kairos Document." They said "there is nothing final about this document" and invite criticism from "all committed Christians." Surely we owe them a response to their invitation. In making such a response it is also imperative to keep in mind that South Africans, especially nonwhite South Africans, have had bitter experience with the political theology of apartheid. Although the white Dutch Reformed churches today insist that they do not support a theological legitimation of apartheid, there are still not a few proponents of racial separatism who advocate their peculiar version of "the partisan church." In fact, they tell the Afrikaner story in the form of a "liberation theology" not entirely dissimilar from that of Emanuel Hirsch and some of their opponents in South Africa today, although, of course, to very different political purposes.[8]

The Kairos Document begins with the assertion: "The time has come. The moment of truth has arrived." In its 25 pages it argues that the government of South Africa is totally devoid of legitimacy, is irreformable, and must be overthrown. As in the Bible God "does not attempt to reconcile Moses and Pharaoh," so today the Christian task is not reconciliation but the establishment of justice. The line is drawn between those who represent the aspirations of "the people" and those who work for the reform of a regime "that has made itself the enemy of the people [and] has thereby also made itself the enemy of God." The Church must not entertain the illusion of maintaining a critical distance from the movement of liberation. "The Church must avoid becoming a 'Third Force,' a force between the oppressor and the oppressed." In all its activities the Church must not "duplicate" and, above all, must not "run counter to the struggles of those political organizations that truly represent the grievances and demands of the people."

In the thoroughness of its negation of the *reservatum*, the "Kairos Document" makes Emanuel Hirsch's distortion of the "Kairos doctrine" appear cautious. But surely, it will be objected, this is to overlook the *substantive* question of the difference between National Socialism and, say, the African National Conference. The one cause is unspeakably unjust, while the other is a reasonable and urgent pursuit of justice. As the Latin American liberationists ceaselessly remind us, there is no "moral equivalence" between oppressor and oppressed. They are right, and distinctions must be made. The judgments we come to with respect to the relative merits of political causes is not the most important question at hand, and yet such judgments are important. On the question of making political judgments I cannot agree with Ericksen's suggestion that the difference between Tillich's and Hirsch's judgments is quite arbitrary. Hirsch should have known (and liberation theologians should know today) that movements that deny in principle a normative reason by which they can be brought under judgment are not to be trusted. Hirsch should have known (and liberation theologians should know today) that movements that claim a right to do terrible things to people in order to achieve their purposes will more than likely end up doing those terrible things. It is fair (no, it is necessary) to add that Hirsch in 1934 was not as culpable as are theologians who serve as apologists for Marxist-Leninist revolution today. Of course Hirsch should have taken the ominous doctrines of Nazism, as set forth, for example, in *Mein Kampf*, more seriously, but there never had been a National Socialist regime before. The principles of Nazism had no track record in practice. It was possible, even if recklessly self-deceptive, to accent the positive and hope for the best, as Hirsch did. None of these things can be said of Marxist-Leninism in the 20th century.

I am well aware that, the evidence notwithstanding, such historical-political judgments will be disputed by many today. Whatever has been the experience with revolutions past, it is today argued that *this* revolution is different, *this* socialist experiment has never been tried before, *this* will turn out to be the new order based on Marxist scientific analysis and Christian revolutionary hope. The force of our criticism is thus stymied by appeal to evidence from the future, evidence which of course none of us can possess. In 1934 Tillich had to admit that, despite the troubling evidences, he could not *prove* that Hirsch was wrong in his political judgment. It is conceivable, Tillich had to admit, that National Socialism would establish the new and just revolutionary order for which Hirsch yearned. *The gravamen of Tillich's argument, therefore, was not that Hirsch was wrong in his political judgment but that he was wrong theologically.* In making our political commitments, he contended, it is theologically impermissible to let the *obligatum* devour the *reservatum*, to annul or suspend the eschatological proviso. Hirsch denied that he was guilty of such an error. Juan Luis Segundo denies that it is an error.

The impasse is all too real. Some of those on the one side of impasse will object that my argument makes theology counterrevolutionary, pitting theological truth against revolutionary commitment. One can only say in response that any revolution that requires a compromise of theological truth, or sets itself up as the norm of theological truth, is a bad revolution. It is bad for truth, theological or otherwise, and it is almost certainly bad in its consequences for the people in whose name it is advanced. The painfulness of the impasse is intensified when we recognize that what is at stake is the ordering of our loyalties. For the Christian, the truth of ultimate allegiance is the Gospel of God's justifying grace in Jesus Christ, and the community of ultimate allegiance is the Church constituted and sustained by that Gospel. That community is not a theological abstraction but a concrete, social and historical reality which must be free to proclaim its truth and define its mission. It in turn is created and defined by a proclamation and a grace that transcends all historical moments and movements.

In its institutional forms the Church can be, and frequently has been, inimical to the well-being, the common good, of society. In such instances the Church must be reformed. What must never be done, however, is to attempt to reconstitute or redefine the Church in terms of a program of social and political change. What must never be done is to posit an ideologically defined "people's church" against the Church constituted by the Gospel. What must never be done is to attempt to replace the Gospel itself with an ideology for social transformation which we then call the Gospel. What must never be done was done by some of the *Deutschen Christen* and is being done today in versions of liberation theology. The painful words of Saint Paul (recalled by the Confessing Church in Germany) now make a new and urgent claim upon our attention: "But even if we, or an angel from heaven, should preach to you a gospel contrary to that which we preached to you, let him be accursed" (Galatians 1). This is a hard word, to be sure, and it is understandable that we shrink from exploring its applicability to our own time. But, as Christians in 1934 were not called to speak the easy words of their own choosing, so we might ask whether the contemporary impasse does not lay a similar call upon us. Of course we do not want to deepen the impasse by unhelpful polemic, but neither dare we disguise what is at stake for Christian theology. As Christians and as theologians we must speak the truth in love (Ephesians 4) but, insofar as we have been given to understand the truth, we must speak the truth, as Paul Tillich spoke the truth in love to Emanuel Hirsch.

In his study of theologians under Hitler, Robert Ericksen concludes by asking what lessons we might draw for today. "We can best avoid [their] error," he writes, "by heavily stressing the values of the liberal, democratic tradition, humanitarianism and justice, and by conscientiously probing history with a view towards its significance for our contemporary decision making." I believe Ericksen is right, although I also believe he is too skeptical about the possibilities of grounding the liberal democratic tradition in orthodox theology and clear reason. But the latter point is the subject for another paper. My immediate point can be summed up in one sentence: A political theology is politically disastrous and theologically suicidal when it permits any proposal for the common good to subsume the question of the Good by denying spiritual, intellectual and social space for the Christian saying of Yes and No.

Notes

1. For a good account of Emanuel Hirsch and his times, see *Theologians Under Hitler* by Robert P. Ericksen, Yale University Press, 1985. The other theologians considered are Gerhard Kittel and Paul Althaus. Hirsch citations are from pages 121 to 200.

2. Trutz Rendtorff examines the question of democracy and the Confessing Church in "More than Resistance: What We Need to Learn from the German Church Struggle," *Confession, Conflict and Community*, Eerdmans Encounter Series, 1986.

3. The full text of Tillich's letter is published for the first time in English in *The Thought of Paul Tillich*, edited by James Luther Adams *et al.*, Harper and Row, 1985.

4. Karl Dietrich Bracher, *The Age of Ideologies*, St. Martin's, 1984.

5. Juan Luis Segundo, *The Liberation of Theology*, Orbis, 1976. Pages 110 and 116.

6. McCann in *The Thought of Paul Tillich*, *op. cit.*, page 93.

7. Segundo, *op. cit.*, page 118.

8. For a more thorough discussion of the role of religion and social change in South Africa, see the author's *Dispensations: The Future of South Africa as South Africans See It*, Eerdmans, 1986.

Eight

The Good to be Pursued in Common

DENNIS P. McCANN

The purpose of this volume is to challenge American capitalism, by elucidating the moral agenda implicit in Catholic tradition regarding the common good. Formulating our purpose in this way, however, presents us with a number of problems, the most serious of which is the questionable assumption that the Catholic tradition is of one mind in its understanding of the common good, and that insofar as it is, this understanding is immediately relevant to our political economy today.

I find it necessary to challenge both parts of this assumption. I will argue that it is doubtful whether any such consensus ever existed in Catholic social teaching, if not from the beginning of its modern elaboration during the papacy of Leo XIII, then certainly from the publication of Pius XI's encyclical letter, *Quadragesimo Anno*, whose "principle of subsidiarity" had the potential to turn his predecessor's social theory on its head. (Cf. Duffy,

1949) In any case, whether or not I can succeed in making this historical observation stick, I will argue that the common good, as commonly understood, does not provide a very helpful perspective for challenging the American political economy. The perspective is not very helpful because, once its content is stretched far enough to establish continuity between its origins in a traditional, paternalistic view of society and the church's growing appreciation for the virtues of the modern, democratic state, it inevitably becomes so nebulous that nothing very well focused by way of a moral agenda can be inferred from it. And what sort of challenge to American capitalism could that possibly represent?

As a first step in overcoming this impasse in Catholic social teaching, I hope to provide a basis for redefining the common good historically and procedurally. My definition, "the good to be pursued in common," precisely because it is procedural, clears the public space necessary for historically informed dialogue about political economy. Out of that substantive dialogue, no doubt, various challenges to American capitalism will be forthcoming; but their validity cannot be predetermined by appealing to some privileged notion of the common good that exempts itself from dialogue. The authority of Catholic social teaching, I contend, would only be further compromised, were that to be the case. Instead, any substantive proposals seeking to define the common moral agenda, and hence the common good, for our society today must submit to the procedures of free and open inquiry, that is, they must be tested in a dialogue dedicated to "the good to be pursued in common." Such a dialogue, as is appropriate in our secular, pluralistic society, will inevitably be ecumenical in the broadest sense of that term.

In order to illustrate the consequences of my proposed definition, I will conclude this essay by arguing that the controversy within the Catholic community over a "preferential option for the poor" is best understood not as a repudiation of the common good but as an attempt in dialogue to achieve a new moral consensus, first among Catholics, and then within the public at large, about "the good to be pursued in common." Seen in this light, the partiality, and, perhaps, even partisanship built into this "preferential option," do not disqualify it from consideration; indeed, it is impossible to offer any concrete proposals for this dialogue that would not be partial and partisan, in one way or another. Rather, it is only in working through such proposals that any meaningful moral consensus can ever be achieved. Catholic social teaching, in other words, has everything to gain and nothing to lose by abandoning the pretensions of universality and absolute finality that have clung like an aura to so many of its proposals. Such claims, if they ever can be validated at all, can only emerge as the result of a genuinely public dialogue, and not to be taken as the precondition for one. A first step in this direction, I hope to show, would be to shift to a consistently historical and thus procedural definition of the common good.

The Change in Catholic Social Teaching

Let me begin with a meditation on the history of modern Catholic social teaching. Here I will depend mainly on the recent work of Father Charles E. Curran, *Directions in Catholic Social Ethics* (1985), which I can only hope will become increasingly influential as all of us together move toward the formulation of a social ethic appropriate to the emerging reality of American Catholicism. In the first essay in that book, Curran points out what most of us probably take for granted, namely, the fact that modern Catholic social teaching exists in a particular historical and cultural context, and therefore the necessity of "a proper hermeneutic in explaining it." (Curran, 1985: 6) Only in light of awarenesses similar to Curran's own is it possible to interpret, for example, the conflicting claims of various Catholics struggling with the question of the relevance of Catholic social teaching to American capitalism. For without an awareness, however inarticulate or unacknowledged, of the distance separating the culture in which modern Catholic social teaching has been formed from our own, that is, the ongoing differences between the social milieu in which Papal encyclicals are written and the emerging reality of American Catholicism, it is impossible even to formulate the question of relevance, let alone resolve it one way or another.

Curran's own "hermeneutic" opens up a useful perspective on the problem of the common good, which I wish to explore. By contrasting the teachings of Leo XIII's *Rerum Novarum* (1891) with the new directions that may have culminated in Paul VI's *Octagesima Adveniens* (1971), Curran outlines an important shift in the "anthropological base" of Catholic social teaching. Today, Catholic social teaching offers a moral ideal that emphasizes, both descriptively and normatively, "freedom, equality, participation, and historical consciousness." (Curran, 1985: 20) Leo XIII, by contrast, offered a view of humanity that was "fearful of freedom and equality and looked upon the majority of people as the untutored multitude who had to be guided or directed by their rulers." (*Ibid.*: 7) This history of modern Catholic social teaching thus can be viewed as a series of intellectual developments responding to changing social conditions by which the Popes and bishops, the faithful, and their theologians have gradually moved from the one anthropological perspective to the other.

Within this historical overview, Curran points out that in Leo XIII's teaching the common good was understood paternalistically. Contrary to liberalism, Leo viewed society as an organism "in which the total common good of the society is entrusted to the rulers." Here is Curran's apt characterization of Leo's opinion:

> The picture emerges of a static and hierarchically structured authoritarian society governed by the law of God and the natural law under the protection and guidance of a paternalistic ruler who directs all to the common good and protects his subjects from physical and moral harm. (Curran, 1985: 9)

As Curran points out, such a view admits of no distinction between society and the state. The state as embodied in the ideal ruler directs all things to the common good, which is regarded as substantive, objectively knowable and indivisible. Little wonder that such a view could not reconcile itself with that typically modern, originally American, innovation, namely, the separation of church and state, which forms the basis of our secular, pluralistic society.

Yet, I would argue, Leo's understanding of the common good is faithful to the mainstream of Catholic tradition, if by Catholic tradition we mean the legacy of St. Thomas Aquinas. As Normand Paulhus suggests, in a recent paper asking for a reexamination of *Social Justice: A Meaningless Term?* (1986), Thomistic thought poses the question of social justice not "in terms of the relationship between person and society, . . . [but] between the common good and the individual good." (1986: 4) In the medieval context of Thomistic thought, the common good is not regarded as "an alien good" to be imposed upon (presumably recalcitrant) persons by society, but rather as in its totality intrinsic to each individual as the appropriate expression of the final end of humanity, which is realized in the beatific vision: "Since we are destined to the enjoyment of God, 'the final aim of social life will be, not merely to live virtuously, but through virtuous living to attain the possession of God' (*De Reg.*, I, 14)." (Ibid.: 6) Since the common good thus "includes not only material, but spiritual and religious dimensions within its ambit," social justice, or to give it its traditionally Thomistic name, "legal justice" becomes the virtue by which the ideal ruler orders all things to their proper end, the beatific vision.

Notice that in this Thomistic definition of the common good, none of the presuppositions grounding our typically modern, originally American, separation of church and state can even be formulated, let alone taken seriously: there's no room here for the distinction between state and society, between religious and secular, between public and private. Nor is there any room for a pluralism of religious opinions and political ideologies. Dissent, schism, and heresy can only be regarded as, ultimately, a defect or a departure from the common good, and should therefore be proscribed and persecuted by the ideal ruler. For the common good is substantive, objectively knowable and indivisible.

Everyone knows, of course, that modern Catholic social teaching in fits and starts has gradually abandoned Leo XIII's traditional and Thomistic understanding of the "ethical society-state." (Curran, 1985: 8) Typically, the church's struggle with the modern totalitarianisms of both the Right and the Left is credited with facilitating this transition; but honesty requires us to give equal emphasis to the protracted and, apparently, unfinished struggle for religious liberty within both the church itself and society as a whole. Without joining the lessons stemming from both these struggles, it is impossible, I contend, to understand the problem of the common good — for these struggles are essentially one.

The principle of subsidiarity, which first appeared in Pius XI's *Quadragesimo Anno* (1931), is one of the two chief bench marks in this struggle; the other, of course, is the "Declaration on Religious Freedom" (*Dignitatis Humanae*) from Vatican Council II, inspired by the American Catholic theologian, John Courtney Murray. By insisting that it is "an injustice and at the same time a grave evil and a disturbance of right order to assign to a greater and higher association what lesser and subordinate organizations can do" (Cf. Byers, ed., 1985: 68), the principle of subsidiarity clearly places the burden of proof upon anyone who would either maintain the "authoritarian and paternalistic" society that Leo XIII envisioned or modernize such a society through the imposition of totalitarian programs, whether of the Right or of the Left. Although Pius XI himself apparently did not understand the principle's radical implications, already with Pius XII's wartime addresses we can detect the abandonment of "Leo XIII's ethical concept of the society-state and . . . [the acceptance of] . . . a juridical or limited constitutional state." (Curran, 1985: 12)

Consistent with the thesis I am arguing here, it is noteworthy that the recent Extraordinary Synod in Rome itself has called for study "to examine whether the principle of subsidiarity in use in human society can be applied to the church and to what degree and in what sense such an application can and should be made." *(National Catholic Reporter,* 20 December 1985: 16; cf. Steinfels, 1985: 698-700) Such study, it is to be hoped, may yield insight into the analogous burden of proof that ought to be imposed upon paternalistic, if not actually totalitarian, forms of religious authority. This extension of the principle of subsidiarity, I contend, would not have been possible without Vatican II's recognition of the right to religious liberty. Indeed, with the fateful conjunction of both these bench marks, the question of religious liberty *within* the church, as Murray himself apparently anticipated (cf. Abbott, ed., 1966: 674), itself has become an explicit part of our common struggle with the legacy of the "ethical society-state."

Whatever its wider ramifications, the principle of subsidiarity was first formulated on an *ad hoc* basis as a last-ditch ideological defense against fascism, that typically modern deformation of the church's own traditionally paternalistic and authoritarian social ideal. (Cf. Curran, 1985: 11) As such, it tended to balance the church's traditionally uncompromising hostility to liberal individualism with an emerging antipathy toward "collectivism." In ways that can only give comfort to self-consciously American Catholics, the church's social teaching, under the banner of a *"tercerismo"* that rejected both these modernistic distortions, became increasingly, though often haltingly, open to the ideals embodied in what the National Conference of Catholic Bishops (N.C.C.B.) has come to regard as the American "experiment in democracy."

Curran rightly celebrates these ideals as the new "anthropological base" informing Catholic social teaching: freedom, equality, participation, and historical mindedness. But the question that his historical recitation raises for me is whether, given this new "anthropological base," Catholic social teaching can continue to promote its public moral agenda in terms of a moral claim upon the common good. For each of these ideals, and especially the last one, makes it almost impossible to understand the common good as if it were still self-evidently substantive, objectively knowable, and indivisible. Curran's own exercise in hermeneutics, his unflinching recognition of the cultural biases built into Leo XIII's ideal "ethical society-state," leads me to wonder what sense it makes, once we have become aware of the distance between these biases and our own, to continue using Leo's language of the common good in formulating a moral agenda for our own pluralistic society and culture. I suspect that it makes no sense, if we continue to assume that the common good is substantive, objectively knowable, and indivisible.

Alas, I would be surprised to find much immediate support for my thesis among Catholic social ethicists in this country, despite the fact that virtually all of them are struggling in one way or another with the cultural biases implicit in traditional Catholic "social doctrine" (cf. Curran, 1985: 34-6), and that virtually all of them presuppose the new "anthropological base," not only in their ecclesial and social praxis, but in their theorizing about it as well. Typical of the results of such theorizing is David Hollenbach's important treatise, *Claims in Conflict; Retrieving and Renewing the Catholic Human Rights Tradition* (1979). Here, among other things, Hollenbach retrieves the traditional notion of the common good by identifying it with the aggregate of all "public goods, considered in their interrelatedness and mutual dependence" to which individuals should have access guaranteed through certain enforceable "social rights." (Hollenbach, 1979: 148-9) The public goods emphasized by Hollenbach, however, derive their significance from the new "anthropological base," insofar as they tend to empower "participation in the public life of society, whether in the economic, political or cultural sphere." (*Ibid.*) Yet when it comes to their implementation, Hollenbach appears to be just as paternalistic as Leo XIII. Social justice, in this view, thus is retrieved as "a spiritual and intellectual guiding rule" for empowering first of all the state to ensure equal access to these public goods.

It doesn't occur to Hollenbach to ask the questions I'm asking, perhaps because he is less impressed than I am with the contrast between Leo XIII's world-view and our own. Instead, his translation seems to paper over the rift that I detect between the semantic fields represented, on the one hand, by the common good, and on the other hand, by an aggregate of public goods embodying the values of freedom, equality, participation, and historical mindedness. I am not, of course, disputing either the validity of these public goods, or any person's claim upon them as a matter of right. But I do wonder whether Hollenbach's willingness to identify these with the common good doesn't lead him to be somewhat unimaginative, if not undemocratic, in his conception of the role of the state and its relationship to society. He does, of course, discuss the principle of subsidiarity as limiting the power of state intervention and embodying a pluralist model of social interaction. (Cf. *Ibid.*: 158-9) But he continues to rely upon the state, like Leo XIII's ideal ruler, to enforce a proper distribution of "public goods": "In such a model the large juridical institutions of society would continue to be the chief instruments of communal solidarity." (*Ibid.* :165) That conclusion, despite its thoroughly progressive intent, strikes me as still too uncomfortably close to the legacy of paternalistic authoritarianism.

Habermas and Murray

I propose redefining the common good as the good to be pursued in common. By this I am advocating a deliberate break with the traditional Catholic "social doctrine" that assumes the common good to be substantive, objectively knowable and indivisible. If the common good is to remain a topic for discussion within a self-consciously American Catholic social ethic, it must be understood as historical and procedural, that is, as generalizable only in a public discourse characterized by free and open inquiry, but inevitably partial and perspectival, and hence continually in need of revision and reform. The translation that I propose therefore is not a substantive equation between the common good and "public goods," but a correlation between the common good and the notion of "generalizable interests" outlined by Juergen Habermas in his critical social theory. In order to explain this proposal, let me review some of the key points in the chapter on "Vision and Choice; Practical Theology and Christian Social Ethics" that Charles Strain and I offered in *Polity and Praxis: A Program for American Practical Theology* (1985). There, among other things, we adapted Habermas' theory in ways that are relevant to a revised understanding of the common good.

The overall project of *Polity and Praxis* is not specifically rooted in the tradition of Catholic social teaching. Instead, it is an attempt to define both descriptively and normatively a genre of theological discourse that is represented in the history of most Protestant and Catholic communities in America. Strain and I call this genre "practical theology," insofar as it has been shaped by various attempts to develop a critical theory of religious praxis capable of orienting the public agenda of these diverse communities in a secular, pluralistic society. While our understanding of this genre is heavily influenced by the methodological breakthrough announced by contemporary political and liberation theologies, it is by no means exclusively determined by it. Although practical theology has been characteristic of American Christianity only in the wake of the period of rapid industrialization that accompanied and followed the Civil War, we see it rooted in the protean American experience of the "Errand Into the Wilderness" whose religious aspirations received typical expression in John Winthrop's Pilgrim sermon onboard the Arbella. (Cf. McCann and Strain, 1985: 21-25)

Despite its Puritan origins—nay, precisely because of them—we claim that the genre includes all self-consciously American religious social thinking including that of American Catholics; indeed, as we suggested in *Polity and Praxis*, its procedures are just as applicable to the theological reflections of a John A. Ryan as to a Walter Rauschenbusch, or of a John Courtney Murray as to a Reinhold Niebuhr, or to the recent pastoral letters of the National Conference of Catholic Bishops as to the public statements of the National Council of Churches.

Strain and I are confident of these claims for the genre because we believe that we have discovered the structure of public discourse underlying the whole spectrum of practical theologies representative of American Christianity. Here is where, among other resources, Habermas's critical social theory comes into view. By developing a normative history of communicative interaction capable of revisioning the public agenda of the intellectual tradition, namely Marxism, in which he works, Habermas illuminates the challenges, theoretical as well as practical, that any particular community of faith and/or ideology must face in addressing the problems of a secular pluralistic society. (Cf. Mc-Cann, 1986; 1981) Particularly relevant is Habermas's analysis of what sort of policy recommendations, formally considered, will emerge on such a community's public agenda. Authentically public discourse, that is, free and open inquiry approximating the conditions of what Habermas calls an "ideal-speech situation" (Cf. McCann and Strain, 1985: 50-58), will yield an agenda consisting of "generalizable interests." (*Ibid.*: 152-161)

The contrast between this term and the traditional notion of the common good should make clear its procedural implications. Consider, for example, the difference between the "good and "interests." Any community advocating its own agenda as representative of the common good has already judged its own truth-claim prior to public discourse. The common good under such circumstances is proposed not for open-ended discussion but for acknowledgement and implementation, perhaps, through some social process of intellectual and moral conversion. By contrast, there is a healthy note of agnosticism about generalizable interests. As interests, they are recognized as the fruit of a particular community's moral deliberations, now presented to society as a whole for public consideration. A similar contrast obtains between "common" and "generalizable." To advocate some proposal as furthering the common good suggests an accomplished fact; to warrant it as generalizable is to state an intention, that is, it represents what the particular community of faith and/or ideology hopes to achieve in public discourse. For any proposal to stand as a "generalizable interest," the particular community proposing it thus must commit itself to a process of free and open dialogue with the public at large, out of which some of its proposals may emerge as the object of a true consensus, while others may not. Of course, those that do not become part of the public consensus may be reconsidered by the particular community and revised for public consideration later. But those that are accepted as part of the public consensus stand no longer as generalizable interests, but as truly generalized: at that point, and not before, they can rightfully claim to represent the common good, understood now as the good to be pursued in common.

Habermas's own descriptions of a "generalizable interest" are very much to the point here. In the process of forming a true consensus about a society's praxis, generalizable interests claim to represent "the *common* interest ascertained *without deception*." (Habermas, 1975: 108) His emphasis, which follows through on the chief concerns of his normative theory of communicative interaction, rests on the integrity of the process of public discussion: whatever these common interests turn out to be, they must be "ascertained *without deception*." His explanation, though needlessly opaque, involves a distinction between any particular individual's or community's own "interpretations of needs" and "what *all* can want" as the result of participating in the formation of a "constraint-free consensus." (*Ibid.*; Cf. McCann and Strain, 1985: 154-5) Strain and I see two distinct, though related, procedural questions emerging from this distinction. The first, regarding "the interpretations of needs," we understand as critical self-reflection; the second, concerning "what *all* can want," opens us distinctively ethical reflection.

Habermas's own view of "critical self-reflection" is too restrictive. He understands it primarily in terms of the kind of ideological criticism peculiar to the Frankfurt School, which sees critical theory emerging at the point of creative dialogue between Marx and Freud. Critical self-reflection thus is clearly a form of "consciousness-raising," but for our purposes it remains too individualistic, as if psychoanalytic therapy provided the most illuminating model for pursuing this question. Strain and I, however, correct this distortion by insisting that critical self-reflection is a process constitutive of intellectual community, specifically, communities of faith and/or ideology. What Habermas refers to as "interpretations of needs" we therefore propose to mediate through the critical hermeneutics of various intellectual traditions—and not just ones loyal to Marx and Freud—by which these communities continually renew themselves.

Assuming this correction, Habermas's understanding of critical self-reflection as the process by which each participant acknowledges that the interest at issue is proposed "*without deception*" may seem less utopian. What is at stake here is the authenticity of the discussion internal to any particular community of faith and/or ideology. The individual members that constitute the community in question, each and severally must be able to recognize that the moral agenda presented by the community for public consideration truly reflects a consensus regarding how the community's own traditions are to be interpreted and further developed. Without this inward-looking moment of critical self-reflection the community cannot claim to be a "mediating structure" linking the aspirations of its individual members with the concerns of society as a whole. Indeed, so essential is critical self-reflection to the community's attempt to formulate its public moral agenda that Strain and I regard it as the indispensably distinctive task of practical theology. Every practical theology is always already a critical ecclesiology.

Distinctively ethical reflection focused, by contrast, on the question of "what *all* can want" goes beyond a concern for the authenticity of the community's proposed moral agenda to a concern for its appropriateness vis-a-vis society as a whole. Can the community's proposal become the object of a true consensus involving not just its own membership, but all citizens regardless of their particular communal loyalties? Or, lacking the warrants that can carry conviction in a secular, pluralistic society, must the community's proposal be regarded, not as a generalizable interest, but as the special pleading of another organized "special-interest group"? In order to distinguish the two possibilities, Habermas formulates certain formal conditions that any proposed generalizable interest must meet in public discourse, if its claim upon the public at large is to be recognized as valid. (Habermas, 1975: 113) While an explication of these conditions would take us well beyond the scope of this paper, what is important here is to recognize the moral authority thus conferred upon such interests. They, and only they, cannot justifiably be compromised, either in theory or in praxis. Indeed, Habermas's view of distinctively ethical reflection thus yields a definition of social injustice as "the suppression of generalizable interests." (*Ibid.*) Even in a secular, pluralistic society, justice therefore demands that the generalizable interests that emerge in public discourse be recognized and implemented; everything else, however, remains subject to political negotiation as usual.

Habermas's theory, obviously, is suggestive in its formality, but it hardly provides an exhaustive account of distinctively ethical reflection. Strain and I attempted to make its relevance more explicit by showing how at least one tradition of Christian social ethics, namely, the mainstream American Protestant tradition known as the "middle axioms" approach, does tend to focus on the cluster of intentions designated by generalizable interests. (Cf. McCann and Strain, 1985: 161-169) More to the point here, I believe, is the parallel that could be developed between Habermas's critical social theory and John Courtney Murray's view of the pluralistic society as a "pattern of interacting conspiracies." (Cf. Murray, 1960: 33) Like Habermas, Murray understood civil society as itself based on consensus. Like Habermas's appeal to a normative theory of communicative interaction, Murray used the philosophy of natural law to establish not only the standards of public argument but also what such an argument might produce by way of public consensus. (Cf. Murray, 1960: 102-126)

What Murray's view of America as a network of civil conspiracies adds that Habermas's theory of generalizable interests lacks, of course, is a grasp of the historic significance of cultural pluralism as the actual precondition making public argument in this country both possible and necessary. Murray, I believe, would have no difficulty understanding how and why the plurality of American conspiracies, that is, the historic communities of faith and ideology in this country—Protestant, Catholic, Jewish, and secularist—must act as "mediating structures" enabling their respective individual members to participate in a genuinely public discourse. What Habermas adds that Murray lacks, however, is a sufficiently critical cognitive anthropology and metaethics, that is, a normative as well as descriptive theory of communicative interaction, capable of sustaining the claims of public discourse as itself conforming to the logic of natural law moral reasoning. Ironically, precisely because the current intellectual climate in this country today is far more pluralistic than even Murray could have imagined, we must give up some of the vivid historical resonance of his "Catholic Reflections on the American Proposition" in favor of the more highly formalistic approach that Habermas outlines. Such is the burden of proof anyone must bear today who would attempt to liberate the legitimate claims of the natural law tradition from the legacy of paternalistic authoritarianism. Be that as it may, here I can only note in passing the fruitfulness of Habermas's work for carrying forward Murray's distinctive approach to American Catholic social ethics.

Were I to develop Habermas's theory of generalizable interests in such a context, among other things, I would use it to explore Murray's expectation of "a second great argument" concerning religious freedom *within* the church. (Cf. Abbott, ed., 1966: 674) In light of Habermas's understanding of the role of critical self-reflection in any community's attempt to formulate generalizable interests, this unfinished business about religious freedom becomes the litmus test guaranteeing the credibility of the church's participation in any attempt to form a civil consensus through public argument. In a secular pluralistic society that already acknowledges religious freedom as a matter of constitutional right, the church may disqualify itself from public discourse regarding the common good, unless the commonly accepted procedures of public consensus formation are also respected in the church's internal discussion of its own moral agenda.

U.S. Catholic Experience

The recent performance of the N.C.C.B. in formulating the pastoral letters, "The Challenge of Peace" and "Catholic Social Teaching and the U.S. Economy," leads me to be cautiously optimistic about the likelihood that the American Catholic church will be able to institutionalize a process of adult moral dialogue that lives up to these expectations. Despite equally significant indications of the church's continued inability to appreciate the necessity of dissent in any truly open process of discussion, these letters not only encourage free inquiry but also stipulate in advance the legitimate grounds for a diversity of opinion regarding the specific policies that they recommend, not only for the public at large but also for the Catholic community in this country. I refer, of course, not simply to the bishops' decision, as Archbishop Weakland put it, "to write the letter . . . in public" (Cf. Weakland, 1986: 28), but more to the point, to their frank admission of the role of "prudential judgment" in public policy assessment. In their view, it is perfectly consistent to consent to the basic principles of Catholic social teaching, and yet dissent from the policy recommendations that the bishops actually draw from them. Indeed, the letters appear to encourage such dissent, as an indispensable contribution to the work of the drafting committees seeking to discern a true consensus within the church over the meaning and relevance of Catholic social teaching today.

The full implications of this new pastoral letter process for an American Catholic social ethic have yet to be realized. Here, however, I am proposing a revision in our understanding of the common good that I believe is consistent with the direction this process seems to be headed. If the common good is to remain a stimulus to both critical self-reflection within the church and distinctively ethical reflection regarding the church's claim upon society as a whole, it must be redefined in terms consistent with the process of adult moral dialogue. In a secular pluralistic society, in which by definition there is precious little consensus in matters of substance, the common good should be understood procedurally: it conveys the church's commitment to a genuinely public discourse seeking to define the good to be pursued in common. Such an understanding of the common good is more or less synonymous not only with what Habermas outlines in the theory of generalizable interests but also with what Murray describes as a civil conspiracy.

The Option for the Poor

The preceeding may strike the less patient and more practical among my readers as so much airy speculation, coupled with the usual academic nitpicking. Instead of telling us what he thinks the common good requires of our society today, McCann retreats once more into the deep structures of communicative interaction, in order to reiterate his faith in dialogue. Let me respond to this complaint, whether it be real or imagined, by indicating what difference I think my thesis might make, in terms of the ideological undercurrent that I detect in this symposium's manner of formulating the question of the common good. I refer, finally, to the controversy surrounding the "preferential option for the poor" advocated in several drafts of the N.C.C.B. pastoral letter on the economy.

It is my purpose to defend the option for the poor. Here I find myself in agreement with Michael Novak, or at least with what Novak said in his recent book, *Freedom with Justice: Catholic Social Thought and Liberal Institutions* (1984): "The 'option for the poor' *is* the correct option. Everything depends, however, upon the next institutional step." (Novak, 1984: 192) Though we may disagree on what is involved in that "next institutional step," I take it that for the most part we agree on how, in the kind of secular, pluralistic society that Novak celebrates as "democratic capitalism," ideological and political progress is made toward social justice. It is not made by relying upon the intervention of a paternalistic authoritarianism that sees itself as the arbiter of the common good. It is made through public argument about conflicting interests and discordant moral agendas, some of which may eventually be recognized as generalizable and, hence, as essential to social justice.

The intriguing thing about the option for the poor, even a "preferential" option for the poor, is that it already is formulated as a generalizable interest. The word "option," for all its ambiguity and resonance in the obscurities of European moral theology, is of crucial importance here. For it cuts both ways, both as an exhortation of those who define their religious loyalty in terms of the Catholic community of faith, and as a strategic proposal for policy study among the public at large. It is an option in the sense that it lacks the compelling logic of *apriori* necessity; it is strictly contingent upon a particular "hermeneutic" of the Catholic tradition and contemporary history. Its warrants, in the first place, are particularistic because they are strictly theological: it is an attempt to define what the moral agenda of the American

Catholic community today is and ought to be. Only in the second place is this option pressed upon the public at large, and urged with arguments that make explicit its claim as a generalizable interest.

Like all generalizable interests, the option for the poor provokes both critical self-reflection and ethical reflection. Its power consists precisely in this double provocation. Critical self-reflection responsive to it seeks, inevitably, to renew the church's own self-understanding: what "interpretations of needs" can no longer be taken for granted if this option is pursued by either the church as an institution or its individual members? As the drafts of the pastoral letter on the economy insist, the option "demands a compassionate vision (Lk. 10:33) which enables the church to see things from the side of the poor, to assess lifestyle as well as social institutions and policies in terms of their impact upon the poor." (First Draft, Par. 54; Second Draft, Par. 59) This requirement, I submit, is precisely the kind of hermeneutic task that Strain and I argue is constitutive of practical theology. But in light of Murray's unfinished business about religious freedom *within* the church, I must also insist that such a requirement cannot be met in anything less than adult moral dialogue. Hence the promising, though still all too fragile, connection between the option for the poor and the very process by which the pastoral letter is being written and revised within the church.

Yet the option for the poor does more than provoke the kind of critical self-reflection that may lead to ecclesial renewal. It also invites all of us to a new kind of public ethical reflection. The option for the poor is a generalizable interest, insofar as it advocates the interest of a particular group as of more than mere "special interest." If the option for the poor truly points at "what *all* can want," its advocacy by the American Catholic community amounts to a civil conspiracy, that is, a putative consensus of faith and ideology whose moral claim can actually be generalized, and thus vindicated, in public argument. Here, too, the first and second drafts of the pastoral letter on the economy yield evidence for the kind of public discourse I have described. In neither draft is the option discussed exclusively in religious terms: beyond the paragraphs in which its theological presuppositions are outlined, both drafts explicitly invoke the option for the poor when proposing "moral priorities for the nation." (First Draft, Par. 103; Second Draft, Par. 89) Indeed, if anything, the link between these priorities and the option for the poor is more explicit in the second draft than in the first; although even the second draft, in my view, is less explicit than it could be, if the option represents a truly generalizable interest in our society.

What the second draft hints at, but does not develop fully, is the way in which the option for the poor resonates not only with Catholic tradition but also with the deepest aspirations of the American dream. The ongoing American experiment in democracy, and our collective wisdom continually replenished by deepening insight into "pattern of interacting conspiracies" upon which this nation is founded, both require an option for the poor. The bishops sense this, of course, for they insist that "those who are marginalized and whose rights are denied have privileged claims if society is to provide justice for all." (Second Draft, Par. 89) But the warrants for this claim remain too abstractly Catholic, and not concretely rooted enough in the ongoing public argument that Americans have always conducted about themselves and their sense of national purpose. Yet it is precisely in that public argument that the option for the poor should be most fruitfully provocative.

There is another side to the option for the poor that can be highlighted by thinking of it as a generalizable interest. By seeing it in this way, we can clearly understand that the option for the poor provides not a substantive definition of the common good as such, but a provisional framework for policy deliberation pursuant to it. Within such a framework, a diversity of prudential judgments is both possible and necessary; yet if the option already defined the common good in advance, it is hard to see what there would still be left to discuss, let alone offer dissenting opinions about. A generalizable interest, however, indicates the community's intention of shaping a public consensus regarding society's "needs" and "norms," which will then frame the discussion of policy but not preempt it. Precisely because it is perspectival, and therefore provisional, it may also be generalizable: it all depends on how consensus emerges from the public argument that it succeeds in provoking.

The result of this procedural interpretation should be to throw an obstacle in the path of anyone who would pit the option for the poor against the common good, in order to discredit the former as a misguided innovation in Catholic social teaching. It may be tempting to think that ordinary Catholic people would be more receptive to the message of the pastoral letter on the economy, were it couched in familiar appeals to the common good; but I submit that whatever resistance the option for the poor has generated is itself testimony to its power to provoke critical thinking even among ordinary Catholics. There could be no question of pitting the option for the poor against the common good, were the common good to be seen in appropriately procedural terms. Were such a redefinition to be accepted, it would be clear that the notion of the common good offers no challenge to American capitalism other than the ongoing challenge of adult moral dialogue. In short, were such a redefinition to be accepted, loyalty to that challenge would require us to consider strategic initiatives like the option for the poor. Catholic social teaching would be the poorer, were it to abandon the option for the poor in the name of the common good.

BIBLIOGRAPHY

Abbott, Walter M., S.J., ed. 1966 *The Documents of Vatican II* . London: Geoffrey Chapman.

Byers, David M., ed. 1985 *Justice in the Marketplace: Collected Statements of the Vatican and the U.S. Catholic Bishops on Economic Policy, 1891-1984.* Washington, D.C.: United States Catholic Conference.

Curran, Charles E. 1985 *Directions in Catholic Social Ethics.* Notre Dame, Indiana: University of Notre Dame Press.

Duffy, Thomas F. 1949 *The Implications of the Papal Teaching of the Principle of Subsidiary Function for Political Theory.* Unpublished M.A. dissertation submitted to the Faculty of the School of Social Science of The Catholic University of America.

Habermas, Juergen 1975 *Legitimation Crisis*. Boston: Beacon Press.

Hollenbach, David 1979 *Claims in Conflict; Retrieving and Renewing the Catholic Human Rights Tradition*. Ramsey, New Jersey: The Paulist Press.

McCann, Dennis P. 1981 "Habermas and the Theologians." In *Religious Studies Review* 7:14-21.

McCann, Dennis P. 1986 "Wrestling with Modernity: A Review of Juergen Habermas's *Theory of Communicative Action, Volume One*." In *Commonweal Volume CXIII, Number 3 (February 14, 1986), pp. 89-91*.

McCann, Dennis P., and Strain, Charles R. *1985 Polity and Praxis: A Program for American Practical Theology*. Minneapolis: Seabury/Winston Press.

Murray, John Courtney 1960 *We Hold These Truths: Catholic Reflections on the American Proposition*. New York: Sheed and Ward.

Novak, Michael 1984 *Freedom with Justice: Catholic Social Thought and Liberal Institutions*. San Francisco: Harper and Row.

Paulhus, Normand 1986 "Social Justice: A Meaningless Term?" An unpublished paper given at the annual meeting of the Society of Christian Ethics, Chicago, January, 1986.

Steinfels, Peter 1985 "A Sober Look at the Synod." In *Commonweal*, Volume CXII, Number 22 (20 December 1985), pp. 698-700.

The Extraordinary Synod in Rome 1985 "The Church, in the Word of God, Celebrates the Mystery of Christ for the Salvation of the World." Final Document of the Extraordinary Synod. In *The National Catholic Reporter*, December 20, 1985, pp. 9, 13-16.

Weakland, Rembert G. 1986 "How to Read the Economic Pastoral." In *Catholicism in Crisis*. Volume 4, Number 2 (March, 1986), pp. 27-34.

Nine

Private Goods, Public Goods and the Common Good: Another Look at Economics and Ethics in Catholic Social Teaching

ERNEST BARTELL, C.S.C.

The common good as a normative criterion for the evaluation of economic institutions, policies and systems in the major documents of Catholic social teaching dates back to Pope Leo XIII in the nineteenth century and maintains a resiliency that endures, with greater or lesser emphasis, through documents as recent as the second draft of the U.S. bishops' Pastoral Letter on the U.S. economy. Nevertheless, the context in which the concept is used in papal social teaching and other ecclesiastical documents has evolved in ways that alter the relationship of social sciences to the social teaching of the Church. What follows is a sketch of some of the changes in the evolution of Catholic social teaching

179

that affect the relationship of that teaching to various analytic constructs and fields within the discipline of economics. An attempt will also be made to suggest ways in which the usefulness of economics for an appreciation of Catholic social teaching is both strengthened and weakened by these changes.

Economics in Church Social Teaching before Vatican II

Early papal social encyclicals, such as Pope Leo XIII's major document on labor, *Rerum Novarum*, were grounded very strongly and uncritically in the natural law tradition of Catholic theology. This tradition stressed very heavily the role of human reason in arriving at eternal truths or philosophical absolutes as well as ethical knowledge and understanding. Although the giants of that tradition fully understood the limitations of human reason in grasping the totality of the mysteries of the Christian faith, the tradition that was handed down tended to divide into separate tracks what could be learned from the revealed sources of the faith and what could be learned by human reasoning.

The emphasis on deductive logic in much of the natural law reasoning about human affairs contributed to a somewhat abstract product that offered the security of immutable truths. At the same time, however, a deductive scholastic methodology applied to ethical problems was perhaps especially vulnerable to oversimplified assumptions about the ahistorical and static character of human institutions as understood or experienced by the practitioners. Thus, some contemporary ethicists find in the writings of Pope Leo XIII in the late 19th century an implicit acceptance of paternalistic authoritarian social systems common in western European tradition as a preferred ethical norm for the preservation of order in society.[1] Concepts of freedom, equality and participation are not prominent in the writings of Leo XIII[2], but there is no lack of emphasis on the inevitability of suffering and misery of the poor.[3]

Moreover, the clear logical connections between the social nature of the human person as defined in the natural law tradition and the ethical and social prescriptions flowing therefrom tended to place a high premium on the harmoniously rational and organic ordering of interests and functions as a priority in reasoning about society. Leo XIII is quite forceful in denying that nature has created an adversarial relationship between rich and poor. Rather, "the exact opposite is true . . . nature has commanded that the two classes mentioned [the rich and the poor] should agree harmoniously and should properly form equally balanced counterparts to each other."[4]

The frequently cited principle of subsidiarity flows neatly from this deductive analysis in the natural law tradition. Moreover, the combined tilt towards paternalism and a hierarchical ordering of functions is consistent with organic models of society, so it is not surprising that models for the reordering of economic life suggested by economists working from an analysis of early Catholic social teaching often embodied a corporatist rationale that never received much support within the democratic political culture of the United States, even among Catholics.[5]

In this intellectual environment the common good is easily defined as the ultimate goal of an organic, generally hierarchical, society with functionally well ordered institutions and actors. In this context the common good implies a coherent, organic whole that can in principle be discovered and understood, if not by the less educated majority, at least by wise and paternal leaders and rulers at various levels of society. It appears that for Leo XIII the meaning of the common good was more political than economic.[6] In *Rerum Novarum* the concept is associated most closely with the responsibilities of the state as the central and most all encompassing institutional actor: "For the state is bound by the very law of its office to serve the common interest . . . the state has one basic purpose for existence, which embraces in common the highest and the lowest of its members."[7] Those "who dedicate themselves to the state . . . are to be regarded as occupying first place, because they work for the common good most directly and preeminently."[8] Those engaged in other callings, such as workers, also "serve the public weal," but they do so "less directly."[9]

For Leo XIII, the normative criteria operative in economic life appear to be drawn more directly from concepts of justice than from the notion of the common good. Although the worker receives for his own use a share of "what he contributed to the common good," his entitlement, which is the legitimate concern of public authorities proceeds from "equity", that is, from a norm of justice.[10] Thus, early on in papal social documents a distinction is acknowledged between the justice that governs economic distribution and the more comprehensive and organic common good to which is directed the authority of the state. Obviously, in the logic of a natural law tradition, these norms are neither inconsistent with one another nor do they imply competing claims on resources for the attainment of social order.

The normative character of the common good is more explicit in the writings of Pius XI and Pius XII, where the relationship of the economic order to broad social goals of peace, stability and security is more fully developed.[11] In the labor encyclical of Pius XI, *Quadragesimo Anno* , there is a clear relationship between the common good, which is made synonomous with social justice, and the just distribution of economic income:

> "Therefore, the riches that economic-social developments constantly increase ought to be so distributed among individual persons and classes that the common advantage of all, which Leo XIII had praised, will be safeguarded; in other words, that the common good of all society will be kept inviolate . . . To each, therefore, must be given his own share of goods and the distribution of created goods . . . must be effectively called back to and brought into conformity with the norms of the common good, that is, social justice."[12]

Like Leo XIII, Pius XII makes the common good, the special responsibility of the state in its political and economic activities.[13] Like Pius XI, Pius XII places a high moral profile on the common good, giving it a "pre-eminence and a dignity proper to itself."[14] Moreover, Pius XII, as early as 1941, adds an international economic dimension to the common good which emphasizes relations between the powerful and the weaker nations:

"It is inevitable that the powerful states should . . . play leading roles in the formation of economic groups comprising not only themselves but also that in the interests of the common good they . . . respect the rights of those smaller states to political freedom, to economic development."[15]

Both Pius XI and Pius XII speak of the social doctrine of the Church by which they refer to a body of Church teaching that contains principles of economic order deduced from natural law and a plan for a social order that is consistent with those principles.[16] Not only is a distinction preserved between moral science and the positive social sciences, such as economics, but some indication of the proper relationship between them is articulated. While acknowledging that economics has its own principles, Pius XI makes it clear that economics depends upon moral science. The moral law deduced from natural law determines independently where the "proper place" for economic objectives is in the universal order of purposes, while economics helps only to "determine the limits of what productive human effort cannot, and of what it can attain in the economic field and by what means."[17] Pius XII is more generous to economics and economic life and anticipates later social teaching of the Church by stressing the possibilities for creativity in economic activity and by identifying a functional economic dependence with a violation of human rights.[18]

The assumption of a coherent body of natural law from which can be deduced a properly ordered society implies that the common good has a meaning which can be discovered and understood apart from the knowledge of social reality. The positive "science" of economics helps to determine only what is feasible in a specific social situation. This approach made possible nearly absolute judgments of specific social and economic systems as embodiments of models that could be morally evaluated *a priori* . It also supported calls for radical transformations of existing social orders and led to ambitious searches for alternative models of entire socioeconomic systems, the so-called Third Way between the models of capitalism and socialism that were morally denounced in papal social teaching. The emphasis on order in the natural law tradition of the early social encyclicals and the heavy use of the principle of subsidiarity in *Quadragesimo Anno* and in the social teaching of Pius XII probably contributed to the interest in corporatist models of economic life among Catholic economists in the 1930's and 1940's.

Even in the period between the papacy of Leo XIII and that of Pius XII there was some evolution of economic thought in Catholic social teaching, suggesting at least the possibility that there might be more flexibility in the actual attainment of a common good grounded in an immutable natural law. Leo XIII has been criticized for making the right to private property so nearly absolute as to imitate John Locke.[19] Pius XI corrected that interpretation by stressing the social nature of private property in a manner much more consistent with the teaching of St. Thomas Aquinas, and the teaching of Pius XII preserved that shift.[20] Without diluting the right to private property, the social character of ownership requires that property owners consider "not only their own advantage but also the common good," and public authorities are assigned the responsibilities of defining the duties of ownership when "the natural law has not done so" and of determining "upon consideration of the true requirements of the common good, what is permitted and what is not permitted to owners in the use of their property."[21]

There was also movement, though less, in the appraisals of models of economic systems in the pre-World War II social encyclicals. Unbridled capitalism is severely condemned by all, and socialism is never deemed acceptable. Nevertheless, whereas Leo XIII condemned all models and elements of socialism, Pius XI acknowledged the legitimacy of some elements and the aspirations of some socialist models without accepting the materialistic and atheistic premises upon which they were based.[22] In so doing he implicitly acknowledges the complexity and diversity of relationships between economic systems and abstract goals like the common good. It may also be argued that he implicitly leaves an opening for the greater appreciation by his successor of economic analysis in understanding the common good.

The diversity and complexity of economic institutions, policies and systems and their relation to the common good achieves still broader significance in the social encyclicals of Pope John XXIII, *Mater et Magistra* and *Pacem in Terris* in which the economic dimensions of the common good are internationalized with a twofold emphasis— 1) on the development of underdeveloped countries in an economically interdependent world and 2) on the preservation of moral, ethnic and political pluralism in that process of development:

> "Because all men are joined together . . . we appealed in the encyclical *Mater et Magistra* to economically developed nations to come to the aid of those which were in the process of development . . . It is vitally important, therefore, that the wealthier states, in providing varied forms of assistance to the poorer, should respect the moral values and ethnic characteristics peculiar to each, and also that they should avoid any intention of political domination. If this is done, 'a precious contribution will be made towards the formation of a world community, a community in which each member, whilst conscious of its own individual rights and duties, will work in a relationship of equality towards the attainment of the universal common good.' "[23]

The greater recognition of economic pluralism in the social encyclicals of John XXIII is further evident in a less dogmatic and rigid approach to models of economic systems. For John XXIII there is a structural sin as well as a personal sin, and structural evils as well as their remedies may be found in a variety of economic institutional settings. Thus, there is no repetition of the blanket condemnations of the twin evils of capitalism and socialism as defined and judged by his predecessors. Rather, there is at least an implicit acceptance of some diversity of economic systems in the achievement of economic objectives: "This implies that whatever be the economic system, it allow and facilitate for every individual the opportunity to engage in productive activity."[24]

Moreover, with due respect for the protection of the rights of the individual, John XXIII acknowledges a wide variety by legitimate interventions of public authorities in economic life as expressions of their responsibility for the common good. Without abandoning the principle of subsidiarity John XXIII recognizes the need for government intervention, especially in relation to the distribution of wealth and income, which is an important economic element of the common good for him. Thus, he affirms:

> "...it is within the power of public authorities to reduce imbalances . . . Consequently, it is requested again and again of public authorities responsible for the common good, that they intervene in a wide variety of economic affairs . . . ,"[25]

John XXIII goes beyond the general statements of his predecessors about the responsibility of the state for equitable distribution of income and wealth in accordance with the common good to make some rather specific economic policy recommendations. For example, to counter the deleterious distributional effects on rural populations of the worldwide slumps in agriculture in the postwar period, John XXIII recommends government intervention on behalf of the rural sector in highway construction, transport services, marketing facilities, pure drinking water, housing, medical services, elementary, trade and professional schools, "things" requisite for religion and for recreation, tax policy, subsidized credit availability, price supports, insurance and the provision of capital equipment for rural enterprises.[26] He even uses the principle of subsidiarity as justification for cooperation between public and private sectors, even to the extent of government intervention on behalf of the development of private enterprise.[27]

John XXIII remains solidly within the natural law tradition, especially in *Pacem in Terris* . Nevertheless, his acknowledgment of national and international diversity of economic institutions, policies and systems suggests more openness to the contributions of the empirical observations of economics, not only in applying immutable ethical principles to real world situations, but in the analysis of the effects of economic activity on human welfare. Indeed, it is *Pacem in Terris* that first uses the expression, "signs of the times,"[28] which will later become an important foundation of Catholic social teaching, especially in the *Medellin* and *Puebla* documents of the Latin American bishops. Moreover, John XXIII in *Pacem in Terris* uses natural law arguments about human rights to establish economic rights, which like other classes of rights are based upon the inherent dignity of the human individual.[29]

Although the interrelationships between economic development and social and political progress are at least implicitly present in earlier papal social teaching, they are explicitly linked to the common good in *Pacem in Terris*.[30] Moreover, in this integrated context economic inequality is linked with political and cultural inequality as destructive of human rights and the ability to fulfill the duties that accompany those rights.[31] John XXIII is faithful to the teaching of Leo XIII in articulating the role of the state almost exclusively in terms of the common good: "Indeed . . . the whole reason for the existence of civil authorities is the realization of the common good."[32] That common good is "chiefly guaranteed when personal rights and duties are maintained."[33] Despite the use by John XXIII of natural law to ground his teaching on economic rights and private property, there is in his writings greater emphasis on diversity and pluralism and less emphasis on the notion of a rigid and self-contained body of social doctrine deduced from natural law reasoning than in the writings of his predecessors.

Economics in Church Social Teaching since Vatican II

Moreover, only two years after the appearance of *Pacem in Terris* , the Second Vatican Council with the authorization of Paul VI issued *Gaudium et Spes, Pastoral Constitution on the Church in the Modern World,* which nowhere refers to *the* social doctrine of the Church. This document carefully avoids any implication of a single preferred model of an economic system, especially one implying corporatist principles of hierarchical and organic structures of the sort derived decades earlier from application of early papal social teaching, especially *Rerum Novarum.*

Likewise, in *Gaudium et Spes* the right to private property, even with its social dimension, is no longer derived from natural law. Private property is justified instead by the observable beneficial effects it affords persons, e.g., in the expression of personality and the exercise of duties, and in its contribution to the maintenance of personal freedom.[34] Even the social dimension of private property is explained pragmatically, rather than philosophically, by reference to the need to curb "a passionate desire for wealth and serious disturbances" that can create a pretext for calling into question the right of private property itself.[35]

Moreover, for the first time in a major social document bearing a papal name, the right of public ownership is explicitly affirmed in the name of the common good along with the right of public authority to intervene against the use of private property that is detrimental to the common good.[36] Thus, the space for diversity and pluralism of economic models is extended still further to include systems with at least some characteristics of socialist models.

The concern of John XXIII for a universalized common good that acknowledges international economic interdependence is carried over into *Gaudium et Spes* with a call for international economic cooperation based upon the "solidarity of mankind."[37] *Gaudium et Spes* also calls for international application of the principle of subsidiarity "to regulate economic relations throughout the world"[38] according to the norms of justice. However, subsidiarity is not the only principle invoked for international economic cooperation. In addition, along with the traditional concern for equity in distribution there appears to be for the first time in a major social document of the Church an acknowledgment of the normative criteria drawn from positive economics, specifically the criterion of economic efficiency, when the Council calls for the coordination and promotion of international economic development "in such a way that the resources earmarked for this purpose will be allocated as effectively as possible, and with complete equity."[39] In a manner quite familiar to economic discourse, the norms of efficiency and equity are now joined in Church social teaching.

Thus, the methodological shift from the more rigid deductive logic of earlier natural law argumentation to a more positivist analysis of observable effects in *Gaudium et Spes* creates further opportunity for the use of economic analysis in evaluating economic institutions, policies and systems. Indeed, the evaluation of private property and of public ownership in *Gaudium et Spes* contains the rudiments of a pragmatic social cost-benefit analysis. Limits on public intervention in the use of private property are implicitly set in economic terms by the optimization of the benefits of private ownership relative to the ethical and social costs of private acquisitiveness.

It must also be noted, however, that the decrease in reliance upon natural law argumentation is accompanied in *Gaudium et Spes* by an increase in reliance upon the beliefs of the Catholic faith as revealed in Sacred Scripture to ground the social teaching of the Church. This shift from philosophic argumentation to Scriptural analysis implies that the common good is not necessarily a logical, organic synthesizing principle in a coherent body of social doctrine, but a concept whose meaning must be discovered inductively. That may help account for the fact that *Gaudium et Spes* is unique among major Church social documents to that time by defining the common good, rather than assuming it as a premise of argumentation. While preserving a traditional emphasis on the human person, the definition of the common good is couched in language consistent with an inductive approach to social teaching: "the sum of those conditions of social life which allow social groups and their individual members relatively thorough and ready access to their own fulfillment."[40]

Certainly *Gaudium et Spes* does not go so far as to ground the principles of Catholic social teaching in economics or any of the positive social sciences. However, the greater incorporation of economic principles as well as the shift of emphasis in that document away from philosophic argumentation based on natural law premises to positive inquiry into the sources of revelation does indicate an evolutionary trend that continues in subsequent social documents of the Church. Thus, in opening a long discussion on human society and the social nature of man *Gaudium et Spes* calls attention to "Christian doctrine about human society" in recent social documents of the Church, but then states that "this council is merely going to call to mind some of the more basic truths, *treating their foundations under the light of revelation.*"[41] The trend towards greater reliance upon the Gospels has continued in subsequent documents of Church social teaching, especially those issued by the General Conference of Latin American Bishops at Medellin, Colombia in 1968, and at Puebla, Mexico in 1979, and even the current drafts of the Pastoral Letter on the U.S. economy.

This change of emphasis also shifts the methodological issue facing the use of economics in Catholic social teaching from an emphasis on establishing logical relationships with a scholastic philosophical tradition to the challenge of interpreting the place of economics in the revealed mysteries of the Catholic faith. On the one hand by the time of *Gaudium et Spes*, economics in its diverse dimensions had become much more fully integrated in Catholic social teaching than it was in the days of Leo XIII and even Pius XI. On the other hand little attention had yet been given to the rules for the appropriate use of economics as a set of tools to understand and apply the social message of the Gospels. This lack of clarity has continued to disturb the development and understanding of Catholic social teaching, especially through the debates about liberation theology after *Medellin* and *Puebla* and into the current discussion of the U.S. bishops' Pastoral Letter on the U.S. economy.

In retrospect the hand of Paul VI is evident in the social teaching of the Second Vatican Council, which began during the term of his predecessor, John XXIII, and finished during his term. The more vigorous incorporation of economics into Catholic social teaching along with a more openly inductive methodology observed in *Gaudium et Spes* brings an increase in the specificity of policy recommendations to the first two social encyclicals of Paul VI, *Populorum Progressio* and *Octogesima Adveniens*. In *Populorum Progressio* Paul VI discusses economics rather directly, distinguishing between analysis of economic structures, e.g., markets, public agencies, corporations, and analysis of economic ideologies. He is forcefully harsh in his judgment of economic structures which permit the economic domination of some peoples by others, and bases some of his criticisms upon the empirically observable "gap . . . widening between the development of some and the stagnating, even deteriorating condition of others."[42]

Paul VI develops still further the concern of John XXIII for economic equity in the international economy with expanded attention to the measurable inequalities growing between developed and underdeveloped countries. He explicitly speaks of quantitative economic growth, endorses industrialization of poor countries and especially incorporates several criticisms of the inequitable distributional effects of international markets. In *Populorum Progressio* he appears to incorporate the economic analysis developed by the United Nations Economic Commission for Latin America during the 1950's and 1960's to argue for a bias against developing countries in the terms of trade of international markets, along with some elements of dependency theory that followed in economics literature.[43] He extends to the international economy some of the same natural law principles of economic equity that Leo XIII used for domestic economies. His call for greater equality in bargaining strength between poor nations and their trading partners, e.g., rich nations or multinational corporations in international markets, resembles the call for equity in domestic labor markets, and he is vigorous in his denial of the justice of international free trade when the trading partners are in "very unequal situations."[44]

In the documents of Pope Paul VI there is repeated reference to the diversity of economic situations, functions, institutions and organizations as well as to the pluralism of options for action by Christians in society. It is not surprising then when he affirms that the Church "does not intervene to authenticate a given structure or to propose a ready-made model."[45] At the same time, he makes it clear that the Church is not content to limit its interventions "to recalling general principles."[46]

Nevertheless, Paul VI continues to use the concept of the common good, especially in various human rights settings, e.g., before the law and in the media. However, it is when the discourse shifts beyond the dictates of law to the instruction of the Gospel that Paul first introduces the concept of the preferential option for the poor that was to be developed as a principal moral and social norm in the *Puebla* documents and used in the letters of the Canadian and U.S. bishops on their respective national economies, as well as in the final report of the 1985 extraordinary Synod of Bishops.[47] It is worth noting that the norms of economic equity which Paul frequently espouses, especially with appeals to the Gospel, do not imply specific measures of quantitative equality. Rather, the inequalities he condemns are those which are "excessive" or deprive others of "the necessities of life."[48]

Paul VI's later encyclical, *Octogesima Adveniens*, explicitly elaborates a double edged quality of positive sciences that is quite different from that contained in the teaching of Leo XIII. He acknowledges the "significant flowering" of the "human sciences" and their role in "subjecting to critical and radical examination the hitherto accepted knowledge about man."[49] However, he also worries about scientific change that "threatens to drag [the world] towards a new positivism," and about the "methodological necessity and ideological presuppositions" that "make it impossible to understand man in his totality" because they

> "too often lead the human sciences to isolate, in the various situations, certain aspects of man, and yet to give these an explanation which claims to be complete or at least an interpretation which is meant to be all-embracing from a purely quantitative or phenomenological point of view."[50]

Populorum Progressio contains what is perhaps the strongest statement in the evolution of social teaching on property in papal documents to support public intervention in the use of private property, and the rationale in the statement is clearly an appeal to the common good: "The common good, therefore, at times demands the expropriation of an estate if it happens that some estates impede the common prosperity . . . "[51] This statement is followed by authorization of confiscation of property revenues, which "are not to be left to men's good pleasure," and by authorization to prohibit both "plans for excessive profit made only for one's own advantage" and efforts by the rich to transfer income abroad in search of higher returns.[52]

Unlike earlier papal social encyclicals, *Populorum Progressio* lacks the evenhanded condemnation of extreme models of economic systems of the right and left. There is no overt critical analysis of socialism, but there is severe condemnation of an "unbridled liberalism" which makes "profit the chief incentive to foster economic development, competition the supreme law of economics, private ownership of the means of production an absolute right."[53] Moreover, the criticisms of market capitalism, as suggested by the treatment of the international economy described above, are based upon functional analysis of the operation of market economies, rather than upon philosophical or ideological criticism of models of economic systems.

In the absence of comparable treatment of socialist economies and given the functional treatment of private property in the document, it is not surprising that many readers found in *Progressio Populorum* an opening for socialist institutions in Catholic social teaching. Perhaps in response to this reaction *Octogesima Adveniens*, issued four years later, contains an evenhanded condemnation of both Marxist and liberal capitalist ideologies.[54]

However, Paul VI stops short of absolute condemnation of all socialist experiments. Instead he acknowledges the attraction of contemporary socialist developments to some Christians and distinguishes among three levels of expression of socialism: "a generous aspiration and a seeking for a more just society, historical movements with a political organization and aim, and an ideology which claims to give a complete and self-sufficient picture of man."[55]

Paul VI expresses his doubts about the ability to turn these distinctions into an operational reality. Nevertheless, these distinctions, as well as references to the yearning for "liberation . . . from need and dependence"[56] were subsequently interpreted to allow for the introduction of Marxist analysis, presumably without the objectionable features of the ideology, in the interpretation of economic history by Catholic theologians, economists and other social scientists, most notably among Latin Americans, who were able to find further support for objectives of economic liberation in the *Medellin* and *Puebla* documents.

In *Evangelii Nuntiandi*, Paul VI relates still more closely an economic interpretation of human history to the Gospels by linking economic liberation to the Church's spiritual mission of evangelization:

> "Peoples, as we know, engaged with all their energy in the effort and struggle to overcome everything which condemns them to remain on the margin of life: famine, chronic disease, illiteracy, poverty, injustices in international relations and especially in commercial exchanges, situations of economic and cultural neocolonialism . . . The Church has the duty to proclaim the liberation of millions of human beings . . . This is not foreign to evangelization."[57]

Both the *Medellin* and *Puebla* documents are marked by the distinctive characteristics of contemporary papal social teaching: an emphasis on Gospel foundations rather than upon natural law, increased integration and specificity of economic analysis, a sense of institutional as well as personal sin, along with a clear link between economic liberation of poor peoples and nations with the transcendent evangelical message of the Church. Nevertheless, the *Medellin* document on justice retains from earlier papal social teaching a focus on personal virtue, reference to the common good and balanced criticism of the extremes of liberal capitalism and Marxist systems, both of which are criticized for their ideologically determined social priorities.[58]

The *Puebla* document is outspoken in its affirmation by the General Conference of Latin American Bishops of "a clear and prophetic option expressing preference for, and solidarity with, the poor."[59] The Latin American bishops develop the biblical basis of this priority extensively and acknowledge the tensions, conflicts and accusations, including that "of propounding a dangerous and erroneous Marxist ideology."[60] There is also reference to the importance of personal conversion, but, extending the thought of John XXIII, also a strong emphasis on injustices perpetrated by economic structures, the "mechanisms of oppression."[61]

Among the specific actions pledged by the bishops is one with significance for economic analysis: "We will make every effort to understand . . . the mechanisms that generate this poverty."[62] However, elsewhere in the document there are criticisms of the views of the human person inherent in "classical" economic liberalism and Marxism, in which economic efficiency and individual freedom are explicitly rejected as the bases of human dignity when they result in a religious notion of individual salvation which is blind to the demands of social justice.[63]

The *Puebla* document goes beyond criticism of the two familiar ideological extremes, however, to criticize a third view of the human person, one based upon consumerism, which is embodied in any system of "production and selling . . . done in the name of such values as ownership, power and pleasure, which are regarded as synonomous with human happiness."[64] By thus "blocking off access to spiritual values, in the name of profit people promote an unreal and very burdensome 'participation' in the common good."[65] For the authors of the *Puebla* document this threat of consumerism to the proper ends and goals of the human person is considered the "most pervasive" of the three dangers.[66]

Laborem Exercens, the major economic encyclical of John Paul II, was issued, like *Quadragesimo Anno* and *Octogesimo Adveniens*, as an anniversary sequel to the labor encyclical, *Rerum Novarum*. Nevertheless, it embodies many of the major shifts in method and focus of later social teaching, including a much stronger grounding of social teaching in Scripture, which is the basis for the encyclical's major contribution to the theology of work, namely, that through work the human person shares in divine creation. Although retaining a traditional concern for the individual human person, the analysis in the encyclical is also based heavily on social observation rather than on natural law reasoning of early labor encyclicals and contains considerable specificity, including endorsement of analyses made by two United Nations organizations and of specific labor policies like co-management. As a result there is less explicit recourse to the common good as a moral norm.

Although interpreted in the United States alternately as "socialist economics" and as deserving of the cheers of John Locke and Adam Smith,[67] it contains a brief, but strong geographic universalism with some emphasis on distributional inequities imposed on developing nations by public and private institutions acting in international markets.[68] Of interest to the economist is the fact that the criticisms of capitalism and socialism are based much more on empirical observations of the practical effects of specific systems on persons and on the production and distribution of goods and services than upon the specific theoretical premises of the models upon which they are based. Specific effects of historical experience with both capitalism and socialism are criticized, while at the level of principle the emphasis is on criticism of a materialism which cuts across ideological lines and which gives priority to economic targets over broader human goals.[69]

The recent Pastoral Letter of the U.S. Catholic bishops, *Catholic Social Teaching and the U.S. Economy*, while solidly grounded in traditional Catholic social teaching, clearly reflects and extends recent characteristics and trends in that teaching. The moral teaching of the letter is based very heavily upon interpretation of Scripture, and explicitly acknowledges sources outside those of revelation, ranging from pre-Christian Greek and Roman philosophy to the U.N. Universal Declaration of Human Rights and Duties.[70] The letter is also explicit, however, in its dependence, not only upon Scripture and philosophy, but upon "empirical analysis" for its discussion of the economic "signs of the times."[71] The Pastoral Letter explicitly affirms the ability of empirical evidence to help set an agenda for economic reform, and it even goes so far as to call upon Catholic universities to engage in the necessary research.[72] After nearly a century of Catholic social teaching such an affirmation highlights the extent of methodological evolution in Catholic social thought. From a relatively self-contained body of philosophic reasoning embellished by Scriptural citations and offered to social sciences like economics for application in the design of economic systems, Catholic social thought now presents itself as a framework for ethical and moral policy analysis based upon an interactive body of Scriptural, philosophical and empirical analysis.

The Pastoral Letter continues to invoke traditional principles and appeals to the common good as the basis for universal justice and human rights, but immediately includes "economic freedom, power and security" in those goals, thereby acknowledging the economic rights first articulated by John XXIII in *Pacem in Terris*.[73] Moreover, the Letter explicitly links the preferential option for the poor to the common good: "Dedication to the common good, therefore implies special duties toward those who are economically vulnerable or needy."[74] After acknowledging the importance of meeting the economic needs of the lower middle class, "if the common good is to be truly common," the document explicitly endorses the preferential option for the poor as developed by the Latin American bishops in the *Puebla* document.[75] As interpreted by the U.S. bishops there is created an "obligation to evaluate social and economic activity from the viewpoint of the poor and the powerless . . . Those who are marginalized and whose rights are denied have privileged claims if society is to provide justice for all."[76]

Following another precedent of recent Church social teaching the Pastoral Letter moves boldly into specific recommendations for public economic policy, which occupy almost 40 percent of the total document. Again following recent precedents in Catholic social teaching there is considerable analysis of the impact of the international economy upon the poorest nations of the world with explicit reference to the international common good, and over 25 percent of the chapter on specific economic policy issues is devoted to that subject. While acknowledging the claims of dependency theory, the analysis in the Pastoral Letter reflects the debates about and evolution of thought on economic dependency in economic literature since John XXIII first raised the subject in a major Catholic social document. Thus, the Pastoral Letter emphasizes the interdependence of international markets and focuses on specific issues that complicate the participation of the poor countries in international markets for goods, finance and investment capital.

Some Implications for the Usefulness of Economics

The evolution of the meaning of the common good as well as the shifts in methodological underpinnings for Catholic social teaching over a century of major papal and regional documents suggests change in the usefulness of economics within Catholic social thought. The change is not, however, simple and direct. On the one hand there is evidence for increased incorporation of economic analysis in identifying the priorities and agenda for economic reform as well as for policy evaluation because of greater openness to positive and historical analysis. On the other hand there is less clarity than before in the appropriate analytical relationships between economics and the multifaceted sources of Catholic social thought, which increasingly include Scriptural interpretations, whose operational applicability to contemporary economic decisionmaking is not immediately evident.

There is more opportunity for using the tools of economic analysis, not simply in applying Catholic social thought to institutional reform, but in developing the analysis of Catholic social teaching itself. At the most obvious level economic analysis can help in both the creation and the evaluation of policy options in areas where reform is warranted by social teaching. For example, the economic status of farmers has been an explicit concern of Catholic social documents at least from John XXIII's *Mater et Magistra* to the Pastoral Letter of the U.S. bishops. Today university supercomputers have the capacity to predict the effects of various federal agricultural policies upon output, income and regional income differentials with considerable specificity. In principle the use of economics is akin to the use of economics envisioned by *Rerum Novarum*, that is, as a tool to put into practice the principles of Catholic social thought.

However, the strength of the tools of modern positive economics lies more in providing consistent bases for practical evaluation of specific policies rather than for constructing broad generalized models of alternative economic systems. Modern technical developments in economics can support the desire for specificity of practical reform in contemporary Catholic social teaching, but has little to add to traditional searches for "Third Ways" between opposing ideological models of capitalism and socialism.

Two substantive economic components of the common good that are consistently affirmed in recent Catholic social teaching (regardless of methodological differences among documents) are 1) the continued emphasis on the distribution of economic income, wealth and opportunity and 2) the regular inclusion of an international perspective, even in documents for national consumption, like the Pastoral Letters of the U.S. and Canadian bishops on their respective economies. These two emphases taken together create opportunities as well as challenges for the helpful use of economic policy analysis for contemporary ethical concerns. Economics can help by predicting measurable effects of policy on economic variables. At the same time any student of elementary economics is made aware of the definitional and statistical difficulties of simply measuring poverty, which for many people is a bit like pornography—easy to recognize, but hard to define. The U.S. bishops explicitly acknowledge the problem, suggesting an opportunity for more thorough analysis. The application of economics in the U.S. for understanding distributional implications of alternative policy changes is often not so carefully developed as are the allocative effects of those changes. This is especially true at the international level.

Recent public discussion, for example, of the high cost to consumers of the "voluntary" quota imposed on the import of Japanese autos tends to ignore the distributional effects of the presence or absence of those quotas on incomes and expenditures of the poor. Thus, if the poor tend not to be buyers of new cars, and if some of their incomes can be shown to be adversely affected by removal of quotas, then the ethical criticism of quotas is apt to be less harsh than conventional trade analysis with its macro-aggregation of domestic consumer and producer effects would suggest. (Of course the adverse impact could be off-

set by other appropriate measures for income redistribution.)
Such omissions and deficiencies are serious for ethical analysis if
the preferential option for the poor requires, as the American
bishops affirm, that economic policy decisions "must be judged
in light of what they do for the poor, what they do to the poor
and what they enable the poor to do for themselves."

The use of economics in matters with ethical or normative
content obviously extends beyond simple examples such as this.
In fact theoretical analyses within public finance and welfare economics extend conventional microeconomic theories of choice
to include not simply material goods traded in the marketplace
for private purposes, but also those which are intended for public purposes and which may not be suitable for private exchange, e.g., national defense. Even one who believes in the ethical neutrality of the analytic methods of positive economics
wherever it is applied will acknowledge that positive economics
brings at least one norm or class of norms of its own to these
discussions, and that is one based upon a rigorously derived
principle of optimization, which intuitively means to affirm the
rationality of choosing more rather than less of any desired object of choice under certain assumptions about the relationship
of those choices to the rest of reality.

A bureaucrat in a socialist economy can use the principle to
ration raw materials among various enterprises in such a way as
to maximize total output of the economy in conformity with socialist values. Defenders of free enterprise as an economic system can defend this system by demonstrating that, under certain
behavioral assumptions, the competition of firms trying to maximize their own profits will result in the maximum total value of
output expressed in market prices. In welfare economics it is
common to speak of maximizing a hypothetical objective function that includes the private and social goals of an entire society. The concepts of social opportunity costs and social tradeoffs are drawn from such extensions of microeconomic
principles of rational choice.

Furthermore, the economic theories of rational choice, including those that incorporate probability and uncertainty, e.g.,
game theory, have been extended to non-economic areas, espe-

cially to political decisionmaking.[77] John Rawls believes that a theory of justice "is a part, perhaps the most significant part, of the theory of rational choice."[78] It is tempting to conclude that such theories can offer the rigor of positive analysis to the normative concepts of Catholic social teaching. However, in all such applications, from the social welfare functions of welfare economics to "maximin" game theoretic analyses of political decisions there are assumptions about the autonomy of the individual person that do not appear to be fully consistent with principles of Catholic social teaching about the human person that are central to the definition of the common good in that teaching. The rational decision maker in all these applications of microeconomics is an autonomous individual who maximizes a set of self interests according to rigorously determined conditions, such as the efficiency conditions of economic cost-benefit analysis.

Typically, the actor is assumed to be egoistic in the determination of self interest. It is true, however, that there is nothing in the logic to prevent the individual from including social goods in a personal definition of self interest, thereby leading to voluntary tradeoffs between competing objectives, e.g., the accumulation of income and the desire to support certain social objectives. Nevertheless, there is no place in this calculus of rationality for acts of commitment, generosity or sacrifice unless there is tradeoff with some other perceived and theoretically measurable good, e.g., the satisfaction or utility of feeling good or even the "gamble" of salvation or sainthood. Any elements which are not susceptible to such tradeoffs do not enter into the calculus of choice except as limits to the individual's willingness to engage in such tradeoffs and hence to the usefulness of the calculus. To say "give me liberty or give me death" excludes quite a number of "rational choice" solutions.

Based upon this calculus of rationality, the social welfare function of an entire society as defined in welfare economics becomes the aggregation of the individual welfare functions of the members of that society, each acting autonomously and rationally to maximize individual sets of self interests in consumption and social goods. The social welfare function defined in this way falls short of the common good of Catholic social teaching on several counts. The common good of traditional Catholic social teaching was derived heavily from a natural law that is presumed to exist independently of the perceptions of individuals acting autonomously and even independent of aggregations of those individuals. Even fifty million Frenchmen can be wrong in the face of an "objective" moral law. In the natural law of the Catholic tradition the dignity of the human person, including women and racial minorities, is derived independently of the perceptions of sexist or racist societies. The rights that flow therefrom, including the economic rights identified explicitly as such in Catholic social teaching since the documents of John XXIII, are derived independently of pay scales determined in the marketplace or even in the voting booth.

Moreover, the social nature of the human person as derived from natural law creates economic responsibilities that may or may not be acknowledged in the welfare functions of individuals acting autonomously. The extent of those responsibilities may independently impose ethical limits on the possibilities for rational maximization, especially of incomes and wealth, of some individuals that they would not autonomously choose. As indicated by the earlier review of documents, the importance of those limits in Catholic social teaching has grown along with the awareness of economic interdependence. As a result there is also growing emphasis in Catholic social teaching on economic distribution, state intervention and especially on the limits of the marketplace, the playing field of autonomous economic decisions, as a normative determinant of the social goals inherent in human nature.

The shift in emphasis from natural law reasoning to theological interpretation of Scriptural sources of Catholic faith for the moral grounding of Catholic social teaching in recent documents like the *Puebla* document and in the Pastoral Letter of the U.S. bishops on the U.S. economy has reinforced these tendencies along with the elaboration of concepts of human solidarity and the preferential option for the poor. This development further separates the premises about the human person in Catholic social teaching from those inherent in the theories of rational decisionmaking grounded in an economic theory whose definition of the human person is implicitly determined by the aggregate behavior of autonomous maximizers.

If there happens to be consensus among the members of society about ethical priorities based on Church teachings about the human person there may obviously be some logical convergence between the use of the optimization criteria in economic welfare analysis and the common good. In such cases economic analysis can help to identify and empirically clarify explicit tradeoffs and opportunity costs (i.e., the value of foregone alternatives) of specific economic policies aimed at broad goals embodied in the common good. The link between peace and economic justice, for example, has been made in the Catholic social teaching at least since *Populorum Progressio* of Paul VI, and the U.S. bishops specifically refer to the political, economic, social and moral opportunity costs of U.S. defense expenditures.[79] Clearly, the bishops find the principles of normative economics useful, though there are obviously opportunities for much more detailed analysis than they offer themselves in these complex areas.[80]

At the same time the methodology of economics can help to identify and clarify tradeoffs of economic targets that are only implicit within the broad scope of policies affecting the international common good and thus not always immediately apparent. This can be especially useful in analyzing policies that have effects on the distribution of wealth and income, which are a central concern in Catholic teaching about the common good. Failure to analyze these adequately can lead to inconsistent, even incompatible, policy recommendations.

In their Pastoral Letter on the Canadian economy, for example, the Canadian bishops deplore the vulnerability and marginalization of the world's poor in the international economy. Yet they propose for Canadian labor greater emphasis on "socially-useful forms of production" in which they include more labor intensive industries and more national economic self-sufficiency. They fail to note that the measures necessary to achieve these objectives would presumably entail either import restrictions against the labor intensive products of the poor of the rest of the world or a decline in wage levels of Canadian workers to levels of their poorer competitors abroad.[81] The U.S. bishops are consciously aware of the conflicting priorities that economic interdependence generates, especially of those that arise between domestic needs and those of the Third World poor. They explicitly ask the questions of who benefits from specific policies and how can costs and benefits be shared, while they refer explicitly to the problems of job displacement in the U.S. created by free trade with low-income countries.[82] In so doing they acknowledge the fundamental principle of economic scarcity and implicitly suggest opportunities for further application of economic analysis.

It is when there is no consensus that a divergence becomes apparent between behavior prescribed by the ethical teaching about the human person in Catholic social teaching and the aggregate behavior of "rational" maximizers. For a subscriber to Catholic social teaching this divergence reveals the inadequacy of welfare analysis based on the optimization of existing aggregate behavior as a measure of the common good. It is not surprising then that the U.S. bishops decry the lack of a "common moral ground" and the "decline in the nation's sense of a common social purpose" as an obstacle to social justice in the United States.[83]

It may be objected that the assumptions of autonomous individualistic behavior in economic welfare analysis more closely represent the variety of liberal pluralism that characterizes contemporary American democracy than does a common good defined independently of the evaluations of the members of the society. Some economists have noted the divergence and have reduced the latter approach to "an authoritarian system of preference determination" that is "incompatible with a normative theory of public finances in a democratic setting."[84] The U.S. bishops themselves have recourse to something akin to democratic principles in defending the rights of the poor to participate in the economic decisions that affect their lives.

In mainstream economic analysis of the optimal provision for public and private goods the premise, as expressed by Richard Musgrave, is that, while the provision of public goods cannot be based simply on the "idea of voluntary exchange," nevertheless, "the satisfaction of social wants must be based on the preferences of individual consumers or voters," and not on a source independent of the preferences of the individuals in the group.[85] Normative economics extends the rationality of economic maximization beyond the marketplace to the provision of public goods, even to the socially optimal provision of marketable goods like food and housing that may be inadequately provided to some members of society through private markets.[86] However, its analytical basis for doing so requires acceptance of a given aggregation of individual preferences, e.g., about income distribution, as the basis for analysis. If that aggregation is not ethically acceptable according to a reading of the common good in Catholic social teaching, the usefulness of economic analysis is limited. Even then the dismal science can at least help clarify the gap between the ideal and the actual and perhaps the directions where individual conversion is most needed.

Classically oriented economists since Adam Smith first compared the loss of one's little finger to a disastrous destruction of China have tried to apply principles of rational choice derived from market criteria to the provision of social goods without reference to moral criteria other than self interest. Following Adam Smith's allusion to the impact of interpersonal relationships on personal decisions, some economists defend a "robust zone of indifference" in human behavior "where one has no cause to be concerned over the effects of one's acts on others."[87] The robust zone of indifference, however, applies only to strangers and not to communities of persons, i.e., not to "family, neighborhood, . . . club, . . . tribe, racial or religious group or . . . nation," all of which are communities in which other mechanisms of distribution are called into play.[88] Given these definitions, Catholic social teaching about the universal common good of an increasingly interdependent human community, and about a deliberate option for the poor, would appear to sanction something less the robust of indifference for economic behavior based on market criteria.

Nevertheless, some economists have ingeniously tried to extend the theory of rational choice to the ethical order by using it, for example, to define an ethical norm for income distribution based upon maximization of self-interest under certain premises assumed to be ethically neutral. Mancur Olson, for example, has interpreted the Rawlsian analysis of economic justice under the "veil of ignorance" as a special application of "maximin" analysis when applied to the distribution of income in which the members of society maximize their self interest when they agree to maximize the income of the worst off member. Olson adds an assumption of the diminishing marginal utility of income, as validated in the probability reasoning of game theory, to the Rawlsian assumption of ignorance of all information that could create an incentive for self-interested behavior and concludes that the members of society act rationally when they opt for equality of income distribution.[89]

Such analyses are technically impressive and suggest normative criteria for decisionmaking under certain conditions of ignorance, e.g., in the provision of insurance for an uncertain future. They do not, however, resolve ethically loaded tradeoffs relevant to the common good, e.g., between personal liberty and the social consequences of maximizing behavior in economic matters that influence the meaning or content of that liberty. Nor do such analyses resolve the conflict between the priority given to autonomous personal preferences in microeconomic analysis and the priority given to independent criteria such as the social nature of the human person and human solidarity derived from natural law reasoning and Scriptural interpretation in Catholic social teaching. Rawls acknowledges that personal beliefs are given from outside the theory of rational choice, but in so doing creates a marketplace of competing beliefs in his theory of justice when he assumes that the parties involved, e.g., members of society "are conceived as not taking an interest in one another's interests. They are to presume that even their spiritual aims may be opposed, in the way that the aims of those of different religions may be opposed."[90]

Nevertheless, creative extensions of rational choice analysis into value laden areas of investigation help the economist to clarify the points at which value premises shape the analysis. The use of positive economic analysis to interpret Catholic social teaching in the American context, for example, helps to identify the points in public discourse about the Pastoral Letter of the U.S. bishops at which debate turns from ethics and economics to political ideology and to polemical defense of personal or group self-interest.

The methodological challenges of relating economics and Catholic social teaching are lightened somewhat by the evolution in that teaching away from the importance given to an authoritative self-contained body of doctrine in earlier documents to the acknowledgment of individual conscience in later documents, especially in those of the U.S. bishops. This acknowledgment, coupled with openness to the role that empirical observation, the "signs of the times" and positive analysis can play in the formation of individual conscience goes a long way towards acceptance of a pluralism of perceptions and behavior in the quest for social policy.

The U.S. bishops explicitly acknowledge the possibility of different conclusions among those who share the same moral objectives and "welcome debate" from Catholics and others.[91] Indeed, the prospect of openness of Catholic social thought to historical economic analysis, including Marxist variations—as well as empirical positive analysis since the time of Paul VI, has given a new slant to old American criticisms of ecclesiastical authority. The Church, however, does not appear ready to maximize individual conscience at the cost of relinquishing its authority to supply the moral and ethical premises lacking in positive analysis and to demonstrate their applicability in policy analysis.

Hence, if the common good is to have operational meaning for economic applications of Catholic social teaching, the methodological challenges that have arisen with the evolution of that teaching and with the extension of principles of economic analysis to larger areas will need to be addressed. If individual consciences are to be formed in ways that are convergent with an authoritative, transcendent social message and mission of the Church, more attention will need to be paid to the ways in which natural law, Scripture, historical and positive analysis can be linked to provide a moral base for an economic policy that can be persuasive. At issue for the economist are nothing less than the still elusive links between measurable inequalities and economic justice as well as the bridge between the increasingly pervasive use of economistic norms of rational behavior and a social order ultimately based on transcendent values of truth and love.

Notes

1. Charles E. Curran, *Directions in Catholic Social Ethics*, (Notre Dame: University of Notre Dame Press, 1985), p. 8.

2. *Ibid.*

3. "to suffer and endure is human . . . if [some] promise the poor in their misery a life free from all sorrow and vexation . . . they actually impose upon these people and perpetuate a fraud . . . The best course is to view human affairs as they are . . . and to seek appropriate relief for these troubles elsewhere," Leo XIII, *Rerum Novarum*, Par. 27 as reproducd in *Justice in the Marketplace: Collected Statements of the Vatican and the U.S. Catholic Bishops on Economic Policy, 1891-1984* (Washington: United States Catholic Conference, 1985), p. 20.

4. *Ibid.*, Par. 28, p. 20.

5. For an American example see Bernard W. Dempsey, *The Functional Economy: The Bases of Economic Organization* (Englewood Cliffs: Prentice-Hall, 1958).

6. Jean-Yves Calvez, S.J., and Jacques Perrin, S.J., *The Church and Social Justice* (Chicago: Regnery Company, 1961), p. 116.

7. *Rerum Novarum, op. cit.*, Par. 48-49, p. 27.

8. *Ibid.*, Par. 50, p. 28.

9. *Ibid.*

10. *Ibid.*, Par. 51, p. 28.

11. Calvez and Perrin, *op. cit.*, pp. 114-115.

12. *Quadragesimo Anno* as reproduced in *Justice in the Marketplace, op. cit.*, Pars. 57-58, p. 62. Cf. also Par. 74, pp. 66-67.

13. *Christmas Message, December, 1942*, as reproduced in *Justice in the Marketplace, op. cit.*, p. 102.

14. *Message to Catholic Physicians, Sept. 11, 1956*, cit. in Calvez and Perrin, *op. cit.*, p. 117.

15. *Christmas Message, December, 1942*, as reproduced in *Justice in the Marketplace, op. cit.*, p. 98.

16. Vd. Curran, *op. cit.*, pp. 19 ff.

17. *Quadragesimo Anno, loc. cit.*, Pars. 42-43, p. 56.

18. *Christmas Message, December, 1942, loc. cit.*, pp. 103-104.

19. Vd. Curran, *op. cit.*, pp. 23 ff.

20. *Quadragesimo Anno, loc. cit.*, Pars. 45-52, pp. 57-60 and Calvez and Perrin, *op. cit.*, pp. 214ff.

21. *Quadragesimo Anno, loc. cit.*, Par. 49, p. 58.

22. *Ibid.*, Pars. 111-126, pp. 76-81.

23. *Pacem in Terris* as reproduced in *Justice in the Marketplace, op. cit.*, Pars. 121, 125, pp. 168-169.

24. *Mater et Magistra* as reproduced in *Justice in the Marketplace, op. cit.*, Par. 55, p. 115.

25. *Ibid.*, Par. 54, p. 115.

26. *Ibid.*, Pars. 127, 131, pp. 130-131.

27. *Ibid.*, Par. 152, p. 136.

28. *Pacem in Terris, loc. cit.*, Par. 126, p. 169.

29. *Ibid.*, Pars. 18-22, p. 154.

30. *Ibid.*, Par. 63, p. 162.

31. *Ibid.*

32. *Ibid.*, Par. 54, p. 160.

33. *Ibid.*, Par. 60, p. 161.

34. *Gaudium et Spes: Pastoral Constitution on the Church in the Modern World* as reproduced in *Justice in the Marketplace, op. cit.*, Par. 71, p. 192.

35. *Ibid.*

36. *Ibid.*

37. *Ibid.*, Par. 85, p. 195.

38. *Ibid.*, Par. 86, p. 196.

39. *Ibid.*

40. *Ibid.*, Par. 26, p. 175.

41. *Ibid.*, Par. 23, pp. 173-74. Italics added.

42. *Populorum Progressio* as reproduced in *Justice in the Marketplace, op. cit.*, Pars. 29-30, p. 209.

43. *Ibid.*, Pars. 57-61, pp. 215-217.

44. *Ibid.*, Par. 58, p. 216.

45. *Ibid.*, Par. 42, p. 242. Cf. Par. 4, p. 225.

46. *Ibid.*

47. *Ibid.*, Par. 23, p. 235.

48. *Populorum Progressio, loc. cit.*, Pars. 23, 76.

49. *Octogesima Adveniens* as reproduced in *Justice in the Marketplace, op. cit.*, Par. 38, p. 240.

50. *Ibid.*

51. *Populorum Progressio, loc. cit.*, Par. 24, p. 207.

52. *Ibid.*

53. *Ibid.*, Par. 26, p. 208.

54. *Octogesima Adveniens* as reproduced in *Justice in the Marketplace, op. cit.*, Par. 26, p. 236.

55. *Ibid.*, Par. 31, p. 237.

56. *Ibid.*, Par. 45, p. 243.

57. *Evangelii Nuntiandi* as reproduced in *Justice in the Marketplace, op. cit.*, Par. 30, p. 271.

58. *Justice*, Medellin Conference documents as reproduced in David J. O'Brien and Thomas A. Shannon, eds., *Renewing the Earth: Catholic Documents on Peace, Justice and Liberation* (New York: Image Books, 1977), pp. 549-560.

59. "A Preferential Option for the Poor," Chapter 1, *Puebla: Evangelization at Present and in the Future of Latin America, Conclusions*, official English edition (Washington: National Conference of Catholic Bishops, 1979), Par. 1134, p. 178.

60. *Ibid.*, Par. 1139, p. 178.

61. *Ibid.*, Pars. 1136 and 1155, pp. 178, 180.

62. *Ibid.*, Par. 1160, p. 181.

63. *Ibid.*, Par. 311, p. 80.

64. *Ibid.*, Par. 311, p. 80.

65. *Ibid.*

66. *Ibid.*

67. Daniel Seligman, *Fortune*, November 2, 1981, p. 63 and Michael Novak, *National Review*, October 16, 1981, p. 1210.

68. *Laborem Exercens* as reproduced in *Justice in the Marketplace, op. cit.*, Par. 17, pp. 318-319. See the volume of essays on this encyclical, *Co-Creation and Capitalism: John Paul II's Laborem Exercens*, ed. John W. Houck and Oliver F. Williams (Washington, D.C.: University Press of America, 1983).

69. *Ibid.*, Cf. Pars. 13, 14, pp. 310-315.

70. *Catholic Social Teaching and the U.S. Economy*, The Second Draft, as reproduced in *Origins*, Vol. 15: No. 17, October 10, 1985, Chapter 2C, esp. Pars. 70, 84, pp. 265, 267. For several commentaries see the volume, *Catholic Social Teaching and the U.S. Economy: Working Papers for a Bishops' Pastoral*, ed. John W. Houck and Oliver F. Williams (Washington, D.C.: University Press of America, 1984).

71. *Ibid.*, Par. 34, p. 261.

72. *Ibid.*, Par. 253, p. 281 and Par. 335, p. 289.

73. *Ibid.*, Par. 87, p. 267.

74. *Ibid.*

75. *Ibid.*, Pars. 88-90, p. 267.

76. *Ibid.*, Par. 89, p. 267.

77. For one summary see Marvin Staniland, *What is Political Economy? A Study of Social Theory and Underdevelopment* (New Haven: Yale University Press, 1985), esp. Ch. Three, "The New Political Economy," p. 36ff.

78. A. John Rawls, "A. John Rawls," in Robert H. Hartman (ed.), *Poverty and Economic Justice: A Philosophical Approach* (New York: Paulist Press, 1984), p. 113.

79. *Ibid.*, Par. 24, p. 260.

80. See, for example, Ruth Leger Savard, *World Military and Social Expenditures 1985* (Washington: World Priorities Inc., 1985), esp. pp. 22-29.

81. "Moral Crisis" and"New Directions" in Canadian Conference of Catholic Bishops, *Ethical Reflections on the Economic Crisis (Catholic New Times,* 1983) pages two and three unnumbered.

82. *Catholic Social Teaching and the U.S. Economy, loc. cit.*, Pars. 262-264, p. 282.

83. *Ibid.*, Par. 26, p. 260.

84. Richard A. Musgrave, *The Theory of Public Finance* (New York: McGraw-Hill, 1959), pp. 13, 87. Musgrave identifies the latter approach with an "organic theory of the state."

85. *Ibid.*, pp. 86-87.

86. Vd. "Merit Wants," *Ibid.*, pp. 13-14.

87. Charles P. Kindleberger, "International Public Goods without International Government," *The American Economic Review*, Vol. 76, Number 1, March, 1986, p. 3.

88. *Ibid.*

89. Mancur Olson, *A New Approach to the Ethics of Income Distribution* (University of Notre Dame: unpublished lecture, Feb. 13, 1986). Although Rawls disavows utilitarianism, others besides Olson find in his "contractarian" approcah the same principles of equilibrium theory. Vd. Kenneth E. Boulding's review of A. John Rawls, *A Theory of Justice* in *Journal of Economic Issues* , Vol. VII No. 4, December, 1973, pp. 667-673.

90. Rawls, *loc. cit.*, p. 111.

91. *Catholic Social Teaching and the U.S. Economy, loc. cit.*, Par. 32, p. 261.

Part III

Breaking New Ground

JOHN W. HOUCK

Part III examines the common good from various perspectives, with an eye to uncovering new insights. As one of the participants in the conference put it, "As we do not live in a static world, we cannot expect static concepts." There is no doubt we live in a change-prone world:

It has become a truism that modern life is terribly complex and changeable. Since 1945, we humans have changed (and improved in many cases) our material, scientific, and technological bases more than in all our prior history. For example, we have published twice as many books and journals in these three decades as in all the centuries since Gutenberg. We can travel faster and to more places (including outer space) than even our more imaginative predecessors could have dreamed. Our growth in the uses and misuses of energy have been well documented, but it suffices to point out that we have used more energy in these three decades than in all of our prior history. No doubt, we will use in the

213

next two decades more energy than in the prior three decades. This record-setting and record-breaking is the story of our recent history, whether it be in material goods or services, science, technology, education, or medicine.

(Father Theodore M. Hesburgh, C.S.C., *Full Value*)

Given all the activity described, there are ample warrants to justify asking: Are we better off as humans? Has our economic system the conceptual tools like the common good to measure its degree of responsibility? Can we let the economic organization (and actor) focus single-mindedly on its goals, i.e., profit-maximizing, survival and growth, or career advancement, to the exclusion of any consideration of society's best interests? To these questions, Part III provides a spectrum of responses.

In the first essay, the theologian Michael Novak writes enthusiastically about new opportunities and perspectives in examining both the common good and the American business system. Novak reassesses Adam Smith's idea about the pursuit of self-interest, which, according to Smith, is translated by markets and competition into the common good. In place of the common good being attained through the self-interested actions of individuals, Novak would like to substitute a concept known as practical intelligence. He believes the common good is the result of all of us exercising our practical intelligence; that is, we set up institutional arrangements to achieve maximal convenience and minimal expenditure of time.

The second essay, authored by the economist Charles Wilber, is a synthesis of traditional economic thought with the concerns growing out of religious thinking. *Gaudium et Spes* defines the common good as "the sum of those conditions of social life which allow social groups and their individual members relatively thorough and ready access to their own fulfillment." The common good is not a mere summary of individual welfare. Rather, it is a set of social conditions necessary for the realization of human dignity which transcend the arena of private exchange and contract.

John W. Cooper, in the chapter twelve, explores the great de-

bate in the Christian churches over questions of economic justice. He argues, however, that religious-ethical thought too frequently uses the measuring stick of the ideal and has little sense
of the mundane but necessary processes of economic production, distribution and consumption.

The final essay, by the economist Gar Alperovitz, takes a dia-
metrically opposed position to that of the previous writer, John
W. Cooper. Alperovitz argues that the notion of common good is
not achievable under the present institutional values, priorities
and structures of capitalism. In fact, Alperovitz believes capitalism is on a collision course with disaster.

Free Persons and the Common Good

Michael Novak judges that one of the achievements of the U.S.
Catholic Bishops' Economic Pastoral is the importance they attribute to the concept of the common good. Novak answers those
who argue that the common good is a static concept and is incompatible with pluralism and liberty. On the one hand, Novak
wants us to respect the power of the tradition from whence the
concept of the common good came, from Aristotle to Thomas
Aquinas and contemporary philosophers like Jacques Maritain.
On the other hand, he wants us to see the dynamic and open-
ended manner in which the common good can be used. For example, the common good is often mentioned in the sphere of
economics, especially in reference to the poor as a norm arguing
for alleviating their poverty by expanding educational and employment opportunities and removing existing barriers. Novak
writes:

> . . . it is not wrong to appeal to the common good as bench mark
> in order to find the current achievement of the common good
> still inadequate. The concept of the common good is thus like a
> pair of pincers. One of its grips focuses our attention upon the
> concrete achieving, the other upon tasks yet to be met. There is a
> moral dynamics within us, in our own culture and in our souls,

the living legacy of Judaism, Christianity, and the humanism they have nourished.

He examines the difference between the individual, overemphasized in economic discourse, and the person, which is a more holistic concept and compatible with the notion of the common good. Out of this sense of personhood, Novak argues, comes inalienable freedom and responsibility, which is embodied in the Declaration of Independence and the Bill of Rights. Novak would like us to work on the set of institutions, like business and markets, not from the individualistic point of view but from the ethical and personal point of view which Novak believes is the source of liberty and responsibility, and hence, dignity. To Novak, this sense of personhood is God's wish for us.

In the past, it was relatively simple to define the common good because our sense of the person and society was static. Today, however, in a change-prone world, Novak argues that we need more freedom, pluralism and initiative, with people and institutions working on the common good in different ways—and only time will tell what is best. Novak describes the major institutions as the political, economic and moral-cultural; today no one of these is superior to the others. Rather over time and by interaction will we discern the "right mix" of these three in the practical ordering of the common good.

Individualism and the Common Good

The economist Charles Wilber takes on the onerous task of attempting to relate individualist philosophy in economic theory to the concept of the common good. This is a challenge because it has long been thought that the two are incompatible if the common good is rooted in a communitarian vision of society emphasizing both the dignity of the person and the social dimension of that dignity.

As Charles Wilber sets up the intellectual task, he lays out the propositions growing out of the individualist view: People are motivated primarily by self-interest; the market translates self-interest into a form of "the common good"; freedom must be the highest value in social ordering; the role of government is to enforce passively the rules of the game; and any interference by government will impede the inherent stabilizing of the economy. Or, to put it another way, the common good is achievable under this social vision through the operation of freedom, markets, and self-interest.

Charles Wilber's synthesis of the two views starts with the adoption of the externality concept, which has a long history in economic theory. He argues that a widened use of the concept of externality tied in with the more traditional ideas of free markets and self-interest will result in practical policy recommendations similar to those growing out of common good theory.

Positive externalities benefit society; negative externalities hurt society. To Wilber ". . . the market system underproduces private goods with social benefits and it overproduces private goods with social costs." He wants the intervention of the concept of externality to serve as the equivalent to the concept of the common good in challenging self-interest, markets and freedom. Wilber points out that ". . . community is neither created nor maintained by rational self-interest alone."

Claimants to the Common Good: Socialism or Capitalism?

In his essay, John W. Cooper sees a great debate raging in the Christian Churches over questions of economic justice. As outside the Church in more traditional political and economic debates, there are two grand schemes jousting for the peoples' loyalty: socialism and capitalism. He explores some of the ideas and arguments by several thinkers about this critical question over the last two centuries.

John Cooper believes that there are some important questions that must be addressed by the theological tradition before any worthwhile answers can be given to the debate about economic justice in either socialism or capitalism. How should the religious person look at the temporal order: wealth, the role of work, and technology? Can the religious perspective and ethical demands growing out of that tradition offer an informed critique of the difficult processes of production, distribution and consumption? Who is responsible for the creation of wealth and how does wealth creation affect the presence or absence of poverty? What should be the relationship between and among the various economic classes? Can a society be established which treats all the economic classes and actors fairly and which maximizes freedom, prosperity and justice? What is "fair" treatment?

John Cooper examines what he believes to be an intellectual and religious bias in Catholic social teaching with regard to capitalism. Part of the cause of this "bias" has been the relative unfamiliarity of the Latin mentality with the Northern Protestant European development of capitalism. Another source of this bias can be traced to the great concern that the Catholic Church has had for Latin America, particularly as manifest in the development of Liberation Theology; one constant of this theology has been its critique of capitalism, arguing that the Northern Hemisphere has created an economic dependency in the Southern Hemisphere.

Cooper does not see the same historical trends in Protestantism, partly because of the close collaboration in the founding of capitalism by the economic actors and various strains of Protestant thought such as Puritanism, Calvinism and Lutheranism. However, the founding documents of the World Council of Churches (WCC) raise questions about capitalism and socialism in an attempt to develop a notion of symmetry between the two systems. To be sure, no meaningful "third way" evolved. Today, Cooper believes,

Mainline Protestantism, like Catholicism, stands at a crossroads. It will either continue to pursue an increasingly radical liberation theology or it will begin the long task of reevaluating the market-oriented system of democratic capitalism.

Cooper wants Christian theology to come to terms with the reality of the world, the difficulties in producing wealth, and the proper role for economic incentives. He sees that there are four basic paradoxes that the Christian perspective must take into account:

1) the world is good, but fallen;
2) wealth is potentially abundant, but relatively inaccessible;
3) work is fulfilling and alienating;
4) technology is creative and destructive;

He believes that Christianity must question the old assumption that self-interested activity is always selfish and sinful, and it must recognize that self-interested economic activity can benefit more than just the economic actor. It can reach out and contribute to the good of the family or the community or even the larger society. Another assumption that must be critically assessed is that economic production and distribution is relatively easy and that there should be little concern by religious groups about the creation of wealth as they expend all their energies reflecting on the distribution of wealth. He asks the question: Which economic system, socialism or capitalism, is best able to bring about the expansion of wealth?

The Common Good into the Future

In the final essay of this section, the social historian and economist Gar Alperovitz takes issue with the optimism of John Cooper about the future of the common good in the capitalist context. First and foremost, Gar Alperovitz tackles the optimistic assumption about the future of capitalism. In an inquiry into the record of the last few decades, he argues that economic growth and progress have come to a halt and that this spells a dismal future. For instance, he cites the following unemployment averages: 4.5 percent during the 1950s, 4.8 percent in the 1960s, 6.2 percent during the 1970s and, thus far, nearly 8 percent in the 1980s. Likewise, he sees the overall growth of GNP slipping: 4.2 percent in the 1960s, 3.2 percent during the 1970s, and 2.5 percent in the 1980s, assuming no recession and 3 percent growth until the end of the decade. Along with other economic analysts, Alperovitz sees nothing but stagnation and holds little hope for the kind of progressive reform that will expand and enhance the common good.

Other barriers to the implementation of the common good are the fundamental cultural values of isolation, individualism and self-interest that war with any attempt to develop a sense of community, of equity, and social consciousness. Until there is a change in our cultural mores, Gar Alperovitz sees little basis for optimism for the advance of social justice or the common good.

What he champions is a fundamental change in our value system. He calls this a reconstruction that would be essential in order to implement the common good and build a sharing of social values. Without this reconstruction ". . . the disintegrating processes and institutions which undermine the common good will ultimately undercut all longer term reform strategies."

Alperovitz is not optimistic about a quick fix, as his prescription calls for a fundamental change from our present culture. First, and foremost, a realistic assessment of the state of capitalist economies is needed. Second, there must be a profound understanding of the need for fundamental reform. Finally, a long-term struggle through reconstruction to change basic values and institutional arrangements must be initiated. According to Alperovitz:

New political energies cannot be mobilized around failing traditions. . . . Clarity about our situation and its requirements is absolutely essential. Although support for human social programs must continue, the idea of helping the poor enter a system which is acknowledged to be profoundly flawed is inadequate to the longer-term historical challenge we face: There is a need, ultimately, for a new and more expansive conception of the common good.

For Gar Alperovitz, then, there is little hope for the implementation of the common good in the present environment of cultural values and institutional arrangements. He takes issue with the other writers' idea that religiously based social and economic criticism can find compatibility with capitalism. Rather, he argues that the voice of religion should seek fundamental changes in our values, reward systems and equity arrangements.

Ten

Free Persons and the Common Good

MICHAEL NOVAK

One of the achievements of the U.S. Catholic Bishops' Economic Pastoral is its restoration to a place of honor of the classic Catholic concept of the common good. This step alone marks a reconnection of Catholic social thought to its Thomistic origins, at a moment in history in which certain themes of Thomistic thinking are more concretely verified in history than in times past. The fact that the contemporary imagination easily grasps the image of "the global village" (a metaphor first recreated by the Thomist-trained Marshall McCluhan) establishes, e.g., the imaginative context of natural law: a way of thinking about all human beings related to one another in a universal framework of mutual independence and mutual vulnerability. The twentieth-century impact of relativism, stressed by historian Paul Johnson in *Modern Times*, is diminishing. It is not the *in*dependence of cultures and moral systems that now most fascinates humans as their *inter*dependence.

The danger in natural law thinking (and in the concept of the common good) has been thought to be twofold: (1) that it is static and nonhistorical; and (2) that it is incompatible with pluralism and liberty. These accusations have a *prima facie* validity, since the concepts of natural law and the common good were first articulated in the environment of the relatively static and undifferentiated authoritarian societies of the ancient and medieval Greco-Latin world. Yet even Aquinas and his colleagues were acutely aware of the differences between pagan Athens and Rome and Christian Europe. They were aware, too, of national differences, as the pattern of *nationes* at the University of Paris suggests.

Furthermore, in the Twentieth century, leading democratic theoreticians such as Jacques Maritain and Yves Simon (followed in the practical order by Sturzo, de Gasperi, Adenauer, Schumann, Malik, Erhard, and others) brought these medieval concepts into the conceptual networks of democracy, pluralism, and personalism. It would be unhistorical not to observe the transformations such thinkers wrought in the classic notions, which in any case were theoretically open to such development. In their hands, it became clear that human beings are historical animals, whose nature is dynamic, inquiring, and open to the new demands and possibilities of history—including error, conflict, and tragedy. These thinkers wrote, after all, in the maelstrom of the First and Second World Wars. Maritain's work in helping to articulate the *Universal Declaration of Human Rights of the United Nations* illustrates both the power of the tradition of which he was the most able spokesman and the contemporary fertility and openness of his mind. Here, indeed, on the levels of the human spirit, lay the beginnings of the interdependence now widely celebrated, as it has become more concrete and visible through magnificent inventions in the transport and communications industries and through international trade, commerce, and finance.

Nonetheless, the concept of the common good remains uncommonly vague. For the past twenty years, even Catholic scholars have neglected it. References to it in various indices of periodicals during this period are virtually nil. How one can square the common good with personal liberty and cultural pluralism is most unclear.

In practice today, the common good is most often invoked in the context of economics. It is employed chiefly with reference to the condition of the poor, both within particular societies and in the relation between economically successful and unsuccessful nations. Concern with the creation and the distribution of wealth and with some relative equality among the members of the human family leads many to appeal to the common good as a device for inspiring individuals to attend to the condition of the less fortunate. How to produce economic development from the bottom up is itself a complex subject. It is something of a short-cut—increasingly recognized to be both a dangerous and a counterproductive one—to hold that the condition of the poor can better be raised, and thus the common good better served, by entrusting matters to the paternalistic administrations of state authorities.

In the medieval period, the church had not been adequately differentiated from the state; institutions of political democracy and human rights had not yet been established; markets were primitive and other institutions of free and dynamic economic development had not yet been put in place; and the routine of cultural and moral life had not yet been institutionally liberated from censorship and other authoritarian controls. In those days, care for the common good was invested in the authorities of church and state, ideally working in mutually respectful concert, but in practice often in deadly combat with one another. For such reasons, the concept of the common good carried heavy symbolic overtones of paternalism. The concept, moreover, was excessively simple. It was imagined that the common good could be easily known, almost by inspection, and efficiently secured by authoritative administration.

Many of the same symbolic overtones now attach to socialist schemes of the common good. It is helpful here to distinguish between classic authoritarian socialism and contemporary democratic socialism. The tendency of all socialist thought is to deprecate individualism ("bourgeois individualism"), private interests, private property, and "unbridled" markets. Classic authoritarian socialism supplies as an alternative the authority of government over all aspects of economic life. By contrast, contemporary democratic socialism is eager to defend both democracy in political life and democratic, decentralized methods in all spheres of economic life. Classic authoritarian socialism, concerned to check the error of individualism, tends to trust the wisdom of authorities of the central state. Contemporary democratic socialism resists such trust in centralized authorities. It wishes to check the error of individualism by mandatory schemes of democratic cooperation among all participants in economic activities.

Manifestly, classic authoritarian socialism exerts more concentrated discipline than the mere paternalism of the undifferentiated medieval society. But even contemporary democratic socialism seriously underestimates the chilling effect of decisions by committee and by worker sovereignty. Democratic methods are time-consuming and inflict underestimated knowledge-costs. Besides, the dynamics of political decisionmaking bring into economic calculation many inefficient externalities.

These objections, of course, are pragmatic rather than principled. Based solely on them, one may allow many experiments to go forward. However, the record of socialist experiments of many kinds suggests that socialist ideals consistently founder on rude facts of human personality and aspiration. In this sense, many persons formerly inspired by socialist ideals have come to the conclusion that socialist ideals are, even in principle, based upon false premises. This objection is principled, but it, too, is not incompatible with patience regarding continued socialist experimentation. Call this the objection of skepticism.

Just the same, invocations of the common good in the economic sphere are commonly aimed at "correcting" liberal individualism. J. Philip Wogaman, in his paper called "The Common Good and Economic Life: A Protestant Perspective," writes for example that the "common good at least means the repudiation of any purely individualistic conception of the common life." Historically, this is not quite true. The common good was highly respected in history long before the individual was, and long before institutions emerged to protect the liberties of the individual. Indeed, after the Eighteenth century societies that respected individual rights came to be thought more historically advanced than those that did not. In referring his definition of the common good to the individual, however, Dr. Wogaman suggests an important point. Jacques Maritain demonstrates in *The Person and the Common Good* that one cannot understand the classic concept of the common good without understanding the concept of the person.

As every tree in the world is an individual with its unique location in space and time, and with a shape all its own, so it is with every member of every species of plant and animal. To speak of the individual in this sense is to speak of what can be physically located, observed, seen, and touched. In this context, the common good would be either the sum of the goods of each individual member or "the greatest good of the greatest number." A purely materialistic conception of the individual is compatible with a high valuation on each individual. But it is also compatible with the view that the whole is greater than any part and ought to take precedence over any part. It is this latter view that George Orwell satirized in *Animal Farm.* In this view, the human being in the social body is like the steer in the herd, the bee in the hive, the ant in the colony—an individual whose good is subordinated to the good of the species.

A person is more than an individual. As the concept of individual looks to what is material, so the concept of person looks to intellect and will: the capacities of insight and judgment, on the one hand, and of choice and decision, on the other. A person is an individual able to inquire and to choose, and, therefore, both free and responsible. For Aquinas, the person is in this sense made in the image of the Creator and endowed with inalienable responsibilities. The good of such a person, who participates in activities of insight and choice (God's own form of life), is to be united with God, without intermediary, face-to-face, in full light and love. The ultimate common good of persons is to be united with God's understanding and loving, the same activities of insight and choice coursing through and energizing all.

Analogously, on earth and in time, the common good of persons is to live in as close an approximation of unity in insight and love as sinful human beings might attain. Since this requires respect for the inalienable freedom and responsibility of each, and since human beings are imperfect at best and always flawed in character, it is by no means easy at any one historical moment either to ascertain the common good or to attain it. There is a serious problem in learning what the common good is. There is also a serious problem in achieving it. In order to solve both these problems, even approximately, persons need institutions suitable to the task.

But what sorts of institutions are likely to raise the probabilities of their success in identifying and achieving the common good in history? These must be invented and tested by the hazards of history. They are not given in advance. Human beings proceed toward the common good more in darkness than in light.

Two fundamental organizational errors are ruled out, however, by an accurate judgment about the requirements of the human person *qua* person. The specific vitalities of the person spring from capacities for insight and choice (inquiry and love). From these derive principles of liberty and responsibility, in which human dignity is rooted. The human person is *dignus*, worthy of respect, sacred even, because he or she lives from the activities proper to God. To violate these is to denigrate the Almighty. On the one hand, then, it is an error to define individualism without reference to God and without reference to those other persons who share in God's life. A self-enclosed, self-centered individualism rests upon a misapprehension of the capacities of the human person, in whose light each person is judged by God, by other persons, and by conscience itself (whose light is God's activity in the soul). The person is a sign of God in history or (to speak more accurately) participates in God's own most proper activities, insight and choice. The person is *theophanous*: a shining-through of God's life in history, created by God for union with God. This is the impulse in history, guided by Providence and discerned by the authors of the U.S. Declaration of Independence, when they spoke of human persons as "endowed by their Creator with inalienable rights," and strove to invent institutions worthy of human dignity.

On the one hand, then, a self-enclosed individualism falsifies the capacities of the human person. On the other hand, so does any vision of the common good as a mere sum of individual goods (or the greatest good of the greatest number). Even if it were true that a hundred persons would experience more pleasure from torturing one person than that person would experience pain (in some dreadful utilitarian calculus), such an action would be an abomination. The person is never subordinate to the common good in an instrumental way. Persons are not means but ends, because of the God in Whom they live and Who lives in them. The common good of a society of persons consists in treating each of them as an end, never as a means. To arrange the institutions of human society in such a way that this happens without fail is by no means easy. The human race has so far only approximated the achievement of such institutions. The road not yet travelled is long. Over most of the planet's present surface, including most of the world's peoples, persons are still conceived of as means to the ends of the state. Their personal liberty is not respected. Every form of collectivism—in which each member is treated as a means to the good of the state—violates the dignity of the human person.

Fundamental conceptions, therefore, play a large role in the construction of systems and the invention of institutions. To be sure, the capacities of the human person incessantly reassert themselves, so that by trial and experiment human societies are driven back, even despite themselves, to taste the bitter fruit of erroneous conceptions. By dint of error, conceptions that are true keep coming to light in history, often at horrible cost. Systems of self-enclosed individualism and of overweening collectivism truncate the capacities of the human person. To attain the common good worthy of human persons, one must look beyond such systems.

Systems and Institutions Designed for the Common Good

Since no other creature in history evinces the capacities of the human person for insight and choice, a social order worthy of human persons is not likely to resemble any other order in nature. A merely mechanical or procedural order, for example, is likely to miss the most crucial component of all, human character; that is, the complex of moral and intellectual skills through which each person slowly fashions his or her unique capacity for insight and choice. Even if one lists all the observable descriptions of individuals on file cards, and even if two (or more) individuals by some chance were represented by identical sets of such file cards (however long), still, these descriptions, as Gabriel Marcel pointed out, would fail to predict the differences between such individuals that would emerge as soon as one began working with them in close colleagueship.

In this sense, each person is an *originating* source of insight and choice, irreplaceable, inexhaustible, beyond even an infinite set of descriptions. (Even at the end of a long life together, husband and wife remain elusive and prove inexhaustible one to the other.) A person's character, as one comes to know it, does provide grounds for predicting behavior ("in" character or "out" of it); but a lively sense of inquiry and choice ceaselessly allows persons to grow in character and to be converted in finally unpredictable ways. No one responsible for choosing personnel for specific tasks will doubt how great differences among persons can be, how unpredictable success is, and how misleading *curricula vitae* and references can be. Human persons are alive with possibility, both for good and ill.

How, then, can we imagine a system designed according to the capacities of human persons? The most sustained treatments of this problem, approached in this way, have been advanced by F. A. Hayek in *Law, Legislation and Liberty* (3 vols.) and in *The Constitution of Liberty*. Hayek's work has been sorely neglected by Catholic social thinkers. To comment further on them here would overburden this essay, for significant space would have to be assigned merely to exposition. But I would be delinquent if I did not at least mention that the consonance (and disagreements) between Hayek's work and such works of Jacques Maritain as *Man and the State* and *The Person and the Common Good* cry out for systematic attention.

The first point to stress is that the problem of the common good has three sides. (1) How can free persons come to know it? (2) How can it with highest probability (nothing in history being other than contingent and probable) be achieved? (3) Through which complex of institutions may it be pursued with maximal respect for human persons?

Since recent discussions of the common good arise most often in the context of economics, it is proper here to concentrate upon the economic system best suited to achieving the common good of free persons. In the fuller treatment, much more would need to be said about political systems and institutions, and about systems and institutions in the moral and cultural order (churches, universities, associations of writers and others, the media, families, civic groups, and the like). Given this self-imposed limitation, let us discuss each of the three questions above in order.

The Veil of Ignorance

It is not so easy to know the common good of free persons. There are three reasons for this. First, even in trying to determine one's own economic good—in the full context of one's own political, moral, and cultural goals—one often feels confusion and uncertainty. Should one buy this house? Take this position? Accept this contract? All such decisions are made in ignorance of the future. Not all the relevant contingencies can be known, and many that can be known are not certain to fall into place. Choice falls in the realm of uncertainty and practical wisdom, not in the realm of logic and certainty. It follows that it is no easier to know the economic good even of one's best friends and nearest neighbors.

Secondly, each of us is necessarily ignorant about the economic good of those in trades, professions, industries, technologies, and circumstances of which we have no experience.

Third, the economic good of the entire nation—on a high level of abstraction from particular persons or groups—may be easy enough to sketch in a "wish list": low inflation, low unemployment, steady growth, credit available at low cost, a stable currency, gains in productivity, a proportionate improvement of the national environment as compared with environmental damage, the steady advance of the poor out of poverty, care for those unable to care for themselves, and the like (almost *ad infinitum*). Yet the sustained investigation of the trade-offs among these many competing goods has won the historical sobriquet of "the dismal science." One can easily imagine the reasons why this is so. The phrase "the common good" sounds simple and clear. But upon inspection this good turns out to consist of many goods. And these are not only not in natural harmony with one another but often in direct conflict. Moreover, it is not easy to rank these goods in a preferential order. One person's set of preferences is not likely to be the set freely chosen by all others.

It is tempting to cut this gordian knot by abolishing freedom and imposing a single view of order, according to someone's plan for the common good, in accordance with that person's scheme of social justice. Short of that, each person is free to try to persuade his fellow citizens that some scheme of preference, some vision of the common good in ordered rankings, is superior to others. Even so, however, the veil of ignorance is not ripped away. However beautiful any scheme may appear in theory, it may result in practice in declines in so many of the goods anticipated that the entire scheme falls into disrepute. The appeal of Catholic schemes of the common good would be far higher, for example, if the actual practices of Catholic nations had led to more admirable results. The prestige of socialist schemes has suffered from the deficiencies apparent in actual socialist experiments. And so forth.

The fundamental point, however, is that once one introduces the good of personal liberty among the social goods to be included in the common good, it becomes clear that "the common good" is a concept of a special heuristic kind. Free persons typically have pluralistic visions of the common good. The scheme of one differs from the scheme of another, neighbor's from neighbor's. Free persons conceive of the good in often mutually incompatible ways. Human ignorance is such that it is virtually impossible to settle such disagreements even on the theoretical plane. And even if they could be settled on the plane of theory, it is not certain that any one settled vision would be treated kindly by historical reality.

Therefore, if we were to accept the ideal of the common good as a general ideal, and even if we were to agree upon a particular vision of the common good, we would still be operating in considerable darkness and uncertainty. Whatever the common good is, it is not easy to know.

Achieving the Common Good

Those who use the notion of the common good frequently exhort their fellows to "attend to" it, to "intend" it, and to "aim" at it. This conception no doubt goes back to Aristotle, who thought of all things in nature and history as "in motion," tending to an equilibrium that is their natural fulfillment or place of rest. Indeed, he defined "the good," in the most generic and unspecified sense, as that to which each natural thing aims. He conceived of a human person, for example, as an animal in motion toward self-realization, at whose (always incomplete) achievement such a person would be able to act well in such uniquely human capacities as inquiry, insight, choice, and decision. In their childhood, Aristotle observed, humans are moved to action by pleasure and pain, feeling, emotion, memory, and passion. The impact of these influences never fades, but gradually the fully developing person comes to order them under the gentle (even "democratic") sway of persuasive insight and self-directed choice. Through self-knowledge, one comes to self-mastery and the fluid, easy, satisfying possession of all one's powers. Since most humans do not achieve this, one must be patient with them. In the *polis*, Aristotle wrote, one must be satisfied with a "a tincture" of virtue.

Yet in Aristotle's Athens, as in the Paris, Rome, and Orvieto in which St. Thomas Aquinas reconceived Aristotle's notions to meet an entirely new context, city-states were only small towns and the many functions and institutions of modern societies had not yet been differentiated. In those ancient and medieval contexts, one person, in effect, could paternalistically "see to" the common good. Often this meant little more than defending the citizenry from hostile attack, improving productive assets such as the supply of water, passing reasonable laws, and caring for the poor. "Golden ages" of prosperity and peace came properly to be celebrated. Yet all this was not incompatible with a fairly rigid set of fixed inequalities, in which resignation to their own lot and station was thought for the lowly and underprivileged to be a high civic good. Compared to the surrounding rudeness of primitive life in the countryside, such small city-states shone out with civilized beauty. Nonetheless, rivalries among the privileged nobles within them were brutal, conspiratorial, and murderous, as one learns from Machiavelli and, considerably later, from Shakespeare. In addition, the *vox populi* was relatively mute, and state and church controlled virtually all channels of commerce, industry, and economic advancement. It was against such *anciens regimes*, Max Weber points out, that the "free cities" and "city republics" of the early modern era began their revolt.

Slowly, an important idea entered human consciousness. One did not need to think of the "common good" as a vision "aimed at" or "intended" or imposed by a singular ruler or set of rulers. One had to think of it also as something *achieved* through the participation of all citizens. On the way toward this achievement, sustained thought proceeded through three steps. First, the state had been experienced as the agent of excessive taxation, torture, censorship, and repression. Second, government to be just must be based upon the consent of the governed. Third, citizens retain inalienable rights, endowed in them by their Creator, upon which the state could not by any means trespass. Made in the image of God, persons capable of insight and choice are worthy (*dignus*) of a sacred respect. In this way, the idea of the limited state, based upon the inviolability of personal rights, slowly emerged in human thought. Thus, as Maritain puts it, the long centuries of Jewish and Christian teaching about the dignity of the human person, working like yeast in the dumb dough of history, sought completion in institutions worthy of that dignity.

This development posed a radical challenge to notions of the common good. First, the freedom and dignity of human persons (made in the image of God) became a primary criterion for any social order truly ordered to the common good. Second, the advent of personal liberty destroyed the simplicity of the concept of the common good. Now each human being was held responsible for forming his own conception both of his own good and of the common good. Traditionalists feared that such radical pluralism would end in anarchy. This was not necessarily so. It would have been so if the concept of the common good depended upon a unity of moral aims, intentions, and purposes. Instead, the concept of the common good was radically transformed. It no longer meant an aim, intention or purpose. The common good came to represent, on the one hand, a social achievement and, on the other, a benchmark.

It is one thing to aim at, to intend or to make one's purpose the common good. It is another thing actually to achieve a social order in which free persons have opportunities to pursue their own visions of the good, both personal and communal, both private and public. The liberals of the late Eighteenth century set in motion the sorts of institutions that would with high probability realize such an achievement. Because of the veil of ignorance mentioned above, they came to the insight that free persons could not be expected to agree in advance about common intentions, aims, or purposes. A society respectful of the freedom and dignity of persons would have to forebear any direct and conscious assault upon the common good. Under conditions of pluralism, that citadel could no longer be taken by frontal assault. On the other hand, it could with high probability be taken by an indirect, less paternalistic route. The order proper to subservient humans is one thing. The order proper to free men is another. The former can be an order ordered by an orderer. Formed in the mind of one, it can be made to "inform" the actions of all. The latter must be allowed to emerge from the free rationality of many. Arising from the intelligent decisions of many, from decisions taken in matters closest to their own hands, such an order can achieve a far higher quotient of practical intelligence than was embodied in any prior order.

How can this be so? We have already seen that it is difficult for any one person to be certain even of his own personal economic good. It is in principle impossible for any one person to comprehend all the concrete economic transactions that render the common good alive and vital in every nook and cranny of the economy. It is even impossible for any one person to comprehend all the goods that must be intended by the phrase "the common good" in a modern economy, even on a high level of abstraction. Economists try their best to do so. Yet even they will be the first to insist that they can tell you, from their science, probable gains and losses from particular courses of action, but that they cannot tell you which of the many goods society might want to pursue, it *ought* to pursue or how to rank them.

Yet all these testimonies to unavoidable human ignorance do not entail that a human economic order must be devoid of practical intelligence. On the contrary, under certain institutional arrangements and according to a set of rational rules derived from much experience, societies of humans that use such institutions wisely and obey their rules (amending them as experience teaches) can suffuse their own economic order with levels of practical intelligence never before attained. While we must doubt that any human economic order can be fully intelligible, designed as it must be for daily use by imperfect, highly fallible, and sinful persons, nonetheless, existing societies do differ markedly in the quotient of practical intelligence that infuses their daily economic life. For practical intelligence is infused into economic transactions in every corner of society by persons employing their own practical intelligence to the maximum degree possible. Social systems differ in their openness to the practical intelligence of individuals.

Here a brief digression may be clarifying. In a classic passage, Adam Smith pointed out in 1776, in the most revolutionary book ever written (whose full effect upon China, the USSR, and the Third World awaits the Twenty-first century), that he had never known persons who said that they intended the common good ever do very much to advance it. He made it plain that he was speaking from observation. Such observation made him doubt the prevailing ideology, in which to seek one's own interest was held to be immoral. To the contrary, he observed—again, as a matter of observation, subject to empirical testing—that when persons diligently pursued their own interests, about which they were relatively quite knowledgeable, the sum of such actions cumulatively recorded on a national scale demonstrably raised the common good of the nation.

In this passage, in my opinion, Smith injured a powerful insight by speaking of "interests" rather than of practical intelligence. To block the path of a merely exegetical argument here, I will not assert that Smith *intended* to say "practical intelligence" or even that the logic of his argument in that context requires that he *should* have said it. In another context, one might well make that textual argument. To take a short cut here, however, I will merely assert that the word *interests* is incorrect and should be rejected. One should not make the claim that when each person seeks his own interests, then, as if by an invisible hand, his successfully achieving those interests adds to the common good of all.

On the contrary, the more accurate analysis is that when each citizen acts with the maximal practical intelligence that he can bring to bear upon the economic activities in which he is engaged, he adds to the degree of social intelligence available in his environment. When all other economic activists conduct their affairs with equivalent practical intelligence, then the entire social texture is rendered more luminous by the cumulative effect of all such acts.

There is a further factor at work. Of all forms of human life, economic activities are perhaps the most universal examples of human interdependence. Almost no one today can live in total self-sufficiency and self-enclosure, like Robinson Crusoe, totally independent of exchange with others. The farmer does not build his own combine or drill for and refine his own gasoline, does not weave his clothes or build his own television set, and does not even grow the tea, coffee, spices, oranges, or other foodstuffs upon which his family relies in his own home. For this reason, virtually every economic good or service passes through physical places of exchange, governed by rules that allow for maximum convenience and minimal expenditures of time; in short, through markets.

I said earlier that the concept of the common good has been translated from the realm of aim, intention, and purpose to the realm of practical achievement. The common good must be achieved; but the best way to achieve it has been discovered to lie not in intending it directly, but rather in establishing institutions and rules that encourage citizens to maximize the practical intelligence with which they infuse their daily tasks. Thus, by an indirect route, citizens of practical intelligence help to build up the social intelligibility of the whole. In this intelligibility lies the common good: an achievement of practical intelligence throughout the whole. But I also said that the concept of the common good also names a benchmark against which the common good as practical achievement is measured.

It may well be that in the economic sphere the rule-abiding institutions of the market maximize social intelligibility and that their practical fruits in prosperity, progress, and an orderly, cooperative spirit are indisputable. Nonetheless, many other social pathologies and problems may rise into view: the problems of those with little or no income, the disabled, the unemployed, and others who can scarcely enter into markets. The concept of the common good, in this sense, obliges us to lift our heads to confront the social whole again, in order to discern where some citizens may be being excluded, where needs are unmet, where fresh and unforeseen problems are arising.

The modern market system arises from impulses of the Jewish and Christian inheritance of the West, which instructed our forefathers that the dignity of every human being is beyond price. That insight led to the liberation of economic activities from the repression common to traditionalist states and to the vindication of the creative economic energies of free citizens. Analogously, a market system functioning within a Jewish, Christian, and humanist culture will always be subjected—quite properly—to claims of a transcendent sort, obliging citizens to attend to the full dimensions of human life both within and outside the economic sphere. The common good as benchmark reminds us that no contemporary achievement of the common good has yet met the full measure of legitimate expectation. The human race is a pilgrim race. At no point can we ever say, "We have attained sufficient liberty for all," "We have attained sufficient justice for all," etc. The ideals to which we are bound always demand that we do still better.

Therefore, it is not wrong to appeal to the common good as benchmark in order to find the current achievement of the common good still inadequate. The concept of the common good is thus like a pair of pincers. One of its grips focuses our attention upon the concrete achieving, the other upon tasks yet to be met. There is a moral dynamism within us, in our own culture and in our souls, the living legacy of Judaism, Christianity, and the humanism they have nourished. Our hearts are restless until the destiny that draws us is fulfilled. That destiny always measures us and levies fresh demands upon us. We come, thus, to the third question concerning the common good.

The Institutions That Serve the Common Good

Once we cease thinking of the common good as a substantive account of what the world ought to look like when all our work is done, and try to think of it as a form of concrete achieving and a benchmark, our minds are led naturally to the institutions through which we can realize this achieving in a concrete, practical, regular, reliable, and routine way. Fresh impulses in human life come usually with passion and emotion; abiding impulses find shape in institutions. *"Politics begins in mysticism,"* Charles Peguy used to say, *"and mysticism always ends in politics."*

Those who first called themselves liberals—and were called liberals—had in mind three liberations (which helps to explain why the appropriate liberal flag is always a *tricouleur*). They intended, first, to liberate humans from tyranny and torture; second, to liberate humans from poverty; and, third, to liberate humans from censorship and other oppressions of conscience, intellect, and art. For each of these three liberations, they invented appropriate institutions: *in the political order*, limited and conditional government, institutions of human rights, representative democracy based upon checks and balances, and free political parties; *in the economic order*, the relatively free market, patent laws and copyrights, labor unions, corporations of many sorts, ease of credit and business formation, the stock association and the business company; *in the moral and cultural order*, religious liberty and the separation of church and state, the free press, rights and practices of free speech, and the independence of universities, the media, and other private associations, from the state.

Each of these institutions was designed to protect the pluralism appropriate to free persons. Each was also designed defensively, not so much to define the common good substantively for all, as to secure for all, against the encroachments of others, the right and the opportunity to pursue the good as each saw fit; and to construct checks and balances against the mighty. The first liberals were well taught, and undoubtedly confirmed through experience, the practical bite of Jewish and Christian teachings about the sinfulness, folly, and unreliability of humankind. They feared utopianism and fanaticism from any quarter. In a sense, they trusted reason, but not the reason of any particular man or party. They wished to assure a hearing for all, and to block a *dictat* from any.

The great liberals were in two important senses not ideologues. First, they trusted experience, observation, and experiment. Second, they were by temperament and choice conservatives, although decidedly not traditionalists. That is, they had great respect for the *tacit* knowing that accompanies experience, habit, tradition, and practical judgment. They were skeptical of "men of ideas" and "the idea class." They did not believe that their grandparents were less wise than they, but they did not fear to carry forward the work their grandfathers bequeathed to them. To their right, they opposed traditionalists, Tories, and the *ancien regime*. To their left, they opposed the socialists, the Diggers, and the Luddities. While they were acutely aware that theirs was a new party, representing a profound revolution in the affairs of humankind, they gladly identified their roots in ancient ways of thought from Aristotle through Aquinas ("the first Whig"). Indeed, most were for a time identified with the Whig tradition; Edmund Burke, Alexis de Tocqueville, Lord Acton and others belonged to this company. To recite some of their names—Montaigne, Montesquieu, and Bastiat in France; Adam Smith, Cobden, and John Stuart Mill in Britain; Madison, Jefferson, Franklin, Hamilton, and Lincoln in the United States—is both to fulfill a duty and to enjoy a privilege. In recent times, their tradition has been extended by A. F. Hayek and Ludwig von Mises; by Raymond Aron and Jean-Francois Revel; by Paul Johnson, Irving Kristol and Robert Nisbet; and by many others.

Because the liberal party is not utopian; because it does not offer a simple picture of paradise on earth; because it is preoccupied with checks and balances to shortsightedness, folly, and vice; because it patiently awaits the outcome of experiments and monitors unintended consequences—for all these reasons, the liberal party forms a view of the world more suited to the middle-aged mind than to the youthful mind. The artistic and the literary intellectuals have sought and found more dramatic materials elsewhere. In ideological combat all this proved for many decades a disadvantage. Today, however, in the closing years of our century, the harvest of forty years of frantic ideological experimentation is coming in. It is a harvest of many bleached bones, lying upon dry fields, that echo with the cawing of crows. It is no wonder the liberal party is enjoying an international rebirth. It is always an autumn party, looking to the spring.

Just the same, there are three themes still incomplete in the liberal intellectual inheritance, one in each of the three liberal orders. In the political order, the popular desire for security, as contrasted with the desire for liberty, has proved stronger than anticipated. Throughout the democracies, electorates have been wooed by the promise of governmental subventions, subsidies, and securities. Vigilance, the price of liberty, has not been exercised. The story of the Grand Inquisitor suggests that, ideally, human beings want liberty but, when they have it, grow irked at its responsibilities and insecurities. There are only recently belated signs that the public is beginning to awaken to the costs and dangers of Leviathan.

Yet it is natural enough that families, provident for their future, desire under modern conditions the sort of security that rural living once afforded. It is not mean of them to do so. But the provision of universal security does choke liberty, innovation, and advance. As parents who overprotect their children reap unintended consequences, so some forms of compassion reduce citizens to a dependence upon the state not altogether different from serfdom. The liberal party cannot only speak of liberty. It must distinguish rigorously among the legitimate and the illegitimate desires for security. The liberal state is certain to be to some extent a welfare state. The limits to that extent await defining.

In the economic sphere, the liberal party has thought too little about the dilemmas of the underdeveloped countries. Caught between cold-blooded traditionalist economies and hot socialist ideologies, many educated persons in the Third World hardly know of liberal ideas and institutions, except as these are reflected in Marxist and socialist literature. They do not recognize that the liberal order begins from the bottom up, from universal property ownership, from open entry into markets, from ease in incorporating small businesses, from the extension of credit to the poor, and from the awakening of economic creativity and activism in every sector of the population. Institutional realities that could be taken for granted in early North America and in Europe are novel to those still living in societies whose institutional traditions antedate the modern era.

The liberal party must think through the small steps, the tacit knowing, and the accumulated wisdom by now taken for granted in their own historical achievements. The virtues, habits, attitudes, and aptitudes appropriate to a traditional society are not identical to those needed to make liberal political and economic institutions function as they ought. "Remembering the answers" to questions long ago socially resolved requires sustained, empathetic work. It is easy to forget how much blood and bitter learning went into our own habit-building and institution-building. Still the liberal hypothesis is that liberal institutions express a system of natural liberty, open to all cultures everywhere. The hypothesis is universal in its range. But, as for that other Kingdom, so in this world also, the gate is narrow and the road is straight. Not down every cultural path can free and creative economic development acquire momentum.

In the moral and cultural order, the liberal party in its youth rebelled against a repressive *ancien regime*. Now in its maturity the liberal party faces a far more deadly foe of liberty: relativism, decadence, hedonism, nihilism. In its early phase, the liberal party tended to concentrate upon the illegitimate restraints imposed by authorities from without. In its maturity, it must now concentrate its fire upon an illegitimate *absence* of all restraints from within. The Statue of Liberty, presented to the United States by France a century ago, is a symbol of true liberty: a woman, not a warrior; bearing in one hand the torch of enlightenment against darkness, and carrying in her other hand a tablet of the law. This Lady, unmistakably purposive, disciplined and serious in countenance, is a proper symbol of liberty, as the neon-lit pornography shops in mid-town Manhattan are not. Were moral decadence to become the symbol of liberal societies, liberty were lost. It is not necessary to be Puritan—there is ample room for sensuality and pleasure in the liberal view—to grasp that liberty is primarily an attribute of spirit, of intellect, of light, of reasoned law. Liberty is primarily an *idea*.

That, in the end, explains why liberty must always be rediscovered by every generation afresh, particularly as each in its maturation works its way through the passions and enthusiasms of youth. How a social order can be designed simultaneously to serve the common good and to respect the conscience and intellect of every free person is not an insight given by unaided nature. The institutions that make that achievement possible, and the ideas upon which such institutions rest, must be thought through again by every generation in a fresh environment. For it is by thinking that such ideas perish or survive.

Politics does, in fact, begin in mysticism. And mysticism must, in fact, end in politics. Human beings live in institutions as fish live in the sea. Only through certain institutions can free persons exercise their liberties. To understand and to invigorate these institutions is the best—the only—way to realize a common good worthy of free persons, and to push ever higher the benchmarks of what a free people may together accomplish.

Eleven

Economic Theory and the Common Good

CHARLES K. WILBER

It is frequently argued that adherence to an individualist philosophy requires acceptance of a laissez-faire economic policy. The goal of this paper is to see if the individualist premises of free market economic theory can yield interventionist economic policy conclusions similar to those derived from the Roman Catholic concept of the common good. If it is possible then adherents of the common good concept can find allies among those who hold some form of individualist philosophy.

The common good concept is rooted in a communitarian vision of society.[1] Because of this it emphasizes both the dignity of the human person and the essentially social nature of that dignity. Therefore, both civil and political liberties on the one hand and social and economic needs on the other are essential components of the common good.

Gaudium et Spes defines the common good as "the sum of

those conditions of social life which allow social groups and their individual members relatively thorough and ready access to their own fulfilment."[2] The common good is not a mere summation of individual welfare. Rather, it is a set of social conditions necessary for the realization of human dignity which transcend the arena of private exchange and contract. For example, "such goods as political self-determination, participation in the economic productivity of an industrialized society, and enjoyment of one's cultural heritage can be obtained by an individual only through participation in the public life of society."[3] Such conditions or goods are essentially relational. To exist they must exist as shared. Claims on these goods are social rights such as freedom to assembly, work, adequate health care, etc.

In short, individual persons have rights to those things necessary to realize their dignity as human beings. These rights are derived from a person's membership in a community, not from his or her nature as an isolated individual.

In contrast economic theory is rooted in an individualist conception of society. Society is seen as a collection of individuals who have chosen to associate because it is mutually beneficial. The common good is simply the aggregation of the welfare of each individual. Individual liberty is the highest good, and, if individuals are left free to pursue their self-interest, the result will be the maximum material welfare.

Economic theory attempts to provide a rigorous demonstration that rational individuals, left free to engage in voluntary exchange, will construct competitive market institutions that yield optimal levels of individual freedom and material welfare. In the absence of market failures this economic theory of individual rationality indicates that intervention by public authorities lowers efficiency and thus the level of output.

What can be said about the justice of such free market outcomes? While there are differences of opinion among economists the free market argument is based on a process-oriented view of social justice.[4] In this view the process or rules of the game justifies the outcome and not vice versa. Further, a just social process is one that rational individuals would have unanimously agreed to in a state of Lockean nature.[5]

Using the concept of externalities I argue in the next section
that an individualist based economic theory can, in fact, provide
a legitimate basis for public intervention into the market process.
Specifically I argue that individual rationality can provide an economic basis for the type of public employment and welfare
programs derived from the common good philosophy embodied in the Bishops' Pastoral Letter on Catholic Social Teaching and the U.S. Economy.[6]

Externalities, Efficiency and Free Market Economics

Historically, economic theory developed within an individualist and utilitarian philosophy. Modern economics is usually dated
from the 1776 publication of Adam Smith's *The Wealth of Nations*. This book initiated a tradition in economic thinking
which continues today. The core of the analysis is the model of
competitive market capitalism. It is believed that an uncoerced
person can be depended upon to act rationally to maximize his
or her individual self-interest; and more importantly, it is
thought that an automatic, self-regulating mechanism to manage
economic affairs is possible if it is built on basic human nature.
The forces of competition ensure that the economy produces
those goods which people demand and does so by the most efficient means.

Thus, from Adam Smith to this day, mainstream economists
have argued that the best way to overcome scarcity and to maximize personal freedom is to rely on the individual's pursuit of
self-interest in a private property system regulated by the force
of market competition, where the government simply acts as the
neutral umpire of the rules of the economic game. In order to
maximize his or her income each person has to provide something (product, service or labor) which others want and are willing to pay for and this will maximize overall production. Thus,
as each individual attempts to become better off, society, made
up of the individuals living in it, benefits. Therefore private

profit and public welfare become reconciled through the automatic and impersonal forces of competition.

The final result is not only a particular economics, but also a particular social philosophy. It can be termed the "free market" or "laissez-faire" tradition within economics. This was the dominant view of economics until the 1930s in both England and the United States, and, after a forty year eclipse, has once again become the dominant position in economics. It can be summarized under a few propositions:

1. People are motivated primarily by self-interest described best by Adam Smith as an "innate propensity to truck, barter, and exchange."
2. A free market economy, through the forces of competition, converts that self-interested behavior into the common good by forcing firms to produce what consumers demand and to do so in the most efficient way.
3. A free market economy requires freedom of choice—of where to invest, of what job to take, of what product to purchase, and so on.
4. Problems in the economy, including poverty, are due either to governmental interference with the free market or are the result of physical and human nature. The scarcity in physical nature requires time to overcome. In addition there are physical causes—i.e., accidents, birth defects, diseases—that prevent people from earning a living. The perversity of human nature means some people will always fail and thus be poor; some people are lazy, immoral, or improvident.
5. Public authorities can and should do little besides enforce the rules of the game and provide those goods—i.e., defense—that the private sector is unable to produce.
6. There is an inherent stability in the market economy, and since supply will create its own demand, that equilibrium stability will generally be at a position of full employment.

Adam Smith and free market adherents theorize as if the economy is composed of a multitude of isolated individuals whose actions are *independent* except when they engage in exchange with each other. However, as industrialization and density of population increase the world becomes less like that. In fact, individual acts of production and consumption become ever more *interdependent*. In economic theory these interdependencies generate *externalities*.

Many privately produced goods generate externalities, both positive (social benefits) and negative (social costs), which affect people who are not involved in the transaction. Pollution is a social cost inflicted on others by those who produce and those who use automobiles. Since the pollution cost is not borne by the producer or individual consumer, too much pollution is produced (and too many automobiles). When one neighbor maintains his or her house, it raises the value of all the houses in the neighborhood. This is an example of a social benefit reaped by all the neighbors. Since not all the benefits are captured by the one maintaining his or her house, there is less incentive to do so and thus less "maintenance" is produced.

What problem do externalities create for the efficient operation of a free market system based on self-interested rational individuals? The existence of externalities results in market failure. That is, the market system underproduces private goods with social benefits and it overproduces private goods with social costs. When, because of externalities, social costs and benefits diverge from private costs and benefits, what is best for each individual is not what is best for society. Government, having the power to compel payment or compliance, has been seen traditionally by economists as the institutional mechanism to correct these market failures created by individual self-interest maximization.

Now I want to apply the concept of externalities in two situations that demonstrate how individualist economic theory can be made compatible with a communitarian conception of the common good.

Corner Solutions, Crime and Negative Externalities

In this section of the paper I want to explore those situations where the optimal free market solution is what economists call a "corner solution."[7] Economists see the market system as a process of solving maximization and minimization problems. Maximization problems involve maximizing some output with given inputs and minimization problems involve minimizing the cost of inputs to obtain some given output. Any solution in which one or more of the inputs or outputs are given a zero value is called a "corner solution" because in mathematical terms it lies at the corner of the set of all possible solution values.[8]

In fact, the free market system's optimal solution to the problem of maximizing society's output given input resources may be a corner solution in which the incomes of some workers may be zero (or at least below the poverty level). This could be the outcome when it is not efficient for any employer to hire a certain type of labor at a positive (or above the poverty level) wage. Given their skills these workers are not needed to produce maximum output. Thus, their incomes will be zero since they remain unemployed. Other workers will be employed only if their wage rates are very low (below the poverty level).

This is not just a hypothetical possibility. In very poor, labor-surplus economies efficiency dictates paying unskilled labor a zero or near-zero wage. The market economy's optimal solution, therefore, is a corner solution where some workers face starvation for the sake of economic efficiency. To a lesser degree the same phenomenon exists in the United States. Left to itself the free market yields optimally efficient results that leave some workers with zero incomes (unemployed) and others working, but with poverty level incomes.

The possibility of corner solutions causes a number of problems for a market economy with its foundation of rational decision making by individual actors. First, there is the possibility of high unemployment rates and large-scale poverty.[9] Second, and my interest in this paper, is the individually rational response of "corner dwellers" to their plight. Economic theory usually goes silent at this point. It probably is assumed that these unfortunate workers go on public assistance or get retraining to increase their skills. However, there is a perfectly rational alternative. After weighing all of the profitabilities, costs, and risks, a corner-dweller can choose to allocate part of his or her labor to illegal activities such as prostitution, gambling, burglary, shoplifting, running numbers, and mugging.

This is not to argue that when wages fall below some minimum level every such person becomes a criminal. Rather, the argument is that to some extent the amount of crime committed is a function of the relative wages between unskilled labor and criminal activity. The existence of corner solutions with their zero or near-zero wage rates and the associated crime rates is a relevant consideration when analyzing the legitimacy of intervention in the free market economy.

The existence of crime as an alternative activity to the zero or near-zero wages of a corner solution makes it a concern of society as a whole, and not simply of those workers involved. In short, "low wages themselves generate an externality, crime, that may be a *rational* response to the set of market wages."[10] Unfortunately, this externality usually is ignored by free market theorists.

Whether you believe desperate people are driven to crime by poverty or that weak people are enticed into crime because the risks are not high enough, the fact remains that crime creates enormous costs for the community in the form of negative externalities—loss of life and property, costs of law enforcement, and the psychic costs of fear and insecurity. These types of externalities cannot be corrected by the free market. Public intervention is called for. For example, the Bishops' recommendation to make employment at above poverty wage levels our top policy priority could pay for itself by reducing the relative value of anti-social behavior.

Anti-Poverty Programs and Positive Externalities

Free market economists such as Milton Friedman have long recognized that education is a special commodity that requires government intervention.[11] It has positive externalities since education has a greater value to society as a whole than to the individual alone. For example, an educated person, it is argued, makes a better voter and more generally is necessary to keep our modern, complex society operating. Thus, Friedman has suggested that a voucher system be used to subsidize education. In this plan government would give all parents a voucher worth the cost of a public-school education which the parents could then spend on any type of school they so desired. The government would then reimburse the school for the value of the voucher. Thus, there would be competition among schools providing people with greater choice and quality.

However, many commodities besides education possess positive externalities. Health is certainly one example. Preventing or curing a worker's illness or accident not only benefits him or her but also those who suffer from his lost output. Also preventing communicable diseases and illnesses has benefits to all who are exposed. Thus, the subsidization of health carries the same logic as the subsidization of education.

The argument can be extended. Why not subsidize other basic needs such as food, clothing, and shelter? The free market answer is that these commodities do not have positive externalities. Rather, their total value is captured by the individuals who consume them.

However, this is a short-sighted argument if a portion of the population are corner-dwellers (receive zero or near-zero wages) who are driven to obtain their food, clothing and shelter through criminal activity which generates negative externalities. There are externalities attached to not subsidizing food, clothing and shelter analogous to not subsidizing education. Here again the logic of free market theory leads to practical conclusions similar to those of communitarian theories.

Since free market economists rely on the existence of positive externalities to justify public subsidy of education, they cannot logically refuse to subsidize a number of other commodities that also generate externalities. Of course there may be argument over the best way to do so—jobs programs, guaranteed income system, direct subsidies of specific products and so on. Here again individualist premises lead to policy conclusions similar to those of the Bishops.

Individualism and Interdependence

I have focussed on the issue of externalities because it holds out the greatest hope for understanding between adherents of individualist theory and advocates of the common good philosophy.

Individualist theory holds that society is nothing more than the sum of individuals involved. It is assumed that these individuals are independent of each other. In technical terms that means individual preference functions are not interrelated and the same for production functions. The concept of externalities was developed to handle cases of interdependence. They are called externalities because independence is considered the norm and interdependence the exception.

Communitarian theories of the common good, on the other hand, hold that society is more than a collection of independent individuals. Rather, interdependence—the essence of community—is assumed to be the norm with independence the exception.

As the pervasiveness of externalities, and thus interdependence, is recognized, the practical policy conclusions derived from individualist economic theory converges to those obtained from a more communitarian conception of the common good (for example, the Bishops' Pastoral Letter on Catholic Social Thought and the U.S. Economy).

Conclusion

The purpose of this paper is to demonstrate that with the addition of the concept of externalities, free market individualist theory yields practical policy recommendations similar to those of common good theory. This is important if support for policy is to be obtained from adherents of individualist philosophy.

However, there are other differences between individualist economic theory and communitarian theory. Economic theory abstracts man/woman into a rational calculator of pleasures and

pains. Communitarian theory sees the person rooted in the concrete reality of specific communities. Meaning and dignity come
from being participating members of the community. And community is neither created nor maintained by rational self-interest
alone. We would do well to heed Boulding's caution of 30 years
ago.[12]

> There is a *danger — in a predominantly commercial society,*
> *that people will take economic behavior as the measure of all*
> *things and will confine their relationships to those which can be*
> *conducted on the level of the commercial abstraction.* To do this
> is to lose almost all richness or purpose in human life. He who
> has never loved, has never felt the call of a heroic ethic—to give
> and not to count the cost, to labor and not to ask for any re-
> ward—has lived far below the peak levels of human experience.
> *Economic man dwells in Limbo—he is not good enough for*
> *Heaven or bad enough for Hell.* His virtues are minor virtues: he
> is punctual, courteous, honest, truthful, painstaking, thrifty, hard-
> working. His vices are minor vices—niggardliness, parsimonious-
> ness, chicanery. Even the covetousness of which he is often ac-
> cused is a playful and innocent thing compared with the dreadful
> covetousness of the proud. *On the whole he escapes the deadly*
> *sins*, for his very vulgarity saves him from pride (how much bet-
> ter, for instance, is the commercial vulgarity of Coca Cola than
> the heroic diabolism of Hitler). *But he misses the Great Virtue,*
> and in that he is less than Man, for God has made man for him-
> self, and he has an ineradicable hunger for the Divine, the heroic,
> the sanctified and uneconomic.

Notes

1. For this section on the common good, I have drawn heavily on
David Hollenbach, *Claims in Conflict: Retrieving and Renewing the*
Catholic Human Rights Tradition (New York: Paulist Press, 1979). Also
see Josef Pieper, *The Four Cardinal Virtues* (Notre Dame: University of
Notre Dame Press, 1966); Jacques Maritain, *The Person and the Com-*
mon Good (New York: Charles Scribner's Sons, 1947).

2. *Gaudium et Spes*, Para. 26, Printed in *Proclaiming Justice and*
Peace: Documents form John XXIII-John Paul II (Mystic, Conn:

Twenty-Third Publications, 1984), eds. Michael Walsh and Brian Davies.

3. Hollenbach, p. 147.

4. The laissez-faire advocates among economic theorists base their argument, however accurately, on Robert Nozick's *Anarchy, State and Utopia* (New York: Basic Books, 1974). Economic theorists of a more liberal orientation find Rawls work more congenial. See John Rawls, *A Theory of Justice* (Cambridge, MA: Harvard University Press, 1971).

5. See F.A. Hayek, *Law, Legislation and Liberty* (Chicago: University of Chicago Press, 1976).

6. *Pastoral Letter on Catholic Social Teaching and the U.S. Economy*, Second draft (Washington, D.C.: National Conference of Catholic Bishops, October 7, 1985). For several commentaries see the volume, *Catholic Social Teaching and the U.S. Economy: Working Papers for a Bishops' Pastoral*, ed. John W. Houck and Oliver F. Williams (Washington, D.C.: University Press of America, 1984).

7. This whole section is based on Andrew Schotter, *Free Market Economics: A Critical Appraisal* (New York: St. Martin's Press, 1985), pp. 65-80.

8. A good illustration of a simple corner solution is the old army nutrition problem. Assume we want to provide a group of soldiers with a minimum daily requirement of protein (70gm.) and iron (10mg.) at the least cost. There are three foods available to provide protein and iron and that have various costs per ounce: peanut butter (40gm., 4mg., $0.20), Spam (20gm., 3mg., $0.50), and Jello (60gm., 1mg., $0.30). One result is immediately evident. No Spam would be purchased because, ounce per ounce, peanut butter gives more protein and iron and is cheaper. Thus Spam would have a zero value in the final solution of this cost minimization problem.

9. In the absence of corner solutions, the assumptions of economic theory make it almost impossible for there to be involuntary unemployment. This is because there is always a wage level low enough to make it profitable for some firm to hire workers willing to work at that wage.

10. Schotter, p. 77.

11. Milton Friedman, *Capitalism and Freedom* (Chicago: University of Chicago Press, 1962), pp. 85-107. Some would question Friedman's consistency and motives but that is a different question.

12. Kenneth E. Boulding, *Beyond Economics* (Ann Arbor: University of Michigan Press, 1954).

Twelve

Capitalism, Socialism, and the Common Good: A Democratic Capitalist View

JOHN W. COOPER

Reinhold Niebuhr once told the story of an enthusiastic young pacifist who was participating in a symposium on Christianity and politics. "A Christian," the young man declared, "always considers the common welfare before his own interest." Niebuhr's comment was at once stinging and affirming:

> To set self-interest and the general welfare in simple opposition is to ignore nine-tenths of the ethical issues that confront the consciences of men. . . A Christian justice will be particularly critical of the claims of the self as against the claims of the other, but it will not dismiss them out of hand.[1]

Many discussions of economic justice today illustrate the struggle to understand the relationship between self-interest and the common good. In fact the two main competing ideologies of the modern era—capitalism and socialism—can be seen as attempts to resolve this struggle. Socialism generally assumes that all self-interest is selfishness and attempts to squelch it through the means of the state—a "state" which claims to represent the common good but often merely reflects the interests of the controlling "new class." Capitalism generally assumes that self-interest is inevitable and even necessary in translating individual actions into the greater common good—in its more libertarian versions, capitalism tends to an anarchic preference for self-interest over the common good. What does Christian moral thought contribute to our understanding of this problem of the common good versus self-interest? What does Christianity teach regarding economic justice?

Even before Karl Marx elaborated his theory of socialism and his critique of capitalism Christian theologians were pronouncing judgment on the two major economic systems of the modern era. The motto of the Christian socialists in England was this: "Christianity is the religion of which socialism is the practice." Adam Smith, a moral theologian by training and profession, had made the case for the morality of capitalism in *A Theory of Moral Sentiments* (1759) and *An Inquiry into the Nature and Causes of the Wealth of Nations* (1776). Since then, the question of economic justice has grown in importance and, today, it occupies a prominent place among the moral concerns of the Christian churches.

This essay will, first of all, briefly survey the major theological responses to capitalism and socialism which have been and remain a part of Christian social doctrine. Obviously, the several great religious traditions of the world offer their own distinctive moral-theological judgments on economic systems. But I will limit myself to the range of views included within the orbit of Christianity. The broader issue of various religions' responses to economic systems was first explored by Max Weber and has been examined repeatedly by later generations of scholars.[2]

Furthermore, this essay attempts to set forth a *normative* theology of economics—one which I have designated a "democratic capitalist" approach. In other words, I will argue that democratic capitalism—that triune system which consists of a predominantly market economy, a democratic polity respectful of human rights, and a pluralistic culture—is morally and theologically superior to socialism in any of its various forms. Democratic capitalism, then, is that system which most fully recognizes and affirms constructive self-interest in the service of the common good.

Admittedly, there is some confusion in labels. Some versions of what is called "democratic socialism," in fact, conform to the above definition of democratic capitalism. Mittterand's France, for example, is a putatively "socialist" country with a predominantly capitalist economy, a democratic polity, and a pluralistic culture. France today is closer to the American model of capitalism than to those countries which display the classical characteristics of socialism: nationalization of basic industries, an economically dominant public sector, centralized economic planning and control, equal income distribution, and the total welfare state. The latter is more accurately descriptive of the Soviet type of political economy in which the "totalitarian" control of political and cultural behavior is coupled with near-total control of economic behavior.

Thus, "democratic capitalism" in its economic aspect refers to those systems which rely primarily on markets, incentives, private property, government regulation of the economy, and welfare provisions for the disadvantaged. "Socialism," on the other hand, refers to the system of political allocation of economic goods, predominant public ownership, centralized economic controls, and the total welfare state.

Catholic, Protestant, and Orthodox Views

Christian thinkers have long pondered the morality of capitalist and socialist *philosophies* as well as capitalist and socialist *systems* . The literature on this subject is vast. These issues are far from settled in the universal Christian church today and the future is likely to bring some unforeseen shifts in the debate.

Roman Catholic perspectives have been profoundly shaped by the social encyclicals of the popes, beginning with Leo XIII's *Rerum Novarum* (1891) and proceeding, most recently, to John Paul II's *Laborem Exercens* (1981). In his recent book *Freedom with Justice*, Catholic lay theologian Michael Novak has shown that this long series of papal documents manifests, on the whole, an evolving understanding and appropriation of the so-called "liberal" ideas of human rights and market economics. Yet, ironically, much of this literature is openly antagonistic toward the *philosophy* of liberalism. Liberalism, after all, originated in the more "Protestant" regions of Europe. Novak urges his fellow Catholics to reassess and more fully to appreciate liberalism and liberal institutions as they have evolved to date.[3]

Beyond the popes themselves, the list of major contributors to Catholic social teaching throughout the past several decades includes Wilhelm Emmanuel von Ketteler, Heinrich Pesch, Oswald von Nell-Bruening, Gustav Gundlach, Goetz Briefs, Franz Mueller, John A. Ryan, John Courtney Murray, and Jacques Maritain. While there were many differences between these scholars, their general approach was to posit a Catholic "third way" *between* capitalism and socialism—one which preserved the notions of private property and competitive markets even while it encouraged the labor union movement, governmental regulation of commerce and industry, and an expanding welfare state.

More recently, Roman Catholics have been confronted with an increasingly militant minority—primarily from Continental Europe, Latin America, and increasingly, the United States—which advocates *liberation theology*, the wedding of Christian idealism with "Marxist analysis." Johannes Metz, Gustavo Gutierrez, Juan Luis Segundo, Jon Sobrino, Gregory Baum, Joe Holland, and others have been harshly critical of capitalism in all its forms, and they have sought to lay a theoretical foundation for "Christian socialism" in the Third World and elsewhere. Recently, Pope John Paul II and his chief doctrinal expositor, Joseph Cardinal Ratzinger, have condemned the "more extreme" forms of liberation theology and they have warned against the use of "Marxist analysis." Rather, they call for the development of a genuinely Catholic doctrine of "liberation."[4] Other contemporary Catholics who have presented alternatives to liberation theology include Leszek Kolakowski, Michael Novak, James V. Schall, Dale Vree, and Dennis McCann.

A brief look at the contrast between liberation theology and its critics—chief among whom is the present pope—will illustrate the issues with which all the Christian churches are currently engaged.

The social teaching of John Paul II stands in clear contrast to the Marxist view of ideology and political economy. In *Freedom with Justice*, Novak concludes his discussion of papal teachings with a summary of John Paul II's "creation theology" by contrasting it with the typical tenets of liberation theology.

> Creation theology differs from liberation theology, first, in rejecting the thesis of class struggle; second, in justifying capital as the material embodiment of human labor down the ages, while stressing the priority of labor; third, in rejecting the primacy of the contrast between oppression and liberation, in favor of the contrast between the absence and the presence of creativity; fourth, in emphasizing the strict connection between the human person as the subject of labor and his right to the fruits of his labor, including the right of ownership; fifth, in highlighting the danger of nationalization, collectivization, and socialization in which a "new class" of government administration comes to power, "claiming for itself a monopoly of the administration and disposal of the means of production and not refraining even from offending basic human rights"; sixth, in interpreting the meaning of "socialization" more exactly than ever before, so as to preserve in it respect for the individual human person and his rights to private property . . .[5]

Clearly, the Roman Catholic view of economic justice will continue to develop through the official pronouncements of popes and the often conflicting analyses of its theologians.

Taken as a whole, Roman Catholicism is today at a crossroads, faced with the option of: (1) further Marxist-oriented efforts to develop liberation theology, or (2) less ideologically captive attempts further to develop the Catholic doctrines of human rights (including economic rights), freedom, and justice within the framework of government regulated market economies.

Protestantism has responded to the capitalism-socialism debate in ways that are similar, in some respects, to Catholicism. The seminal modern examination of this subject is Max Weber's *The Protestant Ethic and the Spirit of Capitalism* (1904-5). Weber linked the "unique" system of profit-seeking through the rational organization of voluntary labor with the "worldly ascetic" Protestantism which emerged most fully among the Puritans, Methodists, Pietists, and Baptists. Socialism, by contrast, emerged as a philosophy which criticized and opposed some of the harsher aspects of life during the early industrial era.

Pre-Marxian Christian socialists, like F. D. Maurice and Charles Kingsley in England, sought to enlist the moral force of Christianity in the cause of the laboring classes. They and many other Protestant theologians of the Nineteenth and early Twentieth centuries attempted definitions of capitalism and/or socialism which would be suggestive of needed reforms within existing Western societies. "Socialism" thus became, in many cases, a codeword for reformed capitalism. Among the more significant voices during this era were Washington Gladden, Horace Bushnell, Richard Ely, Josiah Strong, Walter Rauschenbusch, Ernst Troeltsch, and Karl Holl. The conceptualizations of both capitalism and socialism in this aspect of the literature are quite varied and fluid; the overriding theme of the age is a deep thirst for economic justice defined as the betterment of the conditions of life for working men and women. Phrases like "the common good" abound, but they rarely signify a desire for collectivism or revolution.

With the rise to prominence of Reinhold Niebuhr, Protestant Christianity had its first strong advocate of revolutionary socialism. The young Niebuhr was a firebrand. Having cut his political teeth in Henry Ford's Detroit, Niebuhr criticized FDR's New Deal as a ruse designed to save capitalism. Many Protestants would later take up the challenge of the early Niebuhrian *corpus* in an attempt to refine the socialist ideal. Yet, ironically, Niebuhr himself moved steadily away from the Marxian worldview as he developed his own social philosophy of "biblical realism." In the post-war period Niebuhr became the architect of the "realist" school in American foreign policy and a defender of what he called "capitalistic democracy."

Two of Niebuhr's contemporaries, Karl Barth and Paul Tillich, proclaimed their allegiance to socialism and maintained their positions throughout the ensuing decades. While their conceptions of the meaning of "socialism" were somewhat eclectic, the weight of their reputations helped to foster the socialist viewpoint within Protestantism.

Beginning with some of the founding documents of the World Council of Churches, mainline Protestant thinkers began to develop the notion of symmetry between the two major economic systems. Capitalism and communism were dubbed "equally unjust" and an attempt emerged to find a third alternative—similar to the Catholic effort. Yet, no significant "third way" has emerged in Protestant social teaching. In effect, the primary result of these efforts was the delegitimation of capitalism by Protestant theologians—the virtual reverse of the process first described by Max Weber. An untried and non-specific *socialist ideal* came to dominate most mainline Protestant circles, and the stage was set for the Protestant version of liberation theology.

German theologian Juergen Moltmann is the principal architect of liberation theology among Protestant thinkers. At one time known as the "theologian of hope," Moltmann was profoundly influenced by the neo-Marxism of the Frankfurt School in Europe. Revising the traditional epistemology and eschatology of Christianity, he posited a revolutionary version of the faith which sought the overthrow of the capitalist *status quo*. Epistemology came to be dominated by the ideas of class location and praxis, while socialism emerged as a realized eschatology. This Protestant version of liberation theology remains predominant in mainline circles today and is reflected in the writings of scholars like Harvey Cox, Robert Bellah, Gibson Winter, and John C. Bennett. Furthermore, Protestant liberation theology has forged strong alliances with some elements of feminism, pacifism, and Black theology. This phalanx of theological movements has come to be dominated more and more by extreme leftist ideology. Nothing comparable to John Paul II's warnings about "Marxist analysis" has arisen within Protestantism. Yet, an alternative movement now seems to be emerging. Among the relatively lesser-known Protestants who have criticized liberation theology and delineated alternative visions of economic justice are Peter Berger, Richard John Neuhaus, Edward Norman, Ernest Lefever, and Robert Benne.

Mainline Protestantism, like Catholicism, stands at a crossroads. It will either continue to pursue an increasingly radical liberation theology or it will begin the long task of re-evaluating the market-oriented system of democratic capitalism. Tangentially, we might note that Evangelical and Fundamentalist Protestants, having never pursued the attempt to marry Christianity to socialism, will remain pro-capitalist. In the future many will likely become even more vocal advocates of capitalism, tending, at certain points, to a rather chauvinistic and jingoistic boosterism on behalf of "free enterprise."

The Eastern Orthodox Churches have had a much different encounter with the competing systems of capitalism and socialism. This is so partly because much of eastern Europe, as well as the entire Soviet Union, has been under Communist domination throughout most of the contemporary era. In Russia itself there has been a curious mix of socialist idealism and anti-socialist nationalism in the philosophical tradition stretching from Fyodor Dostoevsky through Nicholas Berdyaev to Aleksandr Solzhenitsyn. There was, certainly, at one time, a lively intellectual interest in socialism among both secular and religious thinkers in the East. But that time has, for the most part, passed. At least since the heyday of Stalinism (or its later exposure as a genocidal system) the intellectual fascination with Marxism has been dead. What looked like utopia in theory showed itself to be the exact opposite: the gulag. The Christian-Marxist Dialogue—purportedly so popular in Eastern Europe a generation ago—has led to none of the promised "convergences" between East and West.

Today the literature from inside the concentration camps, and the writings of exiled dissidents like Solzhenitsyn and Mihajlo Mihajlov, define the terms of the search for a new social philosophy. From the Eastern viewpoint, ideological capitalism remains a primarily Western (and, therefore, suspect) phenomenon—this is so even from the most ardently anti-communist philosophers. A radically open-ended quest to redefine both social justice and man himself has begun. One cannot today predict whether Orthodox Christianity will develop its doctrine of economic justice along the lines of the Catholic and Protestant branches of the universal church. But it is certainly clear that, outside of some officials of the state-controlled churches of the Communist states, there is little interest among Orthodox believers in socialism as a societal model.

A Christian Doctrine of Economic Justice

Given the long history of attempts by Christian theologians, clergy, and laity to respond to the issues posed by the capitalism-socialism debate, what can be said about economic justice from a truly global and ecumenical Christian perspective? What type of system best serves the common good? How should the Christian begin to understand wealth, poverty, work, technology, production, distribution, consumption, socio-economic classes, the economy? I can only offer one approach to that emerging sub-discipline of theology which attempts to understand and prescribe a vision of the just political economy. Obviously, a generation or more of concerted effort by theologians from various traditions and backgrounds will be required before we can truly claim that Christians possess a theology of economics. Indeed, the variety of personal approaches and discrete insights which will arise from this endeavor will enrich the collective Christian understanding of economics and economic justice. What follows, then, is my own summary of a "democratic capitalist" theology of economics.

To begin with, Christian theology must come to terms with the reality of the world and of economic activity. Christianity is particularly suited to this task because, like Judaism and Islam, it fosters a positive attitude toward the world, nature, matter, and the human body. The religions of the Far East are much less likely to do so. Christianity has a *paradoxic* view of "this world," even while it recognizes and gives precedence to the "other world." As God's creation, the world is fundamentally good. Yet it is the arena of the struggle between good and evil. It is thus good, but corruptible. Four basic paradoxes follow from Christian presuppositions: (1) the world is good, but fallen, (2) wealth is potentially abundant, but relatively inaccessible, (3) work is fulfilling and alienating, and (4) technology is creative and destructive. In each of these propositions, an aspect of the world of economic activity is judged to be both a blessing and a curse. In each, two extremisms—those which would result from the premature resolution of the paradox—-are avoided. The complexity of the world of economic activity is revealed in these four paradoxes.

First: "The world is good, but fallen". The "fallenness" of the world, is of course, another way of stating man's propensity to sin. In economic matters, human sinfulness emerges particularly in such vices as greed and envy. Economic theory should take account of human sinfulness, especially in its understanding of the nature of self-interest. Two main types of self-interest are expressed in human relationships: that which is creative or socially beneficial and that which is destructive or socially debilitating. The egotistical, destructive, and selfish side of man is often manifest. Theft, greed, avarice, and envy are not essential to the effectiveness of any economic system—yet each is present within every human group. Both capitalist and socialist systems are harmed by destructive self-interest.

Yet, democratic capitalism seems to take better account of the positive, creative forms of self-interest than does socialism. In *The Wealth of Nations*, Adam Smith argued that men are "led by an invisible hand" to promote the common good by seeking their own success. This is so because self-interest is a motivating force for increased efficiency in the production of increasing quantities of goods and services. As the wealth of a society increases under democratic capitalist institutions, so also does the standard of living of its citizens. As efficiency increases, man is relieved from the drudgery which has for so long characterized his existence.

Christian theology needs a vocabulary for discussing self-interest and for acknowledging society's stake in the wealth created by persons when they pursue their own interests. Clearly, the old assumption that all self-interested activity is selfish and sinful is false. At the very least, we must recognize that most self-interested economic activity is directed not merely toward the good of an individual, but toward the good of his or her family. Democratic capitalism is a system which employs material incentives for the betterment of the individual and the community.

The second thesis is this: "Wealth is potentially abundant, but relatively inaccessible." Many commentators assume that the only relevant question concerning economic justice is: "How is wealth distributed?" Yet, wealth can only be distributed if it is first produced. Therefore, Christianity needs an ethic of production as well as an ethic of distribution. Democratic capitalism clearly outproduces socialism. Less well known is the fact that democratic capitalism also distributes wealth more widely and generously than socialism. All societies employ proportional compensation based upon the varying skills and energies of workers and managers. Only democratic capitalism states distribute wealth more evenly and can raise dramatically the spendable income and standard of living of the masses. Stagnant socialist economies offer affluence only to the political elite.

Wealth, or its possession and use, poses another problem which any theology or economics ought to address—the problem of consumption. The Western world has a problem with consumerism—both 1) the pattern of over-consumption and ecologically destructive waste to which modern Western societies are particularly prone and 2) the ideological reduction of man to *homo oeconomicus*. The present pope is a tireless critic of consumerism. The problem of consumerism suggests that Christianity needs an ethic of consumption. Several denominations, such as the Mennonite and Church of the Brethren bodies, have taken the lead in nurturing an anti-consumerist lifestyle called "simple living."

Wealth is only *potentially* abundant, which is to say "relatively inaccessible." Given the proper incentives and a relatively free market for goods, services, and labor the majority of members in any given society can and will produce more than they consume. The disabled can thus be cared for—out of the excess—and the commonwealth will grow. While it is important to recognize the very real ecological limits of the earth, it is nevertheless important to recognize the vast potential for innovation and expansion inherent in the *oeconomie*, the household of the earth. When, for example, people confront the limited supplies and usefulness of fossil fuels, they respond by developing alternative sources of energy. Market competition is crucial to this scenario, it is the most powerful force for innovation ever devised. By contrast, government "planning" is wasteful and often counter-productive. The paradoxic qualities of the world and wealth suggest the complexity of economic realities.

The thesis that wealth is potentially abundant suggests one of the most important features of the theology of democratic capitalism. Democratic capitalism is committed to the perpetual improvement of the living conditions of the poor. The "preferential option for the poor" means precisely that: an economically just system provides an ample sustenance and the potential for prosperity to the poor *without* thereby eliminating the possibilities for greater prosperity for other socio-economic groups. To do otherwise would plunge society into class warfare. To believe otherwise would be to surrender to a Malthusian cynicism which is unnecessary, false, and unChristian. Democratic capitalism encourages the prospering of the poor primarily through incentives, markets, and private property. Through its welfare programs, democratic capitalism provides a permanent sustenance for the permanently disabled or infirm and a temporary "social safety net" for the temporarily disabled.

This is the third thesis: "Work is fulfilling and alienating." Work, also, is a paradoxical reality. It is, as John Paul II argues, essential to human dignity. That which a person creates with his hand or his mind is an extension of his very being. Work is fulfilling. Yet, all work is alienating as well. Any job entails a demand-level and a routine which can be, at best, merely tolerated.

The democratic capitalist doctrine that each person is entitled to enjoy and dispose of the fruits of his labors, after taxes, is one way that the dignity of work is preserved. Worker "input" into management practices and, even more, worker ownership promise ever greater opportunities for humanizing work. Socialism, by contrast, requires all to work for the state, taking "for each according to his ability" and returning, in practice, a miserly and bare subsistence. The extent of a person's political "connections," not his *work*, determines the amount and kind of economic rewards he receives.

Finally: "technology is creative and destructive." Technology is the last of the paradoxical phenomena with which Christianity must wrestle. Much intellectual energy has been wasted in futile arguments concerning the morality of this or that technology. Clearly, technology itself is morally neutral. The uses to which technology is put determine its moral status. In fact, technology can be dramatically constructive or detrimental to human life and happiness. As technological capabilities proliferate so does man's capacity for good *and* evil. No better example of this can be found than nuclear technology—it gives us our most destructive weapon and, at the same time, some of the most promising new scientific breakthroughs (in medicine, energy, transportation, space exploration, and so forth).

Capitalism vs. Socialism

What do these four paradoxes teach us about economic justice? When should we emphasize one side of a paradox and not the other? There are no simple solutions to the complex issues of economic justice. But we must begin to nurture a nuanced understanding of the world of economic activity. We must then proceed to compare the *ideals* and the *realities* of the two competing systems.

Often a writer will compare capitalism unfavorably with socialism because, intentionally or unintentionally, he has *contrasted* the reality of capitalism with the *ideal* of socialism. As each new socialist experiment of the Twentieth century has turned sour—in the Soviet Union, China, Cuba, Vietnam, Tanzania, Nicaragua, and elsewhere—the advocates of socialism have fallen back upon defending an ideal "not yet realized." By contrast, actual capitalist societies always display some faults. As the reality of democratic capitalism has emerged over the past several decades, socialist intellectuals have tried to explain the "true nature" of the capitalist system. If, say the socialists, the living standards of the lower classes have been raised, then they have simply been co-opted—"embourgeoisement"—and the rich capitalists have continued to confiscate wealth that is not rightfully theirs. If human rights and political freedom, as these are traditionally defined, are more prevalent under democratic capitalist regimes, then these rights are, in fact, bogus—while true, collective rights, or "the rights of the peoples" are embodied in socialist regimes.

When we *honestly* compare the realities of capitalist and socialist systems in today's world, it seems clear that one path encourages freedom and justice while the other leads to totalitarianism. During an age when socialism was only an ideal and had not been put into practice, it was understandable that some persons of good will were convinced by socialism's claims to moral superiority. Now that there have been scores of socialist "experiments" in the Twentieth century and roughly half of the world's 160 nations declare themselves to be "socialist," the situation has changed. Where socialism is dominant, and to the degree that it is dominant, freedom and justice wither. Among that minority of nations where democracy and respect for human rights are the norm—the human rights "watchdog" organization Freedom House identifies approximately two dozen—some form of capitalism is also the norm.

Does democratic capitalism as we have defined it serve the common good? Jacques Maritain eloquently expressed the Catholic ideal of the common good:

The common good is common because it is received in persons, each of whom is as a mirror of the whole. Among the bees, there is a public good, namely the good functioning of the hive, but

not a common good . . .
The common good of the city is neither the mere collection of
private goods, nor the proper good of a whole which, like . . . the
hive with respect to its bees, relates the parts to itself alone and
sacrifices them to itself.[6]

It is in the *systems* of democratic capitalism that one finds expression of this personalism, which is neither individualist nor
collectivist. And it is in the socialist "experiment" that one finds
hive-like behavior and the sacrifice of individual persons to
some revolutionary ideal or another.

No one need claim that the democratic capitalist nations have
achieved perfect justice in order to recognize the vast gulf which
exists between the capitalist and socialist experiments. It is not
even necessary to deny the legitimacy of certain "socialistic" reforms of capitalism, such as "welfare state" programs. It *is* important to recognize as moral the principles upon which democratic capitalism rests. A combination of incentives, markets,
private property, social regulations, and welfare provisions can,
in fact, lay the groundwork for an economically prosperous society which also nurtures economic justice.

Democratic capitalism is a system which institutionalizes the
quest for justice. Just as the three branches of the federal government operate in a "check and balance" relationship to one another, so also do the three components of democratic capitalism—the political, the economic, and the moral-cultural
—comprise a unity-in-tension. The political elite, the economic
elite, and the moral-cultural elite live in different worlds. They
operate by different assumptions. Yet, they each have a claim on
the public conscience and on issues related to the common
good. When an issue arises, the viewpoints of all three sectors
are aired in the media, the court of public opinion. If one group
feels its opposition to any single proposal strongly enough it ex-
ercises a *de facto* veto. When, as in most cases, the issue is not
so critical, a compromise is struck which represents a balance of
the interests of each of the three sectors.

By contrast, under socialism (both in theory and in practice), the political, economic, and moral-cultural power of a nation is concentrated in a single group—"the leaders of the revolution." That group, because it faces no other power center which might correct its impulses, proceeds to impose its will upon society. This is often the point at which basic human rights are disregarded. "Loyalty" to a social model, a vision of the future, a "revolution," becomes the excuse for unspeakable violations of human rights.

Loyalty is a powerful force in human affairs. This emotion is not entirely unworthy. Every polity needs a civil religion. But what is also needed is a principle of self-criticism—and the institutional mechanisms necessary to place power in check. This is the secret of democratic capitalism. It is no accident that success in implementing democracy and respect for human rights go hand-in-hand with economic prosperity for the masses and cultural pluralism. *Freedom* is a leaven which raises the whole loaf.[7]

Conclusion

Democratic capitalism has proven its moral superiority to socialism in the arena of practical application. It is *not* a "Christian" solution to the problem of social organization—there is no "Christian" political system, no "Christian" economics, no "Christian" boundary to cultural expression. But democratic capitalism *conforms* to Christianity's vision of man and society. The Christian view of man as essentially free and responsible before God and society to "do justice, love mercy, and walk humbly" is confirmed by democratic capitalism—even more so by its institutions than by its ideology. Christian theology suggests the paradoxical nature of the world and of economics. It assumes that wealth is potentially abundant but relatively inaccessible. And it implicitly defends *as moral* those systems which actually produce greater amounts of wealth and distribute them more broadly while respecting the essential freedom of each person.

The various Christian bodies are today debating their positions on the fundamental questions of politics and economics. It is imperative that the widest range of clerical and lay expertise be brought to bear on these crucial issues. The capitalist-socialist debate is too important to be left solely in the hands of ideologues. And it must not be debated in a theoretical vacuum which ignores the actual experimental evidence currently available. Once Christians and other persons of good will have an opportunity to weigh the full range of issues, they will surely reject the socialist option and get on with the task of shaping democratic capitalism into ever closer conformity with the demands of justice.

Notes

1. Reinhold Niebuhr, "Justice and Love," *Christianity and Society* 15 (Fall 1950): pp. 6-8; reprinted in D. B. Robertson, ed., *Love and Justice: Selections from the Shorter Writings of Reinhold Niebuhr* (Gloucester, Mass.: Peter Smith, 1976), pp. 27-29.

2. See, e.g., James Finn, ed., *Global Economics and Religion* (New Brunswick, N.J.: Transaction Books, 1983).

3. Michael Novak, *Freedom with Justice: Catholic Social Thought and Liberal Institutions* (New York: Harper & Row, 1984), see esp. Part II.

4. See Cardinal Joseph Ratzinger, "Liberation Theology," *Catholicism in Crisis* 2 (September 1984): pp. 37-41.

5. Novak, *Freedom with Justice*, p. 162; in the fifth point Novak is quoting John Paul II, *Laborem Exercens*, 14.

6. Jacques Maritain, *The Person and the Common Good* (Notre Dame: University of Notre Dame Press, 1966), pp. 49-51.

7. For a fuller *apologia* for "democratic pluralism and human rights" see John W. Cooper, *The Theology of Freedom: The Legacy of Jacques Maritain and Reinhold Niebuhr* (Macon, Ga.: Mercer University Press, 1985).

Thirteen

The Common Good—And The Emerging Longer Term Historical Context

GAR ALPEROVITZ

Buried within virtually every discussion of social justice issues is a silent assumption—namely, that the emerging political-economic context into which the debate is projected will be roughly the same as that which has characterized the recent past. When we think of the possibilities for the coming period, we tend inevitably to project previous trends; we "remember" the future.

But what if the future is not likely to be a projection of the recent past?

We are fast approaching the Twenty-First century. The related issues of "a preferential option for the poor," and "the common good," I believe, can best be explored by first assessing the emerging longer term historical context for thought and action.

272

The Stalemating of Traditional Reform

The obvious starting point for inquiry is the collapse of liberalism as a serious political force. The problems go far beyond those posed by the conservatism of the Reagan Administration: Thomas Edsell's recent *The New Politics of Inequality* documents how the wealthy and the corporations enforce a politics *among Democrats as well as Republicans* which blocks significant reform. This power is not new; the deeply conservative *ongoing* reality is demonstrated by such real world "outcomes" of the political-economic system as the essentially stable (and highly regressive) distribution of income which has allocated roughly 4-6 percent of income to the bottom 20 percent of families; and 41-46 percent (depending on definitions used) to the top 20 percent *year in and year out, through both Republican and Democratic Presidencies, for at least four decades.*

That the basic distributional pattern has not yielded significantly to "reform" for very long periods of time points to much more fundamental blockages—as does the fact that the American income distribution is one of the most regressive among advanced industrial nations. The distributional pattern is also worsening, not improving: The top 20 percent gained nearly 9 percent in real income in the first four years of the Reagan Administration; the bottom 20 percent lost roughly 8 percent.

Other "outcome" measures illustrate the deeper, ongoing stalemate of traditional reform strategies—and put the fight between liberals and conservatives into sharp perspective: For much of the postwar period the percentage of the nation's total resources allocated directly to the poor for income maintenance, food stamps, welfare and the like has varied between roughly 7/10ths of one percent of GNP and 2 percent of GNP. It is currently approximately 1.7 percent. If the main indirect programs targeted at the poor (e.g. medicaid) are included, a generous estimate of the upper limit would reach between 3 percent and 4 percent of GNP. In what's left of the "war" on poverty, politicians and the press regularly *dramatize* what are in reality pitifully small skirmishes; the revealing truth is that: (1) at any point in time the fight is over tiny fractions of much less than 1 percent of GNP; (2) the overall struggle is essentially deadlocked and moving up and down only very slightly relative to GNP (currently, down); and (3) at best 96-97 percent of our national resources (and, in direct terms, 98-99 percent) *are simply excluded from the debate for all practical purposes.*

Furthermore, though well-educated black professionals have won greater access to economic and political positions, huge numbers of blacks are still economically disenfranchised. There seems no way to mobilize black voters to achieve significantly different distributional policies. Attempts by the Democrats—even when they elect a President—to move serious resources to the bottom end of the income distribution open them to a "divide and conquer" conservative political strategy. Further, the United States is the only advanced industrial nation in which the working class is fundamentally, not marginally, racially divided—and this further undercuts the power of traditional reform.

The Collapse of Growth

The idea of "progress" which underlies many social justice strategies was sustained during much of the early postwar period by strong economic growth. *Even though the relative distribution of income and resources did not significantly shift,* growth improved the lives of most Americans. With everyone on an escalator, the fight over who stood ahead of whom—and how far ahead—could be substantially ignored.

But the escalator has slowed down dramatically in recent years, and in many areas has come to a halt—a fact which closes off another avenue of traditional progressive hope. Indeed, as the final decade of the Twentieth Century approaches, many people are moving downward. There have been eight recessions since World War II and unemployment has deepened each decade. The most recent recession (in 1980-81) reached the near depression level of 10.7 percent unemployment. The dismaying overall postwar trend is ominous: Unemployment averaged 4.5

percent during the 1950s, 4.8 percent during the 1960s, 6.2 percent during the 1970s, and 8 percent during the 1980s (so far.)

The current "recovery," in fact, simply returned the economy to the 7 percent range which existed before the Reagan Administration took office and permitted unemployment to rise to 10.7 percent. For most of the postwar period the 7 percent range itself was regarded as deep recession; that it is now regarded as "recovery" is a further indication of how expectations have been lowered in the face of conservative power. And, of course, it is only a matter of time before the next recession.

Other indicators tell the same story: The overall growth of the GNP slipped from 4.2 percent during the 1960s, to 3.2 percent during the 1970s, and *if* there is no recession and 3 percent growth from here on, the 1980s will average less than 2.5 percent. Since World War II productivity growth has steadily fallen from 3.3 percent per year (1947-65) to a mere 1 percent (1977-84). In 1985 productivity "growth" turned negative. In the key manufacturing sector productivity growth in the years from 1977 to 1983 averaged 1.2 percent per year—one-half Germany's growth rate (2.5%), one-third the French rate (3.5%), and less than one-third the Japanese rate (3.9%).

Serious students of the business cycle point out that with the debatable (brief) exception of the years between 1925 and 1929, at no time during the 20th century has the U. S. economy enjoyed sustained economic prosperity other than in periods of war or war's aftermath. Deepening cyclicality (and occasional financial panic, especially in 1907) characterized the economy from the Spanish-American War at the turn of the century until World War I. During and after World War I (with the exception of the severe recession of 1920-21 and the smaller downturns of 1924 and 1927) military spending and deferred postwar demand financed by war savings helped stimulate the economy. Additionally, American exports took over many former British, German and French markets during the war. And wartime military spending helped expand major areas for new postwar investment in the auto and airplane industries.

The stock-market crash of 1929 and the Great Depression returned the nation to the earlier unstable pattern of the first decades of the Century with a vengence—before World War II in Europe began to pull the global economy up. The second World War and subsequent military engagements in Korea and Vietnam had an even greater uplifting power in the postwar period than World War I. Until very recently, in fact, economic affairs have been dominated by war's direct, indirect and aftermath effects:

First, war and war spending stimulated the economy not only during 1939-45, but also during the Korean and Vietnam Wars: It is often forgotten that military spending was 13.2% of the economy in 1952—and averaged 10.7 percent for the entire decade of the 1950s. The fact that it has now slipped (despite much public debate over the absolute size of the defense budgets) to roughly 6.6 percent of the G.N.P.—just about half the level when Eisenhower took office—has much to do with the sagging trend of unemployment in the final quarter of the Century.

Second, the aftermath of war helped American industry by opening up large-scale investment and export opportunities in Germany, Japan, and all of war-ravaged Europe. (The Marshall Plan was only the largest and most widely discussed symbol of the explosion of economic activity which war left in its wake.)

Third, as a direct result of war American exports went literally unchallenged in global markets for much of the first two postwar decades—and when they were challenged, competitors had the difficult task of dislodging well entrenched in-place American distribution systems. (We forget that the other side of the coin of the so-called "new economic challenge" Japan and Germany now offer is the simple fact that America had a free hand in world markets for a very long time because war had eliminated the competition.)

Fourth, war and defense also helped open up new investment opportunities in jet aircraft, electronics and other domestic industries stimulated by military procurement.

Finally, war provided the political rationale for tough measures to control inflation at high levels of employment. In all three major modern engagements, wage-price controls were authorized by Congress and implemented by the President. Though political support for such measures slowly eroded in each decade, and though they had many administrative problems, Presidents Roosevelt, Truman and Nixon all used controls to facilitate very high levels of production and employment. One measure of the waning effect of war is the fact that Jimmy Carter did *not* have a politically viable rationale to stabilize the inflation that was his political undoing—and that as a result the inflation of the seventies was only controlled by sending the economy into a near depression.

Those who accept the easy optimism of the theory that the current recovery promises a steady upward future should reflect on these facts (and the end of the aftermath effects of war—including especially the re-emergence of Japan and Germany as major competitors.) When the next recession comes, it will likely be extremely severe. Moreover, the debt crisis has made Third World nations very weak customers for American goods, and the weakness of the European recovery adds to the factors which increase the instability and volatility of global (and American) economic affairs. Finally, the possibility of a major financial crisis—given the bloated nature of domestic and international debt, and the weakness of many banks—cannot be discounted.

Liberal economists once argued that we had mastered the ideas—and the politics!—to keep the country moving upward; recently conservatives have sounded the same theme. But the longer term evidence confounds this optimistic idea. The title of a recent book by Felix Rohaytn is apt: America was dominant in world economic affairs, he points out, mainly during a brief *Twenty Year Century*. In any serious historical perspective only the two decades between 1945 and 1965 can truly be deemed successful periods of development.

Viewing the recession and unemployment patterns dispassionately, in fact, it appears that the third quarter of the Century (encompassing the "twenty year" century) may be the odd man out in the Twentieth Century taken as a whole. The final decades seem likely to be less a continuation of progress on economic matters than a return to an earlier, more disquieting reality. The period in many ways is, in fact, beginning to resemble the painful pre-World War I years—and there are even echoes of the economically volatile final years of the Nineteenth Century.

This is not to say that a major depression is likely (though it is possible)—nor that none of the New Deal and other economic reforms have meaning. It is rather to observe that the economic power of such reforms, absent war spending and its aftermath, has been greatly exaggerated . . . and is fading.

The Present in Perspective

Such long-term political-economic trends establish a difficult context for proposals involving "the common good" and "a preferential option for the poor." Arthur Schlesinger, Jr. and other liberal writers recurrently urge that there is some inherent cycle of political activity which operates in American life: periods of conservatism are followed by periods of liberal resurgence. The pendulum of politics may swing back and forth, but ultimately there is an underlying forward, progressive political thrust to history. Such a view, explicitly or implicitly, still tends to govern the thinking of many reformers. But it is just this assumption that is called into question by the patterns we have reviewed.

An alternative view of recent American history runs roughly as follows: The spate of reform measures which provided the informing experience of recent progressive theory occurred primarily as a result of the collapse of the economy prior to and during the New Deal. Thereafter, the deeply conservative nature of the American political and social system was masked by the prosperity of the postwar period. The reality is that during both the Truman and Eisenhower eras the dominance of the "conservative coalition" of Republicans and Southern Democrats made impossible any significant extension of New Deal reforms, particularly as they affected low and moderate income groups on distributional and employment matters.

The (slightly) premature capture of the Republican party by extreme conservatives in 1964 set up a momentary but exceptional opportunity: Lyndon Johnson's defeat of Barry Goldwater gave Democrats a very large—but temporary—majority in the House of Representatives. This allowed a skillful President to en-act the Great Society programs: the war on poverty, Medicare, Medicaid, etc. Though the programs in turn established constituencies which thereafter fought tooth and nail to hold on to gains they had not previously been able to achieve, ultimately the underlying conservatism of the nation was re-asserted. It was Jimmy Carter who began the movement towards cutting back social programs, and though neither Republicans nor Democrats can yet take on the elderly, Ronald Reagan mainly galvanized and accelerated a retreat from the mid-1960s interlude that was historically inevitable, and already underway.

The argument is obviously more complicated than a capsule presentation can suggest. We need to distinguish carefully, for instance, between those ongoing reforms (e.g. Social Security, environmental protection) which have been supported by the middle class—and those which deal with the lower class. The main seeming exception, however, proves the rule: The Civil Rights experience forced the nation to accept procedural reforms to allow blacks with education into the middle class, but it collapsed when redistributional or job issues were addressed. A more elaborate form of the argument leads also to the conclusion that we live not so much in an era of *new* conservatism, but rather in a period of *return to the basic conservatism of the system*. Contrary to another political observer, Richard Reeves (whose recent book describes "the Reagan detour"), it is the years between 1965-75—not the years since 1980—which appear as the interruption in a remarkably stable postwar pattern.

There is, however, a fundamental difference between the earlier postwar years and the present period: the war and war-related boom are over and the world economy is facing increasing difficulties. The trajectory of slower and more episodic growth, and rising unemployment, is likely to continue—and with these come ever greater pressures on the political-economic system.

Addressing Deeper Problems

The prospects for implementing progressive measures in a context of political stalemate and deepening economic pain are exceedingly limited: The inherent conservatism of the system is compounded by economic difficulties—and racial divisions further weaken the impulse towards reform.

Though the true depth of America's problems has rarely been confronted, the possibility that we face a long, even permanent, stalemate is beginning slowly to sink in. Two widely discussed documents—the draft Catholic Bishops' pastoral letter on the economy and a recent book by sociologist Robert Bellah and associates, *Habits of the Heart*—illustrate some of the questions which must be clarified in assessing the relationship of social justice issues to alternative contexts and alternative theories of social change.

Habits of the Heart moves beyond superficial optimism to argue that the difficulties of the political-economic system derive from a deep cultural flaw—what the authors term "radical individualism." Our inability to develop a politics of conscience which could alleviate the pain of the poor, our growing indifference to the unemployed, our quiet retreat on matters of racial and, increasingly, sexual discrimination—all, in the view of the authors, reveal that our "habits of the heart" (Alexis de Tocqueville's term for cultural mores) no longer sustain a powerful interest in the values of an equitable community. At the core of our consciousness, we do not even know how to speak about what it means to be creatures of a common culture, tradition, history. Accordingly, we do not have ways in which to understand the requirements of a viable politics of mutual concern.

Though Bellah and his associates are supportive of many commonly discussed reform measures, they are skeptical that there are meaningful short cuts to a politics that can achieve equity, social justice, democratic participation and the common good *in the absence of a transformation of American culture*. Hence, their appeal, first, for a dialogue on *this* question, and, second, their support for educational and institutional reforms which might slowly help knit together and renew a conception of community which can "counter-vail" against the destructive tendencies of radical individualism.

The Catholic Bishops, in both drafts of their letter on the economy, operate from a very similar set of assumptions; their argument (though different in many particulars) is a religiously based expression of the theoretical view that a reform of ideas, cultural mores, and "habits of the heart"—whether occasioned by secular reflection or religious moral concern—is *the* central requirement of a renewal of a politics of social justice.

The essential viewpoint of both documents has considerable appeal—especially for those whose own work concerns cultural matters: educators, religious leaders, writers. The fundamental hope is, through a renewal of ideas and attitudes, that the common good and a preferential option for the poor can both ultimately be achieved. There is also a fundamental assumption that the emerging context is permissive for change.

These ideas may be contrasted with a different, more radical viewpoint: namely, that the problems we face are far more deep-seated. Therefore, attempts to reform culture without a simultaneous direct assault on (a) the dominant economic institutions of the society, and (b) the situational logic and motivational requirements of capitalism, must fail. The institutional and systemic view would regard well-meaning arguments which emphasize cultural reform as not only in error, but seriously misleading: It is an approach which confuses people as to what must be done if basic problems are ever to be solved. Hence, the problems (and pain associated with them) must grow. Violence and political polarization are a likely result of failure to face reality. The longer we promulgate illusions about the nature of our difficulties in the emerging historical context, the worse they will become.

If *Habits of the Heart* urges a change in individualism, and the Catholic Bishops urge a renewal of concern out of religious conviction, the more radical view would urge a change in the system as essential if social justice is to be achieved—however long that may take, and however difficult the task. The contrast between the viewpoints may also be understood as one concerning the timing and priorities of change: The idea that the common good can only be obtained by changing the form of the community (or system) first is radically different from an immediate emphasis on reforms to improve the lot of the poor in the existing system.

Transitional Documents?

Both of the two documents we have briefly reviewed are instructive because they mirror the general approach many reformers take to social justice questions. Despite the essential caution of their basic arguments, however, it is striking how the new context has forced the authors of each to lean toward the radical conclusion: *Habits of the Heart*, for instance, repeatedly acknowledges that the major institutions of economic life encourage a narrow materialism, fuel a radically self-seeking individualism, erode the inherent rewards of craftsmenship and meaningful work, and tend to destroy what remain of many neighborhood and community bonds. The book also traces this institutional logic—and its power to affect individual motivation, character and experience—to the larger systemic logic of capitalism: that the over-riding drive of profit-seeking, of economic growth, of materialism are inherent features of the way the system operates. Personal self-seeking behavior, and individualistic ideas, egotism and greed, come with the territory as it were.

Individual consciousness is, of course, narrowed not only out of hunger for more, but out of fear of less: The economic system's recessions, depressions, plant-closings, and general instability teach the individual that it is better to hold on to what one has—or attempt to add to it—*today* because what little one has may be lost tomorrow. Similarly, private investment decisions regularly pull the rug out from under families and communities which have come to depend upon individual firms. Little wonder that "taking care of Number One" is an idea that people take seriously, very seriously indeed, in such circumstances.

It is not difficult to find extensive and sophisticated supporting analyses of the destructive power of the market (two of the best are Karl Polyani's classic *The Great Transformation* and, in the American context, Garry Wills trenchant critique in *Nixon Agonistes*. Nor are these ideas profound or difficult: They are the common experience of most Americans who understand that the "rat-race" is real, that "the system" has power—and who know in very practical terms the consequences of disobeying its major rules of operation. On these basic matters not only does the emperor have no clothes; he hasn't been wearing any for a long time.

But if the fundamental economic institutions are at the root of many of our problems, and if the operating logic of the system sustains and intensifies the realities which destroy community and press us all towards "radical individualism," is it possible to avoid the radical question? Can we expect serious change without a change in the institutions and the operating logic of the system?

Habits of the Heart comes very close to this question, but in significant part because it implicitly assumes the emerging context will be a continuation of the relative stability of the recent past, it does not confront it squarely. The book sticks closely to cultural problems isolated from the deeper economic trajectory. In doing so, however, it does challenge several illusions which stand in the way of the broader argument that America must face the need to reconstitute an integrated conception and experience of community at all levels: individualist "expressive" therapies which encourage honesty of communication and integrity of relationships are shown to be another way to escape *individually* from the larger problem. So, too, the workaholic to whom money-making and career once meant everything—but who now looks almost exclusively to family life for personal meaning—is recognized as seeking refuge and avoiding community. The radical organizer who "empowers" individuals to obtain their rights may help them achieve the fair self-interest of the poor; he does not, however, thereby automatically build a broader conception of community which transcends empowered individual self-interest. Even those who in the name of community attempt to rehabilitate a nostalgic idea of localism based on earlier traditions avoid the question of how to build community in the here and now.

Given its narrow assumptions about the emerging longer term context, and despite a thoughtful general argument, it is not surprising that when the book comes to prescription it begins to stumble. A cultural transformation is required to achieve a new "balance" of community and individual; we need to recover "our social ecology"; we need to "reconstitute the social world." The difficulty with such ways of formulating the importance of the idea of the common good is not with what is said but what is so conspicuously left unsaid. The eminent European cultural historian, George Mosse, once observed that American liberals were "socialists of the heart"—he meant that they wished the egalitarian and communitarian outcomes of a socialist vision *without facing the hard-headed and difficult political and institutional requirements*. Another historian, William Appleman Williams, in his *Contours of American History* and other writings, has specifically taken up the question of whether the strategy of attempting to rehabilitate ideas and culture without simultaneously challenging the underlying institutions and logic of the system can succeed. Williams' conclusion is that it cannot, but whether one agrees or disagrees with his historical research, the challenge posed by this question must be faced as we enter the approach period to a new century.

It is a painful challenge, and it must be stated precisely: The question is *not* whether a rehabilitation of the ideal of community as opposed to the ideal of radical individualism is important. About this, many who urge values of equity and social justice would agree: The reconstitution of a coherent ideal of a mutually responsible community is at the core of the idea of the common good. The precise question is whether advocating this strategy is misleading in the absence of clarity about whether or not much more fundamental change is needed—and in the absence of a stategy which explicitly *integrates* cultural, institutional and political efforts. If one agrees (a) that a transformation of culture is necessary, but (b) it is unlikely that this can be achieved absent very fundamental changes in the system (even if over a long period), the issue needs to be confronted, and the implications explored.

This assessment, in turn, depends upon how we understand the period of history into which we are living. Nor is the problem avoided by urging a transformation of culture as (implicitly or explicitly) a "first step" towards the larger conclusion—even if that were intended. In *Habits of the Heart*, it is not: the stated goal is very traditional, despite the new philosophical approach—namely, a re-energizing of reform to achieve a better "balance" (again, this term is key) to control the existing corporate system, not to transcend it. In places their language is quite slippery, but the authors are fully aware the approach is closely related to European and Japanese "corporatism." And the rather modest specific economic proposals, including neighborhood and community corporations and Federal chartering of corporations, have been urged by many reformers for at least two decades (See my book, *Rebuilding America*).

The Catholic Bishops' letter is more forthright: First of all, it is about the economic system. Second, rooted as it is in the more communitarian tradition of Catholic social thought, the Bishops (and various Papal writings upon which they draw) are less fearful about taking on capitalism itself. In the encyclical on human work, *Laborem Exercens*, John Paul II states in paragraph 14:

> [T]he position of "rigid" capitalism continues to remain unacceptable, namely the position that defends the exclusive right to private ownership of the means of production as an untouchable "dogma" of economic life. The principle of respect for work demands that this right should undergo a constructive revision both in theory and in practice...

Thirdly, the letter understands the economy as a historical fact—a system that is not immutable; and it is also more aware of growing pain in the emerging context. Nevertheless, the letter's basic view of how to achieve both the common good and a preferential option for the poor is highly confusing. In urging both an extension and refinement of traditional social programs (especially for the poor) and in proposing new, more collectivist strategies (for the common good), the Bishops cloud a number of fundamental questions concerning the depth of the current stalemate, the nature of the emerging context, and the resulting implications. Their "reform" ideas are offered side by side with proposals for cooperatives, community corporations, worker-owned firms, and local, regional and national economic planning put forward explicitly as initial efforts aimed at building a new economic system.

Accordingly, although the Bishops suggest concepts which imply that the common good and a preferential option for the poor might ultimately require transcending capitalism, they do not forge ahead into this controversial terrain. Their fundamental premise is essentially the same as *Habits of the Heart*: If we can reconstitute a more moral, humane and deeply rooted vision of community, then perhaps one day we can (it is hoped) bend the existing capitalist system to meet these ends. The leaders of the major corporations, and the corporate system, are to be in not outside the consensus they urge.

Neither Liberal Nor Conservative Nor Radical

Further perspective on the central question may be gained by attempting to think through some of the possibilities for the decades to and through the end of the Twentieth Century and on into the new century beyond. The notion of a deep stalemate implies that neither liberal nor conservative nor radical politics is likely to do much to solve fundamental problems during the coming generation. The platitudes of the current Administration and the nostrums of the Democratic opposition are both likely to be called into question. Projecting the dreary scenario implicit in the longer trends suggests the period of history we are entering may well be characterized by:

—A continuation of recurrent, ever deepening recessions—i. e. an extension of the pattern of the eight recessions since World War II during which unemployment worsened each decade.

—The continual circulation of what jobs there are, musical chairs fashion, around America's internal Continental empire—so that at one moment New England might be down and the Southwest up, then the Far West down and the South up, and so on. There would likely be periodic severe dislocations in specific industries and localities (e.g. farm, steel, oil, textile, etc.), but the young would move on geographically, chasing the moving jobs and blaming themselves for failure. Occasionally, in bad economic moments the nation might exchange one President for another, but mainly the electorate would simply observe the faltering up-down cyclical process, and the job rotation.

—Periodic urban explosions, and some domestic terrorism, when, for instance, black American youth watching their counterparts on television in South Africa also decided to try to take matters into their own hands as conditions in the ghetto worsened. The sporadic and shifting terrorism would likely be the occasion of sporadic and shifting repression. Total repression would be unnecessary.

—Periodic mild wars of intervention—and an occasional large one—might be followed by periods of public discontent and weariness which would restrain policy-makers until the next outburst. Perhaps the time between wars would lengthen—as the space between Korea and Vietnam was longer than the space between World War II and Korea. Perhaps, over time, slowly public discontent would limit major interventions.

—Occasional major confrontations between the Superpowers would bring the world ever closer to a nuclear exchange but would continue to avoid disaster. The arms race would continue, slowed occasionally by public protest and mounting costs.

—Political oscillation would continue between Democrats and Republicans, with neither able to muster solutions to the system's major problems, but neither fully collapsing. Republicans would proclaim very tough rhetoric, but on balance intervene in significant ways abroad less (restrained by the loud objections of Democrats); Democrats, vulnerable to the charge of being soft on Communism, would end up intervening more often, thus continuing the historic pattern of the 20th Century.

—The slow delegitimation of existing political parties and the economic system would occur—as no group or party would be able to solve the steadily accumulating economic, social, and military problems—and as cultural strains, together with a moral crisis, developed and expanded—between black and white and brown, between religious fundamentalism (left and right) and secular politics, between new age and post-materialist younger generations and the old.

Though other possibilities clearly exist, in my judgment, the context of a *continuing stalemate* is the most likely enduring and enveloping context of the coming period of our history— certainly far more likely, given the underlying trends, than sustained conservative economic gains or a resurgence of progressive reform powerful enough to change basic distributional and employment patterns in more than marginal ways. Such a context is one of historical decay—and potential instability: As some have observed, domestic violence and repression could easily tilt into some form of fascism, and dovish opposition at home to intervention abroad could bring upon itself severe repression. With time and a sustained nuclear build-up there is a statistical liklihood of human, political, or mechanical error leading one day to a thermonuclear exchange.

Pierre Proudhon in 1860 wrote: "All the traditions are worn out, all the creeds abolished; but the new program is not yet *ready*...Hence what I call *the dissolution*. This is the cruellest moment in the life of societies..." Unfortunately, beyond the present moment of seeming calm there may well be fundamental similarities between his time and the period of history we have begun to enter.

Reconstruction

If one believes the economic system is on the whole moving positively, and in the right direction—then what is needed is to help others up into that system. The "common good" is achieved, largely if not entirely, by improving *what is* for all to enjoy. The underlying premise of liberal reform is that social and economic progress *in the existing form of community is possible*, that any stalemates are temporary, and may be overcome.

If, however, the stalemate is deep and fundamental, then there is no significant possibility of a preferential option for the poor within the system. To the extent that the moral integrity of the community as a whole requires that the lot of the poor be improved, the "common good" cannot be achieved without a fundamental change in the system.

It may be that this is impossible. Or that it may take a long time, a very long time. In the first case, those who affirm values of the common good which require that the poor be helped have no option other than to assert their moral vision and stand fast (or, of course, abandon their affirmation of the value.) In the second case, they must build for the long haul—again, if, that is, they affirm the value.

If the stalemate and a need to change the system are acknowledged, issues of strategy come immediately to the fore—as do questions regarding the form and structure of alternatives. Since most Americans have implicitly assumed that the form of the American community would likely endure for a very long time (for all practical planning purposes, implicitly "forever")—give or take a minor reform—we have little real experience with either question.

Before his death the philosopher Martin Buber attempted to define a strategic concept which he termed "reconstruction"— an idea different from reform and different also from revolution. Reconstruction as a strategy aimed to draw upon whatever strains of tradition, values, experience, and spiritual strength that existed to slowly rebuild the conception *and the material institutions of community*. Buber especially urged that without a different experiential basis *in the institutions of everyday life*, the ideal of the common good could never sustain itself against the institutions of profit and power, nor could the people themselves sustain the ideal. (Hence, the inevitable failure both of liberal reform and of cultural reform on its own.)

Reconstruction of underlying institutions implies a long and difficult social process—much longer and more painful than most American reformers have traditionally assumed. Though not a revolutionary theory, Buber's idea also gives first priority to the larger problem of the integrity of the community itself. In a society which experiences itself as a moral community, a preferential option for such poor as exist is more likely (if not normal); absent the reconstruction of the experience and institutions of community, the prospects are highly limited. But there is no way to short-circuit history: Unless the community is rebuilt, the disintegrating processes and institutions which undermine the common good will ultimately undercut all longer term reform strategies.

Difficult as it is to contemplate fundamental change over long periods of time (and difficult as it is for Americans to give up notions of a "quick-fix") the idea of reconstruction may be especially relevant to our emerging long term situation: Ironically, with reform blocked and revolution highly unlikely, the painful, decaying, frustrating emerging context may be the only context in which a strategy of this kind could work. In a situation of intensifying stalemate, people with firmly held values are likely to be forced in increasing numbers into an ever deeper analysis of their plight—and, however slowly, of the need to reject superficial solutions to fundamental problems.

Even if the context were to permit a slow, evolving, organic reconstructive process, however, Buber's idea as it currently stands is clearly inadequate. Buber emphasized the importance of local cooperative institutions, but it is obvious that in a huge industrial nation, far more than the quiet evolution of local cooperation is required. If the ideal of reconstruction were to be taken seriously, there would have to be a slow re-building of institutions at every level—towards increasing accountability to the community—and a rebuilding also of structures which give priority to values other than those of profit.

A strategy appropriate to the transition from one century to the next might include local neighborhood, worker-owned and municipal enterprises. Over the coming decade this strategy would need to be be extended to regional institutions which (in a context of deterioration and the failure of both the giant corporation and big government) might slowly become more independent of the market demand for expansion and for continual relocation and dislocation. The original idea of grass-roots democracy in the TVA (before its co-optation) is worth resuscitating.

Various students of American history are also right, I believe, to remind us of how extraordinarily different our very large nation is from virtually all other industrial nations—and to suggest that our unique Continental geographic scale ultimately requires devolution to some form of regional self-determination. If the idea of reconstruction were accepted, a still longer term vision of a society of substantially, if not totally independent regions, confederated in a reconstructed national political structure, would have to be fleshed-out, debated, and proposed as an answer to the problem of bigness, otherwise there would never be a serious response to the legitimate questions which lie just beneath demagogic exploitation of hostility to "big government."

The notion of intermediate scale is also important in considering alternative structures of economic planning—especially structures which can encourage and sustain local community-based economic institutions. The "dynamic logic" of the market—the logic which undercuts both the individual and the local community—must ultimately be arrested if the social fabric of local community institutions is ever to be reconstructed. But "planning" at the national level is too distant—and at the state and local level, too small-scale. The region is also the unit of appropriate size for this function.

Though Buber's concept of "reconstruction" is particularly relevant in a context of long-term stalemate (and though it is essential to breaking out of traditional "either-or" dead-end reform-versus-revolution thinking), I believe it is also inadequate for our own time in history because it does not sufficiently take account of anger and frustration.

The period we are entering is one in which resentment is all but certain to build (it already is growing rapidly). People are being exploited, dislocated and discarded. Either the inevitable anger will be directed at the elites and institutions which obstruct real solutions to real problems, or scape-goats are likely to be found: especially black and Jewish ones at home, and an "evil empire" with designs on freedom abroad. Moreover, if the inherent instabilities of our situation push us irrationally to war, in the nuclear age we could easily eliminate the possibility of achieving the common good forever.

Those concerned with social justice issues commonly do not like to face up to anger; by default they usually leave the mobilization of resentment to the right-wing. But face up to it we must: The growing anger will require a rational political focus, else it may well destroy us. This requires that as the stalemate deepens and economic and social pain increase, linkages must steadily be fashioned between a vision of community, a strategy of reconstruction, and an outspoken and tough populist critique of those institutions which oppose the needs of the vast majority.

Beyond Stalemate

New political energies cannot be mobilized around failing political traditions—nor on the basis of confused ideas about fundamental issues. Clarity about our situation and its requirements is absolutely essential. Although support for humane social programs must continue, the idea of helping the poor enter a system which is acknowledged to be profoundly flawed is inadequate to the longer term historical challenge we face: There is a need, ultimately, for a new and more expansive conception of the common good.

This brings us, finally, to the question of materialism. Even with all our problems, the United States is still the wealthiest nation in the history of the world; were the GNP today divided equally it would provide each family of four with $65,000. At some point we must clearly get off the "more is better" ladder. Ours is perhaps the only nation which could truly begin a slow transition towards a society of real equality—and of less materialism, less work, and the more humane and meaningful development of self, of relationships, of community.

There is, in fact, a steadily growing contradiction between our extraordinarily productive potential and our language of economic pain, burden and sacrifice. The effort to develop an integrated conception of the relationship of materialist strategies to a longer term non-materialist vision should go forward. As we approach and enter the new century, the necessary personal choice will be the same as the national choice: to draw a line and say enough is enough, and then to begin to build a fulfilling future beyond the dying era of economic necessity—and to help others, here and abroad, to do the same.

Part IV

The Challenges to Business and Society

JOHN W. HOUCK

In the Heart of the American Century, which ironically lasted from 1945-1975, Adolf A. Berle, an astute observer of the power of the modern corporation and capitalism, wrote in *The 20th Century Capitalist Revolution*:

> For the fact seems to be that the really great corporation managements have reached a position for the first time in their history in which they must consciously take account of philosophical considerations. They must consider the kind of a community in which they have faith, and which they will serve, and which they intend to help to construct and maintain. In a word, they must consider at least in its more elementary phases the ancient problem of the "good life," and how their operations in the community can be adapted to affording or fostering it.

It is clear that Berle, drawing from the majestic perspective of St. Augustine, is highlighting the fact that the powerful organizations and institutions within society must be held accountable for the social effects of their respective decisions.

"Social responsibility" is the term which many writers in Part IV employ when referring to the reality we envision with the concept of the common good. Implied in both of these terms is the fact that the corporation, while pursuing profits diligently, even zestfully, is at the same time pursuing service to the society which gives it ground to work in and the legal prerogative to operate.

In the first essay, the ethicist Richard De George argues that the challenge to American society, and its major institutions, like business and labor, is to respond as generously and imaginatively to the challenge of the common good. He goes on to make the point that it will be the moral obligation of government to fill the vacuum if the moral demands of social justice and the common good are not met by institutions such as business.

In the next essay, Gerald Cavanagh, S.J., expresses alarm about the set of values that we all share, arguing that individualism and freedom, while important, are not adequate norms to address the common concerns that should underpin our social lives. He writes, "The new ethic of self-interest, self-fulfillment, and short-term thinking is no longer sufficient for today's complex society."

William Cunningham, representing the perspective of the American labor movement, argues for an active governmental agenda to contend with such issues as unemployment, the minimum wage, civil rights, economic inequality, international free trade and domestic unemployment, and the right to form unions. For Cunningham, the demands of the common good have to be translated into significant public policy proposals.

The chapter, Visual Media and the Common Good, consists of two essays on the role of the media in affecting how we relate economics and business to the common good. Both writers draw on their experiences in making documentaries about the U.S. Bishops' Pastoral on the economy.

David Vogel broadens our thinking to a global context by pointing out that the concerns that we have, growing out of reflections on the common good and the social responsibility of business, must be extended beyond the domestic to the global and worldwide. He argues that justice and the common good are more than national: "Unless we define the 'common good' in terms of both the world economy and America's role in that economy, not only will our analysis and policy prescriptions make little sense, but we will also be guilty of ethnocentrism."

Capitalism and the Demands of the Common Good

For the philosopher and business ethicist Richard De George, the common good is a palpable, substantive norm of judgment about human and social behavior. De George ranks it with the norm of justice in its importance and effectiveness as a test of any ideological pretension, whether free-marketism, welfare statism, or any other pragmatic achievement.

> Both the unfettered market and the welfare state approaches have proven inadequate. Missing in both is a balanced view of human reality. Although we should never lose sight of the dignity, importance, and value of individual persons, we cannot ignore their life in community and human solidarity. We cannot ignore, or consider only in passing—as our ideology has for the past hundred years—the common good.

De George, when examining the common good, sees concrete human beings considered together; he rejects individualism because it ignores the "social animal" dimension of our lives and too frequently treats the individual person as one would treat individual atoms in the physical world shooting about in some kind of container. De George maintains that individualism ignores human solidarity.

In his essay, De George argues that the time is ripe for the exploration of the meaning of the common good for business firms operating within capitalism. Building on recent writings on the social responsibility of business, business ethics, and environmental concerns by a broad range of business scholars and practitioners, De George analyzes the common good in relation to the right to employment, the poor, and international business operations.

First, employment, the *sine qua non* of industrial society and culture, is placed squarely on the shoulders of the contemporary corporations to examine how they impact upon this critical issue in all their operational facets. He avoids two extremes: first, that it is of no concern to private business, and second, that it is exclusively the concern of the national government. According to De George, "The private sector can take positive steps to move towards implementing the right to employment. The challenge is for business itself to come up with new solutions and approaches."

For De George, the poor are more the responsibility of both public programs and private charity than of the corporation. De George states that business has primary obligations to its stakeholders, such as customers, employees, and stockholders. In pursuing the common good he accepts a division of social labor: "But business most often helps best by doing what it does best, and then being willing to give its fair share to local charitable organizations and to pay its fair share of taxes to help the poor."

We also find in De George as we found in other writers the global perspective. Two decades ago, a business ethicist would rarely raise this perspective. However, given the last decade, in which the American economy has truly become part of the world economy (and has in fact lost ground in several competitive markets), any writer must come to terms with the meaning of the common good in the global dimension.

Cultural Pluralism

The long-time observer of American business values, Gerald Cavanagh, S.J., is alarmed about the state of the culture in U.S. capitalism. If a culture be considered a glue holding together the myriad of institutions, private groups, and peoples, Cavanagh makes a very strong case that our cultural glue has dried out. He laments the demise of the Protestant Ethic, that constellation of values that promises material and other rewards for hard work. The Protestant Ethic, which includes qualities such as hard work, self-control, self-reliance, perseverance, rational planning, honesty and an observance of the rules of the game is taken to be a cultural glue that for several decades held the American society together. However, these values of the Protestant Ethic have collapsed in the last generation, and have given way to a new cultural pluralism and self-centeredness. Dedication to hard work has turned into concern for salary and status; self-control becomes self-fulfillment; self-reliance becomes entitlement; perseverance and planning ahead gives way to a short-term view; and honesty and an observance of the rules of the game become the maxim "don't-get-caught." According to De Toqueville (quoted favorably by Cavanagh), "Selfishness blights the germ of all virtue; individualism, at first only saps the virtues of public life; but in the long run it attacks and destroys all others and is at length absorbed in downright selfishness."

There are several claimants attempting to fill the void as the core cultural norm that holds us together. The first claimant Cavanagh deals with is freedom. Freedom is good according to our culture insofar as being free from something supports self-fulfillment, self-interest, and even selfishness. There is too little stress on the idea that freedom is a gift to pursue the *good* personally and socially. Another claimant is our too facile acceptance of "more is better" (or as some call it growthmania) which displaces "Christian doctrine as the ultimate sanction for any course of action."

Gerald Cavanagh has mixed feelings about the effectiveness of the concept of the common good as the basic norm that would move us toward a truly virtuous society. He sees the concept as being too vague, easily becoming a pliable norm in the hands of the powerful who often define the common good as whatever enhances the interests of their own kind. Or to put it another way: "What I do, by definition, must be the common good." He argues that the preferential option for the poor as found in the American Catholic Bishops' Pastoral on the U.S. economy is a more effective norm to guide human conduct and the establishment of human priorities. The reader will want to contrast his defense of the preferential option for the poor with the arguments of Richard De George that the common good is a substantive norm and that the preferential option for the poor is a priority, or heuristic, norm.

Cavanagh suggests that one of the reasons that he is pessimistic about our culture is the powerful hold that both individual freedom and "more is better" have on us; he is doubtful that we can gain consensus on a common set of norms. He suggests that one lesson we might learn from the tightly-knit Japanese society is to rethink our emphasis on self-fulfillment and individualism and to put together a new set of core values: "cooperation, concern for others, compassion, and generosity."

From Concept to Program

In his essay Richard De George talks about the common good as a principle that,

> . . . demands respect for the good of persons in their interrelations, and so for the collective areas in which they are each able to seek their own good. Moreover, to understand one's obligations under this principle, one must view our institutions and institutional practices from a wholistic perspective rather than from a perspective of abstract, separated individuals.

William Cunningham in chapter sixteen sees a definite contrast between De George's concept of the common good and those thinkers who rely on a philosophy of allowing market forces to determine what is in the interests of the common good and what are the requirements of justice. He makes the point early in his essay that there is a false premise in the market mentality which assumes that every citizen is on an equal footing, that wealth does not give some individuals unfair power over others, and that everyone is taken care of by automatic "market forces."

Cunningham believes the market needs restraint and guidance in employment, health, education and the needs of the victims of discrimination and hardship. As might be expected, a major area of concern for this representative of the American labor movement is the fundamental question of employment. Today, Cunningham points out, there is a greater social tolerance for higher unemployment; and that discrimination against women and minorities is also a matter of concern. Due to this discrimination, many women and minorities are stuck on the bottom rung of the economic ladder. He quotes the U.S. Bishops' Pastoral on the economy: "The most urgent priority for domestic economic policy is the creation of new jobs with adequate pay and decent working conditions . . . this goal is based on the conviction that human work has a special dignity and is a key to achieving justice in society."

Two Experiences

What was the subject of speculation or historical analysis by several writers, now becomes the subject (or victim?) of the power of the visual media. Both of the writers, Peter Mann and Bette Jean Bullert, accept that we live in an age of electronic communications, mainly visual through films and television. Therefore the concept of the common good becomes itself enlarged or narrowed, intermediated—even defined and authenticated—by the "images, symbols and stories of media." Both writers trace out examples of this commonly-shared experience, for example, a space-craft crash, starvation of Central African children, or an assassination, which can grip our attention and focus our action. Too often the visual media can communicate reality "as it is," but for both writers the common good is a window into a reality "as it might become."

To illustrate what is possible, Mann explores a five-part film series, "Search for Justice," which deals with the U.S. Bishops' Economic Pastoral. The film is complex as the subject is complex: how do we relate the powerful symbols of cross and flag, Christ and culture; how do we explore the unfinished agenda in being both a Christian and a citizen? The subject also produces the conflict which is to be expected when we are being challenged to practice justice in our daily lives and to apply the common good in rethinking our economic system.

Bette Jean Bullert is a television documentary producer who finds little room in contemporary television for the notion of the common good. She asks herself what she can do to counteract this trend, or how her medium can be used to further community and justice in a complex and conflictual world? She details in the documentary, "God and Money," her belief that there are many stories of heroes (or models), both local and worldwide, who have the sensibility and competence, commitment and effectiveness to justify optimism about the use of the visual media to further the common good.

The Common Good is an International Question

The final essay by David Vogel, of the Business School of the University of California at Berkeley, begins with the very definitive proposition, "Unless we define the 'common good' in terms of both the world economy and America's role in that economy, not only will our analysis and policy prescriptions make little sense, but we will also be guilty of ethnocentrism." He goes on to point out that this should not be a surprise to the reader because the history of capitalism has always been one of an international phenomenon. He points out that each of history's major economic powers—Holland, Spain, Great Britain, and the United States—owed their initial success to profitable endeavors in international trade. However, this supremacy was quickly undermined by other competitors in the international arena. He sees no end to this international character as he chronicles the movement of factories and industrial power from Holland to England to Europe to the U.S. and even to Japan and other competitors around the Great Pacific Basin. Any concern then about the common good has to start out with a global perspective and must include such issues as employment, competition, and investment-savings. He argues that certain economies, by following market-oriented free trade and labor policies, have, on the one hand, helped the less-well off in the Third World, and on the other hand, created a large number of jobs. This is in sharp contrast to the stagnating policies and programs of Western Europe. For Vogel, the common good subsumes many technical questions like employment, industrial capacity and intergenerational taxing and saving.

Vogel is concerned about our shrinking manufacturing base. He believes that some of this shrinkage is inevitable; nevertheless we must channel more resources into manufacturing to provide for future wealth. He is critical of American management values and perspective, arguing that too much of our managerial skill is put into accounting and finance, and not enough into the difficult task of dealing with manpower, work forces, technology, and increased productivity.

Vogel believes that American monetary and fiscal policy have produced a low savings rate; this means that foreign investment flows to the United States, thus draining these foreign countries of capital needed for their own development. He also feels that it is intolerable that we are hurting future generations with our high deficits and intergenerational programs such as Social Security. Vogel makes a plea for the church to urge members to save more and not to deplete the resources available for the Third World and the young.

Fourteen

Business, Responsibility, and the Common Good

RICHARD T. De GEORGE

In 1935 John Maynard Keynes in the Concluding Notes to his now famous *General Theory* wrote:

> The outstanding faults of the economic society in which we live are its failure to provide for full employment and its arbitrary and inequitable distribution of wealth and incomes.[1]

Fifty years later, the American Catholic bishops, writing on the American Economy single out two major moral deficiencies of our system: unemployment and poverty.[2] The parallel with Keynes is both striking and enlightening. It is striking because the two make similar claims, presumably independently and from different perspectives. It is enlightening because after fifty years the same problems are present at the heart of our system, despite our increase in wealth and production and the great strides we have made in many ways. That we still have these same problems with us is an indication that the approaches we have adopted for the past fifty years have not worked to resolve these faults. More of the same approaches are not likely to put us in any better a situation with respect to them fifty years from now. Clearly, new approaches are needed if we are to rid our society of this double blight.

The traditional free market wisdom held that the solution to poverty was an increase in wealth; that the solution to unemployment was an increase in jobs; and that an unfettered free market could produce both. The "invisible hand" would take care of the common good. The post-Great Depression wisdom put its emphasis on government intervention with its monetary and fiscal policies, heavy taxation, welfare, and other redistributive programs.

Both the unfettered market and the welfare state approaches have proven inadequate. Missing in both is a balanced view of human reality. Although we should never lose sight of the dignity, importance, and value of individual persons, we cannot ignore their life in community and human solidarity. We cannot ignore, or consider only in passing—as our ideology has for the past hundred years—the common good.

The Principle of the Common Good

The principle of the common good has been reintroduced into contemporary discussions by the Bishops' Pastoral on the American Economy.[3] What does this principle and the Pastoral mean for American business?

In general business responded with hostility to the first draft of the Bishops' Pastoral. It seemed like a call, if not for socialism, at least for government to do more and more to solve the problems of unemployment and poverty at the expense and freedom of business. The majority of those in the middle class reacted negatively as well, feeling that the Bishops were accusing them of unjustly possessing whatever they had worked hard to achieve, and telling them it was their obligation to give the fruits of their labor not only to the poor in America, but also to the poor of the world.

The second draft of the Pastoral has generated very little reaction, and in fact has been met more with indifference than with opposition, even though it is a much better and stronger document. The second draft calls for fewer specific measures than the first. Instead of making individuals feel guilty and instead of looking only to government for solutions, it raises a challenge. The challenge is for individuals and groups, business firms and government bodies to decide what they should do to help alleviate unemployment and poverty, in the light of scripture and the moral principles the Pastoral enunciates. Instead of preaching specific remedies the Pastoral calls upon each and all of us to come up with appropriate remedies. In this way the Bishops are treating the members of the Church and of the larger society as adults, rather than as children. Instead of attempting to tell us what we should do, they have described and documented problems, laid out principles, and asked us to respond with our consciences, our hearts, and our ingenuity to find solutions. The challenge to business is to determine what it can and must do to satisfy the moral imperatives applicable to it.

Despite the apparent indifference with which business received the second draft, that draft is more radical with respect to business than it might appear. For the Pastoral uses the traditional principle of the common good in a substantive way. To the extent that this principle is taken seriously, the bishops raise the challenge of rethinking a good deal of the way we do business. For that principle enters directly into the heart of economic life. It is co-equal with the principle of justice; but it forces us to rethink the principle of justice itself as well. The emphasis of the bishops on the common good both nationally and internationally is a call to see justice not only in an individualistic way but also in a communal way. Substantively, the principle of the common good demands respect for the good of persons in their interrelations, and so for the collective areas in which they are each able to seek their own good. Moreover to understand one's obligations under this principle, one must view our institutions and institutional practices from a wholistic perspective rather than from a perspective of abstract, separated individuals.

The common good as a substantive principle has both a positive and a negative aspect. Negatively, it commands us not to harm the common good. Positively, it obliges us to do what we can to promote the common good. But concretely, what is meant by "the common good"?

The notion of the common good is obscure if we consider it on the high level of abstraction on which it is frequently defined and discussed. The common good is the good not of society as such or of some superorder. Radical collectivism involves the mistaken claim that the social whole is superior to the individual human beings who make up society. But society does not exist apart from those who comprise it, and society has no independent good of its own. Radical collectivism is as mistaken in its way as is radical individualism, which asserts that only individuals are important. The common good is not the sum of the good of individuals, nor some final end which all people have in common. Each individual person has personal ends, some of which overlap with the ends of others. What all desire are the conditions necessary for pursuing their ends.

The common good is the good of concrete human beings considered together. Individualism ignores the togetherness of human beings. Concentrating on particular individuals, it ignores their interrelations, the common society in which they operate, and the common conditions necessary for them each to pursue their own good. Individualism ignores human solidarity. Unless the common good means the good of human beings considered *together*, it is meaningless.

One understanding of the common good equates it with common *goods*. Parks, roads, common defense, public buildings, and institutions such as courts, legislatures, and armies are part of what can be called the public good, since they are specific public goods provided by government from public funds. There are also common goods that do not require government funding, such as the air that we breathe and the water that we drink. They are not supplied by government, even though they may have to be protected by government if abused. Both of these form part of the common good, but they by no means exhaust what is meant by the common good. What must not be left out is that aspect of the common good that is not reducible to goods at all, but which consists of relations, conditions, systems, and structures.[4] An emphasis on individuals tends to ignore relations and structures that channel actions and that facilitate, promote, or inhibit certain kinds of activities. Concern for the common good leads us to evaluate not only individuals but also the morality of corporate structures, class relations, working conditions, and economic systems. Individuals of good will, because of the structures or systems in which they operate, may be effectively precluded from helping the poor or needy. The remedy here is not to urge individual virtue but to change the structures or the system.

In addition the common good embodies the general conditions that promote human flourishing. These are provided not only through the political process but through interactions among private individuals, by groups at many levels and by the private sector of the economy. The onus to provide or protect these conditions, relations, structures or systems falls on government only to the extent that the private sector cannot, or does not, provide them or acts detrimentally towards them.

The challenge to business is to ensure that the dynamism, the productivity, the individual initiative, and the rewards of the free market in fact promote the common good and not just the good of some individuals at the expense of others. The structures of a free market economy must be made consonant with an acknowledged responsibility for the common good. The task has been implicitly afoot in the concern of environmentalists, in the writings of those in business ethics, and in the call for the increased social responsibility of business. The time is ripe to make the responsibilities of business to the common good explicit, and to systematically draw out the consequences of recognizing its responsibilities to the common good. Our agenda:

What exactly does respect for the common good mean for businesses and what are their responsibilities to the common good?

The Common Good and the Right to Employment

We can begin to answer this question by considering the right to employment, a right not generally recognized in the Untied States, but a right the bishops assert in the Pastoral. The right is derived from the dignity of the human person, but the principle of the common good is necessary to appreciate its full force and strength. For in the light of that principle, the right challenges the individualistic view of labor and management that dominates our present approach to employment.

According to a prevalent view, the doctrine of employment-at-will expresses the true relation between employer and employee. It says that no employer is forced to hire or keep any employee and that no employee is forced to work for any employer. The contract between them is equal and reciprocal; freedom operates on both sides. Either the employer or the employee may terminate the relation at any time, unless precluded from doing so by contract.

That doctrine envisages both employers and employees as independent, freely contracting agents, each pursuing their own good. The doctrine is slowly being whittled away by court decisions, and rightly so, for the doctrine fails to consider the broader context in which both employer and employee exist.

The right to employment arises in a context in which the social organization and structure result in there being too little employment available for those able, willing, desiring, and needing to have gainful employment. The fact that there is not enough work available is not the result of the actions of any one firm or industry. It may reflect production or consumption cycles, structural changes in industries, the lack of need for people with few or no skills, and so on. None of this can be blamed on any firm or group of firms. To this extent the individualistic view is correct. Yet it is the system in which all firms operate and from which business benefits that allows this result. It is the system that allows people to be unemployed because the system does not provide employment. If viewed as a whole, it becomes clear that by allowing unemployment the system is so structured that it treats some people as excess. Hence, if we ask against whom the unemployed can exercise their right to employment, the proper answer is against the system, and not against any individual firm or against government. Concern for the common good means concern for all those who form a part of the system. This means looking at the system as a whole and revising it, with an eye towards justice for all.

The solution to unemployment is obviously to have more employment available. Business can provide jobs. Providing jobs is only part of the task, however. The other part is preserving and increasing the total number of jobs available. This task falls not to government but primarily to the private sector.

From the point of view of the common good, we should look at the good of all those who make up the firm. This leads us to a very different approach in regard to layoffs, plant closings, and discharge in general than does a radically individualistic view. In the case of unemployment resulting from layoffs, those laid off suffer the major burden of any downturn experienced by the firm. Yet the downturn is not typically the fault of those laid off. We can appropriately ask why those who are not responsible for the ills of a firm should suffer the effects of those ills while others do not. If all benefit during good times, it is right that all should share the burden during bad times.

Our society has not completely ignored the unemployed. We have tended to look at their plight as a result of market failure and to handle their needs through unemployment insurance or welfare, recognizing their right to life, if not to employment. Yet although welfare keeps people from starving, it does not allow those able and wishing to work to take full part in the productive work of society, and it prevents them from having the self-respect that goes with so taking part. The difference between recognizing the right to employment and recognizing only the right to life is the difference between being an integral member of society and being marginalized.

The United States with its affluence is one of the few countries of the developed world not to recognize even in principle the right to employment. This is a measure of our failure to appreciate the importance of a wholistic approach to institutions and our failure to consider the common good. Our ideological commitment to individualism erroneously leads us to identify the right to employment with those socialist societies in which the government is the only or primary employer, and hence in which the right to work is exercised against the government. This is a conceptual mistake resulting in an enormous practical price in human suffering. Just as the common good is not equitable with collectivism, so the right to employment is compatible with free enterprise, the private ownership of industry, and the free choice of both employers and employees. The challenge to business is to come up with the means to implement the right to employment in a way that does not involve massive government employment of the unemployed.[5]

At the present time the right to employment is secured for some if an employee has a position with a firm, is productive, and abides by the conditions of employment, as long as the fortunes of the employer make it possible to provide continued employment. Many do not enjoy any job security, even when they get work. Since business benefits from the system our society has adopted, the society can ask business to bear part of the burden of remedying that system so that it is fair to all, respects all, and hence so that employment becomes available for all. To act in this way is to act in accordance with the obligation to promote the common good. The system provides the framework within which each of the firms and workers are to carry on their activities. The system encompasses them, at the same time that they are potentially individual beneficiaries. To understand the system as one that should serve all is to go a long way towards understanding one's obligation to remedy its defects if it fails truly to serve all. Business benefits from the system, but it should not benefit at the expense of others. Hence, business as a whole appropriately shares in the obligation to implement each person's right to employment. Individual firms share in this responsibility to the extent they can respond. Some will be able to do more than others. Some will be able to do very little.

The private sector can take positive steps to move towards implementing the right to employment. The challenge is for business itself to come up with new solutions and approaches. Many companies already have moved at least some way in that direction, as *The 100 Best Companies to Work For in America* [6] documents. There are companies that despite bad times do not lay off workers. If companies realize their interconnection with their workers, considering their common good would lead them to avoid furloughing employees whenever possible. Good companies do not fire employees in order to save money during a slowdown and then hire them back or hire new ones at an upturn. They suffer through a downturn together with their employees. However both might have to give something in the process. Keeping people employed is a way of fighting unemployment, even when done on a small scale. If firms did this, society would benefit more than by having people become unemployed and receiving unemployment insurance, which adds to society's costs in many ways.

To keep competition fair, business may well prefer that all firms be forced to bear the same kind of burden with respect to employment and unemployment. There might, for instance, be tax incentives to motivate firms to retain employees they would otherwise fire. Firms might be required to relocate or provide training for employees when plants are shut down. Unions might cooperate with management in retraining, since management is not obliged to bear the entire burden. Tax benefits for companies providing training programs for the unemployed, whether or not the company hires those people after training, is another possibility. Shortening the work week, sharing work, or providing work for more instead of providing overtime for some are all ways to reduce unemployment.

The government can also provide training and retraining, aid in worker relocation, help match workers with jobs, and ultimately become a temporary employer of last resort.

All of this involves fundamental changes in the way business operates at the present time, and may be perceived as interference with the freedom of firms to carry on their business as they see fit. And of course it is. But the justification for the present system ignores the requirement to provide for the good of all those willing and able to take part in the economic system. The call to provide for the common good is not an easy one. It is for this reason that the bishops' challenge is not an easy one. Theirs is a challenge for society to change, and in this endeavor business can play an active role. The principle of subsidiarity[7] places the burden on lower units—individuals, groups, communities, mediating institutions—to do all they can to meet the demands of providing for the common good, before larger groups are brought in.

If the solution to unemployment is more jobs, and if the private sector creates them, then government need not enter the scene. But to the extent that the private sector is not able or does not choose to, or if the private sector does not succeed in solving the problem of unemployment, then government serves a legitimate function in helping the private sector, or in encouraging the private sector by tax or other incentives to end unemployment, or in coordinating a plan to do it, or finally in attempting to do so itself. The last of these solutions is the least satisfactory, but the challenge to the private sector is to preclude the need for government's doing that. The more the private sector is able to accomplish on its own, the less necessary is governmental intervention. The more the private sector can do with government aid and coordination, the less government need do substantively in providing employment.

The Responsibility of Business and the Common Good

In pursuing the responsibilities of firms for the common good we often obtain better results by thinking small than by thinking big. Many firms correctly claim that they are not set up to handle tasks such as rebuilding the inner city, or solving the problem of poverty. That is true. Yet that is not necessarily what they are all called on to do for the common good. Small businesses must act for the common good on their level, and their actions are as important for protecting and promoting the common good as are those of large corporations. The principles of the common good and of subsidiarity force us to reconsider the importance of small businesses and individual enterprise, and to reevaluate the dominance of our economy by increasingly large and powerful economic concentrations of power.

At its best, business exists to produce products and services, provide work for people, and in the process make a profit. In this sense business serves the common good, thus business is a vocation. It serves the common good both by providing the goods people need or want to develop and fulfill themselves and by making available the service they desire in order to achieve their personal ends. Concern for the common good in this context is concern for people in the person of the employee, customer, or client. Such a view of business is different from one that sees business as existing to make a profit and, in the process, producing goods and services and providing employment. Firms built on the second view tend to forget the common good unless it is necessary to do so to secure a profit. Those built on the former implicitly contain an embedded view of the common good, and serve themselves while serving society.

The differences between the two approaches is at the heart of the difference between a radically individualistic approach and one built on promotion of the common good. If we adopt the common good approach we shall have to reevaluate the morality of takeovers and mergers, the present use of bankruptcy to avoid responsibility, and the wholesale export of production from the United States abroad. The radical individualistic approach does not question the end of profit for its own sake, whereas the common good approach does.

Businesses are typically set up to handle matters of business, and often look at issues from their own perspective and the perspective of the bottom line. The argument of Adam Smith that society is best served when each business pursues its own good is only partially correct. Although business is not established to look out for the public good, and is not composed of elected officials responsible to the public, business is closely linked with others and is responsible for the effects of its actions on others.

To the extent that the business of business is business, its business is not social reform, cleaning up the inner city, caring for the poor, or feeding the hungry of the world. The challenge to serve the common good does not directly demand this. What it demands in specific circumstances will vary from firm to firm and person to person. Yet the consciousness of the effects of its actions on others is necessary if a business is to act morally, and if those within firms are to act morally.

What does this mean in the concrete? Without exception it means acting in accordance with the moral demands to which those in business are subject and to which firms are also subject. The first demand is to do no harm. This is a commonly accepted minimal requirement. Yet when seen from the point of view of the common good it takes on a wider than usual application. For harm to any member or portion of the community is harm not only to those people, but to the community as such. The preservation of clean air, earth, and water are fundamental requirements that follow from the obligation not to harm. They are common goods. But even further, the quality of these goods is fundamental to the quality of human life. The concern is not only for the goods as common but also for the overall quality of life that a people at any stage in history enjoy. The approach that argues that one can buy the right to pollute from those who are harmed, or pay damages to those adversely affected limits harm to specific individuals and fails to consider the harm to the common good. That good not only includes the needs of those directly affected but also of those who will come after us. Concern for the common good links us to our children and their children and their children's children.

No business exists in a vacuum, and no economic system exists in isolation from a political, cultural and historical setting and set of interrelations. Therefore the participants in the economic system are also participants in the social and political system. Corporations and firms, which are economic actors, are also legal and moral actors.[8] To the extent that they exist at the pleasure of society and benefit from the social and political ambiance of which they are a part, they can be expected to contribute to that political and social ambiance. Hence the legitimacy of taxing them. As actors on the social scene, their responsibility not to harm requires them to take proper precautions with respect to their workers and customers, neighbors, and the general public. This responsibility does not come from the nature of capitalism, but from the interrelation of firms with society. These responsibilities are sometimes called social or moral responsibilities.[9]

Positively, business can serve a variety of functions dealing with the common good. We have already noted that business provides employment. It also helps the common good by increasing the total wealth available for distribution and redistribution. These are tasks that business can do as it conducts its business. They are not additional tasks that it takes on itself or that business does instead of government. But fulfilling its social responsibilities is not something that firms do automatically in doing business; and they do not automatically lead to maximal profits in the short run. Hence, the perspective of the common good is necessary not only for managers, but also for investors, and for the ordinary citizen. Investors do not have a moral right to maximal profits in the short run, and they have no right to a profit made possible by a corporation's neglecting or violating its moral responsibilities. The call for business to take a longer perspective than that of the next quarterly report is not new. But our society has not yet moved away from the quarterly report perspective.[10] Concern for the common good demands that we move beyond it, because the common good is served only accidentally and haphazardly by looking only at the short run. Determining how to break our society's fixation on quarterly returns is a challenge for society as a whole, but especially for business.

Unions also have obligations to the common good. The argument that unions have helped raise wages overall, even for non-union members is true. But when wages get so high that the country is no longer competitive with foreign producers who have available cheap labor, then the benefits to workers may be short-lived. Unions can and sometimes do go too far, even if overall they can claim to have helped the worker. Just as business is intertwined with society, so are unions. Just as what is good for General Motors may not be good for the country, so what is good for the United Steel Workers may not be good for the country.

Business is interrelated with society in a multiplicity of ways. Business benefits from the interrelation, and so does society. Because of this, business has obligations towards society. A company that builds a plant in a town provides jobs for people, and serves as a source of wealth that flows through the workers into shops, restaurants, houses, and so on. The town in turn provides a variety of services, and sooner or later charges the business its share of taxes. The company is interrelated with that community. Therefore, a decision to close a plant is not a decision that affects only the company, and hence not a decision that should be made only by the company and only from its point of view. It cannot ignore its interrelation with the town and the workers. There is a community at stake, as well as a private enterprise. There is a commonality of interests and good that must be respected. This is not to speak of some abstract common good but of a concrete common good, a set of common interests and common endeavors. Concern for the common good on the level of the plant and the community requires that plant closings take place in such a way as to protect the common good as well as the private interest of the firm. The United States is moving only slowly to a recognition of this moral demand, and we can learn much from Canada and others who have gone further and done better in this respect than we.[11]

The systematic approach also demands that in some way business and society view the aggregative effects of individual corporate actions. We know in the case of pollution that one firm may produce little enough pollution that it causes no threat or danger to anyone. But many firms each producing that same amount of pollution may cumulatively cause serious problems. Similarly, one firm transferring its production abroad poses no problems. But if many firms do so, the productive base and capacity of the country as a whole may be threatened. A still unsolved problem and a special challenge to business is to determine how to monitor and control effects of individual firms that individually cause no harm, but in the aggregate hurt the common good. The easiest solution is for government to handle the problem. But that is not the only, nor necessarily the best, solution.

Business, Poverty, and the Common Good

Both Keynes and the bishops speak of the dual blight of unemployment and poverty. What is the responsibility of business to the poor and how does poverty relate to the common good?

Involuntary poverty is a cancer in society. In an affluent society it can rob the poor of their self-respect and dignity, and can lead to sickness, malnutrition, illiteracy, crime, broken homes, and other evils, all of which take a toll on the common good and are costly to society as a whole.

Because unemployment is directly related to the economic system, the remedy for unemployment lies primarily within the economic system, even if government may have to intervene or help. We have already seen that a crucial factor in ending unemployment is acknowledging employment as a right, and then taking the right seriously. In contrast, poverty is not immoral in itself. Those in religious orders take a vow of voluntary poverty, and a whole society may be poor and moral. Yet the existence of involuntary poverty in the midst of plenty is *prima facie* evidence of a morally defective socio-economic system. Nonetheless, the problem of the poor will be only partially solved if the problem of unemployment is solved. The impoverization of female heads of households, for instance, has many causes other than unemployment, including male abandonment of families, failure to pay child support, illegitimate children born to teen-agers, and continued discrimination. The social defect of poverty, and so its remedy, lie not only in the economic system but also in the socio-political system. This distinction between unemployment and poverty is important to solving both problems and to understanding the responsibility of business.[12]

In the Pastoral on the American Economy the basic criteria from which the bishops proceed are the dignity of and the respect due to each human person. From these they derive and use the principle of justice, the principle of the common good, and the principle of the preferential option for the poor.[13] The three are not all of the same type. Justice and the common good are substantive principles; the preferential option for the poor (like the principle of subsidiarity) is not a substantive but a regulative, heuristic principle. It is not substantive because it does not give us any specific norm by which we can judge an action or practice or system moral or immoral. As regulative, the principle tells us to consider the impact of our decisions, policies, and practices on the poor. It does not tell us specifically what is allowable and what is not. It tells us to ask about the justice of a practice by considering its impact on the poor. The legitimacy or illegitimacy of that impact comes from the principle of justice; but without special consideration of the poor, they might not receive justice at all. Hence the importance of special consideration of the poor. The principle is heuristic in that it guides our search for appropriate substantive moral judgments by requiring us to consider the poor specifically in our calculations.

Commutative justice requires that those who enter transactions to attain their own ends do so freely, under conditions of reasonable equality. This is the fundamental kind of justice in the marketplace, and respecting commutative justice fosters the common good. Distributive justice deals with an equitable distribution of benefits and burdens by the state and the proper redistribution of wealth to those in need. The major problem of distributive justice in our society is how to manage and reform our various programs that take care of the poor and needy, but do so at high cost for the results produced, and with barely tolerable results in terms of respecting their dignity. Such redistribution is a major responsibility not of business, but of government.

The redistribution required in our affluent country differs both in kind and degree from what is required in poor countries. The preferential option for the poor had its formulation in Puebla and is especially appropriate for the countries of Latin America and other portions of the Third World, where the society tends to be divided into the rich elite and the poor masses. In such a situation the Church, which for a long while was seen as affiliated with the rich, has consciously disassociated itself from the rich and aligned itself with the poor. From that vantage point it can attack injustice and exploitation, hope to counter the efforts of the communist groups who seek the allegiance of the poor, and help change the socio-economic conditions of the masses.

The poor in the United States do not form a class, and a large percentage rotate out of poverty over a ten-year period. Unlike Latin America, the poor in the Untied States are a minority, not a majority. The Church in the United States has not been traditionally associated with the rich. Traditionally associated with the immigrants, the Church has emerged with the immigrant groups into the middle class. The Church has neither the need nor the wish to sever that alliance, unlike the way it wished to sever its identification with the Latin American elite. Thus, to speak of a preferential option for the poor on the part of the Church in the United States must mean something different from what it means in Latin America. Due to the lack of parallelism between the cases, "a preferential option for the poor" has an odd and imported ring to North American ears, and tends to be misunderstood. In the domestic context, "active consideration of and concern for the poor" or "affirmative action with respect to the poor" might profitably replace "a preferential option for the poor."[14]

Concern for the poor should not be at the expense of concern for all. Hence the appropriateness of the notion of justice for all. The fact that the middle class and the rich are better able to speak for themselves than are the poor means that the Church rightly speaks for the latter; yet the Church serves all and must do what it does in a way that preserves justice for all. If we concentrate on the poor in the United States, we tend to concentrate on distributive justice, and therefore on the churches, charity, and government—not on the economic system insofar as it concerns production. The economic system does not concern itself directly with the poor as poor, while the social and governmental systems should.

In our society business as such, and considered only in terms of the economy, has obligations to its stakeholders—its shareholders, its workers, its customers. It has the obligation not to harm. And I have argued that it has obligations to the common good. But there is no direct obligation to those with whom it does not deal and those whom it does not affect. From this point of view it has no special or direct obligations to the poor—individually or as a group—just because they are poor, except to the extent they are poor because they are unemployed. Corporations have obligations in charity. Business shares the obligation of the affluent to help the needy. But business most often helps best by doing what it does best, and then being willing to give its fair share to local charitable organizations and to pay its fair share of taxes to help the poor. Promotion of the common good does not preclude a division of social labor.

Active concern for the poor is not only compatible with, but embedded in the principle of the common good. By providing jobs, increasing wealth, and promoting the common good—which includes supporting just background institutions—business in general fulfills its obligation to the poor. Of course, this does not preclude direct action by businesses located in slums or ghettos to do what they can, nor does it mean that businesses elsewhere need not worry about their actions that do affect the poor through higher prices, unavailability of services, and the like. But not all businesses are so situated.

Just background institutions that ensure the poor have the wherewithal to obtain what they need are a better means of dealing with poverty than direct social intervention by business. The number and plight of the poor will be lessened by the abolition of unemployment. But the development and implementation of just background institutions that treat the poor with the respect they deserve as human persons are the key factors in solving the American problem of poverty. And solving that problem promotes the national common good.

Multinationals and the Global Common Good

The principle of the common good is important on the national level. But it transcends the national level. We can speak of both an international common good and a global common good. The obligation not to harm the international or global common good is evident, for instance, if we briefly consider pollution. Pollution of the ocean or destruction of the ozone layer of the atmosphere are impingements on global common goods needed by all people. Pollution that drifts or flows across borders harms an international common good. The obligation to promote the common good on the international level and on the global level is not less necessary, but perhaps less obvious, than on the national level.

What are the obligations of business to the international and global common good? The answer depends on the transnational involvement of the business in question. A local or strictly national business has no special obligations to the international and global common good beyond contributing its fair share to the support of appropriate group efforts, and its government's legitimate activities in fostering the larger common good.

Multinationals, however, by their activities transcend national boundaries and thus take part in, benefit from, impinge on, and can harm the international and global common good. Multinationals have special opportunities and special obligations with respect to the common good of the countries in which they operate.

An American multinational (MNC) operating in the Third World has special responsibilities and obligations because of the social situation in which it operates. The difference between an American MNC operating in a less developed country (LDC) and the same company operating in a foreign First World country lies in the different background situations and institutions in the two cases. Concern for the common good goes beyond an individualistic approach to multinational operations by focusing on the background institutions of Third World countries and on those at the global level. For the presence of such institutions in sufficient number and kind is a necessary condition for protection of the common good of members of Third World countries and of mankind in general.

The negative obligation to do no harm applies to all firms in all nations. The ability of an MNC to harm with impunity is greater in many Third World countries, where there are fewer legal constraints than in developed countries and greater possibility of doing harm because of the fragility of the weaker economy, the greater dependence on the MNCs, and the disproportion between the resources and expertise of the MNC and the deprivation of the LDC.

In such circumstances the common good demands not only that the MNC do no harm, but that on the whole it help the development of the host country and that it produce more good than harm for the host country. This means that it cannot through a utilitarian calculation justify the harm it does to the host country by weighing that against a greater good to the MNC or to the country of origin. The reason is that on the whole, because of the already inferior position of the LDC, harming the LDC makes it proportionately worse off than the good to the MNC makes the MNC better off. Hence the criteria of acceptable behavior is different for MNCs operating in Third World countries than it is for MNCs operating in First World countries.

MNCs have the opportunity to help development, provide employment, transfer technology, improve the infrastructure, and share their expertise with host countries. For their own successful operation MNCs require and can help build the roads, railroads, communications networks, and other aspects of the infrastructure that developing nations need if they are to develop sufficiently to take care of their own people. They need increased wealth, which the multinationals at their best are able to help them create. The opportunity, however, also exists for exploitation, for undermining the local culture, for contributing to starvation or malnutrition by buying and using prime farm land previously used for local crops in order to grow cash crops for export. The harm done is frequently indirect or unintended, but it is harm nonetheless. Concern for the common good requires self-restraint on the part of the MNC's. The less effectively just-back-ground institutions function within the host country, the greater the temptation to ignore the common good and thus the greater the need for self-restraint.

On the international and global level the common good is best protected by just international and global background institutions. The obligation to promote the common good thus yields the obligation to develop and support such background institutions. The obligation falls to government; but it also falls to international business. The record of both the United States government and of American business has not been exemplary in this regard, despite individual exceptions. The primary obligation expresses itself, for instance, positively in the requirement to form and implement international codes such as the code regulating the sale of infant milk substitutes. The American failure to sign and abide by such international codes is well known. If the codes are poorly framed, then the task is to frame better ones. But when failure to recognize them is simply a function of the self-interest of business, it represents a failure to respect the common good of other nations and of the global community. Although MNC's generally should not interfere with local politics, they can support rather than discourage or fight the development of national and international reforms, laws, or unions that will help defend and enhance the common good of the less developed countries.

Knowledge is social, as are the modes of production. The advances of modern technology do not belong to any company or any nation, because human knowledge does not belong to any company or nation. Human knowledge is part of the common good of mankind. Mathematics has a long international history. It does not belong to the Greeks, Arabs, Chinese, French, English, Germans, or Americans. Science is truly international, as is knowledge in general. Knowledge is also infinitely shareable. It is a common good, even though not equitably distributed. The challenge for those with such knowledge is how to share it with those desiring access to it. The possibility of spreading knowledge widely with inexpensive radios, tape recorders, and television sets, provides opportunities not previously available. However, it requires that such inexpensive products be made and sold at low prices. The transfer of both high and low technology, of knowledge and know-how, is one of the keys to helping LDCs become independent. Such independence represents a common good of each nation for that nation and an enhancement of the global common good. MNCs have gone further than governments in linking nations together. In the process they have often made higher profits than they would have made from similar activities in their home country. Concern for the common good invites a reevaluation of this fact and of those profits, and calls for new structures that will ensure that a greater portion of the profits go to the host country.

The long tradition of natural rights acknowledges the right to property so long as there are not others in need. This principle is repeated by the bishops. Exactly what this requires of individuals and firms on the international level is not settled by this principle. Yet it suggests a reinvestigation of the call for a new international economic order; it suggests the need for a reduction in sovereignty; and it suggests the possibility of a global redistribution system under which affluent nations are taxed for the benefit of those in great need. Concern for the global common good raises a challenge to business to consider the needs of other countries and peoples and to respond with its conscience in developing techniques and fostering background institutions that fulfill those needs.

Reconceptualization of Our Institutions

The bishops' Pastoral calls for serious and deep changes in the way we do business. The challenge to business is to respond as fully, as generously, and as imaginatively as possible. If business fails to meet the challenge, it will be the moral obligation of government to force change to meet the moral demands of justice and the common good. If government fails as well, the moral justification for the system itself will be put in doubt.

The greatest challenge initially is a reconceptualization. Concern for the common good will help us see our society as a whole and help us realize our solidarity with all those of our nation and of the world. Such a reconceptualization has an already existing basis. We have examples of other countries and of individual firms. We are also being forced to reconsider our radical individualism due to foreign competition, environmental deterioration, and growing economic and social pressures. The principles of justice, of the common good, and of active concern for the poor will not by themselves provide specific solutions to the problems of unemployment and poverty. Nonetheless, taking these principles seriously will force us to rethink our approaches to ridding society of these evils, and will encourage us to seek new approaches.

The reconceptualization of our institutions, especially of business, from the point of view of the common good will in turn demand restructuring firms so as to ensure that in acting for themselves they in fact promote, rather than harm, the common good. On the international level it will require restructuring the economic order. The challenge is a large one. The changes required are fundamental, and will require thought, experimentation, and cooperation on many levels by workers, managers, unions and corporations together with those in government, churches, and education. But the dual blight of poverty and unemployment are stains on our society that we can, and must, find ways to eradicate.

Notes

1. John Maynard Keynes, *The General Theory of Employment, Interest, and Money* (New York: Harcourt, Brace & World, Inc., 1964), p. 372.

2. *Catholic Social Teaching and the U.S. Economy*, The Second Draft, *Origins*, October 10, 1985, Vol. 15., No. 17.

3. The bishops speak of the common good in the Second Draft of the Pastoral in the following paragraphs: 75, 83, 87, 90, 101, 108, 109, 113, 115, 122, 234, 247, 251, 270, 284, 285, 294, 295, 306, 309, 310, 311, and 313.

4. For an extended discussion of the role and place of relations and

structures in collectives see Richard T. De George, "Social Reality and Social Relations," *The Review of Metaphysics*, XXXVII (1983), pp. 3-20.

5. For a fuller discussion of this topic, see Richard T. De George, "The Right to Work: Law and Ideology," *Valparaiso University Law Review*, XIX (1984), pp. 15-35; and Richard T. De George, *Business Ethics*, 2nd ed. (New York: Macmillan, 1986), Chapter 9.

6. Robert Levering, Milton Moskowitz, and Michael Katz, *The 100 Best Companies to Work for in America* (New York and Scarsborough, Ontario: New American Library, 1985.)

7. The principle of subsidiarity is a traditional procedural principle in Catholic social thought. The Pastoral uses the principle without defending it. For a philosophical defense, see Richard T. De George, *The Nature and Limits of Authority* (Lawrence, University Press of Kansas, 1985), especially chapters 4 and 8.

8. For a defense of the claim that corporations are moral actors, see, Richard T. De George, "Can Corporations Have Moral Responsibility?," *University of Dayton Review*, XV (1982-83), pp. 3-15. Reprinted in T. Beauchamp and N. Bowie (eds.), *Ethical Theory and Business*, 2nd ed. (Englewood Cliffs, N.J.: Prentice Hall, 1983), pp. 57-67.

9. For a development of the distinction between corporate social and corporate moral responsibility, see *Business Ethics*, Chapter 8.

10. Some privately held firms take a longer perspective and are able to do so because they do not have to justify that perspective to shareholders.

11. For some comparisons of U.S.-Canadian laws in this area, see *Valparaiso Law Review*, 19 (1984), "Rights, Work, and Collective Bargaining."

12. For a discussion of different kinds of poverty see not only the Pastoral, but also the contribution by Charles West to this volume.

13. The bishops explicitly use the principle of the common good 23 times, the principle of justice for all 10 times, and the principle of the option for the poor 7 times.

14. The phrase "preferential option for the poor" has an odd ring to it in part because "preferential option" is redundant, in part because an "option" that is morally required is, if not a contradiction at least paradoxical. This is not to say that the use the bishops make of the principle is mistaken, but that the phrase itself is infelicitous.

Fifteen

The Common Good as an Effective Moral Norm for the U.S. Businessperson

GERALD F. CAVANAGH, S.J.

In the United States there is little consensus on moral norms. Before attempting to examine the common good as a moral norm for the U.S. businessperson, it would be useful to gauge the difficulty of the task of establishing a commonly held moral norm. The openness to moral norms and the ethical climate in the U.S. will have a profound impact on the possibility of achieving a moral consensus.

It is my contention that a bias against explicit moral norms in the U.S. makes it difficult to reach a consensus on the morality of any actions and policies. Individualism, relativism and pluralism all militate against any commonly held moral norms. Our current attitudes have left us with little in the way of an agreed-upon belief system.[1] The collapse of our belief system has come about gradually. As one experienced commentator put it, "Since World War II, we've seen the greatest disintegration of social consensus and the most accelerated pace and degree of change in human history."[2] The fact of this collapse of moral consensus is clear; the reasons for the collapse are varied. One result of this collapse has been its impact on university education:

> The failure to rally around a set of values means that universities are turning out potentially highly skilled barbarians: People who are very expert in the laboratory or at the computer or in surgery or in the law courts but who have no real understanding of their own society.[3]

This collapse must be dealt with in trying to suggest moral norms to aid us in doing the work of the coming decade. Moreover, we in academic disciplines bear much of the responsibility for this explicit renunciation of any belief system or any explicit ethical norms. This occurred in an attempt to be objective and unbiased. A rejection of moral norms is especially apparent in both the social sciences and the business disciplines. Yet in any study which touches human affairs so intimately, experience and reflection show how deceptive it is to claim to be "value-free."[4] That very position is a value position in itself: to reject the conscious and explicit consideration of human values and ethics.

The traditional value system of the United States, the Protestant Ethic, has collapsed in the last generation (see Table 1). The emphasis upon self-control, self-reliance, saving and planning ahead has given way to self-fulfillment, entitlement, and consumption. Even honesty in ordinary transactions has often

Table 1 Change of Values Which Undergird Business System

PROTESTANT ETHIC . . . has shifted to . . . PLURALISM AND SELF-FULFILLMENT	
1. Hard work	1. Salary and status
2. Self-control and sobriety	2. Self-fulfillment
3. Self-reliance	3. Entitlement
4. Perseverance	4. Short-term view: if not successful here, move on
5. Saving and planning ahead	5. Immediate satisfaction: buy on time, little savings
6. Honesty and observing the	6. Obey the law; in any case, don't "rules of the game" get caught

Source: Gerald F. Cavanagh, *American Business Values* (Englewood Cliffs, NJ: Prentice-Hall, 1984), p. 163.

yielded to operating to the limit of the law and avoiding liability. This new ethic encourages self-centeredness and selfishness.[5] Make no mistake: the Protestant Ethic did not insure honesty and integrity, indeed, it often served as a mask for low wages and deceptive practices. Nevertheless, it was a comprehensive, cohesive and motivating value system.[6]

Pluralism and Relativism

The lack of agreed-upon values in American society has led us into a rampant pluralism. If everyone's judgement is of equal value on what is ethical, then it is every person for themselves. This makes it impossible to agree on goals for society or even for the firm. We find it next to impossible to muster a majority for anything but complaint. Major factors in deciding recent national elections were all complaints: get the government off our backs, reduce taxes, and get rid of welfare cheaters. There is agreement on what we do not like, but far less agreement on what we do like and the kind of society in which we would like to live. This then means that there is no foundation for goals, for public policy, or even for private sector planning.

The "common good", as a concept to help us evaluate goals, has fallen out of our vocabulary. When was the last time you heard a public figure talk about "the common good" or even "the public good"? When the only goal set forth for the nation is national, it leaves a vacuum in public discourse. When any policy that would hurt me individually is rejected, when tradeoffs to complex policies are not patiently explained, self-centeredness is encouraged. Since sacrifice is not asked, we drift into selfishness. Paradoxically, the corporate leader, Chrysler chairman Lee Iacocca, illustrates more of the traits of a statesmen in his concern for common good issues — e.g. highway safety, energy use, national debt[7] — than the political leader President Ronald Reagan.

A more common trait in American life is to have little patience with tradition. Each generation wants to forge its own values and ways of living. While this encourages flexibility and innovation, it can also leave us rootless and without common values. It also makes the task of developing any sort of value system, any sort of ethical base, much more difficult. As a result of the above notions of freedom and the lack of respect for past values, it might be said that current American individualism has grown cancerous. Self-willed and selfish men and women choose their own ways of living and working with little concern for the effect on other people.

Self-Interest to Selfishness

Alexis de Tocqueville 150 years ago noted the individualism and enlightened self-interest that he found among Americans.[8] Although he admired the imagination, initiative and resourcefullness that he found among Americans, Tocqueville worried that this self-interest would eventually turn into selfishness. Tocqueville described individualism as a mature, calm and reassuring feeling, which disposes each person "to sever himself from the mass of his fellows and to draw apart with his family and friends." Each individual then retreats to her own comfortable surroundings, and thus "leaves society at large to itself." Tocqueville contrasted individualism and selfishness:

> Selfishness originates in blind instinct; individualism proceeds from erroneous judgment more than from depraved feelings; it originates as much in deficiencies of the mind as in perversity of heart.
>
> Selfishness blights the germ of all virtue; individualism, at first only saps the virtues of public life; but in the long run it attacks and destroys all others and is at length absorbed in downright selfishness.[9]

The consequences of such self-centered attitudes on the part of contemporary Americans are noted in a recent study of American values by Robert Bellah:

> Now if selves are defined by their preferences, but those preferences are arbitrary, then each self constitutes its own moral universe, and there is finally no way to reconcile conflicting claims about what is good in itself. All we can do is refer to chains of

consequences and ask if our actions prove useful or consistent in light of our own "value-systems." All we can appeal to in relationships with others is their self-interest, likewise enlightened, or their intuitive sympathies . . . Where sympathy or already-congruent values are not enough to resolve moral disagreements between ourselves and others, we have no recourse except to withdraw from them.[10]

Freedom as an Inadequate Moral Norm

When asked, most Americans cite freedom as their most important value and even life goal. Freedom is a part of our rhetoric, and attaining freedom is the process of growing to adulthood. We pride ourselves in our free enterprise, free markets, freedom of information, free movement. More than a generation ago the shallowness of this as a goal of Americans was pointed out in a classic study of freedom in America.

> It is now obvious that the *laissez-faire* theory was scarcely more than a rationalization of the economic interests of middle-class business men and promoters, and that it had little to commend it from the point of view of the working masses and their interests. But that ominous fact was long obscured because the theory was formulated in terms of the magic word "liberty."[11]

Freedom is a convenient ideology, since it happily enabled the business person to reconcile his or her selfish interests with his or her altruism. That is, by pursuing his or her own private good, he or she was therefore bettering society. Moreover, Americans are ready and willing to fight for freedom both here and abroad. Note the change in the meaning of freedom today, according to the Bellah study:

> Freedom is perhaps the most resonant, deeply held American value. In some ways, it defines the good in both personal and political life. Yet freedom turns out to mean being left alone by others, not having other people's values, ideas, or styles of life forced upon one, being free of arbitrary authority in work, family, and political life. What it is that one might do with that freedom is much more difficult for Americans to define. And if the entire social world is made up of individuals, each endowed with the right to be free of others' demands, it becomes hard to forge bonds of

attachment to, or cooperation with, other people, since such bonds would imply obligations that necessarily impinge on one's freedom.[12]

Freedom, as the dominant American value, gives each person much scope in determining her or his own life and actions. A troublesome question that arises is: Is there any limit to that freedom? Answers here are difficult. Some would acknowledge that when my actions seriously hurt others that would indicate a limit. Am I free to do evil? If freedom is the important value, it will be difficult to find a counterbalancing value to limit my freedom — especially if there is no tradition of looking to the effect of my actions on others.

Other False Norms

There are other norms that some people attempt to substitute for moral norms. For many, the implicit moral norm in the U.S. today is enlightened self-interest and anything that increases gross national product (GNP) or average personal income. As one commentator has put it, "...the American standard of living began its century or more of rivaling Christian doctrine as the ultimate sanction for any course of action."[13] Growing GNP increases jobs and income, and all other goods derive from these. Hence, an increase in business activity is good. Thus, the practical implicit ethical norm: whatever increases GNP and personal income is good, whatever detracts from them is evil. Note that this proposed "ethical norm" is quite narrow. It presents only a material goal. It says nothing about wasting human and material resources, or about the appropriate or inappropriate means that I may use to achieve this material good. It neglects family values, human happiness or even the effect of my self-interested activities on others. Hence increasing income or even enlightened self-interest can hardly be called an adequate ethical norm.

Contemporary assessments of the business climate find many of the same lack of values. The founder of Control Data Corporation has called Americans "a risk-avoiding, selfish society."[14] We are interested largely in how a given action or policy affects *me* : How will this action effect my career, my life and my development as a person? Will it give me a favorable performance appraisal, so that I am in line for a salary increase and promotion? If so, it is a good action.

Confrontation is a part of the fabric of the United States. We use the adversary system to obtain justice in the courts. Labor has learned that it can only get a fair deal by dealing harshly with management. Business is convinced that it must resist any proposal for additional government regulations. These situations could be handled more efficiently and effectively through negotiation and cooperation. As compared to Japanese society, we notice one cause of the difference. For every 10,000 citizens, Japan has one lawyer, the U.S. has twenty.[15] President Derek Bok of Harvard, former Dean of the Harvard Law School, laments the fact that so many talented young men and women forego other more productive occupations and choose law. He points out that Japan has a total of 35,000 lawyer in the entire country, while we in the U.S. graduate 30,000 every year.[16] The confrontations that follow as this excess of lawyers makes a living for themselves costs us precious time, energy and money and makes cooperation difficult. The atmosphere makes it difficult to speak of goals that could be held in common by differing groups.

The short-term thinking of most business managers is another obstacle in the way of cooperation. Pressured by financial analysts who want to know quarterly returns on investment, corporate managers must try for quick returns out of self-defense. A short time horizon militates against long-term planning, loyalty and cooperation.

The above discussion of the *lack* of moral and ethical consensus is one of the best arguments that could be made for the *need* for clearer ethical norms for our society. No society can long endure without some agreement on what behavior is acceptable and what is not acceptable; what is good and what is bad. If business agreements are not honored unless written into contracts, if a handshake or a person's word is not sufficient to establish trust, business activities would become prohibitively expensive at best or grind to a halt at worst.

The Common Good and the Preferential Option
for the Poor

Let us now examine the common good as a potential ethical

norm for U.S. society. For any norm to be effective and acceptable, it must spring from the shared experiences, needs and convictions of the people. Moreover, this particular version of the common good is rooted in the Christian tradition. A norm of this sort is particularly appropriate for several reasons:

First, we badly need a belief system and a moral consensus in the United States. The Protestant Ethic has collapsed, and self-interest (leading eventually to selfishness) as a personal decision criterion is not adequate for the difficult problems of a complex society. Along with most Americans, we explicit reject as adequate moral norms self-interest and economic goals.

Second, in the United States we already implicitly hold Christian beliefs and moral principles. These principles are bound into the fabric of our society: our Constitution, our laws and our expectations of each other. They have served us well in the past. There is no reason to believe that they are not adequate to the demands of the future. In fact, evidence indicates that they will be more needed and more appropriate in the future.

Finally, I believe Christian ethical principles are the most appropriate and the best ethical principles available to us. While now somewhat neglected, they remain rooted in our experience, and they are sophisticated enough to meet the more complex problems of today.

The basis of the Catholic Church's moral judgments on economic and social life is: "The dignity of the human person, realized in community with others . . ."[17] Or, "Human life is life in community." (Para. 68) This provides a basis for the more specific norm that they propose: "the preferential option for the poor." (Para. 59) They spell this norm out in additional detail:

> First are the duties all people have to each other and to the whole community: love of neighbor, the basic requirements of justice and the special obligation to those who are poor and vulnerable. Corresponding to these duties are the human rights of every person: the obligation to protect the dignity of all demands respect for these rights. Finally these duties and rights suggest several priorities that should guide the economic choices of individuals, communities and the nation as a whole. (Para. 67)

. . . These insights show that human beings cannot grow to full self-realization in isolation, but in interaction with others. (Para. 70)

. . . This duty calls into question extreme inequalities of income and consumption when so many lack basic necessities. . . . Further it sees extreme inequality as a threat to the solidarity of the human community, for great disparities lead to deep social divisions and conflict. (Para. 78)

It is here that one gains a better understanding of the new norm that the Catholic bishops propose: the preferential option for the poor and powerless. This norm insists that any proposed action or policy be measured against how it will effect the poorest and most vulnerable of that society. How that action effects the poor does not automatically determine the morality of the action. However, the norm does demand that the effect of the action on the powerless be one of the first items to be examined. At the very least this sort of policy insures that the poor not be left out of the calculations of the economic actors and policymakers.

The Catholic bishops' then develop their moral principle of the preferential option for the poor. This moral norm stems from "the radical command to love one's neighbor as one's self." (Para. 89) The bishops are at some pains to point out that this moral norm is not intended to pit one class or group against another. It is simply that "the deprivation and powerlessness of the poor wounds the whole community." (Para. 90) Therefore any action or policy which reinforces or encourages such is to be judged in error and wrong.

The preferential option for the poor and powerless has several advantages over the common good when used as a moral norm. First, it is probably less open to bias. When speaking of the preferential option for the poor, it is quite clear whose interests cannot be lost in any calculation. The powerless are front and center. The impact of the proposed action or policy *must* be measured against its effect on them. On the other hand, when using the common good as the moral norm, it is easier to trade off the interests of the poor for the greater welfare of the predominant group.

In deriving a moral norm from the experience of the people themselves, we run a risk: that the norm represent the interests of the predominant group of people in that society. That is, the common good may be determined by white, middle class Americans. As their thinking might go. "If some 'few' people (that is, elderly, handicapped, children and the 35 million poor), fall through the cracks in this ethical analysis, that is unfortunate. However, it is more important to have ethical norms that are beneficial to the majority of that society. If actions or policies benefit the dominant group, then those actions or policies are ethical." Hence moral good is seen through the eyes of white middle-class males, who might be more apt to overlook the negative impact of certain actions on the vulnerable.

Second, the preferential option for the powerless is probably more easily understood than the common good. Unfortunately, the common good is no longer a part of our current vocabulary, except for ethicists and public policy philosophers. Thus, the term loses much of the value it had as a traditionally accepted term. The preferential option for the poor is initially probably no better understood. However, it is at first glance a clearer notion — even though it might initially engender considerable misunderstanding and disagreement. Since it catches the attention of the average citizen, it can then be explained. And, of course, the use of the term in the bishops' letter is not divisive as is often the case when it is used in liberation theology, which is frequently interpreted as pitting class against class, or encouraging adversarial relationships. Rather, the bishops call for the preferential option for the poor and powerless because of community and solidarity. Their intention is to insure that all people are considered.

Finally, using the preferential option for the poor as a norm more readily insures that the common good indeed will be our objective and thus is more likely to be reached. The preferential option for the poor is rather equivalent in its outcome to using the norm of the common good. When solidarity and community is made intrinsic to an application of the preferential option for the poor, it is clear that the greater good of *all* in the group is the goal.

Could the preferential option for the poor and powerless be used by a business executive in her everyday decisions? This is an important issue to be explored. The preferential option for the poor and powerless is more difficult to apply in the private sector than in the public sector. Public sector officials have officially recognized responsibilities for the poor and dispossessed, but this is not the case with business executives. Questions that would be raised by business executives are: How would this business action or policy effect the poor? Is this new product going to benefit the poor? Will this new action bring about new jobs for the poor? Is this new product or process wasteful of resources?

Response of Business and Labor

In a chapter entitled, "A New American Experiment: Partnership for the Public Good," the bishops spell out some specific implications of their moral stance. They point out that "institutional steps are needed today to expand the sharing of economic power and to relate the economic system more accountably to the common good." (Para. 285) They go on to call for "new patterns of partnership" and "new institutional mechanisms for accountability that also preserve the flexibility needed to respond quickly to a rapidly changing business environment." (Para. 286) It is precisely in this arena that the bishops are in fact most in line with current thinking and efforts of business people.

In a recent insightful commentary on the 2nd draft of the bishops' Letter, Elmer W. Johnson, Senior Vice President at General Motors says:

> . . . It is a remarkable document. Even more commendable is the morality of the process the Committee has undergone over the last few years in listening, conversing, digesting. This document could not have been produced except in personal piety and prayerful consideration and with a great deal of moral discourse.[18]

Johnson then describes how the letter is actually charting a course which is very much in the direction that U.S. business firms want to move also. Speaking for the business community, he says:

> To our shame we have found by now that our continued industrial vigor as a nation really hangs, not so much on new technologies or on more brilliant financial deals, but almost entirely on whether we can forge a new kind of human partnership among managers and employees.

Johnson then explains what General Motors is doing to encourage this sort of partnership. He talks about the importance of listening to all people in the firm, and enlisting their best ideas and support. Johnson's new partnership extends to suppliers and customers as well as all those actually engaged in the enterprise.

In the wake of faltering productivity of U.S. firms, poor product quality, the loss of world markets and the loss of jobs and revenue, many other American executives have begun to examine the attitudes of the people who makeup their firm. A concern for quality of product, looking to the long-term good of the firm, and loyalty to that firm are often lacking. These qualities are no more present among managers than they are among hourly workers. The short-term, numbers-oriented and selfish attitudes discussed above are perhaps especially characteristic of the "best and the brightest": the ambitious, able, well educated, "fast-track", upwardly mobile young executive. If selfish, career-oriented objectives are characteristic of managers, how can one expect blue collar workers to have more cooperative attitudes?

For blue collar workers the problems of powerlessness, meaninglessness and isolation are not new. They are well known, and have been studied over the years.[19] The problems have gained particular urgency in the light of the above problems of product quality and declining U.S. productivity. U.S. firms have hence begun large scale programs to reverse these trends. The purpose of these programs are the same: 1) elicit from all members of the organization their best ideas on how to do the work; 2) allow more autonomy in decisions that effect each person's work; and 3) provide an environment that will encourage cooperation and attention to quality. The expected results from such programs are: better quality products and greater productivity, along with the individual experiencing greater satisfaction with work.

The organizational culture of a firm can be influenced by management, ultimately top management. Top management determines the style of operating — whether that style is decisive and authoritarian, or collaborative and cooperative. It seems easier to manage in an authoritarian manner. It takes time to seek advice and to work for consensus. American managers are generally selected on the basis of their intelligence and their ability to make decisions, not on their consensus building skills. Yet that traditional style of management does not foster cooperation. It does not encourage members of the organization to think in terms of the common good. Indeed, in such firms even top management finds it difficult to think in terms of the common good.

While calling for more attention to collaboration and cooperation, management often continues to act in an older mode of status and authoritarianism. Among the sought after privileges of promotion in U.S. firms are: a special parking place, a corner office, key to the executive washroom, access to the executive dining room. In contrast, Japanese firms executives have no special parking place, no separate dining facilities, and their offices are often small and in the middle of the people they supervise. Status and separation do not encourage cooperation.

Consider the issue of executive compensation. Of all the nations of the western world, executive pay in the U.S. is more out of line with the pay of the average worker than in any other country. The rationale for high executive pay is familiar; to reward superior achievement, and to keep top talent at the firm so it is not lured to another firm. To be sure, the contribution of that executive to the financial success of the firm is many times greater than is reflected in that executive's pay. However, there is a downside to this policy: the effect on cooperation within the organization. This is especially true in cases where executives have asked workers to accept a pay freeze or a smaller increase, and have then proceeded to award themselves large increases. This sort of policy says to workers: "Get what you can now. No one else is going to look out for you. When management talks about cooperation, don't believe it. They preach cooperation when it is to their advantage, and discard it when it is not convenient."

Summary and Conclusions

The ethical norms implicitly and commonly used in the U.S. today are not adequate. Whatever adequacy the Protestant ethic had in generations past, the new ethic of self-interest, self-fulfillment and short-term thinking is no longer sufficient for today's complex society. While enlightened self-interest and the resulting "invisible hand" can accomplish much that is useful and good for society, there are many other important public policy issues that receive no attention. That is, a need that is not profitable to the self-interested individual is shoved to the background.

Using enlightened self-interest as the moral norm is inadequate in addressing some of the major problems discussed here, but it also encourages selfish thinking and attitudes. In addition, we in the U.S. resist agreeing on any goals, set of values, or moral norms. We pride ourselves on our pluralism: any American is entitled to do and think what he or she wants, as long as they do not hurt another. All of this makes developing moral consensus more difficult, yet it also makes it more important that it be done.

The Catholic bishops have performed an important service for the U.S. in incorporating in their socio-economic thinking a norm that is gaining acceptance among believers around the world: the preferential option for the poor and vulnerable. They have modified that norm to fit the American experience, and they have applied it to our problems. In doing so, they have focused our attention on community and solidarity: We as people are joined together in the same community, the same nation, and the same planet. Hence the preferential option for the poor once again puts the more traditional ethical norm of the common good in the spotlight, so that it might once again be useful to managers and policy makers.

Cooperation and consensus-building has become important in

business firms over the last decade. Pushed to the wall by Japanese competition, we have learned to our dismay that their business firms are characterized by teams, loyalty and consensus. American manufacturing and service firms now recognize that they can no longer afford the luxury of conflict, alienation and confrontation. If we in the U.S. had kept alive our ethical traditions about the common good and cooperation, we might now be far ahead in building these qualities in the business world. The common good, solidarity and the preferential option for the poor move us toward cooperation, concern for others, compassion and generosity. These are qualities that will fulfill the highest expectations of our social and religious beliefs.

Notes

1. See, for example, Daniel Bell, *The Cultural Contradictions of Capitalism* (New York: Basic Books, 1976).

2. Steven Muller, "Universities are Turning Out Highly Skilled Barbarians," *U.S. News & World Report* , Nov. 10, 1980, pp. 57-58. Muller is an historian and is currently president of Johns Hopkins University.

3. *Ibid.* , p. 57.

4. For an excellent presentation of this point, see William C. Frederick, "Toward CSR-3: The Normative Factor in Corporate Social Analysis." Paper presented at the Social Issues Division, The Academy of Management, San Diego, CA. Aug. 13, 1985.

5. For a further discussion of this new ethic, see Gerald F. Cavanagh, *American Business Values* (Englewood Cliffs, N.J.: Prentice-Hall, 1984), pp. 163-194.

6. See *The Judeo-Christian Vision and the Modern Corporation,* Oliver F. Williams and John W. Houck, eds. (Notre Dame, IN.: University of Notre Dame Press, 1982), pp. 1-19.

7. See Lee Iacocca, *Iacocca: An Autobiography* (Toronto: Bantam, 1984).

8. Alexis de Tocqueville, *Democracy in America* , tr. Henry Reeve (New York: Knopf, 1946), esp. p. 98, 122.

9. *Ibid.* , vol. II, p. 98.

10. Robert Bellah, et. al., *Habits of the Heart: Individualism and Commitment in American Life* (Berkeley: University of California Press, 1985), p. 76.

11. Carl Becker, *Freedom and Responsibility in the American Way of Life* (New York: Vantage Books, 1945).

12. *Habits of the Heart* , p. 23.

13. Thomas C. Cochran, *Challenges to American Values: Society, Business and Religion* (New York, 1985), p. 60.

14. William C. Norris, "A Risk-Avoiding, Selfish Society," *Business Week* , Jan. 28, 1980, p. 20.

15. James Fallows, "American Industry: What Ails It, How to Save It," *Atlantic,* September, 1980, pp. 35-50.

16. Derek Bok, "Our Legal System: Most Expensive, Least Efficient," *Associated Governning Board Reports* , July-August, 1983, pp. 39-46.

17. Catholic Social Teaching and the U.S. Economy , 2nd draft, *Origins* , Oct. 10, 1985, No. 33. For several commentaries see the volume *Catholic Social Teaching and the U.S. Economy: Working Papers for a Bishops' Pastoral* , John W. Houck and Oliver F. Williams, eds. (Washington, D.C.: University Press of America, 1984).

18. Elmer W. Johnson, "Shaping Our Economic Future," a commentary on the 2nd draft of the Cahtolic Bishops' Letter on the U.S. Economy, Dec. 11, 1985, p. 2, unpublished manuscript.

19. See, for example, *Work in America* , James O'Toole, ed. (Cambridge: MIT Press, 1973); *A Matter of Dignity: Inquiries into the Humanization of Work* , W.J. Heisler and John W. Houck, eds. (Notre Dame, IN.: University of Notre Dame Press, 1977).

Sixteen

The AFL-CIO Looks at the Common Good

WILLIAM J. CUNNINGHAM

The stability of a free society stems from the ethics of a society which enables its members to enjoy a sense of dignity. To have a life with dignity, individuals must be able to participate fully in the economic and political life of the society.

The Bishops' Pastoral Letter on the Economy is fundamentally a call for human dignity. The "preferential option for the poor" is a commitment to maintaining the openness and fairness of social institutions. There are a number of factors that contribute to poverty, and one of the most debilitating aspects of poverty is a loss of human dignity. Without some kind of compensating actions, a large share of the population will not have a life with dignity.

The elderly, the poor, and the handicapped must have access to programs that help them cope with their disadvantages, so that they are not isolated from the rest of society. All members

344

of society should have assurance that job opportunities will be available at a decent wage, and that they will not be thrown on the scrap heap because of an injury, old age, or changing technology.

We are seriously challenged by a philosophy which enables people to feel relieved of any responsibility to look after the needs of the less fortunate. It is the notion that there are "market forces" that are appropriate allocative elements of all resources. It assumes that every citizen is on an equal footing, wealth does not give some individuals unfair power over others, and that everyone is taken care of by automatic "market forces."

Not all the assumptions made about "market forces" are true. The market needs certain restraints and guidance that have been available in this nation for a long time. These aspects need to be reviewed from time to time and strengthened when appropriate.

There is an urgent need for social scientists to show the folly of the philosophy of detachment in the areas of employment, wages, health, education and the need to aid the victims of discrimination and hardship.

Employment

The AFL-CIO agrees with the Bishops' view of the fundamental importance of full employment. The Bishops' state in their second draft of the pastoral on the U.S. economy that "Full employment is the foundation of a just economy. The most urgent priority for domestic economic policy is the creation of new jobs with adequate pay and decent working conditions. We must make it possible as a nation for everyone who is seeking a job to find employment. Our emphasis on this goal is based on the conviction that human work has a special dignity and is a key to achieving justice in society" (Par. 135).

Too many Americans fail to sense the urgency of the Bishops' message, including political leaders who seem to ignore the plight of the 8.4 million Americans who need and want jobs; an additional 1.1 million too discouraged to continue the search for work and who are, therefore, no longer counted; and the 5.5

million who can only find part-time jobs. As of March 1986, more than 15 million Americans—12.8 percent of the work force—are wholly or partially unemployed.

Even the "official" unemployment rate of 7.2 percent in March 1986 is unacceptable to a humane society. That rate showed no improvement over the last 22 months, and over the last 18 years, unemployment has been on an upward trend, with each recession beginning from a higher unemployment rate than the previous one.

A few years ago it would have seemed ridiculous to talk about recovery and prosperity with unemployment standing at 7.2 percent. In both 1954 and 1971, it was called recession when unemployment rose to 6.1 percent. In the 1970s, when the jobless rate rose, both Presidents Ford and Carter launched direct job-creation programs because they, like the Bishops, the AFL-CIO, and the Congress that enacted the Humphrey-Hawkins Full Employment and Balanced Growth Act of 1978, accepted 3 to 4 percent joblessness as the upper limit for a full-employment society. That law, which requires the President to report annual numerical goals for reaching 4 percent unemployment, production, real income, productivity and prices, is disobeyed by the Administration.

Unemployment has a terrible effect on the lives of those unemployed in terms of social stability and measurable health effects. Job loss is strongly associated with depression, anxiety, aggression, insomnia, loss of self-esteem, marital problems, divorce and child abuse. Professor Harvey Brenner of Johns Hopkins University found that a sustained 1.4 percent increase in unemployment was directly responsible for 51,570 deaths, including 26,440 heart disease deaths, 1,740 homicides, and 1,540 suicides. This rise in unemployment was also directly responsible for 7,660 additional state prison admissions and 5,520 state mental hospital admissions.

The unemployment rate for black Americans at 14.7 percent in March 1986 was more than twice the average. And the rate for Americans of Hispanic origin was an extremely high 10.3 percent. The rate for black teenagers stood at an astonishing 43.7 percent.

The common good demands that such high rates be specifically addressed.

Arguments that high unemployment is a regrettable but necessary trade-off to restrain high prices are demonstrably untrue. High employment does not push up prices, as opponents of full employment claim. Unemployment rose right along with inflation in the 1970s. Inflation was caused by worldwide food shortages and huge U.S. grain sales to Russia, energy crises caused by the OPEC cartel, runaway increases in housing costs and health-care costs, and high interest rates.

The impact of high interest rates is largely responsible for high unemployment today. The high rates caused a decline in home construction, and hurt investment in new plants and equipment because they made such investment more costly. High interest rates are also responsible for the rise in the value of the dollar which is undermining America's ability to compete with foreign producers.

Fiscal policy has failed to target unemployment as a problem. Instead, fiscal policy has had as its goal cutting taxes for the higher-income brackets in the mistaken belief that the benefits would trickle down to help the less fortunate in society.

Because of the misdirection of governmental fiscal policy, fiscal policy has undermined long-term steps to achieve full employment and specific programs to foster economic growth and employment have been scrapped. Monetary policy has been shaped by fears of inflation, not by the nation's official goal of full employment.

There has been a sharp increase in the number of structurally unemployed. The cutback in training programs and the elimination of public service jobs are serious losses to those who might have used these programs to get a foot on a rung of the economic ladder. Clearly governmental policies which have destroyed so many of our nation's training and direct job creation programs need to be reversed.

Many job opportunities could be created by addressing the urgent need to improve the nation's physical infrastructure. (The problem of deteriorating infrastructure was examined by the Labor-Management Group and published in a 1983 report. The Labor-Management Group is a joint forum of the chief executive officers of the nation's largest corporations and the top elected labor leaders.)

A shorter workweek, particularly when combined with higher overtime pay, could produce a significant number of jobs. A reduction in the standard workweek is long overdue and should be reduced at least to 35 hours. Reductions from the sunrise-to-sunset workday took place throughout the 19th and 20th centuries. The 40-hour workweek became standard around 1940. The gains in productivity of the last 46 years certainly are more than adequate to justify a further reduction in the workweek.

To assure that a shorter workweek is adhered to, the overtime penalty should be raised from time-and-a-half to triple time, and all overtime should be voluntary. These measures would strengthen the incentive to hire more workers rather than requiring workers to work longer than the standard workweek.

Minimum Wage

For most people, income and dignity comes from work. It was found necessary to put a floor under the income from work because of the weaker bargaining position of workers compared to employers. The minimum wage, created to assure that the weakest in society would not be exploited, is an essential part of providing a floor of material well-being. However, the minimum wage has deteriorated sharply in recent years. The last time Congress adjusted the minimum wage was in 1977, raising the minimum wage in steps to $3.35 an hour on January 1, 1981. In the 5 years since then, the cost of living has risen by 25 percent, which means that to restore the same purchasing power, the minimum wage would need to be $4.20 on January 1, 1986. The minimum wage is almost exactly $2 an hour *below* the poverty line, which the government defined as $5.34 per hour in September 1985.

Although most workers earn more than the federal minimum, some 5 to 8 million are paid no more than $3.35 an hour, and some are exploited at even lower wages.

Now, more than 8 years since Congress last acted to adjust the minimum wage, that floor badly needs to be brought up to date. The basic idea of a minimum wage is to provide a floor to wages so that human labor cannot be bought for less than a living wage, enabling employers and producers to compete with one another from a wage base, applicable to all, which prevents exploitation. The minimum wage has fallen so far in buying power that it is in itself exploitive and is no longer sufficient to support even a single person, let alone a family.

Low-wage workers do not share in the general improvement in living standards generated by improving national productivity, unless their wages rise at the same rate as other incomes. The minimum wage ought to be set in terms of average wages rather than depending on *ad hoc* determination by Congress. The AFL-CIO has urged that the minimum wage be set at 50 percent of average wages. The closest relationship between the minimum wage and average wages occurred with the 1967 and 1968 adjustments which put the minimum wage at 53 and 58 percent of average wages. In 1985, the $3.35 minimum wage was only 40 percent of the average wage paid non-supervisory workers.

Arguments that the minimum wage is inflationary or might lead to higher unemployment are disproved by 50 years of experience which shows that modest adjustments in the minimum wage brought neither widespread inflation nor massive unemployment.

Civil Rights

Discrimination against women and minorities clearly plays a role in the high rates of joblessness and low pay among both groups. The lack of adequate child care facilities and employers' unwillingness to provide part-time employment opportunities with fringe benefits, adds greatly to the difficulties faced by women workers.

The current Administration has put a brake on needed improvements in civil rights laws and has retrogressed on enforcement. The budget of the Equal Employment Opportunity Commission (EEOC) and other civil rights enforcement agencies has been reduced. The EEOC chair advocates a policy which would disregard statistical data showing underrepresentation as an indicator of discrimination. Similarly, the Labor Department's Office of Federal Contract Compliance Programs has slackened enforcement of Executive Order 11246, which prohibits discrimination by federal contractors, and the Civil Rights Division of the Department of Justice opposes affirmative action and mislabels affirmative action goals and timetables as "quotas."

The AFL-CIO believes that civil rights laws must be vigorously enforced to deal with discrimination in jobs and other areas like housing. There is a continuing serious need to put teeth into the enforcement of existing fair housing legislation.

Economic Vitality

There is growing recognition that since the early 1970s, the American economy has been showing recurring problems of a serious loss of economic vitality. The AFL-CIO has joined others in the advocacy of an industrial policy to bring about a coordinated approach to those policies that most affect economic growth and the health of American industry.

The United States is still the greatest economic power on earth, but its lead has been decreasing and its manufacturing industries have been severely damaged. An industrial policy would help the nation to sort out national priorities and channel resources into areas that will modernize private and public facilities and restore the national economy to a condition of stable growth. If we fail, we believe the country will continue to lag in productivity growth and international trade, and America's standard of living will continue to decline.

The Reagan Administration's devotion to "market forces" as a substitute for economic policy has dampened the debate on industrial policy, but the consequences of the failure of the Reagan policies to fulfill their promise will revive the interest in a national policy to replace today's uncoordinated policy that produces haphazard results.

A major cause of this loss of vitality are the actions of U.S.-based multinationals in closing plants at home and opening new ones abroad. They are encouraged by U.S. tax laws which defer any taxation of profits from foreign operations until (or unless) those profits are brought back to the United States, and are further stimulated by a dollar-for-dollar credit against U.S. tax liability for income taxes paid to foreign governments.

Recent articles in *Business Week* bemoan the problem of the "hollowing of the American corporation," which is the process of American firms giving up the production of goods and instead becoming distributors of foreign-made products. At the same time, many other countries have implemented aggressive industrial and trade policies to improve their domestic economies at the expense of ours. In steel, auto, electronics, railcars, aircraft, semiconductors, optic fibers, and a host of emerging industries, the advanced industrial countries in Europe and Japan and the newly developing industrial countries have applied a wide variety of strategic government support—from low-cost credit to protection from import competition and government assistance in technology development. The result leaves U.S. producers facing a consistently uphill battle for sales, not only abroad, but also in their own national market.

The AFL-CIO has endorsed the creation of a tripartite industrial policy board which would have representatives from business, government, and labor. The board would develop strategies to ensure the growth of a diversified American economy. Under the policy guidance of this board, a national development bank would invest public and private funds in necessary reindustrialization projects.

Economic Inequality

The Bishops warn that the economic inequality existing in the United States is a threat to human solidarity which will lead to deep social divisions and conflict. Extreme inequality, they warn, in the second draft, undermines human dignity and prevents people from playing a role in social and economic life (Par. 183).

The Bishops point out that 28 percent of the total net wealth is held by the richest 2 percent of families in the United States, 57 percent by the top 10 percent. If homes and other real estate are excluded, 54 percent of net financial assets are held by 2 percent of all families, those whose annual income is more than $125,000. Ninety percent of all families own only 14 percent of these assets (Par. 181). In terms of income, the Bishops note that in 1984, the bottom 20 percent of American families received only 4.7 percent of the total income in the nation, and the bottom 40 percent received only 15.7 percent, the lowest share on record. In contrast, the top one-fifth received 42.9 percent of the total income, the highest share since 1948 (Par. 182). The Bishops' conclusion that "Justice requires that our society take the necessary steps to decrease these inequities" (Par. 183) seems to us inarguable.

The recession and persistent high unemployment, the budget cuts, and the tax policies of the Reagan Administration have contributed to the shift of income from the poor to the wealthy. The recession and high unemployment, together with the trade problems, have put unions at a disadvantage in trying to maintain living standards. The cuts in the federal budget from 1981 to 1986 primarily hurt the poor. The tax policies of the Reagan Administration have shifted the tax burden from the wealthy and corporations to low- and moderate-income wage and salary earners.

The enormous Reagan tax cuts for the wealthy and corporations were based on the argument that the wealthy should receive larger tax cuts because they would save more, and those savings would be used for job creating and productivity enhancing investment. As the AFL-CIO predicted, that argument proved false. In fact, although tremendous sums were given to the wealthy, the savings rate was no higher after the Reagan tax cuts than during the Carter Administration or during the period of the entire decade of the 1970s. The Reagan tax cuts also failed to produce any lasting improvement in investment. And the nation's nonfarm productivity showed no increase at all in 1985.

The revenue drain resulting from the 1981 tax cut has put tremendous pressure on Congress to cut the budget for crucial social programs. The drain amounted to $130 billion, or 70 percent of the expected deficit, for the fiscal year beginning in October 1985, even after taking into account the 1982 and 1984 tax legislation which trimmed some of the abuses and recouped some of the revenue losses of the 1981 law.

Corporations in 1985 are paying merely 10 percent of all federal taxes, compared to nearly 25 percent in the mid-1950s, and year after year many highly profitable corporations pay no federal income tax at all. The 1981 reduction of the 70 percent tax bracket to 50 percent, which greatly benefits wealthy individuals, remains in place, and loopholes widened for income from capital gains and savings remain open. Despite the reductions, the President has urged that the top tax rate be cut further to 35 percent.

Workers' wages and salaries are taxed at far higher rates than "unearned income" on the savings, investments, and estates of the wealthy. The AFL-CIO has called for an end to this preferential double standard. The AFL-CIO also seeks the elimination of the so-called incentives that subsidize mergers, takeovers, plant shutdowns, overseas investments, and other activities that conflict with the national interest. We urge that a basic structure be developed which assures that the poor are off the tax rolls and that the loopholes and escape hatches for the wealthy are closed.

The nation's social values are expressed in the budget of the federal government. The budgets during the Reagan Administration and the proposal for next year are a grave threat to programs which alleviate the hardships for the elderly, the poor, and others in distress.

The Administration has slashed job training programs and calls for more cuts next year. The proposed 1987 budget would jeopardize the health security of the nation with the cuts in programs for senior citizens, the poor, jobless workers, veterans, and federal employees.

The Administration has called for slashes in, or elimination of, a variety of programs which provide income, food, and urgently needed services to the poor and the disadvantaged. At a time when 33 million Americans, including one-fourth of all children, are in poverty and city officials report a sharp rise in hunger and homelessness, the Administration proposes new cuts in programs which help the downtrodden and the hungry. On top of the billions of dollars of previous reductions, the Administration's budget for 1987 demands new cuts which would force millions of the deprived even deeper into the mire of poverty and malnutrition.

The Administration's proposed budget calls for further increases in the defense budget, which has doubled from 1980 to 1986, swallowing up an increasing share of the federal budget and the nation's income. Defense spending should not take place at the expense of needed social programs.

Government actions which ignore the needs of those suffering hardships are exemplified by the House of Representatives recent action to reject legislation that would have required large firms to provide 60 days advance notice of plant closings and assure workers the right to bargain with employers concerning such a decision. In labor's view, along with the training and relocation programs advocated in the letter, displaced workers should be entitled to special severance rights; pension protection, including early retirement options; and also an opportunity to purchase the plant at a fair price, if they so desire.

Trade

The absence of a strong and predictable U.S. trade policy has contributed significantly to the sharp deterioration of the international economic position of the United States. Scores of domestic industries and millions of American workers have been left defenseless against an onslaught of imports spurred by strategies of foreign competitors, the debt burden of developing countries, and the high interest rate policy of the Federal Reserve Board.

In early 1986, America was recording trade deficits that would have been unthinkable not too many years ago. The U.S. merchandise trade deficit in 1985 was 3 1/2 times higher than in 1980. For manufactured goods alone, America has gone from a surplus of $12 billion in 1980 to a deficit last year that reached $113 billion. During this period, exports fell 2.5 percent while imports of manufactured products shot up an astonishing 96 percent. In 1985, the import share of the U.S. market reached 50 percent for apparel, 23 percent for autos, 36 percent for machine tools, 25 percent for steel, and more than 75 percent for shoes. Deficits were experienced even in advanced products like semiconductors and telecommunications equipment.

The Department of Commerce estimated that in 1984 alone, 2.3 million jobs in manufacturing were displaced by trade, with a net loss of 1.1 million for the economy as a whole. In a study on displaced workers, the Bureau of Labor Statistics reported that between 1979 and 1984, 11.5 million workers lost their jobs to plant closure, slack work or layoffs. Twenty-five percent of those 11.5 million are still looking for work and 15 percent have left the labor force entirely.

President Reagan, in his annual Economic Report of the President, wrote that "Our international trade policy rests firmly on the foundation of free and open markets." But such free and open markets that President Reagan bases his trade policy simply do not exist—certainly not in Japan, the European Community, Brazil, Taiwan or Mexico. To the contrary, these nations' trade policies include quotas, stringent inspection requirements, discriminatory standards, export subsidies and incentives, industrial targeting programs, buy-national policies, export performance requirements, barter agreements and co-production requirements.

The Administration asserts that reliance on free trade principles results in higher standards of living both for this nation and its trading partners. The average weekly earnings for U.S. production/nonsupervisory employees have declined more than 9 percent from 1977 to 1985 in constant dollars. The reduction of employment in the manufacturing sector and growth of jobs in the service sector have no doubt contributed to this decline. Average weekly earnings for manufacturing workers in 1985 reached $385. For workers in finance, insurance and real estate, the average was $289. Workers in retail trade averaged $177, and employees in other types of service industries received $261. In the Bureau of Labor Statistics study mentioned above, almost one-half of the displaced manufacturing workers who were fortunate enough to find alternative employment were forced to accept lower pay.

Advocates of free trade believe that current trade policy generates a more productive use of this nation's resources and more rapid innovation. But unemployment is not productive. Nor does a highly skilled machinist contribute more to this nation's wealth in a retail store than he did making sophisticated machinery. Innovation does not benefit the United States if new technology is licensed or sold to foreign concerns, causing the production of innovative goods to be transferred overseas.

The most damaging influence on trade since 1980 has been the high valuation of the U.S. dollar relative to other currencies. The dollar rose 87 percent against the currencies of major U.S. trading partners from July 1980 to February 1985. The overvaluation of the U.S. dollar is the result primarily of high U.S. interest rates, which have attracted tremendous amounts of foreign capital to the United States.

The massive borrowing of the federal government to finance the huge deficits caused by the 1981 tax cuts and the increases in defense spending has put pressure on credit markets and interest rates. At the same time, obsessed by the specter of inflation, the Federal Reserve Board has been following a tight money, high interest rate policy for most of the 1980s.

Many are reassured that the U.S. trade problem will be helped now that the dollar has begun to decline. Despite the decline, the dollar remains some 40 percent higher against the currencies of our major trading partners than it was in 1980. In fact, the dollar has continued to appreciate somewhat against the currencies of Canada, Mexico and Brazil.

The AFL-CIO believes that the current trend in trade policy means not only extreme hardship for American manufacturing workers and the communities they live in, but a loss in the real productivity of the American economy and a crippling of its ability to generate jobs, incomes and tax revenues needed to assure job security and an adequate standard of living for all Americans. The Reagan Administration has reneged on its promise to make Trade Adjustment Assistance funds available to those displaced from their jobs by imports and has targeted the program for extinction.

American workers and their unions have been among the strongest supporters of foreign trade and foreign aid programs designed to lift the people of developing nations out of poverty. Unfortunately, policies are now in place, which countenance and even encourage the exploitation of Third-World workers while undermining American jobs and living standards. As a result, America's chief constituency for effective aid to the people who need it most is being rapidly eroded.

A fair trade policy needs to be developed in the U.S. that deals with the effects of an overvalued dollar, that reacts vigorously to unfair foreign trade practices, and that assures American industry adequate safeguards against a sudden or predatory undercutting of its ability to produce. And the Trade Adjustment Assistance program should be retained and restored to provide adequate compensation to those unemployed because of trade and to improve training.

Trade Unions

The Bishops' Letter on the Economy recognizes the importance of trade unions and the rights of workers to join unions. The Letter criticizes the work of union busters and the unfair employers they serve. The Bishops support needed changes in the nation's labor laws to protect workers' rights.

The nation's labor laws are badly in need of reform to prevent abuses of the law which prevent workers from exercising their right to join unions. In recent years, a growing antiunion sentiment among employers has resulted in an enormous growth in the use of consultants whose job it is to intimidate and frustrate workers who seek to organize unions to rectify problems in the workplace. The use of such consultants often is a signal that an employer is ready to use any method, including breaking the law, to prevent employees from joining a union.

Since 1957, firing for union activity and other unfair labor practices has been increasing rapidly. From 1957 to 1980, the number of unfair labor practice charges filed against employers rose from 3,655 to 31,281, while the number of elections rose from 4,729 to 7,296. In 1957, 922 illegally dismissed employees were ordered reinstated to their jobs by the National Labor Relations Board. That number rose to 10,033 in 1980, a rise of more than tenfold. Professor Paul Weiler of Harvard University estimates that one worker is fired exercising the right to join a union for every 20 who vote in union representation elections.

The chief weapon of union busters is fear, generated through illegal firings, harassment and spying on union supporters, and intensive threats of layoffs or plant closings. Another weapon is delay. Consultants orchestrate every legal objection possible in an effort to discourage workers and destroy their confidence in their union's effort to improve their situation.

An example of the widespread acceptance by business of anti-union efforts took place at the annual American Bankers Association conference in Washington, D.C., when a consulting firm openly offered attendees a "contingency plan" on "what to do if you have a union drive." For $3,000, the firm offered one day of on-site consulting, "tailoring the plan to the needs of your bank," and comprehensive data and information to assist the bank's lawyers in delaying an NLRB election "to assure as much time as possible for the campaign." The intent was spelled out as to "stop any momentum gained by a union and secure the most advantageous voting unit for your bank."

The Virginia Chamber of Commerce brags that it is working "day and night" to prevent unionization in private firms, and that "At the same time, we are working day and night to prevent the organization of public employees. We have helped draft, back and pass legislation preventing collective bargaining by public employees in any area, at any level, in the Commonwealth of Virginia."

How far some firms will go in breaking the law to destroy a union is revealed in a *Charleston Gazette* news report of August

14, 1985, concerning a former employee of a security agency who is now seeking immunity from prosecution to tell his story. His job was to provoke violence in order to help companies get injunctions against striking unions. Besides describing actions to provoke workers on picket lines into confrontations with security guards, he told of blowing up an electrical transformer on one occasion and setting $148,000 worth of lumber on fire on another. Both incidents were blamed on unions in order to get court injunctions.

One major conglomerate decided 20 years ago to implement its goal of a "union-free environment" by means of its merger and acquisition policies. The company began to expand in "right-to-work" states in the late 1960s and to acquire companies with antiunion policies. Finally, the company adopted the standard antiunion practices developed by union-busting consultants. As a result of the company's threats, intimidation and harassment of union supporters, unions have won only seven of 33 NLRB elections held in the company's facilities over the past 15 years. A plant in Athens, Pennsylvania, which had been with the machinists' union for 40 years, was decertified in 1981 after an intense antiunion effort in which supervisors were instructed to grill each worker three times a week and to stress the danger of losing jobs unless the union was destroyed.

Antiunion employers break the law because it is profitable, and they will continue to do so until labor laws are reformed to penalize effectively lawbreaking and, thus, take the profit out of denying workers their rights.

Remedies for workers illegally fired for supporting their unions must be prompt as well as effective. Current practice, requiring discharged employees to wait out lengthy court procedures to get their jobs back, creates hardship for the individual and has a chilling effect on other employees. Because the loss of a job causes family strain, humiliation, fear and intimidation as well as a lost paycheck, double back pay, rather than merely lost wages, should be required to compensate for the losses the worker suffers.

Employers should also be penalized for illegally refusing to bargain. Today, all of the costs of an employer's illegal refusal to bargain rest on the employees. Violation costs the lawbreaking employer nothing, even though he profits through violating the law.

The management consultant could not flourish, or even survive, in an atmosphere that did not encourage such clandestine activity. The United States itself should no longer subsidize repeated, willful violations of workers' rights. For a country that preaches human rights to the rest of the world, debarment from bidding on federal contracts is a minimal action against its own human rights violators.

Election procedures for workers to select a union if they so choose should be sped up or the union should be certified as bargaining agent at once if a substantial majority of the workers have signed authorization cards. These procedures would reduce the current lengthy delays that deny justice.

In stressing the importance of the right to form unions as "a specific application of the more general right to associate" (Par. 103) the Bishops touch on the AFL-CIO's conviction that democracy cannot survive its suppression. Experience at home and in countries beyond our borders bears out the truth of the Bishops' assertion that "violations of the freedom to associate, wherever they occur . . . are an intolerable attack on social solidarity" (Par. 104).

Union Responsibilities

Trade unionists accept the Bishops' comments on the responsibilities of workers and trade unions that "workers have obligations to their employers, and trade unions also have duties to society as a whole." We also recognize the importance of eliminating racial and sexual discrimination. The Bishops noted that "Many U.S. unions have exercised leadership in the struggle for justice for minorities and women. Racial and sexual discrimination, however, have blotted the record for some unions. Organized labor has a responsibility to work positively toward eliminating the injustice this discrimination has caused."

Trade unions do not pretend to have conquered every sign of

prejudice within our ranks, but the labor movement has led the nation in rooting out systematic, institutional discrimination. Such discriminatory provisions as existed in union constitutions were eliminated at the formation of the AFL-CIO in 1955, and the trade union movement became a leading participant in the civil rights coalition that secured passage of the Civil Rights Act, the Voting Rights Act, the Fair Housing Act and the Equal Pay Act. We did so because long experience has taught us that equal rights are essential for all workers to achieve the solidarity that alone can make a union strong enough to win gains in the workplace. Convinced that divisiveness based on racial, ethnic, religious or sexual distinctions has done nothing but harm to workers in their struggle for dignity in the workplace, unions have resolutely sought to eliminate such biases wherever they exist.

The Bishops encourage unions to seek ways to improve their relationship with management through cooperative efforts. Trade unions are engaged in all of the approaches cited by the Bishops including profit sharing, quality of work life programs, and cooperative ownership and increased stock ownership.

Workers and their unions want to cooperate with management because workers feel a stake in the health of the firms where they work. The collective bargaining process is necessarily an adversarial process aimed at developing a contract that is beneficial to both sides. The contract signed by the union and management should, however, lay the basis for cooperation during the life of the contract and ensure the vitality of the firm.

A number of employers have shown a willingness to broaden the scope of collective bargaining and work out ways to increase the participation of workers in decisionmaking. Trade unionists are glad to have this interest and believe that broadening worker participation in decisionmaking will be beneficial to both workers and management by giving workers a greater sense of involvement in their work and a sense that their experience and point of view are valued by management.

Labor and Foreign Policy

Trade unions have long shared the Bishops' view that to be an effective moral force, the labor movement must play a global role (Par. 106). American labor plays an active role in international affairs, morally and materially assisting workers in other lands to build free trade unions, especially in developing countries of Africa, Asia and Latin America. Free and effective trade unions in those countries are essential to the defense and expansion of free and democratic societies. The U.S. labor movement also maintains relationships with other national labor organizations through the International Confederation of Free Trade Unions, the 16 international trade secretariats which group workers by their trade or industry, and the Trade Union Advisory Committee to the Organization for Economic Cooperation and Development (OECD). American unions also play a major role in the International Labor Organization (ILO).

Four foreign service institutes operated by the AFL-CIO reach out to trade unions in other nations, offering on-site educational programs in collective bargaining, labor legislation and techniques of maintaining democratic unions. The institutes also offer leadership and specialized training courses at the George Meany Center for Labor Studies and provide and administer foreign aid for social projects, including the creation of credit unions and cooperatives and construction of housing, schools and hospitals.

The AFL-CIO foreign service institutes are the American Institute for Free Labor Development, formed in 1962 to help strengthen democratic trade unions in Latin America and the Caribbean; the Asian-American Free Labor Institute, founded in 1968 in response to the needs of democratic trade union in Asia; and the African-American Labor Center, founded in 1964. A fourth, the Free Trade Union Institute, was created in 1977 to develop programs and projects between the AFL-CIO and European trade unions, particularly those of the newly emerging democracies of Spain and Portugal.

Conclusion

The AFL-CIO shares the Bishops' view that the federal government must play an active role to provide justice and fairness in American society and agrees strongly with their rejection of any statist or totalitarian doctrines.

The AFL-CIO has steadfastly opposed totalitarian political ideologies and has insisted that democracy is essential for workers to express and promote their rights. The AFL-CIO also recognizes that government must play an active role to bring about full employment, improved working conditions, greater equality, and to promote justice and fairness in our institutions and laws.

The American trade union movement is heartened by the expression of religious and moral values put forth in the Bishops' Pastoral Letter on the U.S. Economy. The AFL-CIO agrees strongly with the sentiments of the Bishops that the economy is not a machine that operates according to its own inexorable laws, and that persons are not mere objects tossed about by economic forces. We welcome the Bishops' support for the role of trade unions in their role of protecting human dignity, and for the support of a positive government role to guarantee human rights and justice.

Seventeen

Visual Media and the Common Good: Two Experiences

(1) Media and the Common Good: The Search for Justice

PETER MANN

Living as we do in the age of electronic communications, our understanding of the common good becomes itself "mediated," that is, defined, enlarged, or narrowed by the images, symbols and stories of media.

For example: Many of us will remember the feelings with which we first witnessed the television broadcast of the Challenger explosion. There was a sense of unreality, of disbelieving shock, as we saw the moments of the flight tick away. We became aware in a new way of the spacecraft as technology enclosing, protecting and threatening human life — the lives of people

364

we knew and cared about. When the spacecraft finally disintegrated, the images kept on exploding in our awareness. We sensed this immediately as a collective grief; we witnessed it together, as a people. Here the common good is rooted in shared experiences of grief, as well as celebration, and media are an incredibly powerful instrument of this common awareness.

Yet media images have an individual history. Afterwards it became almost intolerable to watch this explosion repeated throughout the day on multiple networks. The images had become too painful to see. We turned away, for whatever personal or common reasons, maybe psychic numbing, or a feeling of being manipulated by the networks into voyeurism. Later on, as we shifted into a new mode of investigating the causes of the disaster, we were able to observe the images again and follow the theories as to what happened in those few seconds of flight. Images resonate not only backward, into the past (What happened? Why did it happen?), but also into the future (What does this mean for the space program? For the future of manned space travel?). Yet on a human level those first images remain impossible to comprehend: they go on resonating within us as new theories emerge that the astronauts may have been alive even after the initial explosion until their capsule struck the ocean. For foundational images such as the first moon landing, the Kennedy assassination, and the Challenger explosion, continue to change us and change with us. Such media images are really *compressed narratives* and reading these images is a collective as well as personal activity.[1] Our awareness of the common good today is, partly at least, a transaction with media changes.

The common good is mediated *politically* also — by our institutions and public servants. Our awareness of these is shaped by media, by radio, television, newsprint and the images these bring us. Today, our attitude to media cannot be only one of acceptance and consent. We have to view media with what Paul Ricoeur calls "suspicion."[2] This means critically examining the messages brought to us by media, and bringing suspicion to bear on the self-interest and manipulation implicit in these messages.

Mark Alan Stamaty in the *Village Voice* comic strip "Washingtoon" is a ruthless media demystifier of political pretension. Soon after the 1984 Presidential election he showed Democrat politicians assembled for a weekend meditation seminar with Sri Swami Pollsternanda, a long-haired guru who specialized in helping politicians get in touch with the "opinion poll within." As the politicians meditated, they indeed experienced shifts in their political priorities and value systems. One politician felt the marginalized — the minorities, the poor and unemployed — slipping out of his consciousness, becoming truly marginal. Another got the message from some inner source that a strong defense and cuts in social spending were indeed the voice of truth. Gradually they became realigned for a new agenda. In a sequence of images, the common good — based on traditions, loyalties, and shared memories and hopes — was transformed into personal security, based on power, self-interest, and fear.

The same principles apply to media images of the global community. Children had been starving for a long time in Africa, but a piece of film picked up by NBC via satellite from the BBC showed these starving children to American homes, and people were galvanized to action. This is the strength of television. As a worldwide communication system it spans the globe and connects together the world community. It brings us almost *instantaneously* gripping and troubling images of freshly breaking news. It works best when it communicates events, stories and symbols which evoke powerful feelings. It is weak in showing the connections between events, the relationships between its images and the political, social or economic nexus which undergirds the news. The attention span of commercial television is too brief, its themes exhausted too quickly, its obsession with packaging and entertainment too paramount for it to become an ongoing pathway to understanding, conscientization, and conversion. In the words of Neil Postman, the visual language of television "denies interconnectedness, proceeds without context, argues the irrelevance of history, explains nothing and offers fascination in place of complexity and coherence."[3]

In another sense, everything depends on the awareness we ourselves bring to media images. We can perceive the starving African as a "helpless victim" or as a "struggling underdog." The first perception may lead to compassion and charity. The second has the seed within it of solidarity and justice, which is the awareness of a relationship. Media can "mediate" the common good, but we must also say that it is only through a deep awareness of the common good will we perceive images not only as illustrations of reality "as it is," but also as a window onto reality "as it might become."

Media can make us conscious of our common humanity and of our solidarity with people. But media can also narrow our consciousness, and turn us away from the common good toward a privatized and individualistic vision of the good life. Robert Bellah sees the culture of American individualism, rooted as it is in the value of freedom as being free of ties to others, and in the individual self as the one firm reality, coming to a certain climax in the culture of television:

> Television has no message, in the usual sense of the word. It has no ideology. It doesn't really believe in anything. In some uncanny way it is the last phase of a tradition that began with some nobility, namely the Enlightenment, in pushing the notion of debunking, unmasking and criticism to its final end...At the same time that this unmasking is taking place, there is no call for any change. In fact, the feeling conveyed is that there is nothing that can be done about it. The hidden message, meanwhile, is that material accumulation is the only goal that makes sense. This concept is not presented as something debatable; it is simply there and taken for granted...The essential message of television is that nothing makes any difference.[4]

Bellah is referring here to prime time, commercial television. If his perception is correct, the struggle for the common good must challenge the privatized and consumerist vision of the good life presented within such media. Yet within all forms of media a struggle is taking place to define and manipulate the common good by controlling people's perceptions. Political campaigns are increasingly becoming media campaigns, with vast sums of money spent to create the right images and perceptions among possible voters. Media images package political conflicts and issues in terms of slogans and perceptions. What perception of the Soviet Union is conveyed in the phrase "the evil empire"? Or when the Soviet Union defines itself as a "peace-loving socialist democracy"? Or when contras are renamed "freedom fighters"? Politics in the media age becomes more and more a struggle to define and control people's images and perceptions. By controlling images, you have made the first steps toward controlling people. Roland Barthes' warning remains powerful:

> "...consider the United States, where everything is transformed into images: only images exist and are produced and consumed...it (the image) completely derealizes the human world of conflicts and desires, under cover of illustrating it...the so-called advanced societies consume images...(not) beliefs."[5]

Search For Justice

In the age of electronic communications, media must use images, symbols and stories to explore the human world of conflict and desire, not simply to illustrate it. Images must be found which are not used up in private consumption but instead take us to the heart of the common good. To illustrate this I will talk about "Search for Justice," which is a five-part video series on the U. S. bishops' Economic Pastoral. It uses documentary, interview and debate to bring to viewers the stories and conflicts regarding economic justice within American society, seen from the perspective of Catholic social teaching. The individual programs cover the following themes: 1, The Church and the Economy; 2, The Economy and Human Work; 3, Poverty in the Midst of Plenty; 4, Global Impact of the U.S. Economy; 5, Economic Planning.

From the beginning the project was designed to accompany the successive drafts of the pastoral. "Search for Justice" was a collaborative undertaking between the bishops' staff and theologians, representing the Church's social teaching, with a coalition of Catholic television producers under Edward J. Murray of Oblate Media Images. "Search for Justice" is television designed to inform and educate, to move people into dialogue. It was designed as interactive television, to be viewed by groups in parishes and dioceses throughout the country. It was brought to viewers by the Catholic Telecommunications Network of America (CTNA), the bishops' satellite telecommunications network, and through the dioceses and cable systems connected to CTNA. Discussion leader's guides and viewer's guides were provided to accompany the series, which is now being distributed by Paulist Press. In my own experience of showing the series on cable companies on Long Island, of organizing parish groups to view the series, and of following up with a live video discussion in which the local bishop entered into dialogue with representatives of business, labor and the church community about the implications of the Economic Pastoral for our local situation, I found the series to be an effective educational tool. The people who came out to view the series in discussion groups, as well as those who watched the series on cable in their homes, were a cross section of the Catholic community. The series not only reached a "social justice" audience, but also a wider audience which brought to the programs their own experience of work in business and factories and the home, as well as those of poverty and unemployment. It was gratifying that the programs brought groups (who rarely talk with each other) into dialogue about economic values and questions of justice, i.e., business and labor, unions and church groups and ecumenical representatives. As has been the case all over the country, the Economic Pastoral provides a framework for dialogue regarding values among people from the most varied fields in academia, business, labor and the church. A still outstanding task is to get the teaching of the Pastoral into the Catholic educational system at every level. The use of video will be crucial for achieving this.

I would now like to single out certain aspects of the "Search for Justice" which exemplify the issues raised in the first part of this paper. Archbishop Weakland has alluded to the problem of many audiovisual approaches to economic issues: they are eloquent in depicting scenes of poverty and so creating an emotional reaction, but seem less effective in showing the principles underlying economic justice. As we know, the Pastoral is rooted in such principles as the dignity of each human person as made in God's image, the growth of this dignity through life in community, a community covenanted to justice, the rights which flow from the dignity of each person, and the themes of the common good and solidarity with the poor which define economic justice.

How did the "Search for Justice" deal with this tension? From the beginning those producing the series were aware that the message of the Pastoral had to be communicated in ways connatural to television: not primarily through lecture or interview, although these play a certain role in a series with an educational aim and substantial budget restrictions, but predominantly through symbols, stories and feelings.

In our social and political life there is a complex interaction and tension between the flag, as an American national symbol, and the cross as a central symbol of Christianity. To bring together the theme of flag and cross is to evoke complex issues: of Christ and culture, of the power of civil religion, and of the unfinished agenda in being both American and Catholic.

The opening credits of "Search for Justice" show the flag as an unfinished and dynamic symbol, evoking the American experience. The stars and stripes come together from different directions and do not form a simple harmonious image. The cross as a formative religious tradition is woven into the texture of the flag, of American national life. Yet there are many religious symbols which could have been used, just as there are many religious traditions which make up the American experience and its unique church-state relationship. The music to these credits has the same ambivalence: it is a combination of "Oh God, Our Help in Ages Past" and the Battle Hymn of the Republic. Yet this tension is also at the heart of the Economic Pastoral, for as "citizen believers" how can we search for justice?

We can perceive the way the flag is used, and misused, in contemporary media, seeing the flag waved by a Rambo or a Hulk

Hogan in a comic strip world of American good versus Communist evil. We are brought into the tension between patriotism and nationalism which is to love one's country the way one loves one's family — with pride, but also with care and concern for fairness and solidarity with others — rather than with arrogance and boasting about being No.1.

The Economics Pastoral in its second draft deals with this theme that the American experiment is unfinished and we are being called to a new experiment in economic democracy. Memories of past achievements are balanced by an awareness of the suffering and conflict which were part of those achievements. Hopes for the future are shaped by the challenge to conversion in the economic order. The bishops identify key symbols and events in the American experience but they also add: "The American experiment in freedom and justice for all must attend to unfinished business."[6]

The U. S. Experience and Religious Life

One task facing any media project is to evoke people's stories. For media works more directly via stories and the feelings they evoke than by rational discourse and abstract argument. There are many voices within the American Catholic community, and Catholic pluralism is a reality affecting parish life, individual dioceses and regions and the whole church. This reflects partly the pluralism of the wider American society, and partly it expresses the unique history of the American Church as formed by waves of immigrants into an extraordinary ethnic diversity. A new reality has emerged in what has been called the end of the Immigrant Church and the accession of American Catholics to the economic, social and political establishment.[7]

This realignment has important implications for pastoral strategy today. To what extent have Catholics been absorbed by American life and culture and where have they retained the distinctive strengths of Catholicism with its sense of community, sacramental life, and fellowship within a transnational body?

Whatever the results of these inquiries, this new reality of American Catholicism will only enter the consciousness of the church community when individual Catholics and Catholic groups can be seen and heard telling their stories, sharing their experiences and discovering together what unites and what divides them.

Effective use of the media is a key to this communication. For this is where people are. They no longer come together in the basement of the parish church and they can no longer be adequately reached by the traditional means of ministry. Through the VCR revolution the image is equalling the easy dissemination of print. There has to be a video ministry for the electronic age and Catholics should develop this in their own way, without necessarily emulating the methods and ideology of fundamentalist mass media and televangelism.[8]

The identity and uniqueness of Catholicism is at stake. For powerful forces, within modern society — and media are among these forces — tend to homogenize people and erase what is unique to individual cultures and traditions. (Other forces tend to fragment people and encapsulate them within their own milieu.) Some would argue that Catholics in the United States are so pluralistic that they no longer have a real awareness of belonging to one Catholic church, that their Catholic identity is shattered. If this is so, then communications media will be essential in the task of reintegration. For the same media which privatize and isolate can also become the pathways to communicating a new sense of belonging to a community and seeking the common good.

"Search for Justice" brings together the many voices of Americans, and American Catholics, regarding economic justice. We experience Catholic identity and diversity, as well as a powerful witness that Jesus was on the side of the poor and that is where the bishops belong also. At the same time, we hear strong rejection of the bishops' position, that it is "none of their business," or that they are confusing the issues of economics and religion. There are many stereotypes in these witness segments, but also a deep desire for justice and a profound solidarity with the poor.

"Search for Justice" does not only let these conflicts emerge verbally. It brings stories of the "have's" and the "have nots" in visual form. We see the enormous inequalities in our society and the passions and conflicts created by these conditions. The final section of each program is a debate, in which people from the Catholic community enter into dialogue with a panel of experts to discuss these economic issues. These debates are not concerned with the sensational or the trendy. They show people of faith grappling with the realities of our economic situation and asking themselves how they can move from individual voluntary charity alone into the wider dimensions of justice.

Conclusion

The Catholic bishops in the Economic Pastoral are calling all of us, Catholic or not, to a new global vision of justice in an interdependent world. They are also challenging us to practice justice in our daily lives and to reshape our economic system in accordance with the dignity and equality of all persons on this planet, the overriding importance of the common good, and a deeper solidarity with the poor. The effective use of media is essential to these challenges.

Notes

1. Cf. Peter Mann, "Journey into the Image: Religion, the Arts, and Telecommunications," in *Reflections on a Theology of Telecommunications: Image, Model, and Word* (Center for Religious Telecommunications: University of Dayton, 1984), pp. 27-40, esp. 30.

2. Cf. Paul Ricoeur, *The Conflict of Interpretations. Essays in Hermeneutics* (Evanston: Northwestern University Press, 1974). I have drawn some of the implications of Ricoeur's hermeneutic of suspicion for communications media in my book, *Through Words and Images* (New York: CTNA, 1983), p.10.

3. Cf. Neil Postman, *Amusing Ourselves to Death: Public Discourse in the Age of Show Business* (New York: Viking Penguin, 1986).

4. Robert N. Bellah, "The Sociological Implications of Electronic Media," in *The Electronic Media, Popular Culture, and Family Values:*

A Proceedings Report (United States Catholic Conference, 1985), pp.13-21, esp. 17. Also, Bellah & others, *Habits of the Heart: Individualism and Commitment in American Life* (Berkeley, University of California Press, 1985).

5. Roland Barthes, *Camera Lucida. Reflections on Photography* (New York: Hill and Wang, 1981), p. 118. The Barthes' text is developed in *Through Words and Images*, pp. 4-6.

6. The Second Draft. *Catholic Social Teaching and the U.S. Economy, (Origins* October 10, 1985, Vol. 15: No. 17), #10.

7. Cf. John A. Coleman, *An American Strategic Theology* (New York: Paulist, 1982), pp. 163-181, with references. I have developed some media implications of Coleman's theses in *Through Words and Images*, pp. 21-27.

8. Cf. Peter Mann, "The Problem of the Electronic Churches," in *Through Words and Images*, pp. 8-10.

(2) Television and the Vision of the Common Good

BETTE JEAN BULLERT

Imagine for a moment that you are an anthropologist from outer space. In a faraway space station, you twist your antenna and tune in to an evening of prime time television in the United States. This is what you might see and perceive about the creatures who inhabit that strange land.

Surrounded by dazzle and glitter, flashing lights and anxious laughter, people take pleasure in competing against each other for unseen prizes, hidden behind big doors. Happiness means winning in a contest, and rewards come in the form of applause, refrigerators and cars. Nobody likes to lose, not even in games of chance. The losers disappear behind curtains. The winners remain until they, too, are conquered.

In a crowded police station, filled with the din of typewriters and office chatter, a cop answers a call. Next, she is driving down a dark alley at dusk with her partner. They hear the shrill screams of a woman, and then the sounds of gunshots. The screaming stops. A man emerges from a nearby building, and runs quickly down the alley. Sirens blare, and a chase ensues. The police car comes to a halt. Guns are drawn, and someone fires. A man lies in the street, in a pool of blood.

In shimmering buildings that reach to the sky, a middle-aged white man dressed in a suit vies for more power and influence. J. R. Ewing leans back in his office chair, smiling, pleased with a recent business deal that promises to turn a tidy profit. But his satisfaction is only momentary. Now there is something else he wants, and it eludes him.

From a few brief glimpses of prime time, an anthropologist from outer space would get the impression that in America, happiness is measured in consumer durables. The world is a violent,

375

fast-paced place. Violence is the ultimate communicator, and the gun speaks the loudest. The thirst for control over others and the environment seems insatiable. In business, the quick, the clever and the corrupt win, although this doesn't prove so true in matters of love. Success is portrayed as personal triumph, the victory of one private individual over another. Ambition and the desire to possess are driving forces in everyday life. Friendships exist as fleeting alliances. Characters lead circumspect lives, and they are preoccupied with interpersonal relationships and with their own pleasure.

A moral seer like Robert Bellah would agree with the space anthropologist's impressions. He observes that the culture of radical individualism provides much of the content of prime time television.[1] Failure is seen as personal failing, success means private success, frustration is a personal problem. In stories where political corruption and interpersonal mistrust are ever present, viewers are left with the sense that they, as individuals, can only count on themselves. Their private worlds are the only ones that really matter, and the public arena is a dangerous jungle. The dominant message is that we live in a Hobbesian universe where the aggressive dominate, integrity is in short supply, double-dealing is to be expected, and nobody can really be trusted. Furthermore, there is nothing you can do to change fundamentally this situation. This is simply the way life is. Like a spurned rival storming into J. R.'s office, arms akimbo after discovering another shady business deal or illicit affair, viewers feel powerless, unable to affect or even articulate the forces that shape their lives. Corruption and selfishness appear as personality traits of particular individuals, not indicative of any broader systemic cultural or institutional problem. J. R. Ewing is just a bad guy.

Given the predominantly individualist nature of prime time programs, it should be no surprise that when, on rare occasions, reference is made to "the common good," it is expressed in terms of personal, psychological turmoil. At best, characters intervene to stop a particular wrong, only to have another appear in the next program in a slightly altered form. Emotional crisis and injustice are hydra-headed in television series. The battle brings forth the decency of some and the lack of courage of others, but the rhetoric of "the common good" evaporates in the tussle of individual egos.

One reason there is no room for the vision of the common good on prime time is that the concept of the common good presupposes a notion of community which is absent in the programs. This notion lies outside the experience of the characters and outside the parameters of their discourse.

Prime time television reflects in a general, yet distorted, way the dominant reality within which many of us live. Mistrust and fear combined with a sense of futility lead many of us to turn inward, and to retreat to the coziness of private homes, where we can accumulate more material comforts, and pursue private satisfaction. This retreat is reinforced by frequent commercials and advertisements that pump out the massage: "To be is to buy, and to buy is to be happy." Contained in this consumerist message is the subtler promise of personal fulfillment, to be acheived by ourselves, for ourselves, often in isolation from one another with the help of expensive items, like boats, and other trappings of "the good life."

Fortunately, there is another reality in our culture that coexists and runs counter to the individualistic and consumeristic way of life. Across the country, there are pockets of community where a moral language is kept alive, nurtured by religious praxis and compassion, where speaking about the common good is not met with befuddlement and confusion. In this other reality, to speak of the common good is to refer to a shared commitment and vision of a more just and peaceful world.

From Seattle to San Antonio and from Los Angeles to Miami, there are groups of committed activists who engage in little acts of courage when the need arises. They express their commitment to the vision of the common good by addressing particular and specific common goods. Sometimes the issues are local, other times national or international, but the unifying vision is one of justice, peace and human dignity. Sometimes these local heroes are part of political or community organizations, and some have come from Catholic parishes. They are modern-day peacemakers, and they are the bearers of a communitarian tradition.

Here are a few examples. In Seattle, Dona Ahern and her community organization confront politicians and bureaucratic decision-makers to prevent them from dumping the city's garbage in the neighborhood where the poor live. In the Midwest and nationwide, the late Ruth Youngdahl Nelson, a former national Mother of the Year, spoke out and organized against the build-up and use of nuclear weapons. At the age of 79, she drew attention to the issue by going out on a tiny boat with others to protest the coming of the Trident submarine. In San Antonio, hundreds of the city's poor mobilize their neighbors to get out to vote for a municipal bond for streets and improved drainage. In Bethesda, a young photographer named Marlow Boyer used his camera to show a mutual humanity shared by Soviet and American citizens, despite the climate of fear and suspicion that divides the leaders and much of the citizenry.

These men and women are testimony to the communitarian tradition. They act out of a sense of justice, using nonviolent action, and are sometimes inspired and supported by their religious beliefs. In this consumeristic culture, they stand out as moving examples of the different ways citizens are pursuing the vision of the common good, and rejecting the self-oriented individualistic attitude projected on prime time television. Unlike the self-serving J. R. Ewings on television, and other fictional characters that do not step outside their privatized, interpersonal worlds, these local heroes take seriously their vision of a better world and the human community, and they actively take up issues to help realize it.

God and Money — A Documentary

Television is a selective mediator of reality, local heroes and their missions are seldom characterized in weekly series, but they do show up once in a while in Movies of the Week and occasionally in public television documentaries. As an independent documentary producer, I ask myself how the medium of television can be used to present the vision of the common good, and to show the viewing public what community looks like. Can the medium be used to present a vision of the present and a vision of the future where viewers can see themselves as actors in the public arena, being active rather than passive in the face of injustice? There are already many examples of local heroism and solidarity in real life and in history.

GOD AND MONEY, which I co-produced with John De Graaf, is an hour-long documentary about the U.S. Catholic bishops' pastoral letter on the economy. The program was funded by the Corporation for Public Broadcasting, and it will air nationally on PBS. The bishops' pastoral deals with complex issues and beliefs about our economic system, our national priorities, and a moral vision.

In the program, we follow the debate about the letter locally, through the eyes of parishioners in Seattle, and nationally, in the Catholic intelligensia. We try to convey the hopeful spirit of the pastoral by using strong local characters in Seattle, San Antonio and Boston who maintain active and positive stances while facing various economic obstacles. Since the visual media operate on a kind of logical positivism, "that which cannot be expressed visually, doesn't exist," we show what the Catholic Church already has been doing to promote economic change through the Campaign for Human Development, and the subsequent controversy about the Campaign. We profile three types of projects: The citizen's lobbying organization, the cooperative and the community organization. Through these visually rich projects, and with our strong local characters, we illustrate for viewers the major themes in the letter of solidarity, community and the common good.

In Boston, we videotaped members of the Boston Harbor Lobstermen's Cooperative tell their story. The lobstermen were slowly being pushed out of the harbor as urban developers were claiming the waterfront. Before the co-op, the lobstermen epitomized the "rugged individualists" who were highly suspicious of each other, and only concerned with their own individual well-being. As Tom Morrell put it: "You'd look at another fisherman and you'd say, 'He must be the bad guy. He must be stealing my lobsters as someone is poaching my gear' or something. And everybody was pointing a finger at each other. And now, with the formation of this co-op, everyone's kind of together. You know, you say, 'These guys aren't really as bad as I thought they were years ago.' "

The Boston lobstermen's sequence shows the transition from a highly individualistic view of the world to one where these men see themselves as brothers. They work together now. This is a transition the bishops believe our whole society needs to make.

Another model is the grassroots community organization. By focusing on specific characters and local issues, we show in tangible terms what the Church has been doing to build community and work for the common good. We present two examples of this, one in Seattle, and the other in San Antonio.

In Seattle, we found Dona Ahern stuffing envelopes in a cramped office of the South End Seattle Community Organization (S.E.S.C.O.). Dona is a lifelong Catholic, a mother of six, and a community activist. Several years ago, triggered by a serious auto accident, Dona felt called to express her faith more actively in her community. The South End is the poorest area of the city. Through the efforts of Dona and other members of S.E.S.C.O., the organization has succeeded in pressuring politicians and public officials to allocate more city funds and resources to the community. They have attracted hundreds of thousands of dollars in block grant money for improvements in streets, parks, and the creation of a health clinic. In working for these local common goods, Dona and her neighbors show in concrete ways what it means to serve the common good.

In San Antonio, we found Communities Organized for Public Service (C.O.P.S.) which is a community organization similar to S.E.S.C.O. and it is based in the poor Catholic parishes in the barrios. When Beatrice Cortez and Helen Ayala, both leaders in the organization, grew up in San Antonio, there were no paved streets or sidewalks in the poor areas where most of the Hispanics lived. Each year, the rains would flood entire areas, turning streets into rivers of mud. Most years, someone would die in a flood-related tragedy. The Hispanic poor were just not organized.

In 1973, Ernesto Cortez (no relation to Beatrice Cortez), an organizer of the Industrial Areas Foundation, and members of the community began laying the groundwork for one of the most successful community organizations in the country. By training its members to confront politicians at accountability sessions, and by using a number of nonviolent tactics, C.O.P.S. has later been successful in bringing needed services to the barrios, and changing the political complexion of San Antonio by increasing Hispanic representation throughout local government.

When we visited San Antonio in the spring of 1985, C.O.P.S. was working to pass a municipal bond for improved streets, drainage and libraries. We saw a community of empowered people, who pulled together and devoted a considerable amount of time and energy to getting out the vote for the bond.

The external expressions of serving the common good are evident in the paved streets and sidewalks in the poorer areas of San Antonio. The internal ramifications are clear in the empowerment of the members of C.O.P.S. One member, George Ozuna, put it like this: "People now have hope. They have a sense of, if we continue doing what we're doing, things will get a lot better, and our lives will be enriched. C.O.P.S. also gives me a sense of power, that we can do something, that we can change our lives, that we can have an impact on our future that used to be in the hands of someone else. But now it is in our hands. Now we control our destiny."

In the course of producing GOD AND MONEY, we found many other examples of people working within parishes, in ecumenical and secular groups, and in their neighborhoods who were trying to bring about better lives for themselves and their communities. By working for social and economic improvement in specific, local situations, and struggling with localized issues, these bearers of the communitarian tradition serve as inspiring models. They point the way out of situations of despair and frustration, by showing in concrete terms that community *is* possible, and that people can change their conditions by working together.

Two important purposes are served when we portray stories like these in our documentary. First, by presenting our characters, such as Dona Ahern and George Ozuna, the viewing audience can get momentarily a glimpse of this other world where activism replaces passivity and hope replaces despair. For a moment, viewers can come to see the world as our characters see it, and see that they, too, can have an active role in changing the environments in which they live. Second, in the act of videotaping our key characters, we affirm the importance of their work. We keep alive their vision of the common good for themselves and their viewers.

The Making of Documentaries

GOD AND MONEY tries to capture the hopeful message of the bishops' pastoral. It shows how real, tangible people are serving the common good in particular places, and for them, that pursuit is worthwhile. The program is one example of what one can do with the medium of television, and it was produced by two independent producers. Consider some of the other programs that show community and solidarity that have been made by independents.

Ann Carrigan produced and directed ROSES IN DECEMBER, a documentary about the life and death of Jean Donovan, who was a Maryknoll lay missionary murdered in El Salvador. Ms. Carrigan dug deep into Jean Donovan's life to understand what motivated an upper middle-class, management consultant, with all the material comforts she wanted, to give up her lifestyle, and ultimately her life, in the service of the poor and for the cause of justice. The program was funded in part by the Corporation for Public Broadcasting. Later, a dramatic film called CHOICES OF THE HEART, was made for television, based on her documentary.

Julia Reichert and Jim Klein have produced several documentaries that capture the solidarity of women and workers in the labor movement. One of these, UNION MAIDS, tells the story of

three women who helped organize a trade union against stagger-
ing odds. The women bring to life a turbulent era in American
labor history in the 1930's to the emergence of the C.I.O. They
faced goon squads and red baiting, experienced hunger and sit-
downs, and bore witness to the truth that people can organize to
create better working conditions.

John de Graaf has produced some of the most powerful pro-
files of local heroes on the public airwaves. His characters' lives
illustrate a commitment to conscience and justice. MOTHER OF
THE YEAR is a profile of Ruth Youngdahl Nelson and her family.
A former national "Mother of the Year," and a devout Lutheran,
Ms. Nelson was a long time critic of nuclear weapons. She taught
her children that the purpose of life is to serve the whole human
community. At the age of 79, she joined her children in a block-
ade to protest the coming of Trident submarines. Motivated by
her Christian faith, she took many risks. The program looks at
the motivations that led her to risk ten years' imprisonment for
civil disobedience.

These are just a few of the programs by independent producers who work project to project, grant to grant, on shows
that present issues of justice and show examples of solidarity.
The producers are out there, trying to survive in a society with
less and less money for their work. The joke among independent producers is that you have to be independently wealthy to
survive as one. Independent producers run the gauntlet whenever they want to produce a show, and many talented documentary producers with terrific story ideas never make it to the production phase, not to mention broadcast.

Here is the process of making a documentary—viewed from
the inside. A program starts with an idea, and this concept reflects the values, interests and intentions of the independent producer. Then there has to be a story of general interest that can
express the idea, and the compelling characters who can tell it.

After articulating the story, and finding the characters, the producer than has to find a way to fund it, which usually means
writing dozens of grant proposals to private and public foundations, humanities commissions, and the Corporation for Public
Broadcasting. Many worthy projects never come to be because

producers can't secure the proper funding. Funding, by far, is the toughest hurdle for independents, and the situation is getting worse.[2]

With funding, the producer then moves on to the next phase, the actual production of the program. In production, the story begins to take shape. With a crew, the producer/director records on film or on tape the story as it has been developed. This is an evolving process, and producers face many choices along the way that determine what they have to work with in the editing room. What questions will bring out the characters' views on particular topics best? How can we illustrate in tangible visual terms what the story is about? How can we best convey the story and its characters to the viewers?

These questions and concerns carry over to the editing phase as well. The story is shaped by and adapted to the actual visuals from production and the precise quotes from the interviews. In this process of sifting through the material, the story becomes slightly different and more precise, a synthesis of intention and material. This becomes the finished program.

Now with a finished program, the independent producer must face a second set of challenges, getting the program on the air. Even when a documentary is funded by the Corporation for Public Broadcasting, there is no guarantee that PBS will broadcast it. With a completed show, the producer then has to run the gauntlet of PBS executives and station managers. If lucky, the producer will attempt to promote the show in the press to demonstrate public interest in the subject.

At PBS, programming executives determine if the program is suitable for a national broadcast. Sometimes they require major changes in the already completed script, substantial re-editing, or major changes in the program's focus. In some cases, they request that independent producers add entirely new sequences that require more shooting, or substantial re-editing. All these revisions and changes are to be done at the producer's expense unless he or she is a lucky recipient of a PBS grant.

When PBS accepts a program for national broadcast, it simply means the network will make it available to PBS affiliates if they want to run it. PBS does some initial promotion for the broadcast which includes a preview for the stations. At this stage, the producers must contact all the major affiliate stations and urge them to carry the show and schedule it at a decent time. Most independently produced programs don't fit into an established series (the series tend to commission their own programming), so they have to be scheduled as "one-off specials," sandwiched in between ongoing series, or late at night. The aim is to get scheduled during prime time on a week night, if possible.

With a broadcast date, the producer then has to contact the major television critics in the markets where the program will air. This means preparing and sending out press kits with a copy of the program, and making follow-up phone calls. This can be very expensive, and again, it is done at the producer's expense. Finally, the producer hopes for coverage and favorable reviews in the press, and a receptive viewing audience. When the program airs, the gauntlet is over.

Over the years, independent producers have provided many lively programs that put before the viewing public the themes of solidarity and community, and present hopeful portraits of modern-day peacemakers. As cinematic essayists and sometimes visionaries, in documentaries like ROSES IN DECEMBER, UNION MAIDS, MOTHER OF THE YEAR, and GOD AND MONEY, independent producers have shown how the medium of television can serve and nurture the vision of the common good.

The Role for the Catholic Church

The Catholic Church has long been the bearer of a communitarian tradition in our society. One of its goals is to create a world of love, justice, peace and community, and to get its message out to the public. If the Church wants to reach the public, it must use the public airwaves. By forging links with independent producers in public television, and by supporting them in their efforts to produce programs of mutual interest, the Church can help sustain the vision of the common good for a general audience. In this effort, the Church and independent producers can be allies.

Here are some specific ways we might work together. The Church can continue to cultivate more peacemakers who can be the subjects of inspiring documentaries. It can continue to create more living examples of community building, such as C.O.P.S., that show that community IS possible and working for the common good is a worthwhile activity. The Church can continue to work in a more ecumenical fashion with people of other faiths, and with secular organizations deeply concerned with issues of social and economic justice. The Church can help keep alive the vision of the common good by not backing off from the concrete challenges and obstacles that thwart its realization.

The Church can help support independent producers and their programs by actively funding more independent projects, regardless of whether or not the producer is an insider. It can show its good intentions by using independently produced programs that are already available. The Church can promote programs on public television that sincerely grapple with ethical questions, and it can help with promotion and publicity. For example, when an independent producer's program is sent out to affiliate stations, local Catholics can urge the affiliate to carry it, and to schedule it at a decent time. This would be a tremendous help. When a program comes along that is good in conveying communitarian values, compassion and solidarity, let the people at the 'Corporation for Public Broadcasting and PBS know about it, and that the viewer would like to see more. Perhaps together one could produce a documentary series on the topic of the common good, where public television, the religious community, and independent producers can share their work, and their vision.

The gift the Church can offer a society of isolated individuals is the message of community and the common good. The Church can begin to revive the language of the common good in the public vocabulary by actively supporting independent producers with a similar vision.

NOTES

1. Robert N. Bellah, "The Sociological Implications of Electronic Media," in *THE ELECTRONIC MEDIA, POPULAR CULTURE AND FAMILY VALUES,* A Proceedings Report, USCC, 1985, p. 13.

2. For additional information on this, see "Sponsors Call the Shots on Public Television," *VARIETY,* November 13, 1985, p. 93, and "The Assault on Public Television," by John Wicklein, COLUMBIA JOURNAL-ISM REVIEW, January/February, 1986, p. 27.

Eighteen

The International Economy and the Common Good

DAVID VOGEL

Any analysis of the relationship between capitalism and the common good must begin by recognizing that capitalism is not a national system, but an international one. We live in a highly interdependent global economy. The way we manage the American economy affects the distribution of income and wealth throughout the world. And by like token, the impact of the policies we choose to follow in the United States is constrained by political and economic forces beyond our national borders. Unless we define the "common good" in terms of both the world economy and America's role in that economy, not only will our analysis and policy prescriptions make little sense, but we will also be guilty of ethnocentrism.

The international character of capitalism is not a new development. On the contrary, capitalism was a global system from the very outset: historically, international economic exchanges long preceded domestic ones. Economic historians disagree as to whether or not the emergence of market economies in Western Europe in the fifteenth and sixteenth centuries was made possible by the colonization of Africa and the Americas. But there is no question that the two emerged together: each of the major economic powers of Western Europe—Spain, the Netherlands, and England—owed their initial affluence to their success in international commerce. As early as the seventeenth century, international merchants had accomplished a goal which had eluded each of the ancient world's would be conquerors: the integration of the vast majority of the world's inhabitants into one economic system.

While we have recently become more aware of the importance of international trade, it is by no means clear that the world has in fact become more interdependent. When measured as a percentage of global GNP, international capital flows were probably more extensive in the nineteenth century. If one measures economic interdependence in terms of the international movement of human capital, then there is no question that the world was far more economically interdependent during the nineteenth century; this century has witnessed no movement of people comparable to the migration of millions of Africans, Europeans and Asians to North and South America during the 1800s.

Contemporary Trends

The casual observer might be left with the conclusion that there is nothing unique about the contemporary world economy. However, there are two developments which deserve our attention. One has to do with the dynamics of international competition; the second concerns the position of the United States.

If one examines the dynamics of international competition it becomes evident that the pace of economic change has dramatically increased. For all the dynamism of the world economy over the last six centuries, the fact remains that the rate of change has for the most part been a gradual one. Compare, for example, how long each of three nations were able to dominate the world economy. Holland's dominance of world finance, trade and manufacturing lasted approximately 125 years, from 1575 through 1700. Britain's also lasted a little more than a century, from approximately 1750 through 1870. By contrast, "America's century" endured less than 30 years. It took the nations of Western Europe and North America more than a century to make the transition from predominantly agrarian societies to industrialized ones. Japan accomplished the same feat in less than a third of the time, while the emergence of the newly industrializing nations of East Asia—Korea, Singapore, Taiwan and Hong Kong—as major centers of industrial production has been even more rapid. These four Asian nations, with under 2 percent of the Third World's population, now account for almost 7 percent of its GNP, close to 20 percent of its total trade, and nearly 60 percent of its manufactured exports.[1] For over five hundred years, the world's economic center was in Western Europe; now, in just the last two decades, we are seeing it move to the Pacific Basin. If the current difference in growth rates between the Atlantic and Pacific Basins continues, by the year 2000 the Asian-Pacific GNP will be equal to that of the United States and Western Europe combined.

Nations which dominated a particular segment of the world economy were formally able to maintain their leadership for several decades. Consider, for example, how long Britain was able to maintain its leadership in textile manufacturing, or Germany in steel production, or the United States in the design and assembly of automobiles. Can anyone now point to a particular industry product or technology and state with some degree of assurance which nation's producers will control it twenty-five years from now—or even ten? It used to take decades before the citizens of one nation could develop the skills and acquire the technologies necessary to compete successfully with the world's most efficient producer. Now, thanks to improved global communications, a decline in transportation costs, the prevalence of "turnkey" factories, the willingness of multinational firms to license technologies, and the global increase in technically trained personnel, what once took decades now takes years, or even months. In the highly innovative semi-conductor industry, for example, the gap between the introduction of a new production technology in the United States and its use in Japan is now measured in months.

In addition, the number of countries capable of making and then exporting any product—whether it be wheat, textiles, automobiles, aircraft, or computers—has dramatically increased over the last decade. This trend shows no signs of abating: the world marketplace is becoming increasingly competitive, particularly as Third World nations seek to increase their exports of agricultural products and manufactured goods and even, in some cases, services to the industrialized countries. And notwithstanding the recent increase in protectionism, the world economy still remains a relatively open one. Never in the history of capitalism have so many citizens had the opportunity to consume the products produced by workers and farmers in so many different countries. We are now far closer to the ideal world of Adam Smith than at any time since he wrote the *Wealth of Nations* more than two hundred years ago.

Accompanying this increase in both the intensity of international competition and the pace of economic change has been a shift in the global position of the American economy. America has always been part of the world economy. During the nineteenth century, our cotton exports provided the raw material for Britain's textile industry, while our industrial revolution was largely financed by British and Dutch capital. Likewise, many American firms have had extensive overseas investments for more than half a century—in some cases even longer. Yet throughout most of the lifetime of the individuals now alive in the United States, the world economy was relatively invisible. From the end of the Second World War through the early 1970s, international competition was something which took place outside the United States. Thanks both to the physical destruction of our major industrial competitors and the wartime buildup of our manufacturing capacity, American business emerged from the Second World War with an unparalleled and overwhelming competitive advantage. During the 1950s and 1960s the United States accounted for more than half of the world's Gross National Product. At the same time, American based multinational corporations and firms took advantage of the strong dollar and America's military preeminence to increase their investments in Europe, Latin America, and Asia. The result was that while the rest of the world was both aware of and highly dependent on America, the reverse was not true.

However, this state of affairs has been irrevocably altered.[2] Between 1950 and 1970, our exports of goods and services as a percentage of GNP remained relatively stable, ranging from 4.9 to 6.4 percent. In the space of only one decade, between 1970 and 1980, they more than doubled, to 12.9 percent. Since then they have increased still further. We now export only a slightly lower percentage of our GNP than does Japan. Much the same pattern is true of imports. Ranging between 4.2 percent and 6.0 percent between 1950 and 1970, they increased to 12.0 percent in 1980. And this was even before the United States began to run substantial trade deficits! 80 percent of American manufacturing firms now face competition from overseas producers, while approximately one-third of our farm acreage is exported. American financial services also face increased foreign competition, as Japan has replaced the United States and Great Britain as the world's leading exporter of capital.

The result is that many of the most critical factors affecting the American economy now lie outside our control. Over the last decade, our inflation rate has been significantly affected by the price of oil—a price which since 1973 has been set outside our borders. The single most important factor now determining the expansion and contraction of investment in different sectors of our economy is international competition. The decline in employment in many of our most important industries, such as steel, textiles, and automobile production, is directly linked to their inability to compete with foreign competition. Similarly, the shift in the regional center of gravity of the American economy from the Northeast to the West and the Southwest is related to the relatively higher growth rates of the Pacific Basin. Most dramatically, the economic catastrophe that currently confronts

American farmers is directly linked to their loss of export markets. In summary, the ability of the American economy to provide its citizens with the goods and services they need and want has now become dependent on the ability of American corporations to compete successfully in the world marketplace.

With this background in mind, let me now turn to a number of specific social and economic issues and seek to relate them to the "common good."

Employment

We can all agree that providing jobs for those citizens who wish to work is the *sine qua non* of a just society. By this criteria, the American economy has performed extremely well over the last two decades. Much has been made of the nation's official unemployment rate, which, though somewhat declining in recent months, remains relatively high by historic standards. But a more accurate index of the capacity of the American economy to create jobs is the percentage of the adult population that is currently employed. That figure now stands at approximately 65 percent—the highest in the peacetime history of the United States and the second highest in the industrialized world.[3] The American economy has had to cope with three dramatic demographic changes in recent years: the entrance into the workforce of the baby-boom generation— now all out of college and seeking employment, the increase in the number of women desiring full- or part-time work, and a significant increase in immigration, both legal and illegal. Given these three developments (the first two are unprecedented), what is remarkable is not that the unemployment rate is higher than it was a decade or two ago, but *that it remains so low.*

The contrast with Western Europe is striking. While the United States added 30 million net new jobs between 1970 and 1980, Western Europe experienced a net decrease in job creation. Since 1980, America has created 9.7 million additional jobs—more than the combined total for all the other major industrial economies. Not only have the unemployment rates of most European nations been higher than in the United States since the 1980s, but, unlike America, which has absorbed 12 million immigrants, the Europeans have been sending their "guest workers" home.

There are several explanations for this contrast. One reason has to do with differences in the rate of entrepreneurial activity in the two regions. The "Fortune 500" have added no new jobs to the American economy in more than two decades. Virtually all of the increase in employment in the United States has been due to newly established companies. We are currently in the midst of an entrepreneurial revolution in the United States; since 1980, Americans have been starting new businesses at the rate of more than 600,000 per year. Even though many fail, they have played a critical role in both absorbing new entrants to the labor force and re-employing workers unemployed elsewhere in the economy. For a variety of institutional and cultural reasons, far fewer new businesses have been formed in Europe. As a consequence, workers displaced due to the economic difficulties of many of Europe's traditional industries have experienced much more difficulty in finding other jobs.

However, virtually all the new jobs that have been created in the United States are in the service sector, where wages tend to be considerably lower than in manufacturing.[4] On the whole, those industries in which employment is increasing most rapidly tend to pay their employees considerably less than those sectors where employment is declining. Real hourly wages in the private sector have been virtually stagnant since 1973 and have actually declined during the past five years; the average 25-34-year-old male experienced a 26 percent decline in his real income between 1973 and 1983. The European pattern is markedly different: thanks in part to the strength of unions in Europe, those European workers who are employed have experienced considerably greater wage increases than their counterparts in the United States.

The result is ironic. The social-welfare policies of the United States have long been viewed as inferior to those of the European social democracies. Yet, acting solely through market mechanisms, America's labor polices have been far more egalitarian. We have taken a relatively stagnant wage bill and divided it among an increasingly large number of workers. The real beneficiaries of our market-oriented labor policies have been the least well-off, who otherwise would have been unable to find any employment at all. By contrast, the European have created what is in many significant respects a two-tier society: those who are employed are relatively well off while those who are not are bearing the full brunt of Europe's relatively slow growth rates. Those who criticize the American economy for creating an increasing number of low wage jobs should pause to consider the alternative.

Yet, while the American pattern has done much to foster the common good, it does not augur well for our long-term prosperity. After all, the idea of economic activity is to create wealth using as few, not as many, inputs as possible. Ideally we want an economy in which people become richer by working less, not more. A recovery based on more people working at lower wages may satisfy our sense of fairness, but in economic terms it also means that each worker is less productive. The growth in labor productivity in Europe remains significantly greater than in the United States precisely because the Europeans have substituted capital for labor, while America has done the opposite. Since, in the final analysis, living standards are fundamentally a function of the rate of productivity growth, America's spectacular record of job creation may well prove to be a mixed blessing.

Competitiveness and Manufacturing

In fact, the disproportionate growth of employment in the service sector—and the parallel decline of our manufacturing sector—is extremely troubling. Those who profess to be indifferent to the enormous deterioration in the international competitiveness of American· manufacturing on the grounds that America is becoming a more "mature" service economy are being extremely short-sighted. The British experience should persuade us that a nation that loses its manufacturing base cannot long remain an affluent society. It is not only that services do not (and probably cannot) pay as well as manufacturing. Equally as important, much of the service economy is in fact dependent upon the prosperity of the manufacturing sector. The customer base of our transportation companies, financial institutions, health care organizations, insurance and consulting firms, and advertising agencies consists largely of manufacturers. If our manufacturing base leaves our border, many of our service jobs will follow. Nor is the shift to high technology a panacea. Not only do high-tech companies employ relatively few people, but they, too, are dependent for many of their customers on manufacturing companies.

A certain shrinkage of our manufacturing base is inevitable—even desirable. It makes little sense—either economically or morally—for Americans to continue to produce products that can be manufactured more cheaply either in other industrial nations or in the Third World. But as the Japanese have demonstrated, there is no reason why an affluent, relatively high-wage society cannot remain competitive in manufacturing, particularly in the manufacture of relatively sophisticated products. For it to do so, however, requires that the manufacturing process itself become more sophisticated and knowledge-intensive through, for example, the use of computered-added design, engineering, and assembly. But while the "office of the future" may be in America, the "factory of the future" is in Japan: the sophistication of our manufacturing technology is well behind that of the Japanese. Unless we channel substantially more resources into upgrading our production technology, we may find it increasingly difficult to provide our citizens with increases in real wages in the future. Increasing worker participation can also improve productivity; however, it is no substitute for more capital investment. Yet America is currently investing a smaller portion of its GNP in plant and equipment than any other capitalist nation.

Why is America lagging behind Japan? Much of the blame rests with American management. The pressures corporate managers are under to maximize short-term earnings have made it nearly impossible for all but the largest and most profitable companies to make the investments they need to keep their manufacturing operations competitive. It is clearly difficult for managers to plan for the long-run future of their companies when they are spending all their time worrying about when or if they will be the next victim of a hostile takeover. As a result, American workers have less advanced equipment to work with than their counterparts in Japan. And often, instead of upgrading their own firm's operations, managers have sought to improve their bottom line by acquiring another company— thus compounding the problem. Such "paper entrepreneurialism" simply redistributes wealth from the stockholders of one company to another; it adds nothing to our overall capacity to create additional wealth.

The performance of Japanese manufacturing firms in the United States demonstrates that America can retain its competitive advantage in manufacturing. But it can only do so if American companies are willing to commit themselves to this effort. Yet with a handful of exceptions, the culture of American companies does not place a high value on manufacturing: production managers continue to be paid far less than MBA's with skills in finance and accounting. As a Japanese executive recently noted:

> Who is doing the most to create jobs in the United States? Japanese manufacturers. Meanwhile, American executives are putting people out of work in their pursuit of the almighty bottom line. How is it that Japanese companies can turn out products in the United States at a profit and American companies cannot? We can hardly be faulted for concluding that there must be something wrong with American management methods.[5]

There are no easy or obvious solutions to this problem. But unless we find a way of changing the priorities of American business, we are unlikely to remain an affluent society.

The Trade Deficit

After running a substantial merchandise balance of payments surplus every year between 1893 and 1970, our merchandise trade balance moved into the red in 1971. Since then, we have run deficits every year but two, and the size of these deficits has increased considerably during each of the last four years. In 1985 our trade deficit—the difference in value between the goods we exported and imported—amounted to nearly 150 billion dollars. This is unprecedented, not only in the history of America, but in the history of the world. While this deficit will diminish somewhat over the next few years due to the recent considerable decline in the value of the dollar, it is still likely to remain relatively high in the foreseeable future. From the perspective of American workers, deficits of this magnitude are a disaster: millions have lost their jobs due to foreign competition, and while most have eventually found other employment, it is often at reduced wages.

Yet if one looks at the American trade deficit from a global rather than an exclusively American point of view, it can be seen as a blessing. It has provided a unique "window of opportunity" for millions of people throughout the world to improve their living standards by selling their output to the United States. For the workers of the industrializing nations of Asia, exporting their products to the United States has played a critical role, in enabling them to increase their nation's share of world GNP. For the governments and people of Latin America, desperately seeking to earn the foreign exchange necessary to pay back their bank loans and thus maintain the confidence of the international financial community, increasing their exports to the United States is essential. In 1984, 45 percent of the exports of the 17 largest debtor nations was purchased by the United States.[6]

While it is true that in many cases Americans are losing well paid jobs to less well paid Third World workers, however, for the latter, exporting their products to the United States has meant a significant improvement in their living standards. And, in fact, the average wage differential between the industrializing Third

World and the industrial world has significantly narrowed in recent years. The dramatic growth rates experienced by the economies of East Asia over the last decade demonstrates that Third World nations need not remain mired in poverty—provided they can gain access to the markets of countries richer than they. In short, instead of bemoaning our trade deficit, we should be celebrating it: it reflects a much more equal distribution of the world's wealth, income, and productive capacities.

We certainly have a moral responsibility to assist those Americans who have lost their jobs as a result of foreign competition. For the most part, they are the victims of economic forces beyond both their control and that of their companies. At the same time, however, to help them keep their current jobs by erecting trade barriers is the height of irresponsibility. On what moral basis is the job of an American worker preferable to that of a South Korean or Brazilian worker? Protectionism is morally wrong not simply because it forces American consumers to pay for maintaining the jobs of workers whose wages are usually well above the national average. (Import controls on manufactured and agricultural products cost American consumers $56 billion in 1984, with the cost per job saved averaging more than $100,000.) The more important reason why protectionism is morally indefensible is that it directly transfers wealth from relatively impoverished workers in the Third World to relatively affluent ones in the United States. The burden of economic adjustment should be borne by the American taxpayers through job retraining programs, not by foreign workers—or American consumers.

A similar analysis can be made of the problems currently confronting American agriculture. There are many reasons for the economic disaster currently facing many of America's agricultural producers. Some—like the overexpansion during the 1970s—are due to the farmers' own shortsightedness while others, like the overvalued dollar, are the result of policies pursued by the American government. But among the reasons why most American farmers are in trouble is that the farmers of so many other nations have become much more productive. Total world food production increased by one-third between 1972 and 1985. Thanks to both the increased use of fertilizers and the relaxation of price controls, a nation such as India, which formerly imported food from the United States, is now self-sufficient. Due to the system of market incentives instituted by the Deng Government, Chinese farmers have likewise become much more productive in recent years. In short, America's declining share of world agricultural output means that the rest of the world has become far better able to feed itself. This should be regarded as a positive development, not a negative one.

The case for free trade in agricultural products is even more compelling. The average gap in income between American farmers and those outside the United States is enormous. Quotas and other restrictive measures that limit the entry of agricultural products from Third World countries consign millions of the world's least well off citizens to perpetual poverty. If we wish, for example, to improve living standards in the Caribbean, the most effective course of action we can undertake is to eliminate our quotas on imported sugar. Our current protectionist policies cost Third World sugar exporters $7.4 billion in 1983—the equivalent of almost 30 percent of all foreign aid from the North to the South.

One critical measure of the ethical performance of an economy is how well it treats its poorest members. But certainly this applies even more forcibly to the global economy. As one of the world's richest nations, America has a moral responsibility to do all it can to further a more just worldwide distribution of income. And we have a special responsibility to the citizens of those Third World nations who are making sacrifices so that their children can enjoy a living standard that more nearly approximates our own. The most important way we can meet both these responsibilities is by doing everything possible to keep our borders open to the agricultural and manufactured products of the Third World. If we want to enable Third World producers to help themselves then free trade is the most effective form of foreign aid that we can possibly provide.

There is nothing wrong with the efforts of American government and business to make American industry and agriculture more internationally competitive. Indeed, as I suggested earlier, this should be seen as an important national priority. But it is critical that this goal be pursued in ways that add to, rather than subtract from, the efficiency and productivity of the world economy. In the final analysis, protectionism is wrong for much the same reason that many corporate take-overs are morally indefensible: both are zero-sum economic strategies.

America has long prided itself on setting an example for the rest of the world: it was the Puritans who first introduced the idea of America as a "city upon a hill," providing a model of ethical behavior for the rest of the world to emulate. I would like to suggest that we think about our trade policies in this light. It is certainly true that there is no such thing as free or fair competition in the world marketplace; nations employ countless mechanisms—some legal under the GATT accord and many not—to promote the products and services of their nationals and discourage their citizens and firms from purchasing from abroad. Many of the industrializing nations that complain the loudest about American restrictions on their exports themselves have erected barriers against imports from the United States. And compared to both the European Community and Japan, our borders are far more open.

However, American should not imitate the restrictive trade practices of Japan and the European Community, nor demand reciprocity from the Third World. Rather our free trade polices should set an example for the rest of the world. We should follow principled economic policies even if our competitors do not. Our trade deficit is usually viewed by economists as a sign of the weakness of the American economy. And to a certain extent this is an accurate assessment. But from a moral point of view, the very magnitude of our trade deficit should make us proud: what other nation would allow foreigners such extraordinary access to their domestic market? We have long prided ourselves on our relatively open immigration policy. Should not the same principle also extend to our import of goods?

Foreign Investment and Savings

However, there is one area where America has behaved irresponsibly from the perspective of the long-term welfare of the world economy. In recent years, we have become a net importer not only of goods, but of capital. During 1984 and 1985, foreigners invested more than $200 billion in the United States; currently 1 percent of America's tangible assets and 5 percent of its public and private securities are owned outside the United States. In 1984, the United States became a debtor nation for the first time since the First World War. In principle, there is nothing wrong with foreigners' owning an increasing share of America. Over the last half-century, Americans purchased substantial assets overseas: we certainly have no right to complain when foreigners now do the same in our country.

In terms of the welfare of our citizenry, the inflow of foreign capital into the United States is a positive development. Normally, we would have expected unemployment in America to have significantly increased as our merchandise balance of trade account has deteriorated. But as we have seen, this has not happened: even as our citizens purchase an increasing share of goods made overseas, our economy has continued to generate new jobs. The reason is a simple one: the flow of foreign capital into the United States has counterbalanced the sums we transfer overseas to pay for the goods we import. In this case, however, what is good for America is decidedly not good for the rest of the world. For America is consuming a disproportionate share of the world's savings. If our goal is a more equitable distribution of world resources, we are behaving irresponsibly: the capital being invested in the United States should instead be creating jobs in Europe, Asia and Latin America.

Traditionally, the export of capital has been a means by which the benefits of industrial development have been spread to other nations. Virtually all rich nations invariably become capital exporters. And in so doing, they help develop the economies of their competitors. Thus the world's first major economic power, the Netherlands, provided much of the capital for the Industrial

Revolution in Britain. British capital in turn helped finance the industrial development of the United States. During the 1950s and 1960s America paid for much of the economic reconstruction of Europe while during the 1970s American bank loans channeled extensive sums of money into a number of Latin American countries. American investments have also played an important role in the economic development of Asia. By like token, over the last decade, Japan has become the world's most important source of capital. In many respects Japan is the OPEC of the 1980s.

Seen in this light, America's current position with respect to world-capital flows is rather bizarre. Given our need to both reindustrialize and rebuild our infrastructure, there is a compelling case to be made that America, at least at this point in its history, should not be exporting more capital. But there is certainly no reason why it should be importing it! Certainly, in this area there is a case to be made for national economic self-sufficiency.

What is responsible for this situation? There are many factors, including relatively high American interest rates, the confidence of foreigners in the long-term future of the American economy, a desire on the part of foreign manufacturers to both get around and reduce the likelihood of protectionist legislation in the United States and the decision on the part of many American-based multinationals to invest their profits in the United States rather than overseas. But among the most important reasons why we are importing so much capital is that America's savings rate is so low; indeed it is by far the lowest in the industrial world. In effect, we are living beyond our means: we are allowing—even encouraging—foreigners to do our saving for us.

Efforts to increase our savings rate are proving extremely difficult; indeed the failure of our savings rate to increase since the passage of the Economy Recovery Act of 1981 constitutes one of the most conspicuous and troubling failures of Reagan's economic policies. Nonetheless, we must do all we can to remedy this situation. In the short-run, through some combination of increased taxes and reduced spending, we can work to reduce the federal deficit, thus reducing the government's drain on both our savings and those of the people of Western Europe and Japan. In the long run, we need to reform our tax system so as to provide Americans with more incentives to save and fewer inducements to consume—precisely the reverse of our current tax policies. Perhaps religious institutions could play a role in promoting the value of thrift among our citizens—a virtue which was at one time a central component of the Protestant Ethic, but which has been allowed to atrophy. However we go about this effort—and there are clearly no simple or painless solutions—our underlying goal should be clear: increasing our savings rate should be seen as a moral imperative. We owe it both to ourselves and to the rest of the world.

It is true that if we import less capital, our merchandise balance of trade deficit will also decline since, by definition, capital and trade accounts must balance. But what is critical for the long-term growth of the American economy is not so much the amount of our trade deficit as the absolute volume of goods imported into the United States. To the extent that increased domestic savings are translated into an increase in domestic investment, our economy is likely to grow more rapidly. This will in turn enable us to purchase more than the rest of the world without increasing our trade deficit. The world economy need not be a zero-sum game. By increasing our own ability to generate wealth, we can help not only to improve the living standards of our own citizens, but to provide a more solid foundation for the long-term prosperity of the entire capitalist world.

Sacrifices and Intergenerational Fairness

Increasing our savings rate will in the short run make us all worse off. It is therefore extremely important that these sacrifices be made as fairly as possible. Making our economic system fairer is a complex and multi-faceted challenge. I would, however, like to examine one dimension of the fairness issue that I think has not received sufficient attention from either ethicists or policy-makers. That is the issue of intergenerational fairness.

Over the last two decades, the United States has been engaged in a radical redistribution of wealth and income—so radical that had it been formally proposed as a public policy, its advocates would have been dismissed as left-wing political fanatics.[7] This redistribution has not taken place among social classes but across generations: we have been engaged in a massive transfer of wealth from people below 65 to those older than 65. This has been accomplished principally through two mechanisms: the indexing of social security and other public pensions, and inflation—which has significantly increased the value of homes purchased before the mid-1970s. The former has been particularly important: in 1982, 35 percent of the entire federal budget went to help the elderly through a combination of pensions welfare payments, and expenditures on health care.

We have reason to be proud of our generosity toward the elderly. Up through the 1960s, the widespread poverty prevalent among this segment of our population was a national disgrace. Thanks in large measure to the indexing of Social Security benefits, the percentage of elderly living below the poverty line is now actually lower than that of the population as a whole. Yet the rest of the population has paid a considerable price for this progress, primarily through increased Social Security taxes—a tax which is highly regressive. And, while we have indexed Social Security benefits, we have not indexed wages. As a result, the increase in Social Security benefits has lagged behind the rate of increase in wages. Even more troubling, while we have indexed the welfare payments to those over 65, we have not, of course, chosen to do the same for welfare payments to the rest of the population—a policy which primarily hurts the young.

There clearly is no reason why an elderly person should be poor, particularly since the remaining poverty among those over 65 could be eliminated at a relatively modest cost. The real moral problem presented by our current Social Security system involves our payments to those over 65 who are relatively affluent. Virtually all of these people are receiving far more in Social Security benefits than they have contributed. In fact, the average recipient of Social Security now has more financial assets than the average contributor to it. In effect, our current social welfare system is transferring wealth from less affluent individuals and families under 65 to more affluent families and individuals above 65. This is morally intolerable. Why should my daughter, who receives only slightly above the minimum wage, help to pay for her grandmother's condominium in Florida? Why should not all Americans—both those working and those retired—sacrifice equally to improve the long-term performance of our economy? Any effort to make the American economic system fairer must explicitly address this issue.

Moreover, the financing of our Social Security system and our international indebtedness are related. What has enabled the United States federal government to run such large deficits without significantly expanding our money supply—and thus creating inflationary pressures on the economy—has been the willingness of foreigners—most notably Japanese—to purchase a significant share of Treasury bills and bonds. Thus, in effect, Japanese workers, with a per capita income only three-quarters of that of Americans, are saving nearly 20 percent of their income so that Americans over sixty-five can have incomes well above the average for all Americans, let alone the Japanese. Yet, in the long-run, it will be other Americans who will pay for this misallocation of resources. A growing portion of the wealth generated by the next generation of Americans will be sent back overseas to pay back the money borrowed by their parents and grandparents.

The Japanese Example

Any attempt to re-examine the ethical and social foundations of capitalism needs to come to grips with the Japanese experience. Japan has developed a form of capitalism that is markedly different from that which we have known in the West. Much has been written about the extraordinary economic achievements of the Japanese, and deservedly so. Here is a nation with no natural resources, its infrastructure devastated by the Second World War, and much of its population on the brink of starvation in the late

1940s. Yet within the span of a generation, it has become the world's second largest industrial power—now exporting billions of dollars of capital each year. Moreover as the first non-Western nation to compete successfully with the Western powers, Japan has become a model for a number of Third World nations both in Asia and increasingly in Latin America.

Certainly, there is also much about Japan not to admire. Domestically, Japan, for all its heralded emphasis on worker participation, is by far the least democratic of any advanced capitalist society. The same political party has been in power for more than a generation. Its welfare system remains extremely penurious, and until the 1970s, its economic growth was achieved at a price of extraordinary damage to its physical environment and the health of many of its citizens. Internationally, Japan has pursued a set of extremely nationalistic policies. Its trade policies are the most restrictive of any industrial nation—an issue which is of concern not only to the United States but also to the other nations of Asia. It also places more barriers to foreign investment than any other capitalist nation. In addition, Japan provides relatively little foreign aid and refuses to open up its borders to immigration.

Nonetheless, Japan does demonstrate that the values of fairness and cooperation, on one hand, and rapid economic growth on the other, are not—as is frequently assumed in the West—incompatible. Japanese institutions cooperate with each other to an extent inconceivable in the West: there is extensive cooperation both between business and government and within the private sector itself. Firms frequently collaborate on research projects and the Japanese practice of having companies own each other's stock gives firms a stake in each other's survival. Industrial relations in Japan are also far more cooperative than in the West. Moreover, Japan has by far the most egalitarian distribution of income and wealth of any capitalist society. While only a small proportion of Japanese work for the highly profitable companies that export their products to the rest of the world, the Japanese have structured their economic and political system so as to enable the rest of their population— particularly those who still depend on the land for their living— to share in the overall success of their economy. In sum, Japan is both a highly communitarian society and a highly efficient one. In attempting to restructure our capitalist institutions so as to maximize the common good, we might be well advised to see what we can learn from the Japanese variant of capitalism. At a minimum, we should certainly learn how to better compete with them.

The Challenge for the Church

Attempting to reconcile the interests of Americans and the citizens of the rest of the world is an extremely difficult undertaking. We live in a highly competitive and interdependent world economy in which the economic interests of citizens, workers and consumers in different countries are frequently in conflict. For many throughout the world, the international competition does frequently appear to be a zero-sum game; hence the recent resurgence of economic nationalism in the European Community, the United States, Japan and many Third World countries. Yet, at the same time the Catholic Church has a unique opportunity to advance a vision of the common good that is truly international. The Church, after all, is the world's most preeminent multinational institution; its existence long preceded both the modern world economy as well as the most extant nation-states. Today a growing share of its members are in the developed and developing world. Although the bishops have spoken out on the issue of international military conflict, they have paid much less attention to international economic conflict. The challenge for the Church is to apply its moral teachings in a way that will illuminate our understanding of the dynamics of the relationship between the U.S. economy and the rest of the world.

Notes

1. Steffan Linder, *The Pacific Century* (Stanford: Stanford University, 1986), p. 39.

2. Michael Priore and Charles Sabel, *The Second Industrial Divide* (New York: Basic Books, 1984), p. 185.

3. Warren Brookes, "Statistics Reveal Real Unemployment Pictures," *San Francisco Chronicle*, March 3, 1986, p. 27.

4. John Young "Global Competition: The New Reality," *California Management Review*, Spring 1985, pp. 12-13, and "The False Paradise of a Service Economy," *Business Week*, March 3, 1986, pp. 78-81.

5. Hajime Karatsu, "The Deindustrialization of America: A Tragedy for the World," *KKC Brief*, No. 31, October 1985, p. 2.

6. *Economic Report of the President*, February 1985, p. 107.

7. The data in this section is based on Lester Thurow *The Zero-Sum Solution*, (NY: Simon & Schuster, 1985), pp. 247-252.

Contributors

Gar Alperovitz, historian and political economist, is president of the National Center for Economic Alternatives, a Washington-based research organization. Previously, he served as a Legislative Director in the U.S. House of Representatives and the U.S. Senate, and as a Special Assistant in the Department of State. His most recent books include *Atomic Policy: Hiroshima and Potsdam* and *Rebuilding America* (with Geoffrey Faux).

Ernest Bartell, C. S. C., is the Executive Director of the Helen Kellogg Institute for International Studies at the University of Notre Dame. Father Bartell earned a Ph.D. in economics from Princeton University and was the president of Stonehill College, North Easton, Massachusetts. His published works include *Costs and Benefits of Catholic Schools* and *Economic Problems of Nonpublic Schools*.

Bette Jean Bullert, a graduate of Boston University and Oxford University, is an independent television producer. Recently, she co-produced with John De Graaf *"God and Money,"* which is a documentary examining the dialogue concerning the United States Catholic Bishops' Pastoral on the Economy.

Gerald F. Cavanagh, S. J., is a member of the Department of Management at the University of Detroit. Father Cavanagh has been on the Board of Editors of the *Academy of Management Review* and was national chairperson of the Social Issues Division of the Academy of Management. His published works include *American Business Values* and *Blacks in the Industrial World: Issues for the Manager*.

John J. Collins is a member of the Department of Theology at the University of Notre Dame. He received his doctorate from Harvard University and is the author of several articles and books, including *The Apocalyptic Imagination in Ancient Judaism, Between Athens and Jerusalem, Daniel: With an Introduction to Apocalyptic Literature* and *Proverbs*.

410

John W. Cooper is Dean for Academic Affairs and Associate Professor of Philosophy and Religion at Bridgewater College, Bridgewater, Virginia. He is co-editor with Michael Novak of *The Corporation: A Theological Inquiry* and he was the principal researcher for Novak's *The Spirit of Democratic Capitalism*. He is also the author of *The Theology of Freedom: The Legacy of Jacques Maritain and Reinhold Niebuhr*.

William J. Cunningham, a graduate of Wayne State University, Detroit, Michigan, is a research economist with the AFL-CIO in Washington, D. C. and has been involved in the field of economic research since 1975. Currently, he is chairman of the Productivity Committee, which is part of the Labor Research Advisory Committee to the Bureau of Labor Statistics.

Charles E. Curran teaches and researches in the field of Theological Ethics at the Catholic University of America. Father Curran is a former president of the Catholic Theological Society. His published works include *American Social Ethics: 20th Century Approaches*, *Directions in Catholic Social Ethics*, *Critical Concerns in Moral Theology* and *Directions in Fundamental Moral Theology*.

Richard T. De George is University Distinguished Professor of Philosophy at the University of Kansas. He serves on the editorial boards of the *Business and Professional Ethics Journal* and the *Journal of Business Ethics*. He is the author of many articles and books including *Business Ethics, Marxism and Religion in Eastern Europe* and *The Nature and Limits of Authority*.

John W. Houck is a professor of management and Co-Director of the Notre Dame Center for Ethics and Religious Values in Business. In addition to articles and reviews, he has published several volumes, including *Academic Freedom and the Catholic University*, A *Matter of Dignity: Inquiries into the Humanization of Work,* and with Oliver F. Williams, C.S.C., *Full Value: Cases in Christian Business Ethics, The Judeo-Christian Vision and the Modern Corporation, Co-Creation and Capitalism: Pope John Paul II's Laborem Exercens,* and *Catholic Social Teaching and the U.S. Economy: Working Papers for a Bishops' Pastoral.*

Peter Mann is a producer of television programs for The Diocese of Rockville Center, New York. A Benedictine priest since 1965, Fr. Mann has studied theology in England, Switzerland, France and Germany, where he did advanced studies at the Universities of Munich and Muenster. From 1976-1983 he produced or wrote over 125 television programs, including "Search for Justice," a five part series on the Economic Pastoral of the U.S. Catholic Bishops.

Dennis P. McCann is a member of the Department of Religious Studies at DePaul University, Chicago. He received his St.L. degree from the Gregorian University in Rome and his Ph.D. from the University of Chicago Divinity School. Dr. McCann's published works include *Christian Realism and Liberation Theology* and *Polity and Praxis: A Program for American Practical Theology* (with Charles Strain).

Ralph M. McInerny is Grace Professor of Medieval Studies and the Director of the Jacques Maritain Center at the University of Notre Dame. He is also the editor of *The New Scholasticism* Journal and the author of several books including *Ethica Thomistica, History of Western Philosophy, Thomism in the Age of Renewal, The Priest* and *New Themes in Christian Philosophy*.

Richard John Neuhaus is the Director of the Center on Religion and Society, New York. A Lutheran clergyman, he was pastor for seventeen years of a low-income Black and Hispanic parish in Brooklyn. He is the author of several books including *The Naked Public Square: Religion and Democracy in America, Movement and Revolution, Time toward Home: The American Experiment as Revelation* and *Dispensations*.

Michael Novak is a scholar at the American Enterprise Institute, Washington, D.C., and has been an advisor in national political campaigns. Novak was also chief of the United States delegation to the Human Rights Commission in Geneva in 1986. He has received degrees from Stonehill College, the Gregorian, and Harvard University. Novak's published works include: *A Theology for Radical Politics, Ascent of the Mountain: Flight of the Dove,*

The Spirit of Democratic Capitalism and *Freedom with Justice.*

David Vogel is a political scientist in the Department of Business Administration of the University of California-Berkeley. He is the editor of *California Management Review* and the author of several books including *National Styles of Regulation: Environmental Policy in Great Britain and the United States, Ethics and Profits* and *Lobbying the Corporation.*

Charles C. West is Stephen Colwell Professor of Christian Ethics at the Princeton Theological Seminary. Professor West is a former president of the Society of Christian Ethics and the American Theological Society. His published works include *The Power to Be Human, Outside the Camp, Ethics, Violence and Revolution* and *The Sufficiency of God.*

Charles K. Wilber is a member of the Department of Economics at the University of Notre Dame and was a senior consultant to the U. S. Catholic Bishops' Committee on the Economic Pastoral. He was the chair of his department for several terms; his published works include *An Inquiry into the Poverty of Economics, Capitalism and Democracy - Schumpeter Revisited* and *Religious Values and Development.*

Oliver F. Williams, C. S. C., Co-Director of the Center for Ethics and Religious Values in Business, is on the faculty of the Department of Management at the University of Notre Dame, where he teaches and researches in the field of business, society and ethics. He holds a Ph.D. in Theology from Vanderbilt University and has had the experience of a research year at the Graduate School of Business Administration at Stanford University. Father Williams is the co-editor or author of several books, including *The Apartheid Crisis: How We Can Do Justice in a Land of Violence.*

J. Philip Wogaman is Professor of Christian Social Ethics at the Wesley Theological Seminary in Washington, D.C. He is a former president of the American Society of Christian Ethics and a member of the Nestle Infant Formula Audit Commission and the National Council of Churches' Committee on Religious Liberty. His publications include *Quality of Life in a Global Society* and *The Great Economic Debate: An Ethical Analysis.*

Index

414